TRANSFORMING
PARISH MINISTRY

TRANSFORMING PARISH MINISTRY

The Changing Roles of Catholic Clergy, Laity, and Women Religious

Jay P. Dolan, R. Scott Appleby, Patricia Byrne, and Debra Campbell

CROSSROAD • NEW YORK

1990

The Crossroad Publishing Company
370 Lexington Avenue, New York, N.Y. 10017

Library of Congress Cataloging-in-Publication Data

Transforming parish ministry : the changing roles of Catholic clergy,
   laity, and women religious / edited by Jay P. Dolan.
       p.   cm.
   Bibliography: p.
   Includes index.
   ISBN 0–8245–0931–5
   1. Parishes—United States—History—20th century. 2. Catholic
Church—United States—Clergy—History—20th century.
3. Monasticism and religious orders—United States—History—20th
century. 4. Monasticism and religious orders for women—United
States—History—20th century. 5. Laity—Catholic Church—
History—20th century. 6. Laity—United States—History—20th
century. 7. United States—Church history—20th century.
I. Dolan, Jay P., 1936–
BX1407.P3T7 1989
253'.0973—dc19
                                                               89–1304
                                                               CIP

CONTENTS

PREFACE

In the fall of 1988 the Catholic archdiocese of Detroit announced that it was going to close more than forty churches in the city of Detroit. The announcement provoked howls of protest. Priests and people mobilized in an attempt to save their churches. Meetings and demonstrations took place and all the while the cardinal archbishop of Detroit, Edmund C. Szoka, tried to calm the opposition. After weeks of demonstrations, discussions, and pleading the archbishop revised the numbers and announced that only thirty-one churches would be closed. This episode in Detroit dramatized the plight of the Catholic Church in contemporary America. What took place in the Motor City was not unique; similar scenarios have been going on in every major metropolitan area of the country for the past ten to twenty years. Year after year city newspapers carried the news—"St. Patrick's Church to Close," "St. Agnes School Graduates Its Last Class," "Jesuit Seminary Is Sold to Developer." Catholics were not accustomed to hearing news like this. For years they boasted about their growing numbers. In the 1950s and early 60s the dedication of a new church or school seemed to be an annual Catholic rite of spring. That is no longer true. Even though the number of Catholics continues to grow, the institutional church is shrinking.

There are many reasons for the closing of schools, churches, and seminaries. Catholics have relocated to the suburbs and the large city churches of the immigrant era now go begging for worshipers. The cost of quality schooling has priced many parishes out of the business of education. The Catholic cultural ghetto has come apart and denominational loyalty is not as strong as it was in the 1940s and 50s. Fewer men and women are choosing a vocation to religious life with the result that there are not enough priests and sisters to staff all the churches, schools, and seminaries of Catholic America. To combat the shortage of personnel lay men and women have taken over the work of the sisters and priests. This is most evident in the classroom, but it is noticeable in many other areas of Catholic life as well. As this major shift in roles has taken place, Catholics have begun to rethink the traditional understanding of priesthood and ministry. As a result of this a new theology of ministry has developed and book stores are now stocked with row upon row of books that explore every conceivable aspect of ministry in the church. Much of this literature is useful, but some of it is as frivolous and faddish as Madison Avenue's latest self-help book.

The new theology of ministry has also sparked debate and controversy, and many church leaders, including Pope John Paul II himself, are wary of some of the new trends taking place in the church. In a recent document on the role of the laity in church and society, "The Lay Members of Christ's Faithful People," the pope cautioned against the blurring of the distinction between clergy and laity and warned against the "too indiscriminate use of the word 'ministry'." It is clear that with the pope joining the debate the discussion will take on a more ecclesiastical tone and church authorities will want to place limits on the range of public debate.

Much of the discussion on ministry in the United States has concentrated on the theological and pastoral dimensions of the issue. The historical dimension has been noticeably absent. This book attempts to correct that imbalance.

The heart of this book are the three essays on the priest, sister, and lay person. Each of these essays ranges over a fifty year period, 1930–1980, and examines two major issues—the change that took place in the understanding and practice of ministry among a specific group of people (priests, sisters, or laity) and how this altered their relationship with the parish. In Part IV I have attempted to integrate the essays and some of their major points into a broader social context with a primary focus on the parish over the course of these fifty years. I end the essay with my own interpretation as to why such substantive and dramatic changes took place in the American Catholic Church at this particular moment in time.

This book is important because it provides a much needed historical perspective to a debate that will have decisive impact on the future of Roman Catholicism in the United States. Catholics cannot think and act as if there was no yesterday.

As Americans and as Catholics we will never understand who we are unless we know who we were. In studying the past we can also better understand the present and appreciate the work of our predecessors who blazed the trails that led us to this present age. An understanding of history is also necessary if we are going to be honest and truthful with our use of the past. Memory has an inclination to be selective as well as forgetful and in the search for a usable past a person can innocently, or intentionally, distort the truth. A knowledge of history enables a person to judge the accuracy of the usable past that people wish to endorse. When it comes to the discussion of ministry in the American Catholic Church, a knowledge of the past can be especially helpful.

Historical studies of ministry in twentieth-century American Catholicism are as rare as the bald eagle. A few studies of the priest do exist and even fewer historical studies of women religious are available; as for the laity and their apostolic work in church and society the historical cupboard is virtually empty. For this reason these essays by Scott Appleby, Patricia Byrne, and Debra Campbell are pioneering studies. Nothing like them exists. In breaking new ground they not only reveal how rich the history of American Catholicism was in the thirty years that preceded Vatican Council II, but they also make sense out of the changes that have transformed the church in the post–Vatican II era. But these essays do more than fill a vacuum. In examining the changing role of priest, sister, and lay person over the course of the past half century, these essays provide an historical context for the contemporary discussion about ministry. They show that there was life in the church before Vatican II when many important developments took place. Debra Campbell uncovered a very active laity in the 1940s and 50s; involved in a variety of apostolates, these people developed a new self-consciousness as Catholic lay men and women and this provided the foundation for developments in the post–Vatican II era. In studying priests Scott Appleby encountered some impressive "pioneers of renewal" in the 1940s and 50s who were redefining the meaning of priesthood and experimenting with parish structures well before such thinking was fashionable. Patricia Byrne's sisters were already planting the seeds of change in the decade after World War II, a time when convent communities were buzzing with activities aimed at the renewal of religious life. In other words, new types of ministries were already beginning to develop in those years.

In the current discussion of ministry the danger is always present that flushed with the sense of discovery, but ignorant of the past, people will reinvent the wheel and give new names to realities that existed thirty or forty years ago. These essays will help to cure such historical amnesia. This study also reduces the Mt. Everest proportions of the Second Vatican Council, an attitude that views the council as the explanation for just about everything that has happened to Catholics since the 1960s. By placing the council in an historical context, its importance can be more accurately assessed. In fact, I argue in my essay "that World War II had as much influence on the reshaping of contemporary American Catholicism as did the Second Vatican Council."

In addition to providing some historical context for the discussion on ministry this study also represents a major contribution to the history of religion in twentieth-century America. It is a chapter in the history of twentieth-century American Catholicism that has never been told before in such depth and detail.

The idea for this study first surfaced in conversations that I had with Robert Wood Lynn at the Lilly Endowment in 1985. Robert Lynn was deeply interested in the role of church and synagogue in the United States, and through the Lilly Endowment he encouraged many studies of congregational life. We had previously worked together on an historical study of the Catholic parish, and once this was finished we began to discuss the issue of ministry and its relationship to parish life. This study is the result of those conversations. Funded by the Lilly Endowment it got underway in the fall of 1986 and was completed two years later. During this period my conversations with Robert Lynn and his colleagues at the Endowment, Fred L. Hofheinz and Jeanne Knoerle, S.P., continued. I am most grateful for their support because without their encouragement this study would never have come to life.

One of the most unique aspects of this study was its collaborative nature. Many individuals helped to shape it. An advisory committee was active from the very beginning and carefully followed the progress of the essays. Composed of Kathleen Ashe, O.P., John Coleman, S.J., Ruth Doyle, David O'Brien, and Thomas O'Meara, the committee helped to sharpen the focus of the study and reviewed the work of the authors. We are most grateful to them for their active involvement in the study.

The major work of the study was done during the spring semester of 1987, when Appleby, Byrne, and Campbell were in residence as visiting scholars at the University of Notre Dame's Cushwa Center for the Study of American Catholicism. During these months they traveled widely in order to do the necessary research and interviewing that the study demanded. When together at Notre Dame, we shared our insights and continually reviewed the work of one another.

Since the study was based at the University of Notre Dame, a number of Notre Dame faculty took part in it. The principal participants were Philip Gleason, David Leege, Thomas O'Meara, Mark Searle, and Joseph White; they participated in a number of seminars and evaluated the work of the authors from their own particular expertise. Leslie Griffin and Thomas Kselman were also involved in some of the other brain-storming sessions associated with the study. We are most grateful to all of these individuals for their willingness to share their time and talents with us. The essays are much better because of their involvement.

The authors are also most grateful to the many people whom they interviewed in the course of their work. Scott Appleby wishes to thank Howard Bleichner, S.S., of St. Patrick Seminary in Menlo Park, California, and Robert J. Wister of Immaculate Heart Seminary in Darlington, New Jersey, for welcoming him to their institutions and arranging meetings with their colleagues. Joseph Gremillion, one of Appleby's "pioneering priests," was a most valuable resource and consultant, and Murray Clayton, a pastor in Louisiana, provided an impressive example of the priest as "orchestra leader." Barbara Lockwood was most helpful in the typing of Appleby's essay and was ably assisted by Tim Nelson. Peggy Appleby, Scott's wife, deserves a special acknowledgment for holding family and home together during this project, and Scott dedicates his essay to her.

Patricia Byrne, C.S.J., expresses her gratitude to Sisters Bette Moslander, C.S.J., Marie Augusta Neal, S.N.D.deN., Margaret A. Leonard, L.S.A., Mary Daniel Turner, S.N.D.deN., and Lora Ann Quinonez, C.D.P., for their generous donation of time and valuable insight. She also thanks the archivists and sisters of the following congregations for their enthusiastic cooperation: Sisters of the Presentation of the Blessed Virgin Mary, San Francisco, California; Sisters of Charity, Leavenworth, Kansas; Sisters of Charity, Nazareth, Kentucky; Sisters of St. Joseph, Baden, Pennsylvania; and the Sisters of Notre Dame de Namur in Boston and Ipswich, Massachusetts. A note of thanks is due to Gay Weidlich for typing the essay and to Amelia Vasquez, R.S.C.J., for her faithful help and encouragement. She dedicates her essay to Mary Isabel Concannon, C.S.J., in grateful remembrance.

Debra Campbell extends a special thank you to Julian Pleasants, Regina Weissert and her late husband, Ralph, Joseph Gremillion, Janet Kalven, Sister John Sullivan, John Egan, Edward Marciniak, and Edward Sellner for their time and fruitful conversation. Janet Kirkpatrick of the Regis College Archives, Joyce Dietrick at the Grail Archives, and Kevin Cawley of the University of Notre Dame Archives were most cooperative. At Colby College Sunny Pomerleau of the library deserves a note of thanks as does Pauline Wing and Grace Von Tobel who were helpful with the innumerable details connected with Campbell's travels, correspondence, and typing. Debra also wishes to thank her husband, Deane Ferm, for patiently listening to her talk about her work and carefully criticizing her written work.

Delores Fain, secretary at the Cushwa Center, performed heroic work in meeting a variety of needs for all of us who were involved in this project. She deserves a very special acknowledgment for her patience and kindness throughout the entire study.

JAY P. DOLAN

·PART I·

Present to the People of God: The Transformation of the Roman Catholic Parish Priesthood

INTRODUCTION

> When I first began teaching at this seminary I was considered a "liberal" because I wore street clothes on seminary grounds on days when I was not teaching. In the mid-sixties I was considered a "conservative" because I wore clerical garb on days when I was teaching. Just recently, our new bishop was on the grounds and, as it was my day off, I was in street clothes. A colleague refused to introduce me to the bishop. I guess I'm a "liberal" again.[1]

> What is my most important role in the parish? Being there, being present to the people, as a sign of the Church ... as a sign of themselves. Sometimes I am there to do something specific—to teach, to listen, even to cast a vote—and other times, I'm not really doing anything, but my presence is important. They complain when I'm absent from an important event or meeting.[2]

The preceding half-century, from the Great Depression to the Reagan revolution, has been a time of economic and political upheaval, social dislocation, and cultural transformation. A cursory listing of major events, programs, and movements reshaping American self-understanding—the depression and recovery, the New Deal, American participation in World War II, postwar prosperity, the cold war, the great society and the unsuccessful War on Poverty, the civil rights movement, Vietnam, Watergate, the industrial technological revolution, the women's liberation movement, Hispanic and east Asian immigration, Reagonomics—confirms the judgment that we live in an era of social change unprecedented in American history.

It is not surprising, then, that this period also witnessed American Catholicism's "third romance with modernity." The church had successfully neutralized the "acids of modernity" for a full century longer than many of its Protestant counterparts. Well into the 1950s, American Catholic parochial life remained relatively untroubled by the odd modern trends of secularism, ecumenism, pluralism, and voluntarism. Even as European and American pioneers in liturgy, theology, and social action sowed the seeds of Roman Catholicism's own twentieth-century revolution, the daily life of the average parish reflected a worldview designed to counteract modernity's radical skepticism about the supernatural. Catholic parishioners inhabited a multi-layered religious "world" peopled by saints in heaven (the "church triumphant"), repentant sinners in purgatory (the "church suffering"), and the Catholic faithful as yet on earth struggling toward righteousness (the "church militant"). They understood God to be utterly transcendent, the divine presence mediated by the church militant in public worship and the church triumphant in private devotion. In either case, the church was necessary for saving communion with the divine, and the church was represented to the faithful in the pews primarily, if not exclusively, by the parish priest.[3]

In the decade after the end of World War II, the walls of this Catholic fortress began to give way to a new design, the outlines and contours of which were not sharply drawn. Catholic priests in the United States whose ministries survived the 1960s and 70s could draw up their own list of epochal, often traumatic, events and movements—papal support of Catholic Action, liturgical renewal, critical biblical scholarship, and biblically based ecclesiologies; the Second Vatican Council with its seeming vindication of the pluralism, ecumenism, and social activism prevalent in the American situation; the ensuing crisis of priestly identity and the radical questioning of the viability of parish life—to support the claim that the previous half-century has also witnessed a profound religious transformation described, variously, as a "shift in paradigm," a "Catholic Reformation," and a "New Catholicism."[4]

In an attempt to describe the attitude of priests toward parochial ministry during this tumultuous period, I have drawn upon a number of sources, including diocesan and seminary archives, parish records, primary and secondary accounts of priestly ministry in books and periodicals, and official documents of the church. I also enjoyed the luxury of interviewing seventy-five priests, ordained at staggered intervals from 1929 to 1981. These interviewees ranged in age from eighty-two to thirty-one, and serve or served in parishes in New York, Boston, Chicago, Baltimore, St. Louis, Memphis, New Orleans, Shreveport, rural Mississippi, Seattle, Tacoma, Portland, rural Oregon, and San Francisco. These "data" were not collected for the purpose of sociological analysis. Rather, the remarks and insights of this group of parish priests, diverse in age, region, and theological orientation, have provided an "insider's view" invaluable to a historian of the priesthood who is himself a layman. In some instances the interviews alerted me to attitudes or programs not sufficiently represented in primary and secondary written material. For example, the interview process did in fact provide an important clue to the continuity I sought in the midst of deeply rooted change and discontinuity in the parish priesthood. Repeatedly, interviewees described their vocation in terms of *presence* in and to the parish community. Individuals did not agree on the nature of that presence or the definition of "parish community." But this preoccupation with ways of being present to the parish community provided a principle of order to an imposing mass of documentation on the fortunes of parochial priesthood during these five decades.

In the following essay, then, I shall describe several such approaches to priestly ministry that have obtained since 1930. I have avoided the term "models" or "types," in part because, during a certain period of this history, participants rejected the very notion that there are, or should be, one or more models of priestly ministry. However, my "ways of priestly presence" are as limited as "models" and "types." As didactic constructs that cannot fully comprehend the complex reality to which they point, they attempt simply to describe the primary characteristics of each distinctive approach to priestly ministry from 1930 to the present day.

Accordingly, I have divided the half-century into four discrete periods, each corresponding to a way or ways of priestly ministry that commanded center stage in the ongoing struggle for identity. During the period from 1930 to 1954, the era of the "ombudsman," priestly ministry was centered in the parish and the priest's presence in the parish was both symbolic and functional. His presence as a symbol of the institutional church and the divine Christ was absolute and unchallenged—and it lent substance to his claim to functional omnicompetence. During the initial period of updating, from 1954 to 1962, "pioneer priests" read the signs of the times and recognized that the all-purpose parochial presence of the ombudsman was no longer possible or desirable. They began to reconsider parochial presence in light of a renewed commitment to the larger secular world. The ensuing decade was by all accounts a period of crisis in religion and in the church as in American society.

During this decade, following the opening session of the Second Vatican Council (1962), there emerged a number of new approaches to priestly ministry, including the social activism of the "urban priest" and the professional specialization of the so-called hyphenated priest. These men reconceived the symbolic identity of the priest in light of the conciliar decrees and forged new standards of priestly behavior, but their ability to integrate these symbolic and functional roles within the setting of the suburban parish, or within the organizational structures of any traditional parish, was open to question. The current period reflects the emergence of a way of ministry that draws creatively upon previous examples: the priest as coordinator, supervisor, "orchestra leader." His symbolic presence, rather than his functional presence, lends distinctiveness to his ministry; better put, his symbolic presence is a primary function of his ministry. His home is once again in the parish, but his notion of his place in parish and world is somewhat different from that of his counterpart in the 1930s.

By identifying each of these periods with a particular approach to priestly ministry, I do not mean to suggest that the featured "way" was the only, or even the statistically dominant, approach to priesthood. Certainly, during the period of crisis this is not the case: the large majority of priests who remained in ministry were not, for example, "hyphenated priests" selectively present to the parish. But most priests were forced to respond in some fashion to the new way that commanded center stage during those years, whether by rejecting it or modifying their own self-understandings in its light. Each of the "ways" in turn characterized a particular stage in the development of the parish priesthood in this century. Each predominated, at least in terms of public visibility, during a particular period. In the essay that follows I shall attempt to describe these ways of priestly presence in historical context with an eye toward identifying the social, intellectual, and religious forces that influenced priests at each stage.

1

THE ERA OF THE OMBUDSMAN, 1930–1954

All I can think of about those years is the amazing growth of
the Northwest and of the church in this region. It was a time,
too, of the security and self-possession which comes with clarity
about your position. Everyone's role was clearly defined. The
laity were supposed to pay, pray and obey. Logistically, in terms
of numbers, not much else was possible or desirable. During
and immediately after the War, this area was booming, and the
"service station" model of parish worked very well. We [priests]
seemed to work twenty-four hours a day, saying Mass, hearing
confessions, baptizing. I was also the Catholic chaplain for the
USO in Bremerton. As a priest I loved this time of my life. I
felt alive, vital.[1]

Priestly existence does not merely begin with a vocation.
Vocation is the continued existential fact in the life of a priest.
The fact that remains is that he has been selected from among
all Christians, not merely from the world. The priest is
segregatus a populo—separated from the people—not in the
sense that at one time he is summoned from the ranks to
assume a position opposed to them and later returns as one of
the rank and file. This is sharply accentuated in the Western
Church through the assumption of celibacy, remaining ever
unmarried, in order to belong to God alone. The vocation is a
vocation of heroes. Celibacy is the deciding test and touchstone
of that heroism. With ordination he becomes a *sacerdos in
aeternum*, a priest forever, with a *character indelibilis*, signed with
the seal of priesthood which will be his mark forever, and
which, God forbid, if he be lost, cannot be burnt away in the
flames of hell. The determination and ordination of a
twenty-four-year-old creates a condition which is settled for
time and eternity. The canonical prescriptions describe only his
external condition.

The inexorability and inescapability which go with his freely
accepted ordination are part and parcel of the existence of the
priest. The decision for the priesthood is an irrevocable one.
That is what makes it so serious.[2]

Prior to the Second Vatican Council, the official Roman Catholic theology of priesthood located the fullness of the apostolic priesthood in the office of the priest. The bishop enjoyed more administrative and canonical authority than the parish pastor, and the pastor enjoyed similar authority over his assistant priests, or curates. Nonetheless, Holy Orders imparted to each lowly curate the sacramental fullness of priesthood. "No office held by mortal man exceeds in dignity or sublimity that of the priesthood," wrote Rev. John A. O'Brien in a popular 1943 exposition of this theology. St. Thomas Aquinas declared that no act is greater than the consecration of the body of Christ, O'Brien reminded his readers. "In this essential phase of your ministry," he declared, "the power of the priest is not surpassed by that of the bishop, the archbishop, the cardinal, or the Holy Father himself. Indeed it is equal to the power of Jesus Christ; for in this role the priest speaks with the voice and authority of Christ Himself." The priesthood is not, O'Brien concluded, a human usurpation of divine authority, nor is its authority "derived from the corporate will of the congregation."[3]

The priest was, in the theological terminology of the day, *alter Christus*. Accordingly, his competence in religious questions went unchallenged by a laity that perceived him as "a man set apart" from the crowd. His parishioners presumed him to be a man of holiness by virtue of his ordination. The church, itself an institution set apart from the sin of the world, guaranteed this. In training the priest for public service, seminaries and clergy conferences held up the image of "the Christian gentleman" as the model of priestly behavior in sanctuary, rectory, and marketplace. Such a man would conduct himself at all times with dignity and reserve, polite to a fault, stern in defense of principle. If the priest also happened to be a kind, generous, joyous, self-sacrificing person, the laity accepted this as a bonus. He may just as likely have been cold, impersonal, and somewhat remote.[4]

In fact there is considerable evidence to suggest that the seminary system of the day promoted this latter approach to priesthood. As a rule, a paramilitary program prevailed at many minor and major seminaries of the 1930s, 1940s, and the early 1950s. Characterized by the stern, otherworldly ascesis of the Irish tradition, or by the supernaturalism of Sulpician piety, seminary life during the first half of the twentieth century was, in a large part, a concerted reaction to two heresies that threatened to infect the Catholic priesthood. As Joseph M. White points out in his comprehensive history of the diocesan seminary in the United States, spiritual and intellectual formation proceeded cautiously in the wake of Americanism (condemned by Pope

Leo XIII in 1899) and Modernism (condemned by Pope Pius X in 1907). The former error included a tendency toward pragmatic evangelization and an emphasis on natural rather than supernatural virtues. In reaction, Rome encouraged seminary faculties to devote themselves to the inculcation of supernatural virtues in their students. Modernism promoted an intellectual synthesis of the apostolic faith and modern sciences, the most challenging aspect of which was the incorporation of higher biblical criticism into Catholic theology and ecclesiology. Rome countered with measures designed to repress open-ended intellectual inquiry and experimentation with curriculum in seminaries and other Catholic institutions of higher learning.[5]

The result in the first half of the twentieth century was a highly regimented seminary system that produced a uniform product—soldiers in the church militant. The system emphasized obedience in regard to hierarchical authority, formalism in regard to spiritual exercises and devotions, and conservatism in regard to doctrine. As Philip Murnion pointed out in a study of ordinands in New York in the 1920s, many of the more talented and creative of them were forced out of the system or made to feel unwelcome. Cardinal Hayes cautioned the class of 1930 against "the heresy of good works" (overactivism) and described in military metaphor the priests he sent forth as "the reserved power behind the lines, troops for relief, assistance, protection, and defense." His advice to his charges: keep out of the kitchen, get along with your pastor, and save your money.[6]

Individualism was suspect. Any expression of distinctiveness of personality in and through the priesthood came under severe scrutiny. Cardinal William O'Connell, archbishop of Boston until 1944, offered a succinct summary of this philosophy: "There is no such thing as the personality of a bishop or the personality of a parish priest. Personal qualities are subject to change. These are transient things on which depend nothing of the certainty of the Catholic Faith."[7] In both its form and content the priestly office was seen as objective and owing nothing essential to subjectivity. Suitable men could acquire and exercise its liturgical and extraliturgical responsibilities in a prescribed and uniform manner. "St. John's tried to prepare candidates so that they could absorb a sacramental character at ordination much as softened wax is impressed with a seal," wrote Robert E. Sullivan of the Boston seminary.[8]

An essentialist, premodern worldview stood behind this theology of priesthood. Roman Catholic theologians in positions of institutional prominence during and after the First Vatican Council (1869–1870) subscribed to a theological system best described as neo-scholasticism. Based on a complex manual tradition derived originally from the summas of the medieval scholastic theologians, especially Thomas Aquinas (1224–1274), it had taken on numerous accretions and was presented in the late nineteenth century as an absolute, unified, self-contained system of thought. The proponents of this system were sometimes called "integralists," for they affirmed each particular principle or assertion of the system as necessary to the completeness of the whole. To approach this body of teaching as a surgeon would approach a human body, with a critical eye for imperfections and a scalpel to pare away organs threatening the vitality of the whole, was just what modernists seemed (to integralists) to be doing. To challenge the doctrine of the Virgin Birth or the Mosaic authorship of the Pentateuch on the basis of the latest findings of biblical research was, in their minds, to challenge the whole web of Catholic doctrine, each strand emanating as it did from one impenetrable and unquestionable source—namely, divine revelation as communicated in scripture and apostolic tradition.

This nineteenth-century medievalism was ahistorical in that it posited unchanging, invisible essences as the principle of identity and reality (a person is a human being by virtue of a *soul*; a priest is a priest by virtue of an indelible mark on the soul), which remained substantially unaffected by the shifting tides of human history (a validly ordained priest remains a priest in spite of his external circumstances). Yet, in one of several post-Tridentine Catholic ironies, neo-scholastic philosophers had, by the early twentieth century, allowed the enemies of the church to define the framework of the philosophical debate, with the church in a defensive posture. Secular humanists, atheists, Marxists, and existentialists of every stripe identified human history with the history of matter or consciousness, denying it a transcendence or a significance reconcilable with traditional Christian theism. In a response that undermined Catholicism's ancient commitment to salvation in and through this world, integralists manning the Roman curia in the nineteenth and early twentieth centuries abandoned human experience as an arena for God's redeeming action. First articulated in the Vatican I document on revelation, this philosophical "extrinsicism" denied that the human person is inherently a "hearer of the word." In this understanding, divine self-revelation comes upon recipients unannounced, and finds them unprepared for an event so utterly foreign to their everyday experience. This attempt to protect the "objective, external fact" of revelation led integralists to denounce what they perceived as a "Kantian subjectivism" and an erroneous doctrine of "vital immanence" (the Spirit is present to the individual prior to external revelation) in the writings and teaching of the modernists.[9]

The integralist, or neo-scholastic, approach also promoted a kind of dualism in European and American Catholic sensibilities during the early decades of this century. A history that had, after all, produced Protestants, materialists, and atheistic communists in abundance certainly seemed to mirror a fallen, secular world. Born to such a world, the faithful were ontogenetically disposed to sin and therefore unworthy to approach the altar of the living God. Their one recourse was to a perfect, self-contained society, the pure history of which was untainted by human error. Aloof from the vagaries and "transience" of human personality, this society mediated to the faithful a deity who was as transcendent and mysterious as human society was vulgar and predictable. This perfect society, embodied by the institutional church of Rome, possessed its own objective body of canon law, precepts, and rubrics legitimated in and of themselves (*ex opere operato*) rather than by the personal, subjective qualities of its members. This objective authenticity accrued to the church by virtue of the commission and promise of its founder, Jesus of Nazareth, whose mission and identity Roman theologians interpreted according to an exalted christology that diminished the savior's full, concrete, and thus potentially troubling, participation in the human condition. In short, the religious world inherited by our American Catholic priests of the 1930s and 1940s sustained a vertical rather than a horizontal faith.

This is not to suggest that the faith was rendered sterile or one-sided in practice. To the contrary, the Catholic faithful, with their "infallible sense of the faith," preserved in their own fashion those vital aspects of the apostolic experience deemphasized in the nineteenth-century neo-scholasticism of the integralists. If the mystifying transcendence of God stood behind the elaborate formalism of the Latin liturgy, a palpable sense of divine immanence fueled the nineteenth-century "devotional revolution," the religious sensibilities of which continued to inform American Catholic popular piety well into our period. One need only review the names of the prominent parochial organizations in New Orleans or Seattle or Boston during the 1930s and 40s—the Legion of Mary, the Holy Name Society, the St. Vincent de Paul Society—to appreciate the profound fascination that the doctrine of the communion of the saints, with the Virgin at its head, held for the religious imagination of the Catholic community. In spite of the reforming efforts of Pope Pius X and German Benedictines to encourage eucharistic piety and revivify public worship at the turn of the century, most American Catholics rejoiced in the delights, or recoiled from the terrors, of the supernatural world by means of frequent access to familiar patron saints and the Virgin Mary, whose association with humanity was uninhibited by the burdens of full divinity.[10]

Nonetheless, this balancing act was accomplished within, and on the terms of, the system of transcendence developed by the integralists. This was true of many aspects of Catholic parochial life. For example, the system of transcendence did not eclipse Catholic social outreach, an impulse as old as the tradition. But social concern was exercised within the parameters of the worldview. The St. Vincent de Paul Society, at least in its initial incarnation, helped the indigent to recover from, or cope with, the debilitating consequences of life in an unjust society and sinful world; it did not presume to bring the resources of faith to bear upon the intractable situation or complex economic structures that had left the neighbor homeless or penniless in the first place. And when the parish pastor interceded with the world on behalf of the immigrant, he did not relax the paternalistic stance by which he dealt with the laity from the sanctuary and boardroom alike. Rev. John Tackney of Brookline, Massachusetts, recalls the personification of this approach in the Boston area:

> In Dorchester in the 1920's and '30's was a man named Monsignor Haviland. A person in that neighborhood would never sell their house without asking his permission. He was called "the Mayor of Meeting House Hill." No government—state, federal, or local—ever did anything without consulting him. That's how powerful he was. He was the most educated, he was the most powerful, he was the most revered. Why? Because the whole parish was made up of immigrants! And he was articulate. He spoke for them. He was the James Michael Curley of Dorchester.[11]

This is certainly social advocacy but, as we shall see, it differed significantly from the approach of the "urban priest" in the 1960's. The Monsignor Havilands of the immigrant church wielded influence with public officials because they represented a powerful constituency—namely, the closed society known as the Catholic Church. Yet the pastor was not "elected" by his constituency. Rather, the parishioners placed trust in the pastor because he represented to them something far greater than himself—namely, the triumphant church extending through time and space. The pastor's action was in behalf of this church. On many occasions, this action coincided with the needs and will of his parishioners. On some occasions, it did not. In a 1930 article entitled "Anticlericalism in the United States," Jerome D. Hannan pointed out that the priest's primary loyalty was not to the local church but to the universal church. Susceptible to the disedifying influences of American society, the laity could not always be counted upon, he complained, to defend the interests of Catholicism. Reporting on an interview he concluded with a "deposed church committee," Hannan wrote:

> There are many reasons why a man should not be permitted to serve on a church committee, even though chosen by a majority ballot. He may be a bad Catholic. That type usually finds a way of squirming into the petty politics of church factions. The objection may arise to him because he has unjustly criticized the pastor's administration of the parish. Finally, he may by deed have interfered in parish administration to such an extent as to have hindered its development. . . . They pretended exasperation. "Then all we can do is give, give, give," they exclaimed. I merely reminded them that they all had an obligation to contribute to the support of the church and that it was not a right, but a privilege, which permitted some of the congregation to cooperate with the pastor in the administration of church affairs. . . . It was clear that they believed themselves to be of right the administrators of the congregation's property, and the priest was merely their hired servant, not the delegate of the Bishop. This is a view that is not so rare as one might believe. It springs from the democratic form of political government under which we live, and from the Protestant method of ecclesiastical government which is everywhere operative about us. Both types of government are essentially laical.[12]

Regarding the laity, the actions and attitudes of the priest were individualistic rather than corporate, independent rather than collaborative. As a rule, the ombudsman-priest did not empower the laity to act within the parish or in behalf of the parish out in the world. Instead, he took it upon himself to act. In the world he alone represented the parish. And in the parish he incorporated various ministries within his own. Better put: it did not occur to him that significant apostolic service might occur apart from his sacerdotal office. Intimations of a different way of priesthood, foreshadowed by papal endorsement of Catholic Action, did not disturb his serenity until the 1950s. There was, on the other hand, a very important sense in which the action of the priest was collaborative and corporate. He was a member of a team not within the parish but within the larger church, his diocese. The successful bishop in the ombudsman era did build a sense of solidarity and loyalty in his diocesan priests. Coupled with the centralization of parochial authority in the clergy, this seemed particularly well suited to a brick-and-mortar age of industrial expansion. Tables 1 and 2 chart the rise in the numbers of priests, parishes, and the Roman Catholic population in selected major U.S. dioceses from 1930 to 1960. In most cases the numbers indicate a steady growth accelerating rapidly in the decade after the end of World War II. But the rate of growth was uneven across these three categories. The total number of parishes increased by 25 percent during the thirty-year period, but could not keep pace with the total Roman Catholic population, which doubled. The number of priests in the United States also doubled, but the greatest growth came in the number of religious, many of whom were teachers in Catholic secondary schools, colleges, and universities. Religious orders established new parishes and helped staff existing ones, but the pattern varied from community to community.

TABLE 1

Increase in Numbers of Priests and Parishes—Selected Dioceses

	Priests				
	Secular	Religious	Total	Parishes	Catholic Population
New York					
1930	844	591	1,435	366	1,273,291
1940	935	760	1,695	374	1,000,000
1950	NA	NA	2,093	393	1,260,328
1960	1,199	1,290	2,489	400	1,581,654
Boston					
1930	769	380	1,149	288	1,019,000
1940	920	509	1,429	323	1,044,359
1950	NA	NA	1,939	359	1,302,985
1960	1,326	1,063	2,389	396	1,625,024
Philadelphia					
1930	750	273	1,023	388	812,550
1940	1,033	407	1,440	389	852,000
1950	NA	NA	1,915	398	1,058,058
1960	1,240	701	1,941	439	1,513,269
Chicago					
1930	767	500	1,267	387	1,250,000
1940	1,048	788	1,836	413	1,400,000
1950	NA	NA	2,196	390	1,691,681
1960	1,264	1,549	2,813	428	2,073,616

TABLE 1 *continued*

Increase in Numbers of Priests and Parishes—Selected Dioceses

	Priests				
	Secular	Religious	Total	Parishes	Catholic Population
New Orleans					
1930	140	210	350	132	343,987
1940	154	248	402	140	330,000
1950	NA	NA	498	158	458,260
1960	219	350	569	180	617,961
Baltimore					
1930	253	552	805	170	305,490
1940	403	867	1,297	173	384,710
1950	NA	NA	647	118	297,546
1960	292	420	712	166	410,714
Portland					
1950	NA	NA	281	97	92,378
1970	227	90	317	150	202,040

TABLE 2

Increase in Numbers of Priests and Parishes in the United States

	Priests				
	Secular	Religious	Total	Parishes	Catholic Population
1930	18,873	8,052	26,925	12,413	20,203,702
1940	22,450	11,462	33,912	13,132	21,403,136
1950	NA	NA	42,970	15,292	27,766,141
1960	32,569	21,227	53,796	16,896	40,871,302

Source: *The Official Catholic Directory*

Given such clerical demographics, one must describe parochial ministry during this period with an awareness of the regional variations in its practice. For example, missionaries made inroads in the rural southeast in the 1940s and 50s, establishing sprawling territorial parishes, often ministered by latter-day circuit riders, in Mississippi, Georgia, Tennessee, and Alabama. These priests were ombudsmen in the fullest sense of the term: the undeveloped character of Catholicism in this region required them to be catechists, administrators, community builders, and teachers in the parochial schools. Because ubiquitous parochial presence was impossible for some rural pastors, they were, by force of necessity, "enablers" and "empowerers" of the laity long before those words came into general usage. In many cases, they were able to succeed only because women religious staffed the schools and provided a type of ecclesial presence and continuity required by a dependent Catholic population.[13] Historian Jeffrey M. Burns has demonstrated that the shortage of priests in parts of Oregon, Washington, and Northern California continued well into the twentieth century and gave a missionary quality to Catholic life there as well. The Extension Society of America, a national organization begun in the twentieth century by Father Francis Kelly to assist small missions, played a crucial role in the development of parish life in rural Oregon and Washington. In many priestless parishes, lay persons led prayer services and performed other duties normally reserved for the priest, who, when he visited the parish, was valued primarily for the sacramental ministry he exercised, which the laity could not. But even the mobile religious orders could not meet the needs of the postwar boom in "Catholic frontiers" such as the Pacific northwest. In Portland, for example, the number of priests simply could not keep up with population growth and the subsequent demand for new parishes. Bishops were forced to compete for religious order priests, to "borrow" diocesan priests from other regions of the country, and to concentrate on the building up of a native regional clergy and seminary system.[14]

The larger dioceses in the northeast and midwest were particularly successful in developing a locally born-and-bred presbyterate. In the 1940s, dependence on foreign-born priests diminished in seminarian-rich archdioceses like Boston, Chicago, and New York. In each case, diocesan (secular) priests came to dominate the parochial ministry and assumed the role of ombudsmen in parishes, which often still retained a distinctive ethnic, immigrant cast. The formative role of religious order priests in the history of the presbyterates in these dioceses was, however, no less pronounced than in the rural areas mentioned above. The national parishes that survived in these cities were often staffed by religious order priests. St. Benedict's parish in Chicago continued to function as a German parish until 1952; on the near north side, the Servite and Scalabrini fathers encouraged Italianization through local *feste*, neighborhood societies, and numerous bulletins and sermons preached at parishes such as St. Philip Benizi. Religious order priests had direct influence in the formation of diocesan priests through parish work, teaching in secondary and graduate schools, and occasional stints in diocesan seminaries. The Society of St. Sulpice continued to exert a powerful influence through its diocesan seminaries, and the Jesuits, Benedictines, and Dominicans set standards for diocesan priests through their teaching and pastoral example. In other urban areas such as New Orleans, which lagged behind in producing home-grown diocesan priests in ample numbers, religious order priests stepped in to augment the pastoral capacities of the diocese. It is impossible to generalize about the nature of their influence on diocesans. In some cases, religious priests served as the model of the traditional ombudsman. But in other cases, as we shall see, they were harbingers of new learning and pioneers of a new way of parochial ministry.[15]

This rapid growth, and the organizational chaos that inevitably accompanied it, occurred at a time when American businessmen were developing and implementing the bureaucratic processes of professional management and long-term planning that would characterize twentieth-century corporate life. These modern innovations were not entirely lost on the Roman Catholic Church. This was the age of diocesan centralization and bureaucratization, presided over by power-broker bishops such as Mundelein of Chicago, O'Connell of Boston, and, at mid-century, Spellman of New York. These men focused much of their attention on the building up of ecclesiastical infrastructures that would extend their influence both outside and inside the church: the chancery office, Catholic Charities, the diocesan seminary system, and citywide networks like the Catholic Youth Organization. By such efforts the institutional church emerged in these decades as a formidable force in American civic and political life. The trademarks of these episcopal administrators—giantism, going first-class, business-like management, an unapologetic Americanism—mirrored the triumphal, highly visible Catholicism of the day.

In this scheme of things, the bishop recruited and formed bureaucrats from his own personnel pool: his loyal priests were his civil service. "I am going to make mistakes," Mundelein told his clergy on the day of his installation in Chicago. "But I am your archbishop and I look to my priests to cover up my mistakes, not to expose, discuss, or criticize them. To whom else can I look for as much consideration? Your archbishop is the one man in this town who is constantly in the spotlight. Shield him as much as you can."[16] Although this type of episcopal leadership has gone out of fashion, it served the important purpose in its own day of putting American Catholicism on the social and political map. In a very real sense, then, it was the institutional security and cultural acceptance won by these "imperial" bishops that made possible the creative leadership of a generation of "pioneer priests" at a later time when the universal church was poised for ag-giornamento. And the success of the imperial bishop in establishing among their diocesan priests a corporate identity, a common goal and vision of priestly ministry, provided a security and stability to the priesthood that a later generation would not enjoy.

However, diocesan centralization was not an unmixed blessing for the parochial ministry. The need for clerical administrators for such worthy agencies as Catholic Charities drained parishes of some of the most competent young ordinands. And many of the brightest seminar-ians were sent to Rome to prepare for careers in the chancery or sem-inary. Meanwhile, the curate who "made pastor," usually after decades of waiting, enjoyed almost absolute power in his parochial realm, and tended to resent the expense of supporting centralized activities or church agencies he could not control or use at the parish level. All of this led, at times, to an otherwise curious (given the efforts at central-ization) lack of coordination of the church's resources, especially in terms of personnel. One hand did not seem to know, or care, what the other was doing. Most important, the natural resources of the parish were not always integrated into the overall pastoral and social strate-gies of the diocese—beyond, of course, the regular appeals for finan-cial support. This was an understandable but regrettable result of the church's efforts to be simultaneously responsive to social and pastoral needs on the local, regional, national, and, ultimately, international levels. Nonetheless, this lack of coordinated planning plagued pastoral efforts not only within dioceses but also from diocese to diocese. Re-porting as they did directly to Rome without coordinating pastoral decisions on a national or regional level, Catholic dioceses ranged, especially in terms of personnel, from one organizational extreme to another. Poor planning, combined with an unequal distribution of vo-cations, produced priest-rich and priest-poor dioceses side by side.[17]

In Boston, for example, vocations were plentiful in the late 1920s and early 1930s, and O'Connell ordained large numbers of priests with little regard for the relatively slower growth rate of the lay population. Parishes grew in size, with a full complement of priests serving each. In 1933, in the wake of the depression, the archbishop reacted to a perceived surplus of priests, and the cost of training new ones, by dis-missing twenty seminarians, reducing enrollments, and lengthening the seminarians' course of study. Twelve years later, his successor, Rich-ard Cushing, accelerated the course of study and expanded again, con-vinced that Boston was suffering a shortage of priests. Soon Boston was overflowing with clerics, so much so that Cushing shared his sur-plus with other dioceses in a kind of lend-lease program. All the while, planning for new parishes, consolidation of old ones, or division of those that had grown too large, failed to keep pace with the developments in seminary output. As this was happening in Boston, other regions of the country also experienced an increase in laity, but often without the ample pool of seminarians available to dioceses in the northeast and midwest. Priest-poor Seattle, for example, waited upon ordinands lent by generous bishops in Michigan and Nebraska.[18]

Given this complex of circumstances, and the demands placed upon priests in both rural and urban settings, it is not surprising that Archbishops O'Connell in Boston, Hayes and Spellman in New York, Rummell in New Orleans, and Mundelein in Chicago, among others, expected almost "universal competence" for a variety of ministries from each man receiving holy orders. Pastoral ministry was, in this context, "quite diversified, predominantly parochial, and isolated from other priests and laity."[19]

The priestly presence in the parish was both symbolic and functional. As *alter Christus*, a man set apart, the priest was a symbol of the universal church and the transcendent Christ. His status in this regard was legitimated by his seminary training and subsequent "accrediting" via ordination by the church—not by his personal characteristics or talents. Indeed his holiness was expressed formally through the rather impersonal and mechanical spiritual practices drilled into him at the seminary. And of these practices—private prayer before and after Mass, the recitation of the divine office, the saying of the rosary, meditation before retiring—only the divine office survived the first three years of priesthood in many cases. "Of course the system did not produce personal holiness," a current seminary rector observed, "because it produced nothing personal at all."[20]

The ombudsman's symbolic presence as representative of a tradition of holiness did not depend upon his own personal attributes, but it served to legitimate his ubiquitous functional presence. And the quality of this functional presence invariably *did* depend upon his personal attributes. This was the supreme irony in the day-to-day life of the parish priest. Seminary training had prepared him formally for a symbolic, liturgical role, the performance of which required a certain predisposition to ordered, meticulous action prescribed by rubrics or canon law. In short, it prepared him for life in the perfect society that was the church. Yet when he set foot in his first parish he invariably found himself in the midst of the rather colorful, chaotic, imperfect society that was the local church. The good news was that his status as symbol of the church universal went unquestioned, his religious competence and spiritual qualities unchallenged. The surprising news was that, by virtue of this very status, he was expected to perform a variety of functions for which he was, in the majority of cases, woefully unprepared.

In this regard his seminary training was both blessing and burden. He became "ombudsman" of the parish community by virtue of his extensive education and "certification" by the hierarchy. In the era before the G.I. Bill made a college education an attainable goal for millions of American Catholics, the diocesan priest enjoyed an embarrassment of academic riches. He had studied six to eight years beyond the high school level to serve a congregation for whom a high school degree was a luxury. The combination of his religious status and his educational background proved irresistible for first-generation American Catholics, and their sons and daughters, who thrust him into a leadership role that called for omnicompetence he did not possess. In this sense his education was truly an embarrassment. He was schooled in Latin, dogmatics, moral and sacramental theology, canon law, and rubrics—subjects that served him well in his sacramental role in the parish. But his training in psychology, pastoral counseling, interpersonal relationships, parish administration, and political skills— aptitudes necessary for successful functioning in a city or suburban parish—was either woefully inadequate or nonexistent. A longtime pastor in New Orleans echoed the words of dozens of interviewees in recalling his first parish assignment:

> I was overwhelmed. I had to adjust to an autocratic pastor and to constant demands upon my attention—though always polite and deferential—by the people. For the first few months I tried to hide . . . I was most comfortable at the altar or in the confessional. It didn't help that the pastor was "unavailable" at the most inconvenient times. . . . Popes, including the present one, like to say that the priest "is in the world but not of it." When I recall my first parish, I know what they mean![21]

Indeed the parish priest lived "between" two worlds, a situation that provoked frustration in those who could not cope and demanded openness and flexibility in those who did. On the one hand, he was trained in the semimonastic environment of the seminary, accepted celibacy, and, once assigned to the parish, lived in a community of priests. In these ways his life was much like that of a religious. On the other hand, as a parish priest, he was required to react to a variety of complex situations "in the world." He truly did it all: he was a cult leader, confessor, teacher, counselor, administrator, recreation director, and social worker. Parishioners seeking employment, a loan, or advice sought him out. He told them where to send their children to school, arbitrated domestic squabbles, and spearheaded fund drives. In urban immigrant parishes he was the liaison to the world beyond the ghetto; in rural areas he was often the link to urban civilization. How inappropriate to *these* aspects of his ministry was the widespread seminary ban on reading material or radio broadcasts that carried news of the outside world!

The demands of the situation awaiting the newly ordained curates were frequently softened by the presence of the pastor, in whose office rested the fullness of parochial ministry, in practice if not in theory. The pastor was, after all, the administrator of the parish, the caretaker of the physical plant, and the supervisor of all its proceedings. Even if he did routinely burden his assistants (if they were fortunate enough to hold that lofty title) with the nuts-and-bolts work of running the parish on a daily basis, the pastor was nonetheless ultimately responsible for the welfare of the parish. Knowing this, he often ruled with an iron hand, affording curates little leeway in the exercise of their ministries. He kept a tight watch on their comings and goings, and scrutinized every aspect of their performance, including their attire and table manners.

Above all, the curate bore the burden of the requirements of priestly presence. Stationed in the rectory and, in a later era, captive to the ring of the telephone, he "manned the trenches" for twenty or twenty-five years until he inherited a pastorate all his own. This was his primary responsibility: to be available to those in need. The laity felt free to take full advantage of this priestly presence. Rev. Bruce Dreier of San Francisco recently described the perdurance of this tendency in a parish in which he was stationed some years ago:

> It was Christmas Eve and I had the midnight Mass *and* the 7 a.m. Mass on Christmas morning. I dutifully attended the reception after the midnight Mass, and rolled into bed around 3 a.m. for my three hours of sleep. At about 3:30 the phone rang and I jumped up from bed, thinking "What a terrible time for someone to die—Christmas morning." The voice on the line said, "Fatha, what are the mass times for Christmas Day?"[22]

Eventually, the majority of curates did adjust to the challenges of parish life, if not as glamorously as the fictional Father O'Malley of Hollywood's 1944 popularization of Catholic parochial culture, *Going My Way*. In a little over two hours on the silver screen, Bing Crosby's character won the heart of the crusty Irish monsignor to whom he was assigned, rescued the parish from the brink of bankruptcy, rebuilt the physical plant after a dramatic fire razed it, and crooned away the personal problems of Gene Heather, his attractive co-star. If the three-dimensional parish curate did not boast a record of success as breathtaking as Father O'Malley's, he was nonetheless satisfied with his lot in life. A system that, by today's standards, appears to have been intolerably restrictive and regimented, was a welcome change in the lives of many young men who hailed from lower middle-class first or second-generation working families in Catholic America. The simple fact that the seminary provided three square meals a day guaranteed happy memories of their time there for many depression-era seminarians. The seminary also encouraged camaraderie (while discouraging personal attachments), organized recreation, an advanced education, and a structured lifestyle—no mean accomplishment in the 1930s and early 40s. And the Roman priesthood meant job security and lofty social standing in the majority of towns and cities in the United States—the occasional manifestation of anticlericalism pointed out by Hannan notwithstanding.

In the same way, the religious world of preconciliar Roman Catholicism, the hallmarks of which were moral clarity and theological certainty, promised spiritual security of a sort to the man who had given everything to follow Christ. Max Kassieppe, an Oblate Father from Germany who preached parish missions in Texas, Oklahoma, and Kansas in the mid-1930s, listed among the "joys of the priest" a "pure heart," "a correct view of life and the world," and "a childlike abhorrence of sin." "We have been permitted to hold in our hands the same Savior that Simeon carried in his arms," he exulted. "Why does not this privilege make us more joyful? We priests are really standing in a torrent of grace. Each day brings us new riches, more graces, and greater merit." Kassiepe's presentation included a sustained speculation on "the priest in heaven."[23]

Although the ombudsman priest of the interwar years was only vaguely aware of the stirrings of a Catholic cultural renaissance inspired by European neo-Thomism, the momentum of that movement swept Catholicism toward the popular mainstream of American life in the decade after World War II. Elitist appreciation of Catholic art, philosophy, and literature, characteristic of the previous decade, gave way in the late 1940s and early 50s to a less discriminating, more inclusive celebration of Catholic religious practice. "Catholic smugness" was complemented by "Catholic pride" with the rapid acceleration of American Catholics from immigrant poverty to middle-class respectability. In all this the ombudsman priest, quietly doing his job in the parish, received an additional boost of prestige that further reinforced a sense of satisfaction about his work. The fictional Father O'Malley serenaded audiences from the silver screen as the very real Fulton J. Sheen represented priests on the radio and, eventually, on television. Catholic propaganda boasting of the superiority of the clerical state rolled from presses as never before. A popular volume released in 1951, entitled *The Greatest Calling*, featured ebullient encomiums to the priesthood from a variety of Catholic cardinals (Emmanuel Suhard), celebrities (Clare Booth Luce), and quarterbacks (Notre Dame's All-American Johnny Lujack contributed a piece entitled "God's Quarterbacks"). Fulton Sheen wrote on "The Need for Zeal," Baseball star Ralph Kiner described priests as "The Real Big Leaguers," and the Most Rev. Edwin Byrne provided a simple exposition of the priest as *alter Christus*. The all-purpose parish priest was finally getting his due.[24]

Unfortunately for him, the proceedings already smacked somewhat of nostalgia. For on the very crest of the Catholic cultural revival rode a new kind of priest, the model for which had been forming throughout the reign of the ombudsman. Unlike the ombudsman, this man was enlivened by the opportunities for change present through the historical process. Engaged with the social and political questions of the day, he cast an eye toward shaping them rather than reacting authoritatively to them. Although his approach to priesthood was not self-consciously formulated until the mid-1950s—when it was transformed by the generation that adopted it—his influence began to tell in the shadows of the Great Depression. To the genesis of this approach we must now turn.

2

PIONEERS OF RENEWAL, 1930–1954

... the euphoria, the enthusiasm which was present within us
during Vatican II, reading *The New York Times* everyday about
what was happening.... I took my vacation over in Rome for
about three weeks during each one of the sessions of Vatican II
because I knew it was the most important thing that was
happening in my lifetime as a priest.... We got a hold of the
documents as fast as we could, we studied them and right after
the council we brought the best theologians in the world
here ... and then we had the synod in 1971 and the
magnificent document *Justice in the World*, which stated that
"Action on behalf of justice and participation in the
transformation of the world is constitutive of the mission of the
Church and the preaching of the Gospel." Well, that was our
Magna Carta, because what we said, in our own arrogance,
was: "We were right all along."[1]

While the ombudsman priest enjoyed his absolute rule in the parish, a
relatively small but increasingly influential coterie of his peers initiated
a series of reform movements in the United States that would spell the
end of his dominance of the local scene. One of the priests at the center of this network of pioneers, John J. Egan, quoted above, recalled
his delight at finding their shared commitment to social justice upheld
by Vatican II as central to the mission of the church. That shared commitment, sometimes expressed in startling ways, called into question
for a time the very viability of the parish as a setting for effective
priestly ministry.

The condemnation of Modernism in 1907 and the measures taken
against it—including the establishment of vigilance committees in certain dioceses and the imposition of an antimodernist oath for priests—
guaranteed that development of the Roman Catholic Church in this
country would proceed within narrowly prescribed limits for at least a
generation. Progressives avoided unseemly speculation and innovation
in matters of doctrine, and channeled their energies into a host of social concerns accompanying American entry into World War I. What
creativity was permitted in theology originated in the older churches
of Europe and, perhaps predictably, located its source of inspiration in

a sophisticated reappropriation of the philosophy of the Angelic Doctor of the thirteenth century, Thomas Aquinas. Yet, in spite of its medieval moorings, the neo-Thomist revival provided the impetus for a fresh approach to Catholic involvement in the world. Unleashed from earlier neo-scholastic devotion to the manual tradition (which owed as much to seventeenth-century Jesuit scholastics as it did to Aquinas), Catholic scholars returned to the original sources with renewed vigor. As historian William Halsey has pointed out, the Thomistic worldview proved a fecund source for the generation of a Catholic subculture in the United States that encouraged patriotism, ridiculed communism, and launched the careers of labor priests and social activists alike.[2] For the natural law tradition at the center of the revival served as a bridge between Catholic philosophy and the rationalism of the Enlightenment which shaped the nation's founding documents. Catholics could agree, by virtue of both natural reason and supernatural revelation, that all humans possess certain inalienable rights, and that the primary purpose of government is to protect those rights. This happy coincidence served as the springboard for full-fledged Catholic participation in the public debate about the proper use of the nation's economic resources.

In 1919 this participation was exemplified by the promulgation of the *Bishops' Program of Social Reconstruction* penned by a priest from Minnesota named John Ryan. The program represented Ryan's application of the principles of Pope Leo XIII's encyclical on the rights of labor, *Rerum Novarum*, to the American situation. In some of its particulars the program anticipated the New Deal. Yet, in spite of a vigorous publicity campaign, it did not hold the attention of the nation during the 1920s. Undaunted, Ryan and his assistant in the Social Action Department of the National Catholic Welfare Council, Raymond McGowan, continued to promote these and similar causes well into the 1930s.[3]

In so doing they served as the inspiration for a generation of depression-era priests who inherited their own social and economic problems. Francis J. Haas, a student of Ryan's at the Catholic University, applied his lessons in the field of labor mediation in the 1930s and 40s. John O'Grady, Ryan's younger colleague, ran the National Conference of Catholic Charities from 1920 to 1961 and was a prominent lobbyist in Washington for social security and federally funded, low-income housing. Iowa pastor Luigi G. Ligutti upheld the tradition by his advocacy for farmers and miners put out of work by the depression. In 1941 his leadership of the National Catholic Rural Life Conference won him national recognition as a champion of the rural parish.[4]

This new pattern of priestly ministry, extraparochial by nature, increased in size and sophistication with each new wave of disciples. In the "third generation," for example, a twenty-eight-year-old priest from Chicago, George Higgins, carried on the legacy after meeting "first generation" social actionists Ryan and McGowan in Washington. In 1944 Higgins joined the Social Action Department and succeeded McGowan as its director ten years later. In addition to Ryan, McGowan, William J. Kerby (who founded the National Conference of Catholic Charities), and Peter Dietz (the noted "labor priest," who founded the first association of Catholic workingmen and the first Catholic school of social service), Higgins counted Haas and Burke of the "second generation" as seminal influences upon his own work. And in addition to these teachers, he also learned much from his own contemporaries in the field, including his colleague at the Social Action Department John F. Cronin, a strident anticommunist who later campaigned effectively for civil rights, and Archbishop Robert Lucey of San Antonio, an advocate for migrant laborers. In turn, the newcomer, fresh from the "Chicago School" of seminary rector Reynold Hillenbrand, affected the thinking and practice of his colleagues and mentors.[5]

This pattern of influence and generational cross-fertilization of ideas and methods created a vital network of communication among priests involved in pioneering ministries in the decades preceding the Second Vatican Council. Whereas the ombudsman, secure in his own self-contained "perfect" parochial society, was somewhat isolated from his brother priests, this new breed thrived on exchange of ideas. They were public men, eager to shape social policy and emboldened by the "credentials" for participation in the political debate afforded them by Thomistic apologetics. In this age of Catholic institutional expansion, opportunities arose for sharing plans, plotting strategies, and attracting other priests into the fold as increasingly complex diocesan structures multiplied and bishops sent their most capable seminarians to Catholic University for advanced degrees in social work, education, and administration. There, priests preparing for bureaucratic roles who might otherwise have had little inclination toward social activism were exposed to the thinking of the NCWC leaders.

Barriers to communication were overcome during this period by correspondence, the chance meeting, the centrifugal force of graduate education, the telephone, and, eventually, the airplane. The increased frequency of commercial air travel in the 1950s, perhaps more than any other single factor, ushered in "the age of the convention" and facilitated the cross-fertilization of ideas and methods necessary for effective social ministry.[6]

In the 1930s, the emergence of this renewed approach to priesthood carried with it far-reaching implications for parochial ministry, the full consequences of which would not be realized until the late 1950s. For the enthusiasm for public action and priestly collaboration reflected an understanding of church and ministry that rejected the notion of the parish as properly a self-contained society. The parish ought not to serve only itself, but generate action on behalf of the world, these pioneer-priests came to believe. They arrived at this conviction through their own experiences in public service and through the influence of two interrelated reform movements inaugurated under the broad banner of the neo-Thomist revival. Both the liturgical movement, popularized in this country by the Benedictines of St. John's Abbey in Minnesota, and Catholic Action, a new method of social involvement defined officially as "the participation of the laity in the apostolate of the hierarchy," demonstrated irrefutably to these men that the mission of the church is geocentric as well as theocentric. As these initiatives penetrated the Catholic consciousness, the image of the priest as a "man of the church" took on new and welcome dimensions for those clerics already committed to social involvement as the primary expression of their priesthood.[7]

These developments were brought to the attention of parish communities in a variety of ways. The neo-Thomist canopy for the renewal, first erected by Leo XIII, gained widespread American attention after Frank Sheed and Maisie Ward, devotees of Claudel, Maritain, and other European exponents of the revival, opened their publishing house in New York in 1933. In May of that year, Catholic radicalism hit the newsstands, quite literally, as Dorothy Day peddled copies of *The Catholic Worker* in Union Square. Meanwhile, the airwaves carried the voice of the "radio priest," Charles E. Coughlin, whose political sermons criticized unbridled capitalism and communism alike and supported the New Deal during Roosevelt's first term. The Catholic press provided a forum for pioneers like John LaFarge, S.J., and Virgil Michel, O.S.B. Writing in the pages of the Jesuit weekly *America*, LaFarge addressed the entire spectrum of social justice issues, and was one of the first priests to consistently examine and condemn the "sin of racism" that plagued American society. In the late hours of Christmas Eve 1925, Michel met with Jesuit Gerald Ellard and Fr. Martin Hellriegel, chaplain for the Precious Blood Sisters at O'Fallon, Missouri. In Hellriegel's study that night the three hit upon a name for the journal of liturgical studies they planned to publish. *Orate Fratres* (later *Worship*), the first American liturgical monthly, introduced seminarians and parish priests to a neoapostolic perspective on the central act of worship of the Roman Catholic Church, the Mass.[8]

Despite the apparent diversity of approach, each of these pioneers pointed to the social encyclicals of the popes as one mandate for their particular work. This was the strength of *Rerum Novarum* and Pius XI's *Quadragesimo Anno* in 1931. By authoritatively stating and developing the bedrock principles of Catholic social doctrine, the popes inspired a Catholic dedication to the new apostolate. But the documents seemed to permit some latitude in the specific application of these principles. This made it possible for disciples as different in their analyses and solutions of the problems as Dorothy Day and John Ryan to claim, not without reason, that their approach to social reconstruction was genuinely Catholic. Pius XI's enthusiastic support of Catholic Action consolidated the momentum in this direction. Catholic labor schools and educational efforts such as Jesuit Daniel Lord's summer school of Catholic Action became commonplace in the 1930s. Parishes formed groups to discuss the social encyclicals, promoted the labor schools, and began to support Catholic Action.[9]

Pioneer priests, sensing a moment of social *kairos*, strove to demonstrate the organic unity of these seemingly disparate initiatives. Twelve years before Pius XII's encyclical on the mystical body of Christ, Michel employed the image to integrate social reconstruction, Catholic Action, and the liturgical movement:

> As images, the pictures of the body and the vine are figures that portray a supreme and multiple spiritual reality: our union with Christ here and now, our life in Him through the Church, our active spiritual and integral membership in the latter. This shows us at once the significance of the social note in the texts of the Mass. . . . In the Mass, Christ is both offerer and the oblation offered; therefore the mystical body of Christ is both offerer and oblation offered; therefore we are all so by general inclusion. . . . Thus, active participation truly becomes a "primary and indispensable source of the true Christian spirit," of union and life in Christ. . . .
>
> We should now be more ready to understand that the liturgical apostolate is immense in its scope and possibilities; that it is something infinitely greater than archaeological artistic interest in the liturgy. We should likewise better understand now what the phrase *the liturgy for the people* means. . . .
>
> A further question, however, must present itself to the reader: How practical is all this? I can but answer with the fullest delibera-

tion: supremely practical in the widest extent and meaning of the term. Without some attainment of the above ideals, there can be no complete union of theory and practice in the life of the Catholic, in fact no successful Catholic Action as the present Holy Father understands it. . . . Love of God and love of man, the liturgical life and Catholic Action—such is the final unity achieved by "the active participation of all the faithful in the most holy mysteries and in the public and solemn prayer of the Church."[10]

While Michel and other theologians developed the ecclesiology to frame these new movements, men like Bernard J. Sheil, an activist priest and later bishop in Chicago, worked for "the Catholic social gospel." As an organizer of Catholic immigrant neighborhoods, Sheil defended the rights of meat packers and steel workers, collaborated with lay communities such as the Grail and Friendship House, and established the Catholic Youth Organization in 1930.[11] Another priest of the influential "Chicago School," Reynold Hillenbrand, worked to coordinate the renewal movements launched in the 1930s and 40s. His story is instructive in that it mirrors the careers of other "pioneer priests" of the preconciliar era.

In April 1936 Cardinal George Mundelein named Reynold Hillenbrand the second rector of St. Mary of the Lake seminary and promised the students and faculty, "I've brought you a man with imagination." Mundelein had prepared Hillenbrand for the post by dispatching him to Rome after ordination. There, living at the Canadian college (the North American College was reserved for seminarians), Hillenbrand came into contact with French-speaking disciples of Canon Cardijn of Belgium. Cardijn perfected the Catholic Action technique known as "the inquiry method," whereby one would "observe, judge, and act" in the world. About the same time, historian Steven Avella believes, Hillenbrand visited the abbey of Maria Laach in Germany and other European centers of the liturgical movement. Upon his return to Chicago, Hillenbrand worked for a time at Holy Name Cathedral with Monsignor Joseph Morrison, who reinforced the lessons learned in Europe. Morrison had introduced the Legion of Mary to Chicago, served as a delegate to eucharistic congresses in America and Europe, and had an abiding interest in the liturgical movement. A third seminal influence on the young priest was his exposure to the methodology of the Catholic Evidence Guild, promoted in this country by Sheed and Ward. In 1935 Hillenbrand heard a talk given at Rosary College in River Forest, Illinois, by Rev. Stephen A. Leven of Bristow, Oklahoma, which employed the guild's tactic of public proclamation of "Catholic truth" to potential converts. Fascinated with the effectiveness of "street preaching," Hillenbrand studied the principles of Catholic Evidence work and began to offer courses on the subject at Rosary. Avella contends that these experiences in Europe and at Rosary College convinced Hillenbrand "to define his priestly mission as one of enabling small groups to become active apostles for the proclamation of the gospel," and prefigured his later work with the labor schools and Jocist organizations.[12]

At the age of thirty-six, Hillenbrand brought his vision of priestly ministry to the position of rector of St. Mary of the Lake. Almost overnight the seminary began to serve the church as Chicago served the nation—as a crossroads of commerce, as the vital urban center of the heartland. The list of pioneer priests and lay persons who lectured there during Hillenbrand's tenure, recorded in the students' *Chronicle*, reads like a *Who's Who* of the Catholic renewal: Ellard and Donald Attwater of *Orate Fratres*; Maurice Lavanoux, founder of the Liturgical Arts Society; Dorothy Day of the Catholic Worker Movement and Baroness Catherine de Hueck, founder of the Friendship Houses; Haas, who spoke on labor problems; Ligutti, on rural life; and John LaFarge, on race relations. Hillenbrand also transformed the Sunday Mass at the seminary into a laboratory of the liturgical movement. He introduced the Dialog Mass and led the congregation in singing the Kyrie, Gloria, Credo, Sanctus, and Agnus Dei. He encouraged his better students, including George Higgins and Daniel Cantwell, to attend graduate school at Catholic University. When some of them took his advice and returned to teach in the seminary, they helped him reshape the curriculum to reflect the renewed approach to priesthood.[13]

Events outside the seminary walls continued to influence Hillenbrand. In 1937 he attended the Summer School of Social Action for Priests held at St. Francis seminary in Milwaukee, a program designed to study Catholic social doctrine, investigate the problem of labor, and discuss the role of the priest in alleviating social and economic injustice. Ryan, Haas, Peter Dietz, Lucey, and Wilfrid Parsons of *America* were featured speakers. Invigorated by the exchange of ideas, Hillenbrand returned to Chicago and obtained permission from Mundelein to organize Chicago's own Summer School of Social Action for Priests, which attracted over two hundred men from fifteen dioceses in 1938. During the next six years, Hillenbrand's activities on behalf of labor increased as he joined the Catholic Conference on Industrial Problems and organized a series of labor schools in Chicago. These schools, designed to encourage the unionization of unskilled workers and discourage communist influence in the unions, were first developed by labor priests such as John Monagahan of Brooklyn, Charles Owen Rice of

Pittsburgh, and Archbishop John T. McNicholas of Cincinnati. Hillenbrand's schools retained the familiar format: brief expositions of U.S. labor history, lectures on the social encyclicals, and a discussion of the principles of parliamentary procedures.

Hillenbrand's long-standing interest in Catholic Action was renewed when he met another priest from Oklahoma, Donald Kanaly, at the Chicago Summer School in 1938. Kanaly alerted Hillenbrand to the urgent need to tap an immense resource in the fight for social justice—namely, the Catholic laity. Working with his protege, seminarian John Egan, and a Chicago attorney, James O'Shaugnessy, Hillenbrand quickly established Catholic Action groups in Catholic high schools and colleges, and among Catholic businessmen, their wives, and single working persons of Chicago. During the war years, Hillenbrand's army of young clerics and seminarians served as moderators for the groups, and began to encourage assistance from all quarters. Cantwell, by now on the faculty at the seminary, supported the effort by forming the Catholic Labor Alliance and the Catholic Interracial Council. Edward Marciniak, a Catholic layman, edited the journal of the former, *Work*, and together with James O'Gara and John Cogley, opened a Catholic Worker House of Hospitality. Two priests helped to implement Hillenbrand's "grand plan" in important ways. Martin Carrabine, a charismatic Jesuit, drew in the younger generation through the Chicago Inter-Student Catholic Action (CISCA). Another Jesuit, Ed Dowling, planted the seeds of the Cana movement of the 1940s by his work with families in the suburbs of Chicago's North Shore.[14]

Hillenbrand was not content to see this constellation of programs confined to Chicago or the midwest. He called upon Louis Putz, C.S.C., who had introduced Catholic Action to the University of Notre Dame and worked for the racial integration of the student body. Through Putz's magazine, *Concord*, and eventually through his publishing house, Fides Press, the two men disseminated material on the YCS (Young Christian Students) and YCW (Young Christian Workers) and served as national chaplains for the groups that sprang up in about thirty-five cities by 1947. In that year, the Chicago-based movement forged bonds with the European Catholic Action movements at the international meeting of the YCW in Montreal.

By that time, Hillenbrand's reign at St. Mary of the Lake Seminary had come to an abrupt end. Cardinal Stritch dismissed him from the rectorship in 1944, a move that went unexplained. He continued to exercise local and national influence in the various movements he helped create until a near-fatal auto accident diminished his capacity for leadership in 1949.[15]

Hillenbrand's story provides but one example of a pattern of influence and leadership in the careers of pioneering priests of the ombudsman era. While the ombudsman stayed in the parish, a small but increasingly influential number of his peers were fashioning a different approach to priestly ministry. These pioneers were talented diocesan and religious priests whose paths crossed in graduate school or professional meetings. They sought one another out and developed networks of communication that would inform and serve the American clergy throughout the conciliar era. The exchange of ideas and initiatives provided mutual support and greater plausibility for a new and invigorating conceptualization of the priesthood as pluriform: the pioneers demonstrated that there was a variety of options available in the exercise and expression of priestly ministry.[16]

Although pioneer priests were leaders, they were also followers. The ombudsman's tight grip on any and all forms of ministry and his pretension to exclusive omnicompetence was not possible for priests who came under the influence of a Dorothy Day, a Catherine de Hueck, or an Edward Marciniak. These lay leaders did not wait upon clerical initiative although, by and large, they were pleased to cooperate with the ordained. Dorothy Day's sole commandment to Catholic Workers—that the eucharist be celebrated among them—was as eloquent as any words of Virgil Michel or Gerald Ellard about the liturgy as the proper source of community and social outreach. Furthermore, in many cases lay women and men generated the ideas and methods for programs that priests later joined, co-opted, or clericalized. This point in no way diminishes the very real, creative, and pervasive leadership of priests like Shield, Putz, or Hillenbrand. But it does signal a new "presence" on the ministerial horizon, even if lay apostolates were still being described within the controlling purview of the hierarchy.

These two considerations lead to a third. As the priest found satisfying work outside the parish community and as lay people came forth to share in and at times lead the effort, the first wave of questions about the purpose and efficacy of ministry confined strictly to the parish appeared in the leading journals of opinion.

In the 1930s contributors struck the confident and self-congratulatory tone of Catholic triumphalism. "Very naturally the inspiration for Catholic Action comes from our pastors, and an energetic and efficient hierarchy," *America* reported cheerily in 1930. Enrollment in seminaries was up, "practical faith and zeal" were manifested during a magnificent eucharistic congress in Omaha, "convert-making" went on apace, and dozens of parochial organizations like the Knights of Columbus, the Women's Parish Sodality, and the St. Vincent de Paul

Society celebrated their vitality at national conventions. "In a word, Catholic public action has been stimulated tremendously during the past year," wrote William Lonergan, S.J. "Our laity have been less content to exercise their faith by the piety of their personal lives: they have taken a very active interest in their Church and its organizations, and in works of zeal and charity."[17]

But by the end of the decade, a note of discontent crept into the descriptions of parish progress toward renewal. "Mr. Patrick Donahoe Lived Catholic Action—While the New Parish Thinks of Talking About It," announced one headline.[18] John LaFarge diagnosed the disappointment as stemming from a lack of education about the true nature and purpose of Catholic Action. Catholic Action will have little effect, he warned, unless "you *know how* to deal with those whose spiritual conquest you seek; and second, that you *know what* you are to bring to them." This requires of the lay apostle "an immense amount of systematic study and planning," he reminded his readers, and a willingness to overcome dependence on the leadership of the parish priest:

> The work of the priest in connection with Catholic Action is to give its members such solid doctrinal instruction and such wise guidance as will enable them to discover *for themselves* how to live the whole of Christian teaching in the circumstances they are obliged to meet. The priest is not to attempt to do for the laymen the work only the laymen can do. . . .
> Father Daniel A. Lord's Summer Schools of Catholic Action have revealed much of what *can* be done. But we need a work more permanent, systematic, and properly equipped financially and materially.[19]

By 1950 LaFarge, along with many other priests, had despaired of the approach of the specialized Catholic Action movements, and was proclaiming the gospel of the "direct apostolate" articulated in Abbé G. Michonneau's influential and aptly titled *Revolution in a City Parish*. LaFarge strongly recommended the book "for people who wish to see how a parish priest, with the teamwork of his assistants, has tackled the problem of hostile, irreligious surroundings head-on, 'not by sighs and wishes but by real activity.' " Michonneau's emphasis was upon the direct approach of "militant and united" Catholics to unbelievers. In a departure from standard practices of Catholic Action, the French priest eschewed organizational tactics and preferred intensified individual initiatives. "The creation of this new and revolutionary atmosphere depends on the common efforts of each and every Christian,"

Michonneau wrote, "it cannot be left to the members of specialized movements . . . every man has his own little world to influence, to change, to Christianize." LaFarge agreed that parish life needed to be "revolutionized." Priests and laity should avoid the technical language of the catechist and speak "in language that the ordinary *secularized* person can understand."[20]

Predictably, this sense of frustration with parochial efforts to implement Catholic social teaching was shared by those pioneer priests who had committed their ministries to social outreach. By the very nature of their work, parish priests occupied a public role that, the pioneers argued, they were not fulfilling properly. Writing in *Worship* in 1952 Hillenbrand complained of "a gap between the pope's teaching and the priest's teaching." He blamed this on the unfortunate tendency toward dualism that continued in parish life: "A priest might say, as one did this summer in preaching a retreat, that we are hearing too much about the Mystical Body and not enough about the Church," Hillenbrand lamented, "[while] the pope says they are identically the same." The laity must not, he warned, identify the church exclusively with the sanctuary or parish. Christian commitment becomes fully explicit in the world beyond the parish. It was incumbent upon the parish priest to "create lay apostles" to witness to Christ in every walk of life:

> Political life is the laymen's field. The priest casts his vote, but he is not in politics, holds no political appointment, is elected to no political office. . . . Family life is threatened, and even more than threatened, from a score of sides. Family life is the laymen's field. The priest has no family. This is not to say that these fields go to the laymen by default. They are the provinces of ordinary human life from which the priest is wisely subtracted so that the dedication to his altogether necessary work might be more complete. The crucial fields are the lay fields. We must therefore have lay apostles. Men and women who will ruthlessly eliminate the dual conscience from their lives. The dual conscience is cropping up all the time. A Sunday Catholic who is a martinet at home. A Sunday Catholic, an employer, who is antagonistic to labor unions. A Sunday Catholic, a worker, who will not join a union. A Sunday Catholic who will not live next to a Negro. A Sunday Catholic who thinks the United Nations is a mistake.[21]

Hillenbrand worried that one of two situations would inhibit the parish's realization of his scheme. On the one hand, he imagined, in some parishes a growing number of people would be willing to participate in the Mass and in Catholic Action, but find the pastor "unfavorable to the idea, or unwilling to further the idea." The reverse could also be the case: in some parishes, the priest would be willing and eager, "and scarcely a parishioner had evinced an interest." To avoid these extremes, he urged pastors to form lay people "not in a priest's spirituality which deals directly with religious things . . . nor a cloistered spirituality predicated on isolation or withdrawal from the problem of lay life." Lay apostles required a formation "of association—of meeting people and working with people—of a great, self-sacrificial charity . . . a formation through all the phases of lay life—domestic, parochial, economic, political."[22]

The frustration and impatience of Hillenbrand, LaFarge, and other pioneer priests was inevitable, and in historical hindsight, understandable. For they lived in an era of "eschatological tension," or, to state it less dramatically, "ecclesiological tension." The church for which they waited expectantly had not yet emerged in the 1930s or 40s. Progress toward its realization was impeded to the extent that the priests "in the trenches" failed to absorb the insights and follow the example of the pioneers. When this reformation of Catholic parochial practice did not evolve as expected, pioneers like Michonneau and LaFarge resorted to the rhetoric of revolution, which increased in frequency and volume as the 1950s approached.

The virtual absence within certain key institutional infrastructures of an organized response to these calls for reformation betokened a preoccupation with other concerns, especially institutional expansion. There seemed little need for a new paradigm of church and ministry prior to the 1950s. With the rare exception of a place like St. Mary's during Hillenbrand's rectorship, seminary curriculum and daily life remained unaffected by the ferment in the Catholic world outside the walls. Seminarians were aware of options, if at all, through their own (clandestine) reading of *America, Worship, The Catholic Worker*, or, in the 1950s, theologians such as de Lubac and Congar. Many complained that the seminaries even lagged behind in publicizing the papal social encyclicals.[23]

The uneven rate of social and religious change in various regions of the country also impeded progress toward a new awareness. Rural Catholicism, for example, produced its own version of the ombudsman. In 1936 only one-fifth (19.4%) of the total American Catholic population was classified as "rural," but rural Catholic churches were more numerous than urban churches. By 1947 urban churches outnumbered rural churches. Nonetheless, there remained a vast difference in the size of the two types of parishes. In 1936 the urban parish averaged 1,939 members and the rural 382. The small size of the rural parish was also an obstacle to the building of parochial schools and other parish facilities. By 1947 only 1,726 (17.8%) of rural parishes had elementary parochial schools and only 309 (3.1%) had high schools. The National Rural Life Conference, working with the Confraternity of Christian Doctrine, developed summer "vacation schools" and correspondence courses to compensate for a lack of parochial religious education, but the burden of catechizing fell to the parish priest. Rural Catholics belonged to homogeneous and relatively stable communities built on strong social and family ties. For the rural ombudsman, the more manageable size of the parish was offset by the fact that nearly one-half of the rural churches had no resident pastor and depended upon priest-missionaries. Thus the pattern of presence of the rural priest to his community reflected this tension: he was intimately present to the small community in which he found himself on a given day of the week.[24]

Large sections of the rural south, for example, were mission territory. In Arkansas, Georgia, Alabama, and Tennessee the focus of parochial ministry was on basic catechism throughout this period. The story of the origin and development of the Missionary Servants of the Most Holy Trinity, founded in the United States by Thomas A. Judge, C.M., in 1929, illustrates the point. Judge was preaching in the mission band at St. John's University in New York in 1915 when he was transferred to rural Alabama. There, with the help of a group of lay women, he developed a method of catechesis that emphasized the inspiration of the Holy Spirit. The approach was moderately successful, and the Missionary Servants spread to rural Mississippi where they served as circuit riders. One priest would be responsible for forming parish communities in two or three separate locations, often fifteen or twenty miles apart. In the 1940s the Missionary Servants exercised a ministry devoted to the sacraments and basic evangelization of an illiterate and semiliterate black population. In the 1950s priests devoted themselves to the staffing of parochial schools. The Rural Life Conference, troubled by the involvement of untutored lay Catholics in rural economic organizations outside the parish and the sphere of religious influence, recognized that the most important task of the rural ombudsman was spiritual formation and doctrinal and ethical instruction. The laity continued to look to him for sacramental and personal presence even as religious sisters shared the burden of administering and teaching in the schools.[25]

Social and economic factors also played a part in New England's relatively tardy response to innovations in parochial ministry. Recent studies of Boston after the depression and of unemployment in Massachusetts demonstrate the perdurance of a vulnerable, marginal economic community, consisting primarily of Catholic workers, well into the 1950s. The ascendance of Boston's immigrant, blue-collar work force to middle-class respectability was slowed considerably by the traditional character of Yankee society. In addition, the benefice structure, which allowed pastors to own and control parish revenues and assets, was not modified by synodal legislation until the late 1950s. Consequently, priests retained for a longer period of time an educational and economic advantage over their parishioners, and parishioners remained in the "deferential" mode in their dealings with pastors.

In the 1950s Catholics in the northeast in general, and in Boston in particular, contributed generously to their parishes and their seminaries. The number of vocations to the priesthood soared. Catholics were proud of their identity and experienced "little or no religious confusion." This sense of internal stability was reinforced by a priestly teaching that had changed little since 1900. There was so little innovation, in fact, that some parish publications were actually reprinting verbatim clerical advice from the turn of the century. In a period when the general population was recovering from the social and economic dislocation of World War II, the church of the ombudsman provided a precise yardstick for thought and behavior in an increasingly relativistic world. Parish priests were not expected to effect change but to provide stabilizing leadership during a period of social transformation. By and large they did so with considerable success and vigor.[26]

In the Pacific northwest, the challenges to clerical leadership were quite different from those in the northeast. Church leaders in the postwar era ministered to communities in which the Catholic tradition was not firmly established. The coastal region from Seattle to Portland experienced a population explosion during the war years as the first wave of "settlers" from both the east and midwest (and from Japan, Hawaii, and the Philippines) migrated to the land of lumber. As a result, institution-building and organizational responsibilities preoccupied the ombudsman in the 1940s and 50s, as in an earlier era in Boston and Chicago. But the ombudsman in the northwest was also of necessity a type of Catholic evangelist. He often did not enjoy the luxury (and the organizational challenges) of a ready-made ethnic community on the same scale as did his counterparts in the northeast and the midwest. Often he did not share the ethnic heritage of the immigrants he served, and they did not share the European Catholic sensibilities with which he was familiar by custom and seminary training.

Furthermore, the region was, and to a considerable extent remains, unchurched. In such an environment, it is not surprising that Washington and Oregon also faced a shortage of homegrown seminarians and clergy.

Catholic bishops responded to these realities by developing a presbyterate composed in part of American priests from the midwest and northeast, and in part of foreign-born priests who accompanied their people in migrations from the Philippines and other Catholic outposts in the Far East. When the spirit of reform captured in the decrees of Vatican II did come to this region, as we shall see, it came rapidly, in part because it met little resistance by way of long-standing societal or ecclesial practices. The ombudsman built the church in this region from the ground up. California followed this pattern in some but not all respects. The church in San Francisco, for example, shared the need for Chinese and Filipino priests to minister to burgeoning ethnic groups; at the same time, the Bay Area was home to large communities of Irish, German, and Italian Catholics whose sons sought admission to the local presbyterate. The challenges in ministering to an ethnic community in a time of rapid social change fostered in the ombudsman, be he Californian or Filipino, a keen appreciation for the sense of corporate identity promoted by Catholic doctrine perceived to be stable in its foundations and unchanging in its expression.[27]

There was a final, and perhaps decisive, impediment to the widespread acceptance of a new model for church and priesthood promoted by Catholic Action, the liturgical movement, and the social apostolate. This obstacle to reform was a by-product of the movements themselves. For all of Hillenbrand's petulance about parochial dualism, his own assumptions about clergy and laity, church and world, were grounded in a Tridentine Catholic ecclesiology, which the neo-scholastic and neo-Thomistic revivals had modified but not eradicated. The work of Hillenbrand and his colleagues was, no doubt, a necessary and important stage in the development of a neo-apostolic ecclesial self-understanding—the image of the church that Vatican II embraced. But, in the final analysis, it retained the essential principles of the ombudsman's worldview. Pius XII did in fact describe the church as a mystical body in 1943, but it was clear in the translation (literal and figurative) that the organs of the body depended for their vitality on the head rather than the heart. Catholic Action sought to empower lay people, but their newfound apostolic energy was derived rather than self-generated. Before the mid-1950s most parish priests had a rather clear idea of the distinction between church and world. The church nurtured souls and prepared Catholics for effective apostolic action "in the world." For the average parish priest, however, "the world" was delimited by the geographical boundaries of the parish or local community. The notion that the vocation of certain parish priests might extend to the inner-city slums, the halls of academe, or the political rally, had not yet taken hold.[28]

That this new way of priesthood was a sophisticated development within an old paradigm of the church was evident in the theology of the priesthood favored by the pioneers. It retained the definition of the priest as *alter Christus* but modified the description of Christ underlying it. Christ was less the contemplative man of prayer, more, in the title of a popular treatise on priestly identity, *The Man for Others*, a man of decisive action on behalf of the world. The image of the Lord as a serene, self-controlled, and somewhat effete teacher gave way to the bold, vigorous, crusading carpenter from Nazareth. In emulating him, the priest was to be a dynamic leader, one whose natural charisma inspired men and women to form a community around his example. Rev. William Russell of Catholic University portrayed Jesus' life as "a dynamo which sends out energy for Christlike living" and helped to form a generation of clerical leaders in the image of *Christ the Leader*:

> Jesus showed strength of character, which means love of truth, of justice, of decency. Our civilization tends to produce "yes men." We are afraid of losing popularity or our jobs if we launch forth in indignation against abuses. And yet, Christ expects us to stand always for honesty and for justice, and to enter into those movements which will bring social justice to the common men and women. We have much to learn from the *strong* Christ as well as from the meek Christ.[29]

Priests were to stand for justice, but they were to do so from within the confines of the sanctuary or the parish discussion group. Russell warned his graduate students against assuming that the call to transform the world required the priest to become *involved* in it:

> Christ taught religion: He refused to be drawn into petty quarrels. To condemn injustice is a duty; to seek to manage secular affairs is another thing. He does not want priests to indulge in secular affairs to the extent that they forget their main duty, to be expert in the things of God. . . . Mixing in business often develops a craving for power, for money, and shuts out the thought of God.[30]

Russell's understanding of the priesthood, shared by the pioneering priests of the generation he taught, was in one sense appropriate to his era and perhaps to our own. It may well be more than a "period piece"; indeed, as we shall see, many priests of the postconciliar era find wisdom in the notion of the priest as "one who sends." But in the late 1950s this theology of the priesthood did not fully reflect the sensibilities of the pioneers, who were dedicated to the transformation of the world through, at least in part, the agency of the priest-leader. Neither was this theology adequate to the task of reconceiving the parish priesthood—a task that many pioneers' students believed to be essential in preserving their shared vision. The international church was at the time struggling to reformulate the desired relation between church and world, and between clergy and laity. In the process thinkers developed a theology commensurate to a new awareness of the interdependence of the people of God.

As the American church became increasingly engaged with modern secular and bureaucratic culture, a process that began in the days of Mundelein and O'Connell, it was drawn inexorably toward its own modern revolution. In the transition many of the younger priests found the dualism of Russell's approach unacceptable. For a time after the Second Vatican Council seemed to institutionalize that revolution, there appeared to be no distinction whatsoever between the previously disparate realities labeled "church" and "world." The priest would no longer be Christ but the apostle, "the one who is sent." His ministry would be "in the world" alongside the laity, his distinctiveness as a servant of Christ open to question. The American manifestation of this transition was prepared for in part by the pioneering priests of the postwar era who attempted to make the parish the base for extraparochial service to the world. In doing so these men introduced an alternative to the model of priesthood perpetuated in the seminaries and by the ombudsmen in the parishes. Yet they were not aware of the full implications of this alternative for the church's self-understanding. They endorsed a biblical model for the church—the mystical body of Christ—without anticipating that sacramental incorporation into the mystical body in baptism might transform men and women into ministers of Christ without further ordination. They read, quoted, and worked with Protestants and Jews but retained a firm, if quiet, confidence in the superiority of Catholicism and in the cultural and religious persuasiveness of neo-Thomist apologetics. They acknowledged the pervasive effects of modernization without endorsing or celebrating them. They would bring a transcendent God to a fallen world rather than seek Christ in the secular city. In short, they were neither radically ecumenical nor radically secular nor radically modern.

In a sense, of course, the pioneer priests *were* "right all along": the church would soon officially and universally recognize and reclaim its mission to the secular world. The process of doing so, however, was at times confusing and disorienting. In the late 1950s and throughout the 1960s many pioneer priests and their protégés felt compelled to reexamine the ecclesiological and theological principles that had prepared them for aggiornamento. For without a new model for church, it seemed, there would be no new parish, no new priesthood.

3

PRIESTHOOD RECONSIDERED: PRESENCE BEYOND THE PARISH, 1954–1962

The social problems of our day criss-cross parish boundaries. The accident of parish geography cannot cope with the substance of social and economic reality. The parish is not a self-contained sociological unit. We must create a juridic entity fitted to the needs and functions of the Church in this day and age. The parish can best serve itself and its people by cooperating in the creation of some type of moral person greater than itself, which is now striving to be born. In our efforts here we have come face to face with this basic question. When we try to reduce the Church to its fundamental elements we think of the parish—church and school. The parish is not meeting our needs. CAN it do so?—I leave open to discussion, but personally I think not.[1]

Roman Catholicism in the United States has selectively appropriated aspects of modernity in three distinct episodes. During the aftermath of the American revolution, Catholic leaders, especially John Carroll, were temporarily successful in efforts to refashion Catholic Christianity in terms congenial to republican-era and Enlightenment mentalities. In hopes of establishing American Catholic independence from foreign influence, Carroll presided over the unofficial use of the vernacular in liturgy, the democratization of local church government through a lay trustee system for the management of temporal affairs, the founding of Georgetown Academy (1789) to provide the church with a native-born clergy, and most striking of all, his own election as bishop by the American clergy (1789). A second "romance with modernity," almost a century later, rekindled the efforts at americanization in quite a different context. Responding to the needs of a huge immigrant working class, James Cardinal Gibbons of Baltimore in 1887 prevented the Vatican from condemning the Knights of Labor, the only national labor union in the United States. His fellow "Americanists" in the hierarchy, including Bishop John Lancaster Spalding of

Peoria, Illinois, and Archbishop John Ireland of St. Paul, Minnesota, opposed ethnic nationalism within the American church, questioned the building of a separatist parochial school system, and praised the American ideals of progress, democracy, and religious liberty as compatible with Catholic self-interest. In both cases, the flirtation with modernity ended rather abruptly in disappointment after a generation.[2]

As indicated in the previous chapter, pioneer priests in the 1940s and early 50s interpreted the "signs of the times" in such a way as to prepare the church, and the Roman Catholic priesthood, for a third encounter with modernity, the effects of which continue to unfold three decades after it began. As in the other two episodes, this modernization process challenged the American church's own self-understanding and precipitated a crisis of identity. ("Crisis" is employed here in its etymological sense, as indicating a "turning point" or "moment of decision," rather than a breakdown or collapse.) There were both continuities and discontinuities between the modernization of the postwar era and earlier crises. There was again in the postwar era a concerted effort to "americanize" the Roman Catholic Church both here and abroad, most successfully in the drafting and ratification of the Declaration on Religious Liberty at the Second Vatican Council. There was again in the postwar era a campaign for decentralization and deromanization, a new respect for the integrity of the diverse cultural settings of local churches, and a (successful) call for worship in the vernacular. However, this third romance with modernity threatened to overturn theological principles that the earlier modernizers, from Carroll to Gibbons, had never questioned. Catholic "updating" in the conciliar era provided the conditions by which it was possible for alternative ecclesiological models to challenge those identified with Catholic thought since the Counter-Reformation.[3]

Furthermore, this third romance with modernity proceeded in two overlapping stages, beginning prior to the Second Vatican Council. It is difficult to identify any one year as the moment of transition, but I have chosen 1954 because of its significance in the lives of two priests, Joseph Gremillion and John Egan, whose stories exemplify some of the important shifts in the approach to parish ministry prior to the convening of Vatican II. The following year, American Catholic historian John Tracy Ellis sparked a nationwide debate about the continued viability of previous approaches to education and the intellectual life in particular, and to the division of labor in the church in general, in a widely disseminated essay entitled "The American Catholic and the Intellectual Life." Although Ellis did not intend to challenge the theological and ecclesiological principles of the twentieth-century Catholic revival, his essay did have the effect of demonstrating the elitist character of the revival and its dependence on European sources. Catholic smugness was tempered by an ensuing wave of questions about the effectiveness of Catholic education and various proposals for the professionalization of the religious who ran the schools and colleges, the laity who increasingly staffed them, and the parish priest who played his own particular role as teacher and spiritual mentor.[4]

As the impact of Vatican II and various crises in American society were felt in the mid-1960s, the infatuation with modernity entered a second stage. The task of "updating" and reform seemed to accelerate to a point at which radical reexamination of parish and ministry replaced piecemeal reform. The resulting confusion and disorientation continued in full force into the early 1970s. In 1972 signs of a "cooling off" period emerged, some measure of equilibrium was restored to parish and ministry, and a new way of priesthood took inchoate shape. But the after-shocks of the period of crisis continued to reverberate well into the 1980s.

These two stages of modernization in the conciliar era were characterized by priests who openly rejected the role of the ombudsman as a satisfying model for parish ministry. These priests experimented with parish structures, participated in extraparochial professions, and saw the presbyterate as a distinct, quasi-independent subgroup with its own rights, privileges, and responsibilities within the church.

The first stage of this postwar modernization began almost imperceptibly in the early 1950s. Neo-Thomism continued to dominate Catholic intellectual life, but there were advances in significant areas. Two encyclicals of Pope Pius XII fostered theological creativity. *Divino Afflante Spiritu* (1943) gave conditional approval to Catholic appropriation of the methods of the higher criticism of the Bible. *Mystici Corporis* (1943), a relatively conservative treatise, employed Pauline theology to describe the reality of the church. A year later, a deeply influential work of Emil Mersch, S.J., was published posthumously under the title *The Theology of the Mystical Body*. This treatise modified the hierarchical focus of Pius's approach by posing a distinction within the body of Christ between the visible, institutional church and "those who live in Christ" outside the institution. In 1950 Pius attempted to forestall further innovation in the encyclical *Humani Generis*, which seemed to condemn the "new theology" emerging in postwar Europe in the writings of priests such as Mersch and Henri de Lubac.[5]

The American Catholic pioneer priests of the 1950s were influenced, then, by Catholic theology in a state of transition. They were schooled in neo-Thomism (and, in some seminaries, in neo-scholasticism) but became conversant with the works of de Lubac, Yves Congar, and others. Even seminarians read these suspect authors "on the sly." But these American priests were reformers, not radicals. They worked within the structures of parish and diocese to reformulate parish purposes and reeducate parish leadership. At the same time they perceived that they were serving an American Catholic laity increasingly sophisticated, able in the professional and business worlds, and woefully underused in church life. These reformers of the 1950s were caught, then, between two worlds, struggling to center the mystical body of Christ in the parish while continuing to appropriate the natural and supernatural language, and the clergy-laity dualism, of Catholic Action.

The early career of Louisiana parish priest Joseph Gremillion, ordained in 1943, exemplified these trends. Gremillion was, like many other bright young seminarians, targeted for advanced studies by his bishop and subsequently exposed to the thought and pastoral style of pioneer priests. At Catholic University he attended meetings of social apostolate groups. On Tuesday evenings the theme was "labor and management"; on Wednesday, "Catholic rural life"; and on Thursday, "the lay apostolate." An affable and gregarious man, Gremillion met and formed friendships with Luigi Ligutti, George Higgins, John Ryan, and many others. He was introduced to the network of pioneers.

Upon his return to Louisiana, Gremillion took up the life of a parish priest. Uncomfortable with the isolation of the ombudsman, he formed alliances with progressive priests and laity who shared his enthusiasm for the social apostolate. One such group was the Catholic Committee of the South, formed in 1940 by priests and bishops desirous of fostering a regional sense of ecclesial purpose among the 1.5 million Catholics in the south, half of whom were scattered in towns and rural areas from Louisville to Dallas (the other half was concentrated in the New Orleans area). Gremillion attended meetings, retreats, and conferences of the CCS in the 1950s and deepened his conviction that such voluntary affiliations of concerned priests and laity could do much to form Catholic consciences and raise consciousness against racism, economic injustice, and a host of moral issues confronting the region as a whole. Gremillion also traveled to Grailville, a school for apostolic formation and a center of liturgical revival near Loveland, Ohio. "The para-liturgical Thanksgiving and presentation ceremonies, the Sunday dialogue Mass, the Advent wreathes and baptismal robes—all of these Grail influences we deeply prize," Gremillion wrote, "but most prized is a world vision [and] . . . their help in awakening the Church in America to the potential of lay missionaries."[6]

In 1947 Gremillion became the founding pastor of St. Joseph's parish in Shreveport, Louisiana. St. Joseph's resembled many parishes of the late 1940s and the 1950s in the south. Suburban and residential, the parish is located in a city that was, in 1950, 33 percent black and 7 percent Catholic. Shreveport was, as its motto proclaimed, "A City on the Grow," located in a petroleum-rich region with a local economy based on cotton, cattle, natural gas, and lumber. The suburban area of Broadmoor, where St. Joseph's is located, remains predominantly white today as it was in the 1950s. Blacks are segregated in thirteen city ghettoes, only one of which borders on the parish. The parishioners of St. Joseph's were, in the 1950s, white-collar workers and professionals— doctors, lawyers, geologists, engineers, brokers, sales managers, regional brand-name representatives—and earned an average of $10,000 per year in 1954. Ninety percent of the parishioners owned their own homes.[7]

As pastor, Gremillion was determined to imbue the parish with the spirit of the social apostolate and to invigorate parish societies with a sense of public purpose. In 1954 he chronicled his efforts in *Journal of a Southern Pastor*. Lamenting that "the scope of Holy Name, St. Vincent de Paul, C.C.D. [Confraternity of Christian Doctrine] activity is much restricted," he organized statewide institutes for the Knights of Columbus to orient their activity to "the really critical problem of our day":

> The fifteen thousand soldiers of Christ who are in the best position
> to bring him into the marketplace have no program for training, no
> marshalling ground, no concerted plan of attack. They exert pre-
> cious little group impact upon the most pressing social issues of our
> changing South: racial discrimination and segregation, civil rights,
> labor-management teamwork, share-cropping, migrant workers, the
> fading family farm, dislocations arising from heightened industrial-
> ization, "the welfare state," education without God, corrupt pol-
> itics. . . . How many Knights really grasp what these social encyclicals
> are all about?[8]

Gremillion believed that the parish should provide a "program for training," a "marshalling ground" for lay action. First, the programs and societies would have to become more sophisticated, and deal in "real issues" if they were to exploit the talents and harness the energies of his white-collar parishioners:

> The bill of fare offered by our parish and organizational life tastes
> insipid to the average college man, hopelessly flat and out of touch

with boiling reality for the exceptional gifted person. Much becomes puerile, an insult to his dignity and capabilities. . . . The college grad finds no attraction in organizing benefits and bingos; "youth work" in the form of athletics and talent nights and teen-town parties . . . he is a trained man in his particular field; he owes Christian leadership to that organ or tissue of the social body of which he is a member. . . . To my mind this vocation has precedence over the demands of the parish proper.[9]

In accord with this vision of the parish as a nursery for the Catholic social apostolate, Gremillion established discussion groups based on the model of Catholic Action. These THINK groups pondered the connections between the gospel message and everyday choices faced by the Catholic laity. He also launched an ambitious adult education program to present the Catholic approach to issues of the day. Most striking was his invitation to Betty Schneider of Friendship House, a movement founded in Harlem by Catherine de Hueck to oppose racial segregation and to serve the indigent poor. The proposal to establish such a house in the deep south in 1954 created controversy. In addition to arousing the ire of parishioners not inclined to favor desegregation, the proposal raised the possibility of legal action, for it violated the state law against races occupying the same residence. In spite of the opposition, a house opened in Shreveport that year.

On another front, parochial education, Gremillion also looked creatively to the future. He wanted lay teachers not only for the CCD classes offered to public school children but for full-time teaching in the parochial school. This inclusion of laity in apostolates or "ministries" (the term was seldom employed at the time) previously reserved for religious was an important development nationwide, because it imparted to the laity a sense of ownership of the parish which became decisive in their later emergence as leaders in virtually every phase of parish life.[10] The parish school at St. Joseph's was staffed by the Sisters of Divine Providence from San Antonio. In 1956 there were eight hundred sisters in seventy schools, hospitals, and mission centers. The demand for teachers threatened to overwhelm the supply of sisters. "More and more our Catholic schools must depend on lay teachers," Gremillion wrote. "Laymen have their contribution to make if they are trained and have a *sense of mission*."[11]

This series of efforts to enlarge the vision of St. Joseph's parish exacted a toll on Gremillion. In spite of his earnest desire to "empower" and "enable" lay people, they depended very heavily upon his initiative, leadership, and presence. Moreover, reflecting the era of transition in which he worked, Gremillion thought of the parish not only as a fellowship of believers committed to the transformation of the world, but as a "family of families," as a community both natural and supernatural in character. Because "the parish is Christ," it must be a holy place, a means to sanctification and grace. Engineering the social apostolate was in itself a full-time job, but, as pastor, Gremillion also was expected to perform many of the traditional tasks of the ombudsman, especially in terms of sacramental presence.

By 1958 Gremillion was ready to move on. A robust young priest when he arrived in Shreveport eleven years earlier, he had developed a bleeding ulcer, high blood pressure, and was "constantly exhausted." Moreover, he had discovered firsthand a trend documented by Catholic sociologist Joseph Fichter, S.J., in the late 1940s. Like their modern counterparts of other faiths, American Catholics were forming associations with other persons not on the basis of parish, neighborhood, or religious ties, but on the basis of similar educational, occupational, and racial characteristics. Apart from this community-building function, many parishes were becoming simply "service station(s) where the people had their religious and spiritual needs satisfied."[12] Like many of his contemporaries, Gremillion grappled with the questions posed by this development: Could the parish accomplish the goals of the social apostolate? Given the "diversity of needs and organs and functions experienced by Christ in His mystical Body," should the priest develop a specialized ministry? Could the parish provide a base from which to address the complex problems of race, housing, education, urban development? Is the parish the only, or even primary, locus of service for the secular priest?:

> "Receive the sacraments and give a good example" is woefully inadequate in this age. We are led to a problem which is much more basic. In the juridic structure of the church the parish is considered to be the fundamental unit. . . . The parish is a geographical entity; mere accident of residence determines its composition. But does function, loyalty, and "belongingness"? Here is a carry-over from the single plane horizontal structure of an agricultural and small town society.
>
> To my mind this single plane horizontal concept of the Church's structure needs re-examination and radical adjustment to parallel the present day complexities of society's vertical institutions.[13]

Gremillion responded to this situation by pursuing professional studies and continuing his priesthood outside the parish. He asked to be relieved of parish duties that he might enter doctoral studies at the

Gregorian University in Rome. His bishop hoped for another canon lawyer for the diocese; instead, looking to the future he envisioned for himself and the church, Gremillion studied the social sciences. He would go on to become the director of social development for Catholic Relief Services in New York, and, after Vatican II, take up residence in Rome as secretary for the Pontifical Commission on Peace and Justice.[14]

John J. Egan, Hillenbrand's protégé in Chicago, also followed a career trajectory leading from parish reform to transparochial social activism. Egan always remained a parish priest. Yet his most significant work of reform, designed ultimately to impact the parish, required him to foster creative movements of renewal that could thrive only outside the parish structure. In 1946 Cardinal Stritch of Chicago appointed Egan chaplain of the Cana Conference. Working together with William Quinn, the secretary for Catholic Action, he built a broad base of popular support in the archdiocese, and throughout the nation, for Cana and the Christian Family Movement (CFM). In so doing he studiously circumvented diocesan and parish structures, preferring to encourage local groups to devise their own programs. His critics have charged that Egan did not successfully incorporate these important movements into parish life:

> Cana conferences were training married couples to have babies, to tend to their domestic knitting, to provide support to the other couples, while CFM told these same couples to get out on the street, reach out to the world's problems of poverty, bigotry, war, population, race—apostolates, once Cana did its work, for which they had little time.... Because of these contradictions and tensions, Cana and CFM never made their way, not even in Chicago, into everyday parish structures as Holy Name societies, sodalities, and Ozanam guilds did in an earlier day. In a sense this was a loss to the Church.[15]

This criticism points to the same challenges faced by Gremillion on a smaller scale: How to bring the world to the parish? How to bring the knowledge and expertise of secular society to bear on the real problems of the needy? In 1954, the year in which Friendship House began its short run in Shreveport, Egan resigned as chaplain of the Cana conference and joined forces with Chicago community organizer Saul Alinsky. Together they opposed discriminatory urban renewal programs and lobbied successfully to provide decent, low-income housing for the poor. In 1962 Egan established and presided over the first archdiocesan Office for Urban Affairs in the United States. The Chicago office was in many ways a grass-roots attempt to coordinate urban renewal efforts across parish boundaries. Thus began an important, precedent-setting alliance among parishes and between church and civic leaders, which other dioceses around the country moved quickly to imitate. This type of priestly ministry was, of course, not entirely new; one need only recall Egan's predecessor in the Chicago social apostolate, Bernard Sheil. But the depth and severity of the urban crisis of the 1960s—the widespread poverty and racial conflict in Detroit, Los Angeles, Chicago, and other metropolitan areas—posed a new kind of threat to parish survival in the inner city. The kind of transparochial move Egan and others initiated seemed necessary to those concerned with the decline of older parishes amid violent racial confrontation and manifest economic and social discrimination. Moreover, John Egan approached the task with remarkable skill and national ambition. The "urban priest" soon became a familiar figure on the religious landscape. He was the inner-city social activist, deeply involved with the technical problems of housing, renewal, and redevelopment.[16]

Every priest's story was different in some respects, but in such ways the parish lost many gifted men who responded to the new theology and the newly sophisticated laity by developing extraparochial expertise. This was, after all, the age of the convention. Reliable and affordable air travel made it possible for national associations of priests, women religious, and laity of enterprising spirit and common concern to caucus and convene with regularity. Ideas were exchanged, networks of support and information multiplied, and the pace of reform quickened in the late 1950s and throughout the 60s. Groups such as the National Catholic Educational Association, founded in 1904, gained momentum from the modern emphasis on organization, specialization, and professionalization. The National Liturgical Conference, which held meetings and liturgical weeks annually, became an important forum for the dissemination of up-to-the-minute developments in theological thought in Europe and the United States. This spirit of fellowship was contagious; one did not need to depend on a formal association or institute in order to feel "connected" to the larger movement for reform.

There was in the late 1950s, for example, an extraordinary series of meetings of the major players in the reform movements, pioneer priests who were veteran networkers and conveners and who knew one another personally. Egan, Gremillion, and Louis Putz, C.S.C., initiated and arranged the three-day meetings, the first of which was held August 26–28, 1955, immediately following the National Liturgical Week.

John Wright, then bishop of Worcester, Massachusetts, provided the guest house of St. Joseph's Trappist Monastery in Spencer. Thirty-eight priests attended the meeting, including John LaFarge, Boston *Pilot* editor Francis J. Lally, Luigi Ligutti, and William Quinn. The organizing theme around which both "bull sessions" and formal presentations revolved was "The Lay Person in the United States." Priests related their specialties and work to the questions of "the peculiar role of the layman," and the means by which "he can most realistically discover and develop his real place in the Church today." Joseph Fichter, S.J., presented his reflections on "the place of sociology in the American church today"; George Higgins analyzed the "present economic conditions"; Hillenbrand reported on the progress of the specialized Catholic Action movement (YCS, YCW, CFM); and, Godfrey Dieckmann, O.S.B., editor of *Worship*, provided an update on the liturgical apostolate. The priests in attendance were delighted with the opportunity to "do the things which distance so often forestalls: exchange thoughts and chew over our mutual interests as kindred spirits in the priesthood of Christ and the Apostolate."[17]

Similar priest-summits were held again in July 1957 in Hinsdale, Illinois, and, in Oxley, Ontario, in September 1959. The 1957 meeting on "The Church and the World" was billed as "a conference of priest-friends interested in communication and rapport between the Mystical Body of Christ and the Creature-World, which Christ seeks to redeem." The conveners invited educators, theologians, sociologists, liturgists, parish and diocesan administrators, seminary men, and family specialists for the purpose of personal contact "to get to know one another better, to understand the 'behind the scenes' thinking of each other that our public utterances, programs, and writings may be better understood, and to cross-communicate among specialists." The participants hoped to "affirm an apostolic outlook" toward the social institutions of the world and thus conquer "the defensive ghetto, fortresslike mentality which has been dominant in the church, U.S.A."[18] The 1959 meeting, planned by Egan and Andrew Greeley, focused on ecumenical concerns and on the topic of "Freedom and Authority in the American Church." The format was somewhat more formal in nature, with papers presented on "The Isolation of the Parish from the Mainstream of Life and the Consequent Changing Mission of the Priest," "The Political Image of the Church in the Non-Catholic World," and "The Relevance of Modern Scripture Studies to the Problems of the American Church."[19]

Through such collaboration, priests "prepared for Vatican II without knowing it."[20] In the late 1950s these clerical leaders perceived that the character of the American Catholic experience was changing. They hoped to harness the forces of social, political, and religious change, and to guide Catholicism along the path pioneered by the liturgists, catechists, and social action priests. But neither priest nor prophet could foresee the social and religious upheavals of the 1960s. Priests who had "planned ahead" were themselves overtaken by the press of events.

Three distinct but overlapping patterns of change conspired to create an atmosphere of crisis in the 1960s. The first was considered in one of the presentations at the 1959 meeting, entitled "The New Catholic Laity—Problems of Abundance and Americanization." The "problem" of the laity had concerned pioneer priests for a generation. By simply observing the definitions of canon law, the ombudsman of the organizational era had relegated the laity to a very precise role within the parish. In the words of a 1950 commentary, the pastor "is superior in prestige to both his priests and laity" and "the immediate source of important decisions regarding all aspects of parochial life." Religious brothers and sisters were subordinated to the clergy due to "the lesser importance of their parish functions and the absence of the powers and privileges received by the priest at ordination"; nonetheless, the church "rewards them with a prestige and rank superior to that of the laity." For their part, the laity was described as "an undifferentiated group of Catholics occupying the large square at the bottom of the organizational chart . . . collectively subordinated to the clergy in functional importance, authority, power, and prestige, and to the members of any religious congregation in functional importance and prestige."[21] The Knights of Columbus, Holy Name, and other parish-centered devotional societies of the organizational era fostered spiritual and financial loyalty to the parish in a time of costly institutional expansion. "So, dearly beloved, you have here now, in parochial treasure, valuable and attractive land that may not be encroached upon by interests of another nature," Syracuse Bishop Daniel J. Curley declared at a church dedication. "I need not tell you that you have, also, an additional parochial debt."[22]

As we have seen, pioneer priests and lay leaders challenged a narrow view of lay participation throughout the ombudsman era. Gremillion and Egan were just two of hundreds of parish priests who filtered specialized Catholic Action movements through the parishes in order to develop lay apostolates. But by 1960 the laity had acquired a new independence from parish and priest alike. The subcultural isolation of the immigrant church had preserved a coherent Catholic identity, which was reinforced through a network of private institutions and affiliations. But, as Catholics of the postwar era obtained access to higher

education through the G.I. Bill, the process of americanization decisively penetrated the immigrant subculture. Once immigrant, working-
class, and predominantly urban,[23] Catholic parishioners in 1960 were
less self-conscious about their ethnic origins, and more likely to live in
the suburbs and participate in business and professional life. With the
election of John F. Kennedy as president of the United States in 1960,
Catholics "had a secure place in the American religious ethos" and no
longer thought of themselves as a minority.[24]

Furthermore, the lay women and men who did continue to express
Catholic identity in terms of commitment to parish institutions began
to assume a more active role in parish planning. The path to greater
lay participation ran through the parochial school. Many pastors
found themselves in situations similar to Gremillion's at St. Joseph's:
burgeoning class sizes with decreasing numbers of religious to teach
them. Lay Catholics stepped into the breach in CCD programs and in
full-time teaching positions. From 1955 to 1965, the percentage of lay
people attending NCEA conferences increased dramatically.[25]

This development—the professionalization of the lay Catholic in the
business world and, increasingly, in service to parish institutions—profoundly affected the role of the parish priest. No longer was he called
upon to be all things to all people; his sphere of competence was severely restricted as his parishioners surpassed him in the ability to ma-
nipulate the secular environment. Furthermore, he was now being
held to a higher standard in his own "area of specialization," pastoral
ministry. Because his parishioners were accountable to their employers,
they began to hold the parish priest accountable for *his* performance—
a demand that had been unthinkable in the era of the ombudsman's
unchallenged rule over the parish. Many observers of American religion, aware that this type of "pastoral accountability" has long been a
feature of Protestant churches, argue that it derives not only from
Protestant congregationalism but from particularly American emphases on voluntary association, local autonomy, and a principle of subsidiarity that the Catholic Church has also fostered in its social teaching if
not in its ecclesiology.[26] And it was, and continues to be, among upwardly mobile and thoroughly americanized Catholics that one finds
the greatest expectations of the parish priest in terms of his expertise
in homiletics, liturgy, counseling, and theology. The pressure began before the council but built in the 1960s as lay Catholics took advantage
of greater opportunities to study Catholic thought and practice in colleges and universities. This first pattern of change emerged persuasively in the late 1950s and was deepened in the next decade by
transformations in the Catholic Church and in American society.[27]

4

PRIESTHOOD REFORMED: EXPERIMENTS IN PAROCHIAL PRESENCE, 1962–1972

I was made aware of social injustices. I wasn't dragged in, but I did not take the initiative. Yet I thought it was part of my priesthood. [Racial tension] was starting to stir up in Boston. It was in the air and in the papers, going out to other cities. I remember the first Sunday I was there (St. Joseph's parish in Roxbury) standing outside after Mass—of course, I hadn't really met black people before—and a woman came up and I said, "You look awfully tired." She said, "I've been picketing the school committee. We're going again this afternoon. You coming?" I said, "Sure!" What else could I say? Well, I'll never forget that. I went up there, I wore the Roman collar, they were picketing the school committee, and the ministers and priests—I was the only priest there—had to get up and read scriptures and there were Irish cops standing around and the black kids were signing, "No more police brutality!" and I was thinking, "What the hell am I doing here?"

I felt I belonged there, but I was upset. The younger priests probably felt I wasn't forceful enough, but they were trying to do too much, joiners, doing everything. For example, we went in for poverty and civil rights. Then the Vietnam War was coming along and they got involved in that. I figured, "One thing at a time! Conserve your strength!" So then the diocese and other priests figure "They're just radical" and write them off. So there wasn't that patience we needed.[1]

Sociologist of religion Peter Berger has eloquently described *The Heretical Imperative* at the heart of modern society. To be thoroughly modern, Berger suggested, is to be faced with the proliferation of opportunities to choose, and to exercise choice in realms that once seemed beyond the scope of human freedom. In matters that once seemed literally immune to change—the time it took to travel from Boston to San Francisco, for example, or, to cite a more imposing "non-negotiable," the gender to which one is born—the scientific and technological revolution identified with modernity has created possibilities. Subsequently, the argument continues, modern women and men have discovered that patterns of human behavior and belief once sanctioned by supernatural law or traditional authority do not, in fact, carry the metaphysical burden of inevitability. In a secularized society that places a premium on material development, both progress and individual freedom assume a high priority, for change requires the possibility to choose against the past. In this scheme of things, one inevitability remains: the more modern that persons become, the less readily will they accept a philosophical or religious worldview that precludes personal choice or sanctions only traditional authority in matters of belief and practice. Heresy (from the Greek, *hairein*, "to choose") takes on the character of an imperative in a modern society.[2]

The reexamination of the respective roles of priest and parishioner noticeable in the 1950s reached a new level of intensity due to the celebration of options in Roman Catholicism and in American society in the 1960s. In the case of the Roman Catholic Church, the Second Vatican Council (1962–1965) fostered a genuine pluralism of theological methodologies and perspectives. And in *Lumen Gentium* (the Dogmatic Constitution on the Church in the Modern World), the council fathers proclaimed that "the Church or People of God . . . does not take away anything from the temporal welfare of any people. Rather, she fosters and takes to herself, in so far as they are good, the abilities, the resources, and customs of peoples." This was hardly an invitation either to heresy or to the wholesale americanization of Catholicism: "In so taking them to herself she purifies, strengthens and elevates them."[3] But it was a recognition, acceptance, and conditional endorsement of cultural pluralism within the universal church—a recognition that was the necessary precondition for the later development of what John Coleman has described as "strategic theologies" rooted in the unique experience of local churches.[4]

In other ways as well, Vatican II seemed, to pioneer priests, a ringing affirmation of their own initiatives. *Gaudium et Spes* (the Pastoral Constitution on the Church in the Modern World) renewed the Catholic commitment to social and economic justice, and urged the layman "not to imagine that his pastors are always such experts, that to every problem which arises, however complicated, they can readily give him a concrete solution." *Dignitatis Humanae* (the Declaration on Religious Liberty), chief architect of which was the American Jesuit John Courtney Murray, reconciled the church with religious pluralism and church-state separation. Both documents depicted the church as the guardian of "common human dignity" and challenged Catholics to study and appreciate "all things human."[5]

The majority bloc that approved many of these significant documents was influenced by a brilliant group of German, Austrian, and French theologians who had collectively forged theological and philosophical foundations for the Catholic aggiornamento. Articulated most persuasively in the late 1950s and early 60s by Karl Rahner, the new "theological anthropology" understood human transcendence to be given in the subject's a priori experience of an infinite horizon (God) as the condition of the possibility of any act of knowing. Experience of the divine presence came from within the human person. Rahner criticized "extrinsicism" (the notion that divine revelation is extrinsic to, or given apart from, the human subject's ordinary experience of the world) and "dogmatic positivism" (the notion that the content of such revelation may be expressed definitively in authoritative religious language). These epistemological insights served to modify an earlier Vatican insistence on the "objective character" of divine revelation. Increasingly, the church began to be seen as the mediator of the individual or communal experience of the divine rather than as the guardian of a once-for-all "Deposit of Faith" from on high. The triumphal stance of the ombudsman era was quickly found to be inadequate in this turn to the human subject and to human history as the arena for divine self-communication.[6]

This new appreciation for "all things human" and for the historic character of divine revelation exercised a profound impact upon Catholic self-understanding. Some Catholic thinkers began to understand religious symbols as human, and therefore radically contingent, expressions of religious experience. Other "absolutes," including the church, were subjected to the relativizing force of critical history. A wave of Catholic self-criticism swept Europe and the United States in the 1960s. In his recounting of the 60s shift in theological paradigm, *Man Becoming: God in Secular Experience*, Gregory Baum expressed a common conciliar-era complaint against the neo-Thomistic heritage:

> I came to regard the distinction between the supernatural, elevated life of Catholics, and the natural, purely human life of other people as a dangerous illusion with devastating effects on the Catholic community. The pretense to have access to a higher life not available elsewhere tended to make Catholics blind to the holiness present in others and, with more damaging effects, insensitive to their own failings and vices. It was difficult for Catholics to learn from others and come to self-knowledge. Believing itself to be alive with supernatural life, the Catholic community was often prevented from discovering

how deeply involved it was in prejudices, in hidden antipathies, and in the promotion of destructive social outlooks which the culture to which it belonged had already transcended.[7]

Such self-appraisal contributed unintentionally to a perception, ironic given the intent of the council, that the church had become secularized, had "lost its soul," and was thus irrelevant. The coincidence of this "identity crisis" with the new political and economic respectability of American Catholics elicited from Gary Wills the judgment that "the Catholics' hour had come, though they did not seem to know it; had come, too late, just as their church was disintegrating."[8]

The Catholic priest had the most to lose in these years of uncertainty. Many perceived a dwindling of the prestige and status previously accorded the priesthood in American society. Prior to suspending his own priestly activities, Ivan Illich told a group of his fellows that "we have only a short time left when the Roman collar will open doors for us."[9] Moreover, the council's Decree on the Ministry and Life of Priests disappointed those who sought clarification, for "no attempt is made in it to give anything like a discussion on the theology of priesthood."[10] The Vatican II emphasis on the "priesthood of the laity" and the church as "the People of God" (rather than as an exclusive and perfect society) demanded a formal and full reconsideration of the role and identity of the priest in this new church. When this effort was not forthcoming, many American priests were left to struggle alone, or with their confreres, toward a recovery of the sense of the priesthood as a special and hallowed commitment that somehow sets recipients apart from other Christians. Barring the recovery of such a sensibility, the retention of the obligation of celibacy scandalized a small but vocal minority of the American presbyterate. Many of their brother priests did not publicly express such doubts, but quietly questioned their own commitments to the religious life. The phenomenon of priests leaving active ministry antedated the council but intensified after 1965.[11]

Adding to the pressures on the postconciliar priest was the unprecedented need for theological and spiritual leadership and education concerning the reforms and their implementation. Without such authoritative leadership the American Catholic community risked fragmentation:

> Changes in liturgy and pastoral practice eroded the behavioral foundations of identity; changes in ecclesiology called into question the long dominant quantitative measures of success and failure; changes in theology brought a new pluralism and uncertainty about faith and morality. The end result was that cultural constraints, which once

nurtured and sustained Catholic identity for many, all but disappeared. The combination of change at home and in the universal Church meant that long taken for granted patterns of behavior, forms of the expression of belief, and moral attitudes became problematic; to be examined, evaluated, retained, discarded, or renewed in terms of contemporary perspectives and needs, a process increasingly personal rather than corporate.[12]

The process of "updating" the laity was haphazard and uneven. All too frequently, for example, changes in the liturgy would be explained superficially and after the fact. As one priest recalled, "they (the laity) were now the People of God, but we continued to treat them like passive children. We had been accustomed to defending any action as rooted in the authority of the Church. So now we told them the liturgy was to be changed because 'the Church has willed it.' That was supposed to be sufficient."[13]

In addition to coping with Vatican II and the new American Catholic laity, the priest was forced to respond to a third pattern of change in the 1960s—namely, the massive cultural upheaval in the United States. Again, the pattern of change emerged from a particularly modern and American expansion of the arena of choice and personal freedom. In fact, the new awareness of personal and societal options was in itself revolutionary and established a dynamic of cultural change that, a generation later, still seems irreversible. Traditional authority was under siege in the antiestablishment and antiwar movements of the Vietnam era, in the sexual revolution and "hippie" counterculture, in the advent of new religious pluralism, and in the civil rights movement. Again, human dignity and self-fulfillment was the stated goal of the renewals and revolutions; the formulation of theories and philosophies of human freedom became something of a cottage industry. Emphasis fell on "personhood" and developing one's potential, whether by political activism, experimentation with drugs, "free love," transcendental meditation, or psychotherapy and "transactional analysis."[14] In all this the priest faced overwhelming competition for the attention and loyalty of Catholics who had, a decade earlier, accepted his ability to speak authoritatively on private faith and public morals. Now he seemed but one among many purveyors of truth.

These were, then, times that required adjustment and adaptation, and strained the capacities of many who had believed that the eternal church would be eternally tridentine. What is striking is not that the American priesthood was significantly transformed by these seismic shifts in church and society—no American institution was left unaffected by the 1960s—but that American priests were able throughout to preserve a real sense of continuity with the past even as they formed new alliances and cast off outdated approaches to ministry. If this was a period of crisis—a turning point, a moment of decision—then one must also conclude, from a vantage two decades removed, that the American priesthood as a whole weathered it quite well, answering the challenge to priestly existence with a firm, if not resounding, yes. Although there were resignations from the priesthood in unprecedented numbers, over two-thirds of the presbyterate remained in active ministry. It is true that some of these simply "hung on"; it is equally true that many more deepened their commitment to the Catholic priesthood after painful self-scrutiny and soul-searching. Although, as I will argue, there was a widespread loss of confidence in parochial ministry in the 1960s, even among those who remained in the parishes full-time, priests continued to see their vocation in terms of service to a local people, a neighborhood, a community. There is both irony and poignancy in the fact that Andrew Greeley, a "weekend" parish priest for the large part of his long career as sociologist, journalist, and novelist, summed up his career under the title *Confessions of a Parish Priest.*[15]

There were many developments in the American priesthood from 1962 to 1972 in response to the patterns of change in church and society, and they may be summarized under four general descriptions. First, in response both to the earlier work of pioneer priests in the parishes and seminaries, and to Vatican II's "preferential option for the poor," many American priests devoted themselves to the problems of the inner city. They fought racism in themselves and others, worked for adequate housing and employment for minorities and the underprivileged, and carried the Catholic social gospel to the slums. These urban priests picketed, rallied, and applauded radical prophets such as the Berrigan brothers; those who withstood the trendiness of the moment went on to further the same causes from *within* political and economic structures. A second development was the rise of the so-called hyphenated priest—the priest-sociologist, the priest-psychiatrist, the priest-novelist—in response to the renewed awareness that the business of the church was the human condition in all its manifestations. By pursuing graduate studies and obtaining advanced degrees, talented priests met the demand for professionalization and specialization, and kept up with their Protestant colleagues in ministry with whom they were in closer collaboration. Third was a formal recognition, by church and society, that the priest was himself a human subject with a particular spiritual, sociological, and psychological profile. Studies of the priesthood, many of them commissioned by the

American bishops, followed upon this insight. Problems that had escaped serious analysis, including alcoholism and loneliness, received careful attention. The fourth development in the 1960s followed naturally from the other three: priests formed official and unofficial structures of support—diocesan senates, clubs, associations, prayer groups—in response to a new, shared sense that the priesthood was now, like much else in American society, a voluntary matter, a personal choice rather than an unquestionable obligation. The sustaining of such a commitment required mutual support and encouragement. In this the priests of the 1960s and 1970s were of course following the example of their pioneering, networking predecessors of the preconciliar era. They were also preparing for the future of the American priesthood, for they caucused, prayed, and shared not only with fellow priests but with gifted women religious, lay women, and lay men. Through such affiliations they were led to discover their own holiness and the forces of spiritual renewal in movements such as Cursillo, Marriage Encounter, and Renew.[16]

URBAN MINISTRY

The pioneer priests' commitment to advancing the cause of social justice in the 1950s took on a new urgency in the 60s. John Egan, who turned almost exclusively to the social apostolate after 1954, was profoundly influential on a national level in the 1960s because his style of leadership was perfectly attuned to the needs of the presbyterate. Less a bureaucrat or company man, more a grass-roots organizer who built coalitions from the bottom up, Egan was not aloof from the hierarchical church, but preferred personal contact to administrative memo. He effectively communicated his own enthusiasm for the social apostolate to fellow priests and seminarians through the formation of the Catholic Committee on Urban Ministry (CCUM), an organization that, one Notre Dame theologian suggested, provided a model not only for the urban priest, but for the postconciliar American church.[17]

Informally begun in 1967, CCUM was the natural outgrowth of earlier social action movements including the Catholic Interracial Council, the Catholic Rural Life Movement, the Catholic Worker, Catholic Charities, and the specialized Catholic Action movements. In response to the civil rights movement and in imitation of Egan's own Office of Urban Affairs in Chicago, many dioceses opened offices of social action and established human rights commissions in the early 1960s. A camaraderie developed among the priests holding similar responsibilities and working in the inner cities of the United States. Many of these men were the Catholic "contacts" for community organizing efforts, and frequently collaborated ecumenically with other religious leaders in their cities. By providing leadership, facilities, and funding, the churches were the backbone of such community organization work. In 1967, in an effort to nationalize and coordinate these various initiatives, church and synagogue leaders formed the Inter-religious Foundation for Community Organization (IFCO) to channel denominational funds to community organizations and to monitor their use. Egan brought together sixteen priests in urban ministry and sought representation on the IFCO board as the Catholic Committee on Community Organization. Now the informal network of support was formalized. Its base was broadened and its name changed to the Catholic Committee on Urban Ministry that summer.[18]

In 1970 Egan left Chicago, accepted a joint faculty appointment at the University of Notre Dame with the Institute for Urban Studies and the theology department, and challenged CCUM to extend its core group to include the hundreds of religious and priests who had joined the social ministry in the 60s. In 1971 ninety-two members of the expanded committee, including a significant number of women religious, met at Notre Dame to discuss a "theology of social action"; six months later, two hundred fifty members reconvened (one-third of them women) to analyze current national social issues and methodology in community organization. Soon thereafter, Egan hired two field coordinators who, in 1971 and 1973, visited over eight hundred fifty social ministers in thirteen states. They discovered in these ministers a profound level of commitment and a pressing need for intensive training in community organizational skills. Egan and his collaborators responded by establishing Notre Dame's Pastoral Institute for Social Ministry, a month-long summer program attended by two hundred sixty priests and women religious in 1973.

At the annual CCUM conference in the fall of 1973, every Catholic organization in the United States with a social action orientation was represented. Other organized groups, such as the provincial social action directors for the Jesuits, acquired "in-service" training at the CCUM conference. As the CCUM constituency grew in such ways, regional offices opened in New England, Texas, Ohio, Colorado, and Minnesota, and regional work began in Delaware, Maryland, Virginia, Louisiana, California, New Jersey, and Indiana under the supervision of the field coordinators and the national office. As lay and clerical leadership emerged on the state level in the early 70s, the work of CCUM became more and more a responsibility of the persons resident in the locality.[19]

The story of CCUM provides an important example of the way in which the American religious style of networking and grass-roots organizing was reinforced by the theological and ecclesiological insights of the 1960s. CCUM relied little on official titles, hierarchial structures of authority, or ecclesiastical preferment; at its core were Christians who had personalized their ministries in one way or another and were acting out of a sense of obligation to a people rather than an institution. Moreover, it followed its own internal dynamic, one stage of which was a necessary centralization in Egan and the national office, but the ultimate outcome of which was an empowering of social action ministries on a local level. Although Egan was forced to leave his own full-time parish ministry, he exercised a "ministry to the ministers," and thereby established in the minds of the future lay, religious, and clerical leaders of American Catholicism a model for effective pastoral presence. CCUM began among priests and women religious but was eventually directed toward the laity. As the organization expanded and enjoyed a measure of success, it relied increasingly upon lay response, initiative, and leadership. Among the pioneer priests and their successors who provided leadership in CCUM and similar organizations there was a strong recognition of the practical (and, increasingly, the theological) need for ministerial collaboration with the laity. Given shape in movements and organizations that developed lay leadership, this awareness marked an important transition between the era of the ombudsman and the postconciliar era.

CCUM was also notable for its effort to coordinate pastoral and social ministry at a time when competition and misunderstanding threatened the relationship between the parish priest and the urban priest (who was often, of course, stationed in a parish). The zeal of social-action priests was contagious, but their vision of the parish (sometimes seen as a source for money, volunteers, and recruits) was often at odds with that of the experienced pastor. In Boston, for example, Msgr. Russell Collins, whose recollection of an "urban plunge" in Roxbury opened this chapter, was attracted to the pastorate of an inner-city parish in 1965 by his former students at St. John's Seminary. These young priests had studied similar initiatives in Chicago and in St. Louis, and planned to "take over" seven inner-city parishes in proximity of the cathedral. By rooting their movements in the broken body and shed blood of Christ celebrated powerfully in the new vernacular liturgy, these men would, they believed, rejuvenate depressed areas, uphold the dignity of the marginated, and, in so doing, bring people to Christ. This idealism and fervor for the new liturgy and the social gospel was inspired by the self-image of many seminarians and younger ordinands: the priest is Christ walking the secular city, healing the wounds of injustice, liberating the oppressed.[20]

What seemed missing at times, however, was an effective and well-developed pastoral strategy based on a sophisticated appreciation of the needs of the inner-city parish. Collins recalls the pitfalls of these inchoate efforts at urban ministry:

> The younger priests shared the idea that the white people who lived adjacent to the black ghettos were guilty because they wouldn't open their hearts and homes to blacks. Well, all their investments were in their homes, they were trying to save. There wasn't enough age to understand these things. You really have to have a solid spiritual foundation. Many of the priests didn't have a sympathy for the parishioners. "The old stuff is out . . . Adam and Eve and all that" and not a consciousness of how sacred religion is to people. We tried to have parish liturgies, but we tended to impose our categories on people. For example, the fact that I was a monsignor meant something to the black community, that the Church was recognizing them. But for us it was the new democratic church, so the young priests didn't want me to wear red or be "monsignor" because it was not their concept of the Church. But it was imposing our mentality on other people.[21]

These first years of widespread urban ministry found priests in search of a common spirituality and prayer life beyond the public celebration of the liturgy. Sociological studies of the postconciliar priesthood have documented a diminished observance of traditional forms of priestly piety such as the reading of the breviary and the examination of conscience, in part due to their private and supposedly archaic character. Yet young ordinands and their more mature mentors found themselves, by the nature of their work, involved in a variety of social and political projects in a secularized environment. What was to bind them together, give them a sense of solidarity with fellow Catholics, brother priests? Ironically, the urban priest found his most daunting task to be the formation of a religious community:

> Also in the city you had people who were "looking for themselves." It was a place of more freedom. Sisters started coming and living in apartments. As regards ministry: when we [three priests] first went in [to Roxbury] we would say vespers together. Then after awhile one or the other would be absent for a demonstration or a meeting . . .

the prayer went and after awhile we were just another social group. We were losing sight of what our role was. It became exclusively a social ministry. They formed the Urban Priests Society [of Boston] and it became power against power, the power of the priests against the power of the chancery. We were supposed to be building up the laity, the books told us, but it was the priests and nuns who were going out and doing things.[22]

The journey to the inner city and involvement in broader movements of social protest affected the priesthood in a number of ways. First, the high visibility of the clerical crusader in a media age altered the image of the Roman Catholic priest in the mind of the American public, and radicalized a small but influential segment of the Catholic left. When Daniel Berrigan, S.J., Philip Berrigan, Mary Moylan, and six others publicly burned draft documents in Catonsville, Maryland, to protest American involvement in the Vietnam War, the scene was beamed across the nation's television screens. The action, calculated for dramatic impact, symbolized effectively for many socially conscious men and women the raison d'être of their religious commitment. It also broke, at least temporarily, Bing Crosby's hold on the popular imagination concerning the personality and style of the Catholic priest.[23]

Second, the fight for social justice was the occasion for ecumenical cooperation unprecedented in its scope and quality. The experience of participating in dangerous civil rights marches in Alabama and Washington forged strong bonds of friendship and mutual respect between Catholic leaders and their Jewish and Protestant counterparts. Such interdenominational collaboration found institutional expression in the late 1960s in groups such as IFCO, the Ecumenical Institute, and the community-development committees that sprang up in various cities and suburbs.[24]

Third, clerical and religious participation in radical protest movements alienated or confused a significant portion of the Catholic laity who felt that the priest had no business becoming personally involved in such controversies. Many believed—indeed, had recently been taught—that the priest belonged in the sanctuary or in the parish hall moderating Catholic Action discussion groups. Within a very brief period of time, the laity found the genial parish priest joined, or replaced, by the intense, "committed" assistant who challenged parishioners to become more actively involved in social and political action in the service of justice. The stark, uncompromising proclamation of the gospel according to social activists divided some parishes into factions preferring one "type" of priest over another. Whether expressed vociferously, in organized efforts to rid a parish of a bothersome priest, or quietly, in Mass attendance based on the identity of the celebrant, such divisions persist in our own time.[25]

PRIEST AND PROFESSIONAL

To further complicate the laity's perceptions of the new priesthood, the activist priest was joined by a second alternative to the ombudsman—namely, the professionalized priest. By 1969 this trend was so prevalent as to be celebrated in a volume on *Hyphenated Priests: The Ministry of the Future*. The so-called hyphenated priest obtained an advanced degree or entered professional life in a particular discipline. He was only coincidentally present to a parish; his working address was usually a university campus or a downtown office building. Moreover, this approach to priestly ministry emerged as a self-conscious adaptation to the needs of the modern, American, postconciliar church. Wrote Joseph Fichter, S.J.:

> No longer can the priest be just a priest. He must be a priest who does something; this is where the professionalism comes in. The day of the general practitioner is gone. We no longer live in a Bavarian village or in an Irish village. We now live in a highly specialized society and every priest needs expertise beyond what he gets in the seminary.[26]

The professionalized priest could point to various twentieth-century precedents and contexts for his role. The centralization and bureaucratization of twentieth-century American Catholicism fostered a regard for fixed procedures and professional conduct. The "ecclesiastical organization man" was described as "a good organizer ... less concerned with theology than with fellowship."[27] In turn the pioneer priest added a concern for functional specialization. Asked in 1954 what advice he would give to seminarians, pioneer priest John LaFarge responded, "Tell them to become real specialists. If they're to do anything important, they've got to be really good in some one thing."[28] Pioneer priests also modified and personalized the bureaucratic style. More than the organization man, they believed the Church to be an instrumental structure flexible enough to encourage personal creativity. Valuing orderliness without identifying it with the traditional rules and regulations of a large and impersonal institution, they formed alliances on the basis of shared interests and skills rather than institutional priorities.

Women religious also set an influential example for priests. As in other areas of renewal, they arrived ahead of the clergy on the professional circuit. A decisive step in this direction was the Sister Formation movement, inspired in the early 1950s in part by Pope Pius XII who urged that full professional training be given to religious sisters preparing for teaching and hospital work. This meant that women religious had a head-start of almost a decade in grappling with the issues of specialization and professionalization. They assumed leadership roles in many of the early ecumenical organizations and conferences on urban and rural social outreach precisely because they were well prepared by formal training and substantial pastoral experience.

One striking example of the leadership and influence of women religious came during the first conference of the Center for Applied Research in the Apostolate (CARA) at the Catholic University in Washington, D.C., in 1965. The new ecumenical cooperation and social-scientific approach to the problems of pastoral ministry was reflected in the long-range goal of CARA "to discover, promote and apply modern techniques and scientific informational resources for practical use in coordinated and effective approach to the Church's social and religious mission in the modern world." The initial CARA conference, on "The Church in the Changing City," attracted a number of experts from a variety of denominational background, including Dr. Lauris B. Whitman, executive director of the Department of Research for the National Council of Churches and an ordained Baptist minister, who reported on Protestant social action efforts in rural communities. Geno Baroni, a diocesan priest involved in community organization in low-income areas of Washington, D.C., described a division in Catholicism between, on the one hand, "those who want the Church to play its customary role as guardian of the values and institutions of the past" and "stay out of politics and controversy"; and, on the other hand, "those who insist that the Church should play a more direct role in social change." Baroni articulated the crucial questions facing parish priests, given the renewed commitment to social activism: What is the present and potential role of the neighborhood parish in programs for renewing the declining areas of the city? What is the role of the parish church as a property owner? As a spiritual organization? As an institution of influence? Is it an act of significant relevance to open parish facilities for neighborhood projects? Should parish or church property be considered for nonprofit, low- or middle-income housing under a federally financed program? Should the parish church or other facilities become a focal point for civil rights rallies or militant community organizations? Can the neighborhood parish serve as a training center for our clergy, seminarians, and nuns?[29]

Sustained, comprehensive, and dynamic answers to these questions came from Sr. Marie Augusta Neal, S.N.D., then chairman of the department of sociology at Emmanuel College in Boston. Drawing upon the experience of sisters in the inner city, and upon her own extensive studies of these questions, she outlined a plan for parish renewal including but not limited to the following proposals:

> a) Wherever the inner-city parish plays the role of a bastion of resistance to change (when it does not, in other words, provide the services needed by the bulk of the population but goes on providing the traditional services of a national church to a dwindling national group) then the old parish form must go. . . . b) Wherever the clergy and the religious in the inner-city deny the existence of inner-city problems . . . then the clergy and religious must be retrained or replaced by trained Christians. . . . c) Wherever the liturgy as lived is sterile, hostile, mechanical, and meaningless to the people of the inner city, all those who share in it must be provided with new experiences which allow the liturgy to effect what it is intended to do—to invigorate the church, to relate it to the world, to seek the unity of Christians and a meaningful relationship with all men.[30]

Neal also submitted concrete proposals for the revision of catechetical and parochial education, and the retraining of seminarians and novices, toward the end of fostering social awareness in Catholics and community-organizing expertise in religious leaders.

The professionalized priest of the 1960s and 70s aspired to achieve in his own ministry something of this interpenetration of pastoral and prophetic roles. He responded to a personal calling rather than an institutional mandate, yet understood his distinctive authority in society as deriving, in part, from his role as an official representative of a sacred tradition. He was also acutely aware of the practical exigencies of secularized American society and of a church recently reawakened to the secular wisdom of the behavioral sciences. Even the oblique wording of the Vatican II Decree on the Ministry of Life of Priests seemed to endorse the advanced study of "the deepest meaning and value of all creation":

> All priests are sent forth as co-workers in the same undertaking, whether they are engaged in a parochial or supraparochial ministry,

whether they devote their efforts to scientific research or teaching.... All indeed are united in the single goal of building up
Christ's Body, a work requiring manifold roles and new adjustments,
especially nowadays.[31]

Heightened awareness of the church's own inextricable involvement
in the redemptive course of human history posed an obvious question:
Should priests be professionally committed to the transformation of
the political, religious, and economic structures of society *from within*?
The priest-sociologist, priest-psychiatrist, and priest-politician would,
as the council urged, absorb the methods and findings of the empirical
and behavioral sciences, purge from them the influence of materialism
and atheism, and appropriate them for the work of evangelization and
social justice. Yet this incorporation of the secular behavioral sciences
into the Catholic worldview affected Catholic anthropology at least as
much as Catholic anthropology influenced the sciences. Priests who
had been trained in a manual tradition that defined the human person
primarily in spiritual and metaphysical terms now developed an appreciation of the complex and ambiguous nature of human personality
and motivations. The application of empirical methods of inquiry to
the perennial problems of human behavior was in itself a departure
for Catholic priest-scholars; the appearance of Catholic Jungians or
neo-Freudians seemed to make legitimate any possible combination of
faith and scientific theory. From within came challenges to traditional
Catholic teaching on a number of issues concerning sin, guilt and creation. There was, for example, a renewed appreciation of interpersonal relationships and human sexuality as an expression of mature
Christian love. Such insights radicalized some members of the clergy.
Once presented as a "higher way" of asceticism, celibacy was now characterized by a small but vocal group as, at best, a hackneyed holdover
from a repressive age and, at worst, a formidable barrier to human
authenticity.[32]
Advocates of the hyphenated priesthood welcomed the new professionalization and specialization as the perfect tonic for an ailing presbyterate precisely because it offered a new way of being present to the
People of God. The new understanding of the person as a complex
psychological, spiritual, social, and economic being demanded a new,
sufficiently complex, pastoral approach. Describing himself as "more
secular than most professional Catholic laymen who are currently
preaching the gospel of secularity," priest-sociologist-journalist Andrew
Greeley admitted that "curiously enough, some of my friends have labeled my activity 'hyphenated priesthood.' Very definitely they are

using the word 'hyphenated' in the pejorative sense." But, he argued, a secularized priesthood was a necessary stage in the development of his "psychological generation" of clergy:

> We have been freed from many of the ideological and organizational inhibitions of the past. We have a glorious opportunity to shape a new, more pluralistic and flexible Church. We can form new relationships with the lay people; we can develop a celibacy which means deeper and richer love rather than sterile bachelorhood; we have the freedom to create more effective forms of education and worship. . . . The priesthood is being converted into a "career" that is exciting and rewarding and challenging. . . . If we have the courage to transcend our timidity and narrowness it seems to me that we will quickly conclude that there has rarely been a time when it's been more exciting to be a Catholic priest.[33]

The priest who would specialize encountered certain occupational hazards, the most pervasive of which was the danger of reductionism. Developing as they had in secularized American institutions, the social sciences often accounted for religious belief and behavior by way of sociological, psychological, or even economic constructs. The priest studying psychotherapy, for example, was tempted in his ministry of forgiveness to conflate the previously distinct categories of "the sinful" and "the aberrant." Where did therapy end and spiritual consolation begin? In 1966 Philip Rieff answered with *The Triumph of the Therapeutic: Uses of Faith after Freud*, which warned that "now, contradicting all faiths, a culture of the indifferent is being attempted, lately using a rhetoric of 'commitment' with which to enlarge the scope of its dynamism. . . . Such a credo of change amounts to a new faith—more precisely, to a counter-faith."[34]

Some observers expressed different concerns about the priest taking on another line of work. How could one man do justice to two or more professional roles, each of which demanded, if done properly, a consuming dedication? What is the distinctive identity of the priest? Priest-poet John L'Heureux probed these difficulties in an 1969 essay in response to Fichter:

> I am not certain what a priest is. The functional notion of the priest—a man who administers certain sacraments, preaches, etc.—is under heavy attack today. There is a more pleasing theory of the priest as a man who helps create community. And then there is the bold approach of Father Fichter who says . . . that a man is *de facto* a

priest, he accepts the priesthood as part of himself, and then he proceeds to become a professional.

The trouble I find with a priest who is only a professional-something-else, where the something-else supposedly *is* the exercise of his priesthood, is twofold: (1) the priest-chemist differs in no way from any other professional chemist nor is there any evident reason why he should be a chemist at all; (2) by this description the priesthood is reduced to a facet of personality or to a personal possession. Being a priest becomes like being Irish ... or, worse, like being a member of an exclusive bachelor's club. . . .

It seems to me . . . that [Fichter] has demonstrated that there is no essential contradiction between being a priest and being something else. Agreed. But he has said nothing about what a priest *is*, why a layman cannot do that work. . . . It would seem that for the priesthood Father Fichter proposes, baptism alone is required.

What then is it that a priest does within the Christian community? . . . He must be Christ for people in a way that other people cannot, and this means Mass, sacraments, preaching. He must engage in this narrowly-defined priestly work at least sometimes and with some degree of regularity. Otherwise he might as well be a social worker.[35]

This problem of distinctive identity of the priest *as priest* was particularly acute for those who were not rooted in parish pastoral work. Learned religious orders with a profound tradition of academic accomplishment such as the Jesuits or the Benedictines naturally provided most of the candidates for postconciliar professionalization. Their customary pattern of selective presence to the parish was now reinforced and deepened by the educational demands of professionalization. Yet they influenced through their seminary and university positions many diocesans who also saw the wisdom in specialization and gradually came to realize that their own parish work required some professional skills along with a distinct temperament. The large majority of American Catholic priests did not leave the parish at all in this period. But in ministering to their parish communities many sought to combine the effective pastoral presence of the ombudsman with the newly earned sophistication about modern existence that came with professionalization.

THE SCRUTINIZED PRIEST
Such self-conscious examination of the role and identity of the priest became commonplace in the turbulent decade after Vatican II. The appearance of a "secularized priesthood" challenged the traditional

notion of the priest as the "man set apart." In the pilgrimage from the margins of society into the mainstream, the priest may have lost a mysterious or glamorous aspect of his identity. It seemed at times that the priesthood was threatened by the relativism popular in the secular culture: the priest was just another professional among professionals, his lifestyle and beliefs a choice no more absolute or sacred than the choice of other autonomous individuals. This perception was reinforced, ironically, by the church's own decision, in the late 1960s, to study the presbyterate as a distinct and unique sociological class. This was both a response to a perceived crisis in the priesthood and a long overdue appreciation of the priest as an ordinary human being with particular emotional, psychological, and spiritual needs. By 1970 "the priest" was a universally recognized and academically approved "object of scientific study."

There had been, of course, sophisticated sociological studies of the priesthood, but none of them approached the scope of the "priest studies" commissioned by the church in the late 60s to counter what was generally perceived as a widespread drop in morale, especially among the majority of priests who were not on the cutting edge of new developments in the urban apostolate, professionalization, and specialization. These priests found themselves in a kind of limbo between two worlds. They had not yet absorbed or personally appropriated the new insights and techniques of the postconciliar priesthood, but they were aware that the ombudsman model was no longer sufficient to their needs or to the needs of their parishioners.

Furthermore, these "average" parish priests were unwitting victims of an unmistakable shift in American values in the direction of what one sociologist described as a "sensate culture." Affluent American society was geared to the values of satisfaction and consumption, and fewer Americans felt self-sacrifice and material deprivation to be the economic necessities they once had been. There was, in other words, less cultural reinforcement for the values of work and self-denial or their accompanying religious expression in fasting, self-control, abstinence, and penance. Pope Paul VI was considered by some embarrassingly old-fashioned when he publicly voiced anguish about the world decline in morality. In this context the priest was truly a countercultural figure: his lifestyle became a "sign of contradiction."

The presbyterate manifested the signs of this strain. Between 1966 and 1972 the number of "church professionals" decreased by 15.3 percent while the American population increased by 4.6 percent. While the number of resignations was greater among women religious, priests also departed at an alarming pace. The largest number of

American Catholic priests on record was in 1967 (59,892), but by 1972 the number had declined by almost three thousand. Young men did not enter the seminary at the rate that older priests resigned or retired. Between 1965 and 1972 the seminary population declined by 55 percent.[36]

To their credit the U.S. bishops responded quickly to this situation even as it unfolded. In April 1967 the National Conference of Catholic Bishops directed its Committee on Pastoral Research and Practices to undertake an extensive study of the life and ministry of priests. The committee of priests and bishops designed a plan for a comprehensive study along eight tracks—historical, doctrinal, spiritual, pastoral, ecumenical, liturgical, sociological, and psychological. The historical, psychological, and sociological studies were published in separate substantial volumes, and the project generated numerous spin-off books, articles, and symposia.

It is beyond the scope of this essay to report upon the numerous significant findings of these studies of the priesthood, but a few comments on the most comprehensive study, the sociological report, are in order. The National Opinion Research Center conducted a survey of six thousand priests, including bishops and major superiors, active and resigned diocesan and religious order clergy, beginning in March 1969. From this sample, the reporters pieced together a nuanced profile of the American priesthood. In comparison with other professions, the priesthood did not appear to be in a state of siege or crisis. For example, priests left active ministry at a lower rate than other American workers changed occupations. Candidates for the priesthood were as "well-adjusted" as their counterparts in other professions. From the results of a Personal Orientation Inventory, the NORC staff concluded that Roman Catholic priests were not highly "self-actualized" but neither did they depart from the norm in this. (The "self-actualized" individual was described as time-competent and inner-directed with a high level of self-regard, self-acceptance, and a capacity for intimate contact with others.) In other words, if the American priest experienced difficulties in adjusting to the stress and strain of contemporary life, he was hardly alone in this.[37]

However, when the survey priests were compared not with their secular contemporaries but with previous generations of American Catholic priests, the case for a morale crisis became stronger. About 5 percent of the diocesan priests had resigned between 1966 and 1969, another 3 percent said that they were definitely going to resign, and 10 percent were uncertain about their future plans. Moreover, the job satisfaction of the typical American curate was not very different from that of an unskilled worker. Only in the area of pay were associate pastors more satisfied with their work situation than was the lowest category of workers in American industry. Two distinctive emotional problems seemed to plague the American priest as well: an insensitivity to his own needs and an incapacity to accept aggressive impulses. Finally, there was a noticeable decline in prayer life, especially among the younger age groups.[38]

Perhaps most disturbing to the bishops who commissioned the study was the erosion of the once taken-for-granted doctrinal uniformity of the American clergy; in its place was a selective and critical acceptance of official Catholic teaching on certain matters. For example, only 36 percent of the diocesan priests and 37 percent of the religious asserted that Pope Paul VI's 1968 reaffirmation of the ban on artificial contraception, *Humanae Vitae*, was a competent and appropriate exercise of papal teaching authority (whereas 72 percent of the bishops did); only 40 percent of the presbyterate fully agreed with the substance of the teaching. A significant number of priests also rejected the official church position on divorce.[39] The NORC report also documented a widespread tendency of priests to ignore rules, especially liturgical directives, with which they did not agree. While bishops and priests did share a strong tradition of social concern, these findings revealed a real and pervasive crisis of ecclesiastical authority, which of course wreaked havoc in postconciliar pastoral practice. As one parishioner in New Orleans recalled in a recent interview, "After the encyclical, one could 'shop' for a particular kind of priest: in one confessional birth control was a mortal sin; in another, it was barely a matter of concern."[40]

These studies described a number of distinctive characteristics of the American priest in the period immediately following Vatican II, not the least of which was his very real need to reconceive his relationship to three groups that had shaped his identity in the preconciliar era: the institutional church, represented by its formal teaching and authority structures; the lay men and women whom he served in the parish; and, his fellow priests. As it happened, he found that a renewed relationship to his brother priests was the necessary starting point for addressing his role in the larger institutional church and in the parish.

PRIESTS' ASSOCIATIONS

The cultural and theological transformations of the conciliar era robbed the American priesthood of a sense of shared corporate identity. In the ombudsman era, this had been provided by strong episcopal leadership, standardized seminary training, routinized parish roles for pastor and laity, and a bond of priestly fellowship forged by service to the institutional church and its thriving local churches. In the 1960s, the appropriate role of the parish priest and his relationship to the institutional church was subject of widespread re-examination. In the absence of a consensus on these questions, priests turned to one another to puzzle over the new situation and to find personal support in their ministries. It is not surprising, then, that the NORC findings shed light upon another trend in the decade between 1962 and 1972: the multiplication of official and unofficial priest associations.

As we have seen, "priest-bonding" had proceeded in a somewhat "covert" fashion in the late 1950s in the various informal networks, vicariate meetings, and small-group weekends organized by pioneer priests. In the mid-1960s, many priests, disappointed by the insubstantial treatment of their concerns in the *Decree on the Ministry and Life of Priests* and feeling somewhat like "the forgotten men" of Vatican II, organized self-consciously to reclaim an earlier tradition of "due process" for the clergy.[41] To institutionalize the Vatican II call for collegiality, "active participation," and "shared decision-making," the American church set about the task of forming quasi-democratic, consultative structures of self-governance on the parish and diocesan level, and strengthened the National Conference of Catholic Bishops. There was initially a great enthusiasm for the priests' senates established by dioceses after Vatican II, for many participants believed that they would not only provide a forum for the discussion of diocesan policies but also encourage reform of the priesthood from within. However, it quickly became apparent that key figures in authority were not committed to the democratization of church governance. Where "misinterpretation" of their proper role occurred, presbyteral senates were renamed "priests councils" and their advisory (rather than legislative) identity clarified by the bishop. Undaunted, priests formed both official and unofficial councils to publicize grievances and to influence diocesan policy-making processes. In 1967, for example, the newly formed Chicago Priests' Association led a symposium at the University of Chicago to acquaint other dioceses in the United States with the purposes and workings of priests' councils. By the end of the decade, however, the NORC study found, many priests had become somewhat disillusioned with the process, believing that real decision-making power was still centered exclusively in the chancery.

The pattern of events in San Francisco, for example, was repeated in dioceses around the country. The initiative to form a priests' senate came from a clergy conference of the deanery in June 1966. Once dominated by Irish and Italian clergy, San Francisco had attracted a sizeable minority of Asian and southeast Asian priests, effectively serving a growing population of Filipino Catholics. These priests depended heavily on the pastor in the first parish to which they were assigned. Many of these pastors recognized a need for diocesan representation of priests of diverse backgrounds and included this among their list of reasons for favoring the establishment of a priests' senate. The deanery representatives forwarded these recommendations to Archbishop Joseph McGucken, who established a committee to draft a constitution for the proposed body. The constitution went into effect in January 1967.

Within a year of the opening of senate deliberations, priests expressed frustration upon perceiving that the deliberative body possessed no real power in terms of setting policy. This frustration came out during an April 30, 1968, meeting of priests ordained nine to seventeen years. The group produced a position paper on ecclesiastical authority that called for genuine collegiality and overdue reforms:

> We wish publicly to endorse the Priests' Senate as representing us in the grave concerns of the apostolate and we give this body our complete support and backing. At the same time, we do not see any reason for having such a body in the first place unless it can become more effective in the practical order. We feel the same about representations on the local scene, particularly in regard to parish councils. We support this trend also, but at the same time want to express our concern lest they be representative groups in name only. We also wish to reaffirm what our younger confreres have already elaborated on in regard to the need for experimentation and for a bold and imaginative re-evaluation of present structures in favor of new forms that will meet more realistically and effectively the crises we are presently facing in the areas of liturgy, religious education, social and racial justice, and peace.[42]

Within a short period of time it became evident to the more progressive members of this group, and to younger ordinands, that the senate had not the will nor the desire to overwhelm episcopal opposition to a legislative role for itself. This was not surprising, given the fact that the senate represented a diverse clerical constituency, a majority of which were older priests unaccustomed to confrontation with the bishop. This disgruntled faction of priests drew support from larger networks more progressive in orientation than their own senate, especially the National Federation of Priests' Council (NFPC), formed in 1968 as an independent association dedicated in part to coordinating and representing priests' concerns on a national level—another way of "ministering to the ministers." The NFPC circulated among San Franciscans a document from the diocese of Providence, entitled "Job Specifications for Parish Priests," which protected the priests from obligations outside his special area of service:

1. The Parish Priest should not perform clerical-secretarial duties; namely, record-keeping, making out of records, ordinary correspondence, counting of money and recording of parish receipts. These duties should be performed by a full-time or part-time secretary.

2. The Priest should not be the parish bookkeeper.

3. The Parish Priest should not be the "monitor" of the parish telephone. A Parish secretary, housekeeper or answering service can fulfill this responsibility.

4. The Priest should not function as the Parish Athletic Director.

5. The Priest should not function as the Parish Social Director for either youth groups or any other parish groups.[43]

Encouraged by this network of national support, 134 priests of the archdiocese of San Francisco formed a separate, independent Association of Priests in February 1969, announcing that "the Church at this time needs to undergo change of a far-reaching nature." Threatening open disobedience of chancery directives, the group adopted resolutions of the NFPC calling for optional celibacy for priests, election of bishops, and more active leadership in ecumenical relations and inner-city redevelopment. In a separate draft of a "pastoral agreement" proposed to the archdiocese, the Association of Priests called for the formation of parish staffs operating in a collegial manner with "objective means" of personnel evaluation. The group resolved that "parish duties shall be balanced with provisions for extra parochial work, on-going education, and adequate leisure."[44]

Similar scenarios, with different particulars, were played out in Chicago, New York, Baltimore, and many other dioceses. In many of these instances, the presbyterate was divided into various factions according to the approach taken toward reform—and the expectations of competing groups as to how far and how rapidly the reforms should proceed. The controversy, and the accompanying sense of "the priesthood under siege," was sustained precisely because the drama of the council and its aftermath had aroused in many the expectation that the priesthood would be significantly reformed. For some this meant the introduction of optional celibacy; for others it simply meant a greater share in ecclesial self-determination. For still others, it meant the right to publicly question the teaching of the church—as it did for thirty-nine priests in Washington, D.C., suspended by Archbishop O'Boyle for dissenting from *Humanae Vitae* (1968).[45]

Priestly collective action took another form in the late 1960s and the early 1970s with the creation of "spiritual subcommunities." On a diocesan scale, groups such as Ministry to Priests and the Emmaus Program were instituted to foster priestly fraternity, prayer, and support. On a smaller scale, diocesan priests began to bond together in groups of five to ten to deepen prayer-life and share with one another a vision of the gospel. An important aim of these groups was to meditate and to discuss ways of being present to God, to one another, and to the parish community. Father Howard Calkins of St. Joseph of the Holy Family parish in New York recalled his first involvement with one such group, Jesus-Caritas:

It was somewhere in those early 70s that I first heard of Jesus-Caritas and Charles de Foucauld. I didn't know much about its spirit nor was I particularly attracted to this curious Frenchman who was more a hermit than a parish priest, but the need for fraternity, for brother priests to pray with, challenge, support, encourage, be responsible to and for, was answered. Our monthly days became a priority and the invitation to become "present to God and present to men," to be "a contemplative in the midst of the world" was gently held out by the mixed group of five men who formed the little fraternity. The Word and the sacrament were central to our meetings— the time spent reflecting on the former and an hour of eucharistic adoration offering that quiet time so needed in the hectic life of pastoral ministry.

The fellowship around the table provided an opportunity to relax. But at the core of the day was the "review of life"—to bring before the brethren a decision to be made, a problem being faced, a hope to be explored, a joy to be shared. The concreteness of the review kept it from getting lost in abstract discussion and slowly deepened the trust and openness within the group. The Spirit spoke in and through the brothers ... the result was an experience of communal discernment. Added to this free yet somewhat structured day were other elements of Fraternity life—it included spending an extended time each day in eucharistic adoration and an extended time each month in extended presence to the Lord—a "desert day." It slowly became apparent that each element of fraternity added to the other—the "desert" offering clarity to one's life, an awareness of one's poverty and time to prepare one's review; the daily quiet time, a necessary anchor to an otherwise frenetic day and an opportunity to "center down," entering into greater intimacy with the Lord and so to be more present to others.[46]

Given the tumult of the postconciliar period, involvement in such groups seemed absolutely necessary to the priests who joined them in hope of preserving their priestly identity and remaining faithful to the spirit in which they took their original vows. And, as we shall see, many of the priests involved in such support groups were also led to collaborate with women religious and lay parishioners in various postconciliar Catholic renewal movements such as Cursillo, Marriage Encounter, and the charismatic movement. Through such collaboration with fellow priests and, eventually, with women religious and lay men and women, many individual priests survived a period of personal crisis that inevitably accompanied the crisis in church and ministry.

In fact I shall argue that each of these four developments in the priesthood in response to the ecclesial and cultural identity crisis of the 1960s—the emergence of the social activist "urban priest"; the pursuit of professional careers by religious order and, to a lesser extent, diocesan priests; the new awareness of the priesthood as itself a unique profession worthy of study; and the building of national, diocesan, and parochial networks of information, advocacy, and mutual support by priests for priests—contributed significantly to the transformation of the priesthood and, especially, to the emergence of a way of priestly presence to the parish in the 1970s and 80s, which kept him in the parish. That these developments also threatened for a time to separate the priest from the parish and thus to threaten the very existence of the parish is the subject of the next chapter.

5

THE ABSENT PRIEST AND THE FLOATING PARISH: THE POSSIBILITIES AND PREDICAMENTS OF CRISIS, 1962–1972

If the life of the curate is humanly intolerable, the structure of his work, restricted as it is by the irrelevant tradition of the past, is frustrating and demoralizing. The system of "calls" whereby a priest is required to remain in the rectory awaiting sick calls or applicants for Mass cards or marriage records is an incredible restriction on the efficiency of work which would hardly be tolerated in any other organization. In some rectories only on his day off, which may be one day a week, is a priest permitted to be away from the rectory or off the premises of the parish plant.

His time is often filled with paper work, fund raising, supervision of athletic and recreational activities. . . . In such a structure, not only is a priest unable to operate out of the rigid confines of the rectory, but there is in his ministry no room for experimentation, for creativity or imagination. None is wanted and frequently none is tolerated. Such a frustrating and unchallenging life is bound to lead to a deterioration of professional commitment and interest. When one is required to spend one's time doing routine, irrelevant, or unchallenging work, one is singularly without motivation to maintain one's professional standards or interests.[1]

Agreement and conflict with the established order also lead to organization and establishment of new structures. The movement of revival arises in the midst of ordered and habitual religous action. It is not concerned in the beginning with the replacement of the old order by the new, but with the reemergence of that spiritual life out of which it believes the old order has issued.[2]

In the long run, it could be argued, each of these developments of the period of crisis would enhance parochial ministry. The presbyterate would emerge professionalized, specialized, and with a renewed

79

commitment to the parochial ministry, now seen as a vocation freely chosen rather than imposed. But the immediate result of these developments, taken separately or cumulatively, was a distancing of the urban and professionalized priest from the parish setting. In some cases, priests physically departed the parish—to enter graduate school, join an office for urban development, or, definitively, to pursue professional life outside the priesthood.

Some priests tried to live in both worlds, retaining parish responsibilities even as they managed full-time extraparochial commitments. Others left one parish setting for another, in the inner city, for which they were not fully prepared. In short, the parish faced unprecedented competition for the full attention and devotion of the priest who found it necessary to "be present to" his professional colleagues and to the larger regional or national church.

Dissatisfaction with the parish as primary locus for priestly ministry had begun during the wave of modernization and americanization in the 1950s; in the 60s, dissatisfaction gave way in some cases to demoralization. The author quoted above voiced a widespread resentment of traditional parish structure in which the assistant was perceived as a "nonperson" with no rights, privileges, or responsibilities of his own, destined to serve at the discretion of his pastor. Professionalized priests joined in the chorus of complaints about parochial ministry and wondered aloud if the parish would survive the 60s.

As the 1950s hope for renewal gave way to the 1960s jargon of revolution, there were even sustained attempts to craft alternatives to the parish. During an April 1968 institute at Boston College devoted to the phenomenon, Episcopalian priest Malcolm Boyd described "floating parishes" and "underground churches" as "a contemporary Christian revolutionary movement in the United States, bypassing official church structures and leadership, and concerned with Christian unity and radical involvement in the world (specifically meaning the black revolution, the peace-liberation movement, and issues connected with the question of poverty)." Rosemary Radford Ruether preferred to call them "free churches," because they were composed of persons liberated from institutional confinement. "One does not have a Sunday obligation to destroy one's soul," she said. There were purportedly "hundreds" of these groups in America and England, clustered in this country in the northeast and in San Francisco. Membership was homogeneous, selective, primarily Catholic, but explicitly ecumenical, and included, in many cases, at least one priest. Rocco Caporale, S.J., a priest-sociologist, provided a technical definition of floating parishes. They were, he reported, "convenanting ecclesial units, neither territorially nor hierarchically located, which maintain functional identity boundaries, and generate more or less enduring autonomous systems of symbolism, control, and rewards." By design the groups were small. In avoiding the size of the traditional parish—the sheer logistics of which overwhelmed any genuine sense of community—these underground groups were, in Caporale's judgment, "escaping from the impersonality of the parish structure."[3]

Although, statistically speaking, very few parish priests participated in underground churches and floating parishes, a larger number did experience a sense of disappointment and disillusionment in the decade following Vatican II. In part this was due to the institutional church's failure to meet the expectations for radical reform raised by the council in the minds of many priests in America and abroad. A series of papal and episcopal pronouncements implementing the reforms of the council, interpreting its decrees, and restating, almost formulaically, preconciliar teaching signaled that the liberal interpretation of the council would not be sustained. In 1968 Pope Paul VI overturned the rulings of a papal commission he had established to study possible revision in the traditional teaching on artificial means of contraception. As with each of the setbacks to the liberal cause at the hands of the hierarchy, the encyclical restated preconciliar teaching in authoritative language that rendered suspect the official rhetoric about collegiality and shared decision-making. Paul VI revealed in the encyclical that he considered the theological commission's efforts to be in the nature of preliminary advice, for "the conclusions at which the commission arrived could not, nevertheless, be considered by us as definitive, nor dispense us from a personal examination of this serious question; and this also because, within the commission itself . . . certain criteria of solutions had emerged which departed from the moral teaching on marriage proposed with constant firmness by the teaching authority of the Church."[4] Nor did the methodology of the moral argument of the encyclical, drawn from Thomistic natural law theory, give the progressives cause for optimism. In the backlash occasioned by the promulgation of the encyclical, the preconciliar phenomenon of uncritical acceptance of the authoritative teaching of the Catholic hierarchy became a fond memory for church leaders. Father Joseph Greer, pastor of St. Patrick parish in Natick, Massachusetts, recently described the impact that the unpopular teaching has had in his pastoral experience:

> Priests are bucking their superiors, and the laity—a much higher quality laity than we've ever had before—isn't listening to the church anymore. You might trace a lot of this back to Pope Paul VI's 1968 encyclical "Humanae Vitae," which forbade the use of artificial

methods of birth control at a time when sixty expert consultants hired by the Vatican were in favor of it and the practice was widespread anyhow. When you look at Vatican proclamations, you have to consider two elements: one is *Ecclesia docens*, the Church teaching, and the second is *sensus fidelium*, the response of the faithful or, in effect, the Church listening. If the teaching has no listeners, that says something about the validity of what is being taught: the listeners are saying something to the teachers. The *sensus fidelium* was that "Humanae Vitae" was off base. The faithful basically ignored it. But, sadly, some people left the Church because of it. I'm not for a watered-down, convenient religious faith—the salt without savor. But this is not the world it was when Joe Greer first put on the biretta at St. John's. If someone asks about birth control, I give chapter and verse on "Humanae Vitae," and then listen for extenuating circumstances. I usually hear some.[5]

Most if not all parish priests faced the challenge of defending, or explaining away, what seemed to lay Catholics to be at best a troubling doctrine and at worst an irresponsible exercise of teaching authority. Not every priest responded as did Father Greer with at least an initial deference to the magisterium. Indeed, responses varied wildly, from interpretation of the encyclical as having an infallible character the slightest dissent from which would be a grievous (mortal) sin, to the open admission that the church had betrayed a sacred trust. The new theological environment promoted a turning to the conscience of the individual in the process of moral decision-making; ironically, *Humanae Vitae* inadvertently demonstrated the wisdom of that turn. The undermining of institutional authority affected the parish priest directly, and served to exacerbate his sense of disorientation and uncertainty about his role in the church and society.

Similar reaction followed upon the promulgation of Paul VI's *Letter on Priestly Celibacy* in 1970. Again, the council raised expectations that priestly celibacy would become optional; Catholic leaders in Holland, impatient with the delay, published a declaration in 1969 calling for this reform. Again the pope responded by restating traditional teaching in absolute terms and foreclosing the possibility of change in the requirement:

The reasons adopted to justify such a radical change in the centuries-old norm of the Latin Church, which has been the means of so many fruits of grace, holiness and missionary apostolate, are well known. But We must say without equivocation that they do not appear convincing to Us. They seem to overlook a fundamental and essential consideration which must never be forgotten and which belongs to the supernatural order. That is to say, they represent a breakdown of the genuine concept of the priesthood.

Considering everything before God, before Christ and the Church, and before the world, We therefore feel it is Our duty clearly to reaffirm what We have already declared and several times repeated: that the link between priesthood and celibacy, as established for centuries by the Latin Church, constitutes for it a supremely precious and irreplaceable good. It would be extremely rash to undervalue it or even to let it fall into disuse. It has been consecrated by tradition and is an incomparable sign of total dedication to the love of Christ (cf. Mt. 12, 29). It is a bright demonstration of the missionary demand which is essential in every priestly life, in service of the risen Christ, who lives for ever and to whom the priest has consecrated himself in total readiness for the sake of the Kingdom of God.

There are priests who, for reasons recognized as valid, have unfortunately found themselves unable to persevere. We know there are only a small number, whereas the great majority wishes, with the help of grace, to remain faithful to the sacred pledges made before God and the Church. It is with great sorrow that We agree to accept their insistent request to be released from their promises and dispensed from their obligations. We do this only after careful examination of every single case. However, the profound understanding which We have for persons, in a spirit of paternal charity, must not hinder Us from deploring an attitude which is so little in accord with what the Church rightfully expects from those who have definitely consecrated themselves to its exclusive service.

For this reason, after mature examination of the matter, We clearly affirm it Our duty not to permit the priestly ministry to be exercised by those who have turned back after having put their hand to the plough (cf. Lk. 9, 62).

They ask Us whether it might not be possible to consider ordaining to the priesthood men of advanced age who have given proof of exemplary family and professional life in their social circumstances, in a situation of extreme shortage of priests, and limited to regions in such a situation. . . . We cannot conceal that such an eventuality arouses grave reservations on Our part. Would it not be, amongst other things, a very dangerous illusion to believe that such a change in traditional discipline could be restricted in practice to local cases of true and extreme necessity? And would it not also be a temptation to others to look to it for an apparently easier answer to the present lack of sufficient vocations?[6]

If Pope Paul left any doubt that the retention of this preconciliar theological and ecclesiological self-understanding would forestall efforts to update the church's teaching on the priesthood, it was removed once and for all by Synod of Bishops convened in Rome in 1971. The synod reaffirmed the teaching of Paul on celibacy—"the law of priestly celibacy existing in the Latin Church is to be kept in its entirety"—and described the priesthood in ontological rather than existential language, retaining the emphasis on the notion of the priest as the man set apart by virtue of an indelible mark on his soul:

> The lifelong permanence of this reality which imprints a sign—and this is a doctrine of faith referred to in Church tradition as the priestly character—expresses the fact that Christ irrevocably associated the Church with Himself for the salvation of the world, and that the Church herself is consecrated to Christ in a definitive way for the fulfillment of His work. The minister, whose life bears the seal of the gift received through the Sacrament of Orders, reminds the Church that God's gift is irrevocable. In the midst of the Christian community which lives by the Spirit, he is a pledge, despite his defects, of the salvific presence of Christ.[7]

To those who had hoped for reform of the priesthood, or at least for the initiation of a promising dialogue with the Vatican, the 1971 synod was perceived as a step backward. American theologian Father Charles E. Curran complained that the schema did not follow "the more inductive theological methodology . . . (it) follows the older theological approach which thinks in terms of an eternal and universal priestly essence or nature which then just has to be accidentally modified in different historical, cultural, or temporal circumstances." He voiced the concern of many of his brother priests that the document represented "an inadequate reading of the signs of the times" and made the "grave error" of embracing a theological methodology that "assumes that there is a theology of priestly ministry which exists as a universal model apart from the lived experience of the present and without the knowledge that the contemporary sciences can furnish about the nature and function of the priestly ministry." Curran argued that there are important and fundamental aspects of ministry found in the scriptures and tradition, but these remain very general and capable of diverse historical manifestations. "This document is based on a theological methodology that has been abandoned by most Catholic theologians today," he wrote. "This methodological error lies at the roots of the false conservatism of this document and prevents it from really coming to grips with the question of concrete models for Christian ministry today." In its place he called for a model of priestly ministry based on an inductive and at least partially empirical methodology:

Thus the more inductive nature of theology and of its systematic reflection on the Christian ministry prevents theology from proposing any concrete models of priesthood which are viable for all ministers, in all different historical situations. A more inductive approach will be able to propose only tentative models and will greatly depend upon the contemporary experience of those who are trying to live the life of the Christian minister in our contemporary society. This more inductive and somewhat empirical approach will also call for dialogue with the behavioral sciences. There is no such thing as the universal or eternal model of ministry which can serve as a concrete model for Christian ministers.[8]

This set of circumstances in the early 1970s—the perceived failure of the 1971 synod, the reduced authority of priests' senates and associations, the departure of a significant number of his brother priests from active ministry, the absence of a theology of pastoral ministry adequate to parish experience—placed the parish priest squarely inside the modern predicament: he was confronted with a variety of options regarding his immediate personal and professional future. He could apply for laicization and leave the active ministry altogether; he could request a leave from his parish assignment to pursue advanced studies, or to develop an urban ministry; he could divide his time between parish responsibilities and extraparochial ministries; he could remain in the parish, an ostrich with his head in the sand, seemingly immune to the pace and comprehensive nature of the transformations all about him; or he could, at his own pace, incorporate into his own parish ministry those aspects and emphases and insights of "the new priesthood" that he found necessary to effective pastoral service. From a vantage fifteen years removed, it seems that most parish priests chose some form of this last option. Even at this time of increased mobility, experimentation and transformation, the vast majority of American priests remained in the parishes, performing the ministry for which they had been ordained. But they were not unaffected by the changes "on the outside."

In the mid-1960s Joseph Fichter conducted a survey of 2,183 diocesan parish priests and 2,216 of their "best" parishioners. It seemed to demonstrate both the perdurance of the older ombudsman model for parish priesthood and the impact of the new developments upon it. The study compared and contrasted the parishioners' perceptions of the priest's role and his self-perception. In summary, Fichter found that the priests were beginning to select from among the multiple functions of the ombudsman model a few preferred functions— namely, counseling, spiritual formation, sacramental ministry, and religious education. Of four images of the parish priest, the priests themselves preferred "the spiritual leader" and "the overburdened professional." By contrast, the parishioners perceived the priest as "the executive" and "the insolvent businessman" and emphasized his administrative responsibilities and role as director or moderator of parish organizations. They expected him to be, in Fichter's words, "the responsible supervisor of the parish unit, and 'all things to all people.' " The study seemed to indicate that, in rejecting the priorities established for his ministry by his parishioners, the parish priest was moving slowly away from the ombudsman model of priesthood that they, and he, had inherited.[9]

Five years later, in 1970, Eugene Schallert, S.J., conducted an extensive survey of priests of San Francisco to measure the extent to which the presbyterate had absorbed and accepted the changes in the church since Vatican II. The study demonstrated that the urban priests and hyphenated priests had influenced the thinking of the presbyterate as a whole but had not "converted" a majority. The study included an "anomie" scale to discern the level of apathy and deadening loss of meaning in priests trained under the old (ombudsman) model and forced to witness its transformation. Only a small percentage scored high on the anomie scale, indicating that the presbyterate had adjusted surprisingly well to the new models. By a significant majority, priests favored diocesan and parish restructuring, and improvement in diocesan programs of priestly formation, renewal, and continuing education. Two-thirds of the respondents approved of extraparochial ministry for priests such as community-organizing, journalism, or sociology; about the same number listed little if any involvement in these, and cited as excuses the time-consuming demands of parish ministry, a lack of the specialized training required for the new ministries, and a dedication to parochial ministry.[10]

In short, parish priests were influenced by their absent confreres and to a significant extent: they began to accept communal, public, and professional aspects of the priesthood as central rather than peripheral. Yet they remained committed to the local neighborhood parish. Although the ombudsman was crowded off center-stage by the urban priest and the professionalized priest, he continued to man the trenches.

J. F. Powers's short stories have captured with considerable tenderness the survival of clerical culture after the council. In one story set after the council, Simpson, the newly ordained assistant at Trinity parish, is troubled that "some people seemed to think there were now two or more schools of thought about everything." He finds a certain comfort in the taciturn routine of his pastor with whom he has, in fact, little human interaction. Nonetheless, he senses a stability and dignity in this type of pastor, and aspires to be, as the title of the story suggests, "One of Them":

> He was determined not to complain. He thought there was too much of that going on these days among the clergy, of all people. He would not, he thought, be happier in another parish, neither in the suburbs nor the slums, for he was not, though fresh from the seminary, one of those who expect to change the world by going out into it. For him the disadvantages in his situation were outweighed by the advantages. At Trinity he could feel that he was still in the church of his choice, with divine worship and the cure of souls still being conducted along traditional lines—no guitars, tom-toms, sensitivity sessions, speaking in tongues—and at Trinity he could also feel that he, though newly ordained and a convert, though keyless and considered a suitable case for pamphlets, was the man in charge.[11]

Although his was no longer the most celebrated "way" of priesthood, the ombudsman was not supplanted by any single "type" of priest during the period of modernization and americanization, from 1954 to 1972. Instead there were a number of options for priestly ministry, none of which won the pervasive allegiance formerly enjoyed by the ombudsman, none of which was entirely at home in the traditional parish. In the heady days before the council, the "place to be" was the suburban parish; in the 60s and 70s, the scene shifted to the inner city and the university. The parish priest riding the crest of reform entered a period of crisis precisely because no clear consensus developed about the preferred direction of parochial ministry. One thing alone was evident to the successors of the pioneer priests: the ubiquitous parochial presence of the ombudsman could no longer effectively serve the proper function of the priest in the world. Disintegration followed upon this awareness: the period of crisis witnessed the parish priest's struggle to integrate his symbolic and functional roles without benefit of a persuasive theology of parochial presence. This had been a relatively easy task for the ombudsman whose pervasive functional presence in the parish was legitimated by his symbolic representation of the transcendent Christ and the eternal church. But the priests ordained after the council sensed that such integration of types of presence in the parish was both impossible and undesirable. It was impossible because the old symbol-system based on an essentialist, supernaturalist worldview was fading from Catholics' sensibilities in direct proportion to their full participation in modern American culture. It was undesirable because perceived as facile and inauthentic. The functional presence of the ombudsman was not legitimated by his personal qualities, by his unique freedom.

However, in the struggle to "personalize" and thus "authenticate" their ministries, urban priests or professionalized priests were as likely to be concerned with providing suitable housing or education for their people as they were with providing them the eucharist. In the most successful of these men, the symbolic and functional roles of the priest were well integrated: their daily actions—their pastoral presence— were in close imitation of the Christ and church they symbolized. Sufficiently sophisticated in the new theology, they could no longer believe themselves to be representatives of a Christ beyond history. If they represented Christ at all, they did so, they were convinced, not by way of an indelible and invisible mark on the soul, but in their flawed humanity. That human Christ had been, certainly, an advocate for the oppressed, even a revolutionary; ministry to the urban poor seemed a most appropriate context in which to represent that Christ. It was not altogether clear to the new priest, however, what business Christ might have in a simple neighborhood parish, and that is why he was, in one sense or another, absent from that setting. Devoted to interpersonal communication, intimate liturgies, and small-scale social action programs, the members of these "floating parishes" attempted to localize and decentralize the Catholic renewal.

As H. Richard Niebuhr pointed out in the second quote opening this chapter, such movements of revival "arise in the midst of ordered and habitual religious action" and are concerned with "the reemergence of that spiritual life out of which it believes the old order has issued." The "floating parish" attempted to meet needs that the parish of the 1960s could not meet. But the "floating parish" ultimately failed precisely because it was not a parish. Whatever the sense of community and religious vision it imparted to its members, the group was not an authentic Catholic parish because it was by definition exclusive, closed to the uncontrollable, unmanageable number of baptized (and possibly indifferent or lukewarm) believers who happened to reside in the neighborhood. The "floating parish" was not, in other words, territorial, rooted in the neighborhood. For all its unwieldy size, the territorial parish remained inclusive and therefore "catholic" in the genuine sense of that term. The perduring challenge was to foster a community of shared faith in a neighborhood the size and "quality" of which could not be easily controlled.

6

THE EMERGENCE OF THE ORCHESTRA LEADER, 1973–

There were in 1985 in the Episcopal Church two hundred and forty-five lay persons for each priest; in the Lutheran Church in America, there were three hundred and seventy-two. For the Catholic Church, the figure was nine hundred and twelve. There is another and key difference between the Catholic and the Protestant clergy: the Catholic priest usually lives next door to his church. As a celibate, he has no family to shield him from whoever may call upon him or from whatever unpleasant tasks he may have to perform. His parish is his family, and his life. He has to be available twenty-four hours a day to baptize, wed, bury, advise, preach, teach, preside, officiate, console, and counsel. A modern-day pastor like Father Greer may find himself at once outmoded and overwhelmed. As a seminarian, he was trained to give until he dropped, but now psychologists tell him that this is unhealthy. He was told to keep a tight check on his emotions, but now he is expected to "feel." He looked forward to becoming a pastor, to having an authority akin to that of a captain aboard ship, but Vatican II and the liberal social currents of the nineteen-sixties and seventies changed that prospect. In addition, the accession of John Paul II, who is a conservative and activist Pope, and the increasing centralization of diocesan bureaucracy have meant that more and more is being asked of American pastors. They are point men in the Church's battles against the enemies of moral standards, such as the advocates of abortion and birth control, and against those who ignore Church law—for example, by arguing that non-Catholics or Catholics not in a state of grace should be allowed to receive Holy Communion. Father Greer and his fellow-priests are expected to revitalize the half to two-thirds of their flocks (nominal Catholics) who do not attend church regularly; to run an efficient parish; and, at the same time, to neglect neither their spiritual growth nor their health—all this without the prerogatives once enjoyed by the clerical aristocracy. For priests of this generation, the life of a pastor has become something of a juggling act.[1]

We flatly reject any ideas that tend to neglect the average Catholic and that opt for an elite Christianity embracing only those with apostolic concerns. Catholics need the career priest to serve them full time; to remind them that Christianity is transcendental; to represent a concern for Christian witness that they, in living their ordinary lives, are not always capable of. To put it in more theological terms, the career priest must be a sign for the average Christian; he must be, as it were, an intensified embodiment of the priesthood of all the faithful.[2]

A persuasive argument could be made that, even in 1989, the crisis in Roman Catholicism, and particularly in the Roman Catholic priesthood, has not abated. Since 1968 approximately ten thousand priests have resigned (as well as fifty thousand sisters and four thousand brothers). Today, approximately sixty thousand priests serve fifty-five million Catholics. Sociologists estimate that there will be a 40 percent decline in the number of active priests from 1980 to 2000, and that, by the year 2000, only thirty thousand priests will be available for sixty-five million Catholics.[3] Those men who weathered the storm of the 60s began to suffer the consequences of a priest-shortage in the 1970s. With fewer associates, the parish priest faced a greater work load, less freedom of action, and a narrowing of his pastoral activities to those sacramental ministries that only he can perform. Although there are indications that U.S. seminaries have a clearer sense of purpose than they have had in two decades, it is impossible to conclude that the recent slight rise in seminary enrollment (after a sustained period of decline) signifies a trend.[4]

At the same time there is evidence to suggest that the priesthood has survived the most difficult period of crisis, is recovering and gaining strength even in diminished numbers, and is meeting the challenges summarized in the opening quote of this chapter with considerable skill. The turning point came in the early 1970s. After 1973 the rate of resignations from the priesthood slowed considerably, leading sociologist Dean Hoge to comment that "probably the bulge in resignations from 1966 to 1973 was a specific product of that period of time—just after a large number of new ordinations and in the midst of rapid change in the church."[5] Contrary to expectations, sociological surveys demonstrated an increase in American priests' self-esteem, morale, and satisfaction with their work during the period from 1970 to 1985. And, in an age when demand for priests far exceeds supply, the chancery offices and diocesan personnel boards are far more likely than in the past to consider the wishes of the individual priest up for transfer.[6] Although it faces serious challenges to its continued efficacy, the parish priesthood of the 1980s remains a vital force in American Catholic life.

Part of the explanation for this continued vitality in the midst of change is the emergence, in the 1970s, of an approach to priestly ministry, a way of presence to the parish community, which consolidated the gains of the period of crisis while retaining many of the strengths of the ombudsman. The priest who follows this way of presence is, given the realities of contemporary parish life, an "orchestra leader." Through various means discussed below, he has absorbed the seminal insights of postconciliar ecclesiology and pastoral theology, including the fundamental principle that each Christian shares in a "royal priesthood" by virtue of baptism; the notion of a priest as the "Christ who sends" or commissions rather than as an apostle who is himself "sent" to others; and the conviction that "empowering" and "enabling" other ministers is one of the distinctive roles of the ordained priest. Accordingly, he perceives each parishioner as uniquely "called and gifted" for service to the church and to the world. As a representative of the universal church, his role is, in the words of the council, to elevate, purify, and bring into closer conformity with Christ the fruits of lay ministry. Within this role his specific function is analagous to that of the conductor of a symphony.

Webster's New World Dictionary gives multiple definitions of the verb "to conduct." It may imply "a supervising by using one's executive, skill, knowledge, wisdom, etc.," "an issuance of general instructions," or "supervision that involves attention to detail." Given his particular temperament and personality, the orchestra leader may in any given situation rely on one or all these leadership skills. In the contemporary parish, he is faced with virtuosi practicing the same piece of music, each according to his or her own interpretation of the score. His job is to bring cohesion and direction—harmony—to these individual efforts. By integrating and supervising their individual efforts, he establishes a community of common purpose. He is no longer the only one who knows the score, but he interprets it for the musicians and by his presence during the performance signifies the group as a whole. The individual members—women religious, lay ministers, his associate priests—may play as individuals without him; or they may play successfully as a group without him. But in his absence the performance will not be an "official" performance, and, for better or for worse, unofficial performances do not play well in most American Catholic parishes.[7]

Three patterns of development in the 1970s led to the emergence of the orchestra leader. First, a new wave of Hispanic and Asian immigrants entered the United States. Effective pastoral presence to these groups required further diversification of ministerial skills and reliance on the expertise developed during the era of the professionalized priest and the urban priest. Second, the American Catholic laity began to exercise a new and unprecedented kind of leadership in and for parishes as the demand for ministerial service diversified and increased, and as prominent spokespersons, especially among women religious, articulated a nascent theology of lay ministry. Third, impetus for an updating of priestly ministry came piecemeal and in various ways from the institutional church or from movements in affiliation with the church such as Cursillo and Marriage Encounter. Some priests learned of the inchoate way of the orchestra leader from seminars, institutes, and postgraduate education programs sponsored by dioceses and led by talented and ecclesiologically sophisticated priests, women religious, and lay persons. Others followed the example of fellow priests or bishops who embodied the renewed attitude toward parochial presence. These three patterns of development followed upon the often traumatic experiences of the conciliar era and occupied the attention and energies of the parish priest. Given the comprehensive nature of these developments, there was, in a real sense, little time to absorb the impact of the various pressures on priestly identity. Yet such time for reflection became necessary during this period.

THE NEW IMMIGRANT CHURCH

In 1965 the U.S. Congress amended the McCarran-Walter Immigration Act in order to eliminate the national origins quota system, which had preserved the overwhelmingly European character of the nation. Almost immediately immigrants from Mexico, the Philippines, and Vietnam crossed the borders, especially in the west and southwest, at the rate of about five hundred thousand per year. For example, the California Filipino community, the large majority of which is Catholic, grew from 40,000 in 1950 to 350,000 in 1984, with the years after 1975 being the most intense period of immigration.[8] Hispanic immigrants made their way in the 1970s to the urban areas of the northeast. The Portuguese settled in southeastern Massachusetts in significant number, for example, and by 1975 fully one-third of the Catholic population of New York City was Puerto Rican. Moreover, this trend shows no sign of abating. There were fifteen million Hispanic Americans in 1980, but population experts predict that their number will swell to thirty-five million by the year 2000.[9]

As in previous periods of American history, immigrants transformed the character of the parish and the neighborhood. Filipinos took special delight in religious processions and the sacral character of the priesthood, demanding that the parish priest be present for the blessing of homes, automobiles, and prized possessions.[10] Although they wished to be served by a Filipino priest, the relationship between immigrant priests and parishioners was sometimes fraught with tension over the question of americanization. For example, in San Francisco's St. Joseph parish a major fiesta and procession in honor of "Santo Niño de Cebu" has been held since 1969. It features the enthronement of a replica of a sacred statue of the child Jesus, followed by Mass, a novena of prayers, a large banquet, and a ball. Designed to inspire "the highest values in upholding sacred traditions of Philippine culture and heritage," the fiesta was supported and encouraged by an Irish pastor but opposed strenuously by his successor, a Filipino priest who argues that the procession and shrine are "un-American" and serve only to increase the alienation between the Filipino and American communities in San Francisco.[11]

The absence of sufficient numbers of immigrant or bilingual priests to serve these burgeoning ethnic communities has created pastoral challenges for many American dioceses. In New York City, for example, the Hispanic community has not produced enough priests to serve the people who are themselves often poorly instructed in Catholic practice. Exacerbating the usual tensions that accompany assimilation of a group into a foreign host culture is the fact that many Hispanics have moved from a relatively stable rural society to the chaotic urban environment of a huge city like New York. Dioceses have responded creatively to this situation by taking a number of measures, including the opening of Spanish Catholic Action offices, sometimes called Spanish Apostolates, to coordinate the assimilation of new immigrants into the public school system, programs of public aid, and other institutions of modern urban life. Spanish has replaced Italian as the major modern language in seminaries. In New York, the archdiocese adopted the custom of sending a portion of the ordination class to learn the language of their future parishioners in their native lands.[12]

The effect of the new immigrant church upon the practice of priestly ministry is complex. On the one hand there is a great demand in the immigrant communities for the sacramental ministry exercised exclusively by the priest (the consecration and celebration of the eucharist in Mass, the granting of absolution for sins in the sacrament of reconciliation, or confession). In some communities, first-generation parishioners insist that the priest also be present to perform a variety of functions shared more efficiently with lay ministers, including baptisms, marriages, spiritual formation, and religious education. Moreover, the administrative and financial concerns of the ombudsman era are by no means a thing of the past in inner-city areas in which the racial, ethnic, or socio-economic composition of the neighborhood has changed rapidly. Pastors must still devote a considerable amount of time and energy to fund-raising. Added in the new immigrant era to the responsibilities met by the preconciliar ombudsman is the expectation that the parish priest will be a relentless advocate for social and economic justice in his neighborhood. This is especially true in inner-city parishes plagued by inadequate housing, unemployment, racial discrimination, and high dropout rates in the public schools. Although their approaches are diverse, they differ in skills and background, and their experience is greatly varied, the clergy is inevitably involved in the housing needs of their parishioners and their community.

The situation in New York in 1981 is instructive on this point. Father Tom Leonard of Incarnation parish in Upper Manhattan had joined a task force for housing under the auspices of the Washington Heights Consortium, an association of thirty-two private and educational institutions, banks, hospitals, yeshivas, and churches. In January of that year the task force supervised the purchase and rehabilitation of over one hundred In Rem buildings (owned by the city due to foreclosure for tax arrears). Under the Tenant Interim Lease program, tenants would assume responsibility for the maintenance and, eventually, the ownership of the building. Although he was not an urban priest of the 1960s, the enduring influence of that experience is evident in Father Leonard's description of the nature of and reasons for his involvement:

> For me, the religious dimension is that the social apostolate is tied into the mission of New York. The Church has to be in dialogue with the world. Housing ought to be a part of the ministry of the Church. Priesthood embraces all aspects of life and has universal interest. It should lead you onward to dialogue with the local community.
>
> I did not have any background in housing. You do not have to be an expert in the field of construction.
> —Get the city manual and learn the terms so that you will not be bewildered.
> —Find out how areas are zoned by the city and what possibilities exist.
> —Keep in touch with the neighborhood planning offices which are knowledgeable about troubled spots.

—Encourage block associations.

—Use your experiential knowledge; as a priest, you have access to many apartments, through school visits, weekly sacramental visitations, so you have seen many apartments when occupied.

—Know key people, i.e., informed people.[13]

Meanwhile, in the black and Hispanic neighborhoods of the South Bronx, Father Roberto Gonzalez, O.F.M. applied for a federally guaranteed loan to make private ownership accessible to the poor by creating a cooperative based on the Sweat Equity program. His initial efforts focused on one abandoned building in front of his parish church of St. Pius, which he envisioned as the home for eight displaced families. Gonzalez came to St. Pius in 1977 unfamiliar with the inner workings of this urban ministry. But the plight of the people quickly drew his attention and his efforts on their behalf.[14] Elsewhere in New York City, in the Manhattan neighborhood known as Hell's Kitchen, Father Thomas Farrelly, an urban priest of the 1960s, continued to organize workers and tenants to protest unfair treatment and inadequate housing in Sacred Heart parish. He remained committed to a vision of priestly ministry as sacramental presence characterized by a devotion to the cause of social justice.[15]

In responding to the pastoral needs of the new immigrant communities, the ombudsman has become, by force of necessity, a supervisor, coordinator, orchestra leader. This is not the first time, of course, that parish priests have been involved in public affairs, such as the struggle for affordable, decent housing or for jobs. The advice given by Father Leonard to "know key people" and to "be visible at community meetings" could as well be a citation from the ombudsman's manual of 1940. Yet the social, political, and ecclesial transformations of the intervening forty years have made an impact on the way in which the parish priest goes about his work. To put it simply, the job has expanded such that one man, or a small team of men, cannot handle it alone. The period of crisis and response, from 1954 to 1972, led to the specialization and diversification of the skills necessary for successful "holistic" ministry to the parishioners in their economic, social, and educational, as well as spiritual and religious, needs. The urban priest's knowledge of the city zoning codes and the names of key social action leaders in the ecumenical community are no less salient to today's pastor than is the priest-psychologist's insight into the dynamics of sin and guilt.

The demands on pastoral ministry have expanded in another way as well—in the sheer numbers and scope of the population to be served.

The ombudsman was often concerned with community and civic affairs to the extent that they affected the lives and fortunes of his own parishioners; the postconciliar, post-1960s orchestra leader understands in principle that his commitment, shared by parishioners, extends beyond the parish for the sake of other Catholics and, increasingly, for non-Catholics. For example, the proportion of non-Catholic students attending Catholic parochial schools has, for a variety of social reasons, increased significantly since 1954. In areas without a parochial school or Catholic high school, priests may serve as chaplains and campus ministers to the local public school, or provide various counseling services to its students, Catholic and non-Catholic. Catholic priests, in other words, may be found in settings that would have seemed quite strange to their predecessors of the ombudsman era. And, in an era of fewer priests and a larger Catholic population in need of sacramental and pastoral ministries, the parish priest recognizes that he cannot comprehend all the specializations required, nor alone provide the personal presence necessary, to serve well the people of God. By the mid-1970s, he realized he needed help. This was a fortuitous realization, for help was coming anyway.

THE LAY MINISTRY EXPLOSION

Eighty percent of all teachers in Catholic schools today are lay persons. There are hundreds of professional lay directors of relgous education in the parishes, and, there are about one hundred twenty-five lay mission volunteer programs. The practice of ministry is now often a specialized, part-time avocation: lay persons are working in pastoral planning offices, campus ministry, bilingual ministry, ministry to the aged, clinical-pastoral education, and Marriage Encounter. In the late 1970s and the 1980s women religious began to assume some roles traditionally preserved for the priest. Sister Dorothy Trosclair prepared for her current work as the canonical pastor of a tiny parish in rural southeast Louisiana as early as 1968 when she responded pastorally to a chronic shortage of priests in the rural communities outside Lafayette, Louisiana. From that time her ministry has been dedicated to the task of "enabling laity" to be ministers. She accomplishes this in various ways—through parish Renew programs, training of catechists, and formation of active parish councils. Trosclair believes that genuine apostolic ministry is the call of all baptized Christians and that "ordination, even if at the hands of the hierarch," is a call from the local community. The role of the parish minister is to be present to this community, to stand as a real symbol of its shared life as the people of God.[16]

Lay ministry emerged within the church both from the top down and the bottom up. The official decrees of the Catholic hierarchy in the late 1960s and 70s promoted lay involvement in ministries traditionally incumbent on the priest.[17] In 1967 Pope Paul VI promulgated the motu proprio *Sacrum Diaconatus Ordinem* restoring the permanent diaconate. In 1972 he issued *Ministeria Quaedam*, which opened to lay men offices and functions previously granted only to candidates for the priesthood receiving minor orders. American lay men, and eventually, women were trained and served as lectors and eucharistic ministers at the celebration of the Mass. The pope's description of the "proper sphere" of lay involvement in the church relied heavily upon the conciliar reaffirmation of a qualitative difference between "the priesthood of the faithful" and "the ordained or hierarchical priesthood," and there has been considerable discussion of the notion that these promulgations were a thinly veiled attempt to "clericalize" the dynamism of lay ministry.[18] Nonetheless, the appearance of nonordained parishioners on the altar performing ministerial functions once reserved for ordained males was a powerfully suggestive example to American Catholics.

Lay ministry also began as a "grass-roots" movement in the sense that many of the first women and men offering themselves as ministers did so in continuity with their previous volunteer or professional work in the parish. The institutions of the Catholic educational system, including the parochial school and the Confraternity of Christian Doctrine, were staffed in the 1950s and 60s by dedicated women religious, and, in increasing numbers, lay men and women, many of whom responded to the priest shortage and to the new insights of postconciliar pastoral theology in the 1970s by assuming ministerial positions on the parish staff. There was, for example, a natural continuity in many such women's lives between teaching in the parish school or in the CCD program and later seeking advanced courses in preparation for a position as Director of Religious Education (DRE) for the parish. Dennis Geaney wrote in 1979:

> The most revolutionary breakthrough in the emerging concept of nonordained ministry is the parish religious education coordinator. In a decade these coordinators have developed into a cadre of thousands of professional educators who are working on parish staffs in the ministry of the Word, a ministry formerly almost exclusively the work of priests and sisters in the parochial schools. . . . The coordinators are, for the most part, women who have been trained in religious education departments of Catholic universities, and have

brought fresh theological insights and pedagogy into the parish structures.[19]

Parish priests were both encouraged and threatened by the sophisticated and sometimes aggressive lay leadership in ministry and in the administration of the parish. In most cases, their first exposure to the phenomenon came in the aftermath of the Vatican II instruction that "in dioceses, as far as possible, there should be councils which assist the apostolic work of the Church either in the field of making the gospel known and men holy, or in the charitable, social, or other spheres. To this end, clergy and religious should appropriately cooperate with the laity."[20] Parish councils were perhaps the first structured way for lay men and women to participate in the planning process for the parish as a whole. Supporters welcomed them as "a skeleton for the body of the liturgical community," given the postconciliar emphasis on liturgy as a celebratory expression of the apostolic work of the church. In many cases, councils generated subcommittees supervising every aspect of parish life, including liturgical planning, education, and finances.

The dynamics of local Catholic leadership were, of course, radically affected by the development of parish councils. Priests who were uncomfortable with the new sharing of power (it was, unfortunately, perceived in these terms by some pastors) could and did take advantage of the ambiguity in canon law that encouraged but did not require of the pastor any particular kind of behavior in relation to parish councils. He could refuse altogether to establish them, establish them and let them lie fallow, convene them occasionally or regularly and veto their legislation (or dismiss their recommendations) with or without discussion. Or he could work assiduously to develop a complementary, collaborative relationship with the council.[21] A great deal depended on an intangible but decisive reality—namely, the personal character of the individual priest. Those pastors who entrusted important decisions to and accepted the sound recommendations of the parish council displayed an openness to change and adaptation that was, given their seminary training, rather remarkable.

In the late 1970s parish councils gave way to, or coexisted with, the development of a parish staff, which included the pastor, associate pastor and assistant(s), the pastoral associate (frequently, a woman religious), the director of religious education, the principal of the parish school, the liturgist, the musician, and any other full-time parish employees. A substantial amount of the literature on pastoral theology from the late 1970s and early 1980s was, not surprisingly, devoted to the articulation of new models of consensus-building, decision-making, and "the power cycle." In this discussion attention was paid to the changing role of the priest:

> In no way is this affirmation of the DRE intended to depreciate those clergy in parishes who have always fulfilled this kind of role, and who continue to do so today. The change, however, is that there is now an additional person, or persons, fulfilling the same role and, more often than not, this person is a woman—a major change—and/ or a non-ordained person, which tends to mitigate the problem sometimes encountered by those whose training and background causes them, unfortunately, to see priests as authority or father figures.[22]

The image of the priest as "father figure" came under attack, perhaps necessarily, in the transition from ombudsman to orchestra leader. Priests who had enjoyed unquestioned authority on matters of theology, worship, and administration now found that they had to strive to keep up with the talented and pastorally sophisticated women religious and lay men and women with whom they worked. As troubling as this situation was, it provided an occasion for grace, a moment of transformation, in the lives of many priests:

> My real conversion to Jesus Christ came in the fourth decade of my priesthood through the ministry of a Sister who led a retreat for diocesans in 1977. She awakened me to my own need to be loved by my people, to have relationships with them on equal footing, and . . . [to the idea that] the Spirit does the real work in the parish, not this ordained person or that lay person. I don't hide behind the collar, never really did. I still wear it proudly. But I realize very gratefully that I am not the only minister in the community.[23]

Women religious and lay leaders also nudged the parish priest toward a reexamination of his role by involving him in a number of movements of renewal designed to tap the personal and spiritual resources of Catholics disenchanted with an exclusively institutional experience of church. One of these was the charismatic movement, which had an impact on parish life throughout the 1970s and into the 1980s. The movement emphasized the immediate gifts of the Holy Spirit, charismatic prayer, and the close personal bonding that accompanies fellowship in the Spirit. Some priests had highly emotional experiences in charismatic prayer groups, which contributed, they believed, to their spiritual development and thus to their effectiveness as ministers. Others were called upon to represent the larger parish, or the institutional church, to the charismatic community. One advocate of the clergy's involvement in charismatic communities recommended that "the pastor, being concerned with the overall good of the parish and of each member, can bring to a charismatic group his experience of the faith of the parish as a whole, showing how it is not only charismatic groups that have faith."[24] A quite different movement, Marriage Encounter, also drew many priests into interaction on a personal and spiritual level with couples seeking to renew their commitments to their marriage. As one priest-participant put it, "The method of Marriage Encounter stressed interpersonal openness and respect for each person's story. It was a tremendous way to learn not only what makes for good marriages, but also to learn what makes for good relationships."[25]

The advent of sophisticated lay ministers subjected the priest to a level of scrutiny he had never experienced. Was he as au courant about the latest trends in parish worship as the sister who had taken a graduate degree in liturgical studies? Was he as knowledgeable about church history as the lay historian teaching adult education courses in the parish? The orchestra-leader-to-be found it impossible in such a world to meet the previous expectations that the ombudsman would possess a general omnicompetence in matters religious. He was faced with the option of celebrating and blessing the good gifts of his lay collaborators in ministry and his specialized young assistant, or of pretending that he, and the parish, did not need them. Such pretense was quickly exposed in an age of education and rapid dissemination of information.

Lay ministry also forced parish priests to reassess the image and stereotype of women ingrained in them by the seminary culture during their formative years. Priests who had the chance to read the persuasive writings of feminist theologians such as Elizabeth Schüssler Fiorenza and Rosemary Radford Ruether in the late 70s and early 80s had already experienced firsthand the skill of female associates in parish ministry. The experience of collaborating with gifted and intelligent women as equals was new and challenging to those priests who attempted it. It was also confusing, as were several elements of the lay ministry explosion.

If the priest did in fact learn to collaborate, he remained ultimately responsible by canon law for the welfare of the parish and answerable on this score to his bishop. How was he—must he—to retain this "bottom-line" mentality in a collegial setting? And if he accepted in principle the plurality of spirit-filled ministries, how was he to articulate his own distinctiveness as an ordained priest? Priests await definitive answers to these questions, but they began the process of formulating them within the framework of the institutional church, which attempted in the 1970s to prepare its ordinands for the priesthood of the 1980s and beyond.

THE REFORM OF THE INSTITUTION FROM WITHIN

One very important result of the priest studies commissioned by the U.S. Catholic Conference was the development of sophisticated retreat programs and institutes dedicated to the continuing education and the spiritual renewal of priests. From 1968 Holy Cross priests of the University of Notre Dame offered annual institutes and summer schools designed to acquaint priests from dioceses throughout the country with the first fruits of the collective effort of Catholic scholars to fortify postconciliar theology with insights from the behavioral sciences. In Menlo Park, California, on the grounds of St. Patrick's Seminary, Sulpician fathers opened the Vatican II Institute in 1977, which hosted workshops, seminars, and retreats for the purpose of acquainting visiting clergy with the latest developments in biblical scholarship, pastoral theology, and ecclesiology. Staffed by a pool of professionalized priests and sisters, such institutes also devoted a portion of their curriculum to examination of the state of priestly ministry, and the health and happiness of the diocesan priest. Instructors led visiting priests in readings and discussions of priestly spirituality and well-being, and offered specific recommendations on practical matters ranging from details of parochial administration to the advantages and disadvantages of team ministries.[26]

The institutional church facilitated the transition to collaborative priestly ministry in a second way: priests modeled themselves after the example of charismatic leaders in the presbyterate. Progressive priests in Seattle, for example, were dissatisfied with the progress, or lack thereof, of reforms in their region during the decade following the council. But, as a young church, they had not formed a strong tradition of clerical leadership. However, in May 1975, Raymond Hunthausen was named archbishop of Seattle, a move that was to consolidate the reform process and revivify the presbyterate. The widespread sentiment of priests interviewed in Seattle is that Hunthausen's arrival was a turning point for the church. The archbishop reformed the bureacracy to reflect what he felt to be the key insight of Vatican II, "shared responsibility" for the church. He erected a three-tiered structure: a pastoral council composed of six priests, three nuns, and eighteen lay persons; a presbyteral council of eighteen priests to implement the vision of the pastoral council; and a financial council composed solely of the laity. To further promote cooperation and collegiality on the parish level, he invited Jesuit Fr. George Wilson, a consultant for a management-training firm out of Cincinnati (MDI), to give a series of workshops on leadership development and a consensual decision-making model to a team of diocesan priests who in turn developed a Parish Leadership Development Program. This was presented to every parish in the archdiocese over a two-year period (1977–78) with the goal of inspiring laity and priest together to "take ownership" of the local church. In response to reported criticism that such programs amounted to a "secularization" of the local church, Hunthausen pointed to the success of such parish renewal programs in actualizing the Vatican II vision of the church as the People of God.[27]

By his dedication to the principle of shared decision-making and consensus-building on the diocesan level, coupled with his well-known and often courageous stance on questions of the nuclear armaments industry in the Seattle area, Hunthausen fostered among the priests of the diocese a collegial, consultative pastoral style characteristic of the parish orchestra leader. As Father Gary Morelli explained, Hunthausen's personal integrity, self-evident love for the church, and thoroughgoing personal appropriation of the spirit of Vatican II combined to make his example of pastoral leadership irresistible to the presbyterate of Seattle—a considerable proportion of whom have in the recent controversies endorsed his leadership enthusiastically at each opportunity.[28]

Indeed, Hunthausen's interpretation of the implications of Vatican II for a postconciliar theology of the priesthood is shared by many of his brothers in the presbyterate and articulated by other American bishops. Archbishop Daniel Pilarczyk has contributed to the developing ministerial profile of the orchestra leader in a recent address. Pilarczyk pointed to the council's relocation of the fullness of the apostolic priesthood in the office of bishop. The parish priest is described in the conciliar documents as sharing in the priestly powers by virtue of his ordination at the hands of the bishop. By defining the priest's vocation in terms of the episcopal office, the council provided an ecclesiological basis for understanding the parish priest to be a "mini-bishop"—one who oversees, coordinates, teaches, supervises, and enables other ministers.[29]

Among those priests who have adopted the pastoral style of the orchestra leader, there is a conviction that the very distinctiveness of priestly identity, subjected to radical reexamination in the 1960s, is to be found in a renewed way of being present to the people of the parish. When Vatican II defined the church as the People of God in every local community and culture, it became necessary to think of the church as a concrete, historical, and particular reality. One important outcome of this emphasis was the priest's renewed identification with those he served in the parish. It is accurate to say that in this sense the people of the parish have become the referent of the priest's symbolic presence. He represents them as the historical embodiment of the body of Christ.

This recent relocating of the sacred, prefigured in the theological anthropology endorsed by the council, has led to two important developments in the American church. First, it has reinforced the historical tendency toward congregationalism by providing a theological vindication of it. This has made the pluriformity of ministry and parish life inherent in American religion easier to swallow for American Catholics. Second, it has provided a compelling rationale for the continued existence of a clergy "set apart" in some way from nonclergy. When the functional presence of the priest, so central to the ombudsman's identity, was rendered superfluous by the realization that the laity could function on their own very well without him, both in the world and in the sanctuary, there was a protracted period of self-examination. Priests looked beyond the parish, with the hope of securing a niche "in the world" alongside the laity. Some were reluctant to be "set apart" as symbols of a supernatural order, for they rightly read the signs of a skeptical age and concluded that such a fate would be equivalent to cultural exile. Their initial optimism and enthusiasm for secularized ministry was shaken repeatedly by disappointments from the left (once secularized, many of the most gifted resigned the priesthood) and from the right (the unexpected and rapid reappearance of the old authoritarianism).

At this writing the presbyterate appears divided on the question of future directions for priestly ministry, and, precisely, the appropriate relationship of pastor to parishioner. The orchestra leader is most comfortable with the role of "mini-bishop," supervising, representing, and coordinating a host of talented lay ministers serving the parish. Another school of thought seems to prefer the return of clergy-laity relations on the model of the ombudsman era. Many institutional leaders experience ambivalence in this situation, faced with two competing models of priestly presence.

For example, some priests grew impatient with the prolonged crisis and sought to reassert familiar patterns of clergy-laity relations. In December 1977 a group of forty-seven prominent clergy and laity members issued "A Chicago Declaration of Christian Concern," which received widespread attention and inspired a formal conference. The signers called for a recommitment of the laity to its "proper sphere" of ministry:

> A wholesome and significant movement within the Church—the involvement of lay people in many church ministries—has led to a devaluation of the unique ministry of lay men and women. The tendency has been to see lay ministry as involvement in some church related activity, e.g., religious education, pastoral care for the sick and elderly, or readers in church on Sunday. Thus lay ministry is seen as the laity's participation in work traditionally assigned to priests or sisters.

> What specifically characterizes the laity is their secular nature. It is true that those holy orders can at times be engaged in secular activities and even has a secular profession. But they are, by reason of their particular vocation, especially and professionally ordained to the sacred ministry. Similarly, by their state in life, religious give splendid and striking testimony that the world cannot be transformed and offered to God without the spirit of the beatitudes. But the laity by their special vocation, seek the kingdom of God by engaging in temporal affairs and by ordering them according to the plan of God. They live in the world that is, in each and all of the secular professions and occupations. They live in the ordinary circumstances of family and social life, from which the very web of their existence is woven.[30]

There are other indications that the question of priestly identity remains a lively question in our own time. The story of Darlington School of Theology at Immaculate Conception Seminary in Mahway, New Jersey, bespeaks the disorientation and frustration experienced by many priests as they have struggled to discern and apply the teachings of the council. In 1974, the faculty began to admit students "who are not candidates for the ordained ministry, but who wish to pursue theological study on an advanced level or to develop competence in one of the various Christian ministries exercised in the church that do not require ordination." Seminarians found themselves in classes with lay men and women, and women religious. Privately, faculty members encouraged women who intended to present themselves for ordination at the conclusion of their studies. Publicly, the school declared that "it must be understood that a broader understanding of the concept of ministry has gained currency among Catholics, especially in recent years; and this, with the growing awareness of the diversity and complexity of the pastoral needs of the church, has made it incumbent on the clergy, as well as the religious and laity, to seek a deeper and more extensive training in the sacred sciences." From 1974 to 1984, many of the seminary faculty downplayed the distinctions between priesthood and other forms of ministry. The seminary changed its statement on purpose three times during that decade, along with its name and location.[31]

By 1987 the seminary was under new and vigorous leadership, and an era of consolidation of reform, and a rejection of reforms perceived as uncritical, had set in. This development is not particular to New Jersey; much has been said and written in the last few years about a perceived "swing to the right" by Catholic seminary rectors and faculty. This "return to order" after a period of intense questioning of authority and priestly distinctiveness is manifest in a renewed affirmation of celibacy as an existential sign of the priest as a "man set apart," in a careful narrowing of the variety of pastoral options open to the priest in his role as confessor, and by a return to the discipline of the ombudsman era in such matters as the wearing of the traditional clerical garments (including the cassock and collar). Opponents of "the new traditionalism" fear that a period of retrenchment is at hand; supporters interpret this as a time of necessary moderation after a generation of extremism. It may be true, as some seminarians interviewed for this project argued, that to be an effective priest in a culture indifferent if not hostile to Christian values one needs definitive guidance from superiors, a shared sense of mission, and the resulting esprit de corps reminiscent of the ombudsman era. However, this corporate identity may come at great cost if, in achieving it, young priests rely on a standardized approach to pastoral ministry or on rigid formulas. It is, of course, quite possible that the styles of priesthood embodied by the priests of the period of crisis (1954–1972) may be judged by future historians as unfortunate aberrations or seen as a passing moment in a longer historical process by which the Roman Catholic priesthood renewed itself in the late twentieth century. Be that as it may, the period did at least demonstrate that the unquestionably complex character of human behavior cannot be comprehended by a set of codes and prescriptions, however nuanced. For better or worse, the human judgment and, one hopes, the human compassion of the priest will remain perhaps the most important aspect of his pastoral service in the future as it was in the past.

Although this brief history has stressed changes and developments in the parish priesthood over the past half century, one is equally impressed by the continuities between the priesthood of the 1930s and the 1980s. For every story of disgruntlement with parish ministry recounted in these pages one could tell two of satisfaction. Msgr. Ray Hebert voiced the feeling of many priests whose ministries span the period under consideration in this essay:

> My first pastor 37 years ago was a wonderful priest who is still active as a pastor. On a number of occasions I have told him that if I had to start my ministry all over again I would be happy to be his assistant. My first years of priesthood were joyful ones. As I recall those years, my experience was not so different from the majority of priests I knew. If you had asked my priest-colleagues at that time whether they were happy in the priesthood I am sure that you would have gotten a resounding "Yes."[32]

The principle of continuity informing the disparate works of these Catholic priests of the United States has been effective pastoral presence to the People of God. In his recent history of the diocese of Syracuse, David J. O'Brien profiled a man ordained in 1930 who in many ways embodied this quality. Father Charles Brady worked among the minority population of Syracuse at the Bishop Foery Foundation where he met and befriended blacks and responded to the daily problems of finding shelter, food, and clothing. Brady was primarily concerned with bringing faith to black people, but this work made him keenly aware of discrimination, poverty, inadequate housing and sanitation, and other problems facing poor and black people in the city. In the late 1950s, he and his associates joined with black groups to encourage open housing and integration rather than relocation programs in Syracuse, an act for which he was roundly criticized. Brady's work was, O'Brien writes, "radical in its simplicity." His description of the priestly style of this man whose career spanned the ombudsman era and the period of crisis could also be applied to many of the "orchestra leaders" of the contemporary period:

> He attended baptisms weddings and funerals . . . . He did not expect to build a church, he had no interest in organizing black people for social action, though when that happened he was delighted, nor did he want to establish an office or agency in Catholic Charities. Nor was he a social worker. Most of all, Brady's work was a matter of presence, of being with people and not for them, of being a servant and not a leader. In the process he was, for a number of people, a revolution, perhaps a revelation . . . . They were, as many recall,

"hooked" not by any particular theological message but by this simple warm priest who was doing good and made them feel good when they helped.[33]

It is this consistent priestly presence which inspires hope that the spirit of Vatican II will continue to elude confinement in extremist programs of both left and right. After a period of crisis and self-doubt, the Roman Catholic priesthood in the United States experienced a modest revival in the 1970s and early 1980s. There was a "disenchantment with disenchantment." Parishioners called for a priest who offered a warm personal presence as well as a persuasive professionalism.[34] As lay ministries were established in the United States, first by decrees from Rome, then by regional and local initiatives, the pastoral vision of Vatican II deepened the ongoing process of transformation of parish ministry. The laity responded to the council's description of the church as the People of God by claiming possession of, and accepting the responsibility for, various charisms. Disenchanted with secularism, the priest could not retreat to the functional omnicompetence of the ombudsman, for only two "functions" remained his alone by virtue of ordination and both were sacramental (consecrating the eucharist and absolving penitents). Both of these acts, and many others of the priest, have come to be understood as aspects of his prior, all-encompassing obligation to be present to the people of the parish as a sign of the transcendent character of their own service. The retention of the vow of celibacy and the image of the priest as "set apart" and "radically other" from the parishioners in this way now serves to disclose the underlying eschatalogical significance of the various functions of the parishioners, many of which the priest alone once performed. Today, the priest often finds himself in a setting in which he may be called upon to do or to say anything in particular. But Catholic parishioners continue to esteem and to require his presence as a radical expression of their own rootedness in God and in the divine work of redemption.

· PART II ·

In the Parish but Not of It: Sisters

INTRODUCTION

The history of sisters in Roman Catholic parishes during the fifty years surrounding the Second Vatican Council is one of astonishing change. For most of this century, convents were so strongly identified with parish schools in the United States that for parishioners and for sisters alike the two institutions seemed identical—at least until the mid-1960s, when both began to come apart at the seams. Then sisters, the most separate of separatist Catholics, became front-line participants in civil rights demonstrations; exemplars of a hierarchical, institutionally oriented church, they emerged as chief exponents of liberal reform.

Today, sisters represent a very different presence in parishes than they did before Vatican II. In those days they were highly visible in church, their habited ranks forming a kind of subdued pageantry, and in the school, where they provided the majority of staff and clearly set the tone. Outside these structures, their activities were rather limited. Now sisters in parishes are less exotic in appearance, perhaps, and certainly fewer. They may provide a fraction of the school personnel, work in social service, teach at a nearby university, serve as chaplain in the local prison, or operate a shelter for battered women. Perhaps a sister runs the parish, or a parish may have no sisters at all.

The striking change in sisters' life and work between 1930 and 1980 cannot be understood apart from their intimate connection with the Roman Catholic Church, both institutionally and symbolically. What happened in the church has happened to sisters, and for many of the same reasons. Religious orders, while highly specialized and distinctive segments of the Catholic population, exist squarely within church structure and see service to the broader community as integral to their mission. This has been particularly true in the history of American Catholicism, where the work of religious congregations made possible extraordinary systems of education and health care sponsored by the Roman Catholic Church. As noted by historian James Hennesey, from the time of John Carroll, sisters have been valued in this country primarily as servants of the church's institutions, and schools became "one of the spinal cords around which religious life in the United States developed."[1]

Sisters and parish schools, while agents of americanization for Catholic immigrants, have at the same time had an ambiguous history of separation from the American way of life. Producing successful American citizens, the parochial school system was nevertheless predicated on the separateness of Catholics, who perceived the American environment as hostile to their religious values. Religious orders, frequently compared with utopian communities or total institutions,[2] understood themselves as set apart, to the extent that separation from the world defined religious life.

Traditionally, religious life for women evolved in two principal forms: the contemplative orders, devoted to prayer and penitence, whose members are technically termed "nuns," and the active congregations, the "sisters," who work directly in the wider society. Active congregations, historically more recent, tended to be overshadowed by the earlier model, and sisters (by their own choice or the will of bishops and Roman authorities) adopted a modified type of cloister in imitation of contemplative nuns. Sisters teaching in parochial schools therefore embraced a rather strict and anachronistic version of cloister in order to ensure isolation from the "worldly" influence of mainstream society, including the rest of the parish.

Convents at the period when this study begins were closed systems, islands of religious ideology, which provided a strong institutional framework insuring the complete integration of both life and work. One sister recalled her congregation during the 1940s and 50s: "We talked school all the time. . . . It was a *life* dedicated to schools and children."[3] Before 1965 the daily regime varied little from one convent to another—strictly communitarian, tightly scheduled, usually in or near the institution operated by the sisters.

Although sisters formed an essential part of parish organization, they had an extraparochial base, in their religious congregations. Some communities, like the Sisters of the Presentation, had become involved at the parish level only with their arrival in the United States. Lacking precedents, they had to devise new roles for themselves in dealing with parish life and parish priests. Pastors ordinarily engaged a religious community through its major superior for a specified number of sisters (appointed by her) to take charge of the school or to do other work in the parish. The contractual relationship of parish and sisters was not with the individual, but with the congregation. A sister's tenure in a given parish could range from weeks to years, subject to congregational demand—and sometimes to pressure from the pastor.

Sisters were paid minimal salaries and usually supplied with housing by the parish, but all other expenses, including food, clothing, education, and medical care were congregational responsibility. Sisters were thus helpers in the parish, to a degree outsiders, and definitely dependent on the pastor. The interrelation of these three factors was to prove significant in determining the direction of the future.

By 1966, of all professed sisters in the United States, 63.7 percent were still involved in teaching or teaching administration; by 1982 the figure had dropped to 29.1 percent. The total number of sisters, moreover, had plummeted from a peak of 181,421 in 1965 to 122,653 by 1980,[4] and the impact of this decline on church-related schools and institutions has been immense. The statistics reflect radical change in women's communities resulting from the interaction of complex factors: a gradual process of professionalization in teaching; the dramatic cultural and ecclesiastical transformations of the 1960s; a theological revolution that interpreted the world in a highly positive sense; and heightened awareness of historical and social problems related to the role of women. If a new order for sisters' communities became clearly evident in the wake of Vatican II (and the council was indubitably catalytic), the evidence of history shows that it was in the making long before 1962.

Research for the present study is drawn largely from the archives and experience of sisters in six congregations or provinces having a history of intense parish involvement and wide geographic distribution within the United States, and to whom the author is deeply grateful:

Sisters of Charity of Leavenworth, Kansas. Founded in Leavenworth (1858), from Nashville, Tennessee (1851), and Nazareth, Kentucky (1812), the community is located chiefly in the midwestern and northern United States, as well as Peru.

Sisters of Charity of Nazareth, Kentucky. One of the first indigenous American communities, established in Nazareth, Kentucky (1812), with sisters throughout the southeastern United States, and one large group in New England, also in India and Belize.

Sisters of Notre Dame de Namur, Ipswich Province. Founded in Amiens, France (1803), moved to Namur, Belgium (1809), the first United States establishment was Cincinnati, Ohio (1840). The province is located chiefly in New England and forms part of a widely distributed international congregation with headquarters in Rome.

Sisters of Notre Dame de Namur, Boston Province. The province was established in 1973 in response to ideological differences within the community. The Boston group shares much geographical territory with the Ipswich province, in addition to houses in South Carolina and various other states. Like the Ipswich province, Boston forms part of the larger international congregation.

Sisters of the Presentation of the Blessed Virgin Mary, San Francisco. Founded in Cork, Ireland (1775), the congregation came to San Francisco (1854). Presently the sisters are chiefly on the U.S. West Coast, in Mexico and Central America.

Sisters of St. Joseph, Baden, Pennsylvania. Established in Ebensburg, Pennsylvania (1869), the congregation was originally founded in Le Puy, France (c. 1650), and came to Carondelet, Missouri (1836). Sisters are concentrated in western Pennsylvania, but are also found in numerous other states, Brazil, and China.

The study presented here, while by no means comprehensive, gives an in-depth view from the perspective of these six communities. The congregations selected are fairly representative of many others whose primary work has been parish schools. Although ethnic composition, period of foundation, charismatic tradition, and differences in geographic situation did create cultural variations from one congregation to another, they were far outweighed by the prevailing homogeneity of religious communities before Vatican II. Despite the considerable diversity within congregations at present, common experience, such as similar educational exposure and the influence of national sisters' organizations, has produced comparable developments in orders, which are quite recognizable across congregational lines. The sample is limited to the degree that it does not include any group that could be considered extremely conservative, nor any, like the Parish Visitors of Mary Immaculate, who worked primarily in parishes without schools. Unfortunately lacking in the selection are any congregations whose membership is composed largely of recent immigrants or women of color. The conclusions of this study may therefore be tied significantly to the fact that it is the story of predominantly white organizations whose history was shaped in the "old" American immigrant Catholic church.

7

SAVING SOULS AND
EDUCATING AMERICANS, 1930–1945

The Catholic Church in America in 1930 exemplified a twentieth-century brand of Tridentine Catholicism, strongly marked by the imprint of nineteenth-century ultramontanism. By the turn of the century in the United States, breathtaking geographic expansion and the conscious construction of a church had given way to concerns about organization and maintenance. Parishes were well-ordered units of a highly regulated church, characterized by a distinctive body of doctrine, hierarchical organization, and sacramental focus. The religious life of Catholics centered on the parish, and the parish centered in the person of the pastor. Congregations of women religious epitomized this style of Catholicism—minutely regulated, fervent, disciplined, and galvanized for action. Convent life reflected the hierarchical arrangement of church in strict rank, unquestioning obedience, and sure possession of a better way.

The first decades of the present century saw the Catholic church well into an intensive process of regularization, and with it religious communities. The National Catholic Educational Association (NCEA), established in 1904, sought to unify and lend support to Catholic educational efforts. By the end of the nineteenth century, dioceses began to organize offices of education, headed by priests, and actively encouraged standardization and uniformity in schools, limited always by parish finances and the power of the local pastor. The 1917 *Code of Canon Law* provided the framework for Catholic life, reinforcing the institutional understanding of church as a perfect and self-contained society.[1] The code provided readily available universal norms subsequently imposed on sisters' constitutions, and also added incentive for the development of Catholic schools. Canon 1374 forbade Catholic children to attend "non-catholic, neutral, or mixed schools, that is, those which are open also to non-Catholics"[2]—American public schools, in other words. Throughout the period preceding Vatican II, the U.S. bishops issued numerous exhortations on schools, much along the lines of their 1919 letter, which, echoing the Third Plenary Council of Baltimore (1884), argued that the Catholic Church, "because of the great combat between truth and error, between Faith and Agnosticism . . . is obliged, for the sake of principle, to maintain a system of education distinct and separate from other systems." Thanks to the increased population and rising economic status of Roman Catholics following World War I, the bishops' desires regarding education became a possibility, and the number of parish schools grew considerably. By 1920 there were 5,852, or 36.5 percent of parishes in the United States with schools—roughly the same percent of parishes with schools in 1900 (3,812 of 10,427 parishes). By 1930, however, the number of parish schools had risen to 7,225,[3] or better than 40.5 percent of all parishes.

Sisters viewed their apostolate ultimately in a supernatural light: the primary aim was the salvation of souls, for which professional preparation and personal holiness were the chosen tools. In the words of one provincial superior in 1930: "We should daily pray . . . for success with the children and by success I mean that we may reach their souls."[4] If sisters' efforts took place in parish schools, they saw them in a cosmic context. Mother Ann Sebastian of the Sisters of Charity of Nazareth drew the community's attention to world conditions on the eve of World War II, citing the "need of valiant men and women, servants of God, to battle with the overpowering forces of evil. And where may the Church better turn to find the stouthearted and brave than among religious?"[5]

This was a world embattled in supernatural warfare, and sisters were called to form the front lines. They were, after all, Catholics, who every Sunday invoked St. Michael the Archangel, praying that he, by the power of God, would "cast into hell Satan, and all the evil spirits who roam about the world seeking the ruin of souls." Yet there was a strong positive component to sisters' conduct of Catholic schools, and it derived largely from the supernatural perspective, with its belief in the God-given dignity of individuals and the sublime purpose of human life.

NEW RIGIDITY IN CONVENT LIFE

The push for more schools following World War I had sharp effects in convents. Communities took on the responsibility of producing more and more sister teachers, which they indeed had to do if they wanted to remain in the parishes. In her study of sisters in the archdiocese of Boston, Mary J. Oates cites the case of a community fired from a parish school in Salem, Massachusetts, in 1924 because they were temporarily unable to provide a teacher for every grade or, as the pastor demanded, to pay the salary of a lay teacher.[6] The study also indicated that during the late 1920s, the Sisters of Notre Dame de Namur in Massachusetts began taking recruits considerably younger, "probably in response to the expanding demand for teachers." While less than 20 percent of the sisters in this province born before 1900 had been admitted under twenty years of age, 53 percent of those born between 1910 and 1919 were still in their teens.[7]

Change in the internal structure of congregations for the sake of institutional works was nothing new. Following the French Revolution, for example, Sisters of St. Joseph, formerly scattered in small, independent houses, adopted a centralized diocesan government mainly to provide the organization and mobile personnel needed for the institutions of a society in the process of industrialization. The Sisters of the Presentation abandoned strict cloister (the rule of enclosure in their convent) in order to staff the parochial schools in San Francisco.[8] In the first half of the twentieth century, what the Catholic Church demanded of sisters was an increasingly rigid internal organization in order to supply qualified and pliant personnel for its rapidly growing institutions. That movement would carry the image of sisters in America as a pious and versatile labor force to its limit.

In addition to pressures from the accelerated demand for schools, sisters felt an increasing rigidity in their lives as a result of new constitutions, revised to bring them strictly into line with church law. These revisions amounted to a process of fossilization, in which the spirit of the founder was made to fit the procrustean requirements of the new *Code of Canon Law.* The result was a certain homogenization of sisters' documents, with a trend toward uniformity and emphasis on institutional works. The tendency is clearly evidenced in the constitutions of the Sisters of Charity of Nazareth written before and after the 1918 publication of the code. In the section concerning the purpose of the congregation (see the Appendix at the end of chap. 10), the 1922 edition no longer envisions Sisters of Charity caring for persons in hospitals and private homes, but only in institutions ("hospitals and asylums"). Their primary commitment to the poor is strikingly muted, and the mystical perception of St. Vincent de Paul—so characteristic of the seventeenth century—of serving Christ in the poor, appears as an anemic reference to "manifesting in their lives the love of Christ for mankind."[9]

Constitutions were often revised by a cleric, or else by the sister superior, without involving the rest of the community. The Presentation sisters preserve the story that their superior, Mother Carthagh Quirke, learned by chance from a visiting Irish Dominican (male), that Rome expected revised constitutions, and she therefore rewrote them.[10]

When the new document was distributed on April 10, 1937, the presiding clergyman, Monsignor John Byrne, felt it necessary to reassure the sisters that "we are not bringing in the reign of law."[11] Nevertheless many women, in all congregations, experienced the effects of a new rigorism. Immediately after their novitiate, for example, sisters with temporary vows were strictly separated from those perpetually professed—even in small houses, at the cost of great loneliness. Superiors became preoccupied with implementing details of canonical prescriptions, and convents more and more assumed the aspect of an efficient, if religious, machine.

NEW REQUIREMENTS IN SCHOOLS

By the 1930s a largely unrecognized shift had already begun in the composition of Catholic life, which was to have long-range effects for parish schools and for the sisters who staffed them. American Catholics started to experience a degree of economic improvement and the beginnings of suburbanization. The urban and suburban mobility of Catholics, coupled with U.S. immigration policies of the 1920s, would erode the need for Catholic schools as an ethnic enclave, while the gradual movement of Catholics into the economic mainstream meant that parochial schools were no longer institutions primarily serving an underprivileged class.[12] The schools remained, however, the chief source of religious education in the parish, and the religious component was ensured by the presence of sisters.

The decisive factor for the history of Catholic schools in the United States, however, was the drive toward professionalization of teaching, which appeared during the 1920s and proceeded from both church and state. In his 1929 encyclical, *On the Christian Education of Youth,* Pius XI spelled out the most comprehensive Catholic statement on the subject to date, including a remark on the importance of good teachers: "Perfect schools are the result not so much of good methods as of good teachers, teachers who are thoroughly prepared and well grounded on the matter they have to teach."[13] American sisters, well aware of how true this statement was, interpreted it as a call to prepare themselves rigorously for teaching as a primary means of inculcating Christian values.

The most immediate and effective impetus for improved teacher training came not from the church but from the state. Faced with a burgeoning postwar population, and alerted by the low academic performance of many draftees of deficiencies in the public education system, state governments worked steadily in the years following World War I to upgrade the quality of elementary and secondary education by imposing increasingly stringent requirements for certification. By 1926 states had developed complex programs for certification, which had serious impact on sisters.[14]

Previous to the war, elementary school teachers often had no special professional training beyond secondary school. Fifty percent of states, by 1920, required only secondary education for teachers, and in 1921 no state required even one year of college or normal school as a minimum prerequisite for basic certification.[15] Under those conditions, sisters frequently had a preparation equal to or surpassing that of public school teachers, thanks to the apprenticeship and ongoing supervision afforded new teachers within convents. The added requirements for professionalization, however, sent sister-teachers, like their public school counterparts, scrambling for normal school certificates and college degrees.

The previous system of motherhouse summer schools was no longer adequate for the formation of elementary school teachers. In fact, from 1895, Catholic orders and colleges had operated summer sessions for sisters. These included the Paulist Fathers in New York, New York City's Cathedral College, Catholic University, St. Louis University, De Paul, Marquette, Fordham, St. John's in Brooklyn, Villanova, Notre Dame, and others. Sisters also began to attend secular universities, colleges, and normal schools, particularly where no Catholic institutions were available. The experience proved enlightening.

Sisters of Charity of Leavenworth stationed in Butte and the surrounding areas went to normal school in Dillon, Montana, during the early 1920s. There they occupied, in sequence, an abandoned hospital, an uninhabited mansion, and a rectory from which the priest had just moved out. Mice, bedbugs, dirt, collapsing ceilings, leaky floors, crowded conditions, and inadequate light bedeviled their studies.[16] These adventures provided exposure to a new world—not, indeed, without restrictions. Proprieties of convent life were still to be observed, and Mother Berchmans Cannan's admonition to summer school students in 1924 is classic: "Where classes are conducted by male teachers, the Sisters will arrange so that there will be 'two together,' even though one can be but a 'visitor.' There will be no exception to this."[17] Such remnants of Victorian mores continued to waste the time and energy of sisters until the 1960s, but they were considered part of cloister.

Elementary teachers needed normal school certificates, but those teaching secondary school required college degrees, which they earned usually on a part-time basis in summer sessions at Catholic or secular universities. The Schmitz Study done at Catholic University in 1927 revealed 75 percent of sisters then teaching high school had four years of college education.[18] They may not have earned degrees, however, because the part-time nature of sisters' education prevented their taking required courses in proper sequence, and they tended to amass extraordinary numbers of credits before graduating. Pressure for academic credentials coincided with the widespread development of high schools, and records of the communities studied reveal the effects in sample educational histories from the period. Sister M. Carthagh Quirke, later superior general of the Sisters of the Presentation, obtained her teaching certificate in 1901, and twenty-one years later earned a B.A. in education from Catholic University. Other women from her community were studying at the University of California in Berkeley for degrees in history and chemistry. Sister M. Alphonsus Maloney, a forerunner of contemporary continuing education programs, obtained a B.A. from Duquesne University at sixty years of age, before embarking on her second term as superior of the Sisters of St. Joseph in 1928.[19]

The apparently delayed and frequently part-time nature of the sisters' educational careers described above is typical. It mirrors the added expense and personal strain entailed for communities by the necessity of sisters' earning college degrees at a time when congregations generally carried heavy debts from building. In her groundbreaking study on sisters' education done in 1940, Sister Bertrande Meyers estimated that a local convent with twelve sisters and a total annual income of $4,200 in 1930 could expect to spend $1,373 on summer school alone.[20] In addition, the sisters had to provide all their own living expenses apart from housing. They sent a substantial portion of their earnings to the motherhouse to provide for the aged and infirm, the training of novices, amortization of community debts, and subsidizing charitable works. Financial distress seriously impeded sisters' ability to pursue studies, and the tension between education and finance is a fairly constant theme in letters from superiors.

The need for sisters to obtain credentials also had repercussions in schools, and occasioned some of the first calls for lay teachers. Mother Berchmans Cannan of the Sisters of Charity of Leavenworth wrote to Monsignor Patrick McInerny in 1932, asking his help to encourage the hiring of lay teachers in secondary schools:

> If every Catholic High School would arrange to take one or two lay members on the Faculty, it would encourage Catholic higher education. Our Sisters would be enabled to acquire their higher degrees during the year instead of spending such strenuous vacations. Here is a worthy propaganda. Will you try to spread it for me?[21]

Religious teachers outnumbered lay by more than five to one in Catholic secondary schools during the mid-30s,[22] and lay faculty were viewed as a temporary expedient until enough qualified sisters could be obtained. But superiors were aware, even at this early date, that lay teachers were a necessity, simply because sisters were unable to fill the needs of the Catholic school system by themselves. That insight was not transferred into serious planning at congregational or diocesan levels, however, and superiors and superintendents alike had to deal ultimately with the relative autonomy of pastors in the matter of hiring.

Advanced degrees had been acquired by a few sisters during the 1920s and 30s, and well before that, for the purpose of staffing colleges operated by their congregations. (The earliest Catholic women's college in the country, Notre Dame of Maryland, received its charter in 1896, under the auspices of the School Sisters of Notre Dame.) The history of Catholic women's colleges is closely linked with the twentieth-century demand for academic credentials. In an era when Catholic institutions of higher learning were exclusively male, sisters sponsored colleges to provide for Catholic women, but also as a way for their own members to acquire an education, which was otherwise prohibitively expensive. Between 1920 and 1938 sixty Catholic women's colleges opened in the United States, twenty-six between 1920 and 1925 alone.[23]

The sister with a Ph.D. in the 1930s takes on human face in the story of Sister Rose Dominic Gabish, S.C.L., for many years dean of Saint Mary's College in Leavenworth, Kansas, and later executive director of the Sister Formation Conference. Her memoirs, written at the request of her religious superior, are one of the treasures in American sisters' archives. Sister Rose Dominic joined the Sisters of Charity of Leavenworth at the end of September 1923. On October 1 she found herself part of the first class of St. Mary's Junior College, and described the reaction this aroused in the motherhouse:

> The rank and file of the community had no experience with novitiate members who were not gingham-clad workers from dawn to dusk except during set hours of prayer and recreation. They found it difficult to adjust to seeing us going around in good clothes, carrying books, and sitting down studying.[24]

Sister Rose Dominic finished the bachelor's degree at Kansas University in record time: "Four years after entrance I had completed four years of college, just as if the novitiate had been non-existent." She also obtained her M.A. from Kansas University, and in 1930 began studies for a doctorate in German at the University of Wisconsin, Madison. In a herculean program, which included two years as teacher and dean of St. Mary's College, she managed to complete doctoral requirements during the Thanksgiving holidays of 1935.

Although sisters like Rose Dominic Gabish were relatively few, they were quite significant for the subsequent history of religious life. Their education and broadened experience proved influential in communities, and collectively they formed a seedbed for eventual change. Sister Madeleva Wolff,[25] who earned a doctorate in English at the University of California in Berkeley in 1925, later served as president of St. Mary's College at Notre Dame, where she pioneered in promoting advanced theological degrees for women during the 1940s, and was a key figure in the evolution of the Sister Formation movement.

A corollary of the educational and professional advancement of sisters was the appearance in 1929 of the first journal for women religious, *Sponsa Regis* (from 1965, *Sisters Today*), published by the Benedictines at Collegeville, Minnesota. It was followed in 1942 by *Review for Religious,* edited by the Jesuits at St. Mary's, Kansas. Both journals were important vehicles of information for sisters before national organizations of religious began to take shape during the 1950s. The first articles murmuring renewal and adaptation began to appear in these periodicals in the last years of the 1940s.

Although major steps had been taken in sisters' educational development, there remained serious limitations, particularly in the area of theological studies. In fact, academic theology was suggested for the first time as part of the Catholic undergraduate curriculum in 1939.[26] Formal theological education remained the preserve of the clergy, and sisters were dependent on clerical interpretation for matters of great importance in their personal and community lives. Moreover, although some novitiate programs required study of theological texts, sisters lacked training in method, and sometimes felt inadequate even to teach religion courses included in the high school curriculum.[27]

The professionalization of teaching, which began in the 1920s, had incalculable consequences for sisters. It forced them beyond the limits of their own institutions in order to obtain certification and set them on the path of intellectual independence. Education of sisters in general and the specialized training of a few for the first time established the potential for competent leadership by women in the American Catholic Church. But the need for education also placed huge financial burdens on congregations, and tested the endurance of individuals by adding relatively heavy studies to rigid and overburdened schedules.

At the same time, the expanding parish schools called for more and more teachers.

SISTERS FOR SCHOOLS, AT ANY COST

In his 1957 study, *Parochial School*, sociologist Joseph Fichter identified an important distinction between parish schools and private institutions where children received an expensive education. Parish schools were rather "religious public schools," financed from a common fund and dependent on the voluntary contributions of Catholics.[28] To this project, sisters donated a lion's share by supplying both personnel and indirect financial contributions.

Parish employees, sisters worked for minimal salaries, and kept their communities afloat by earning money after hours, particularly through music lessons, which comprised almost half of a convent's earned income in lean years. They also suffered gender discrimination, being paid approximately half as much as religious brothers for comparable work in parish schools.[29] Mary Jo Weaver accurately links sisters' financial situation to the prevailing view that women's work (caring for the sick and teaching the young) was unpaid labor, whether done in homes or institutions.[30] There is no question that sisters' economic arrangements with the parish kept them in a position of dependence, the effects of which are being realized only in the present. By walking a financial tightrope, however, sisters supplied an essential part of the unique cooperative effort which created parochial schools in the United States.

Despite determined efforts to professionalize, increasing demands for teachers and financial hardship augmented by the depression often placed insuperable limitations on sisters' capacity to obtain preservice training. Those with patent ability were likely to find themselves in a classroom within days of entering the convent. Such was the case with Sister Mary Isabel Concannon, who turned down a scholarship at Seton Hill College in order to join the Sisters of St. Joseph of Baden, Pennsylvania, in 1931.[31] As a student at Holy Rosary High School in Pittsburgh, Mary Claire Concannon recognized the Sisters of St. Joseph as "excellent teachers, really professional women," and she herself wanted to teach. Moreover, she had often seen a neighbor, Sister Gregory Rieland, enjoying herself during a home visit—singing, dancing, playing the piano—and was impressed that "she didn't give up her love for her family." The twofold image of human warmth and professional competence exerted a powerful magnetism: "I was attracted to those who were for others, and by that call to excellence—that what they did they did so well." She chose the convent rather than college.

Of the sixteen young women who entered the Sisters of St. Joseph at Baden in 1931, five were "educated" (they had completed high school), and very shortly went out to teach. Most of Mary Claire's six months as a postulant were spent at St. Mary's in New Castle, Pennsylvania, as a teacher in the grade school. Two things stood out in her mind from her first experience "on mission":

> The way those sisters embraced me as a young person; and the other impression I have of those very early days was: "This is the list for visiting the sick!" Every day every sister in that house went out to visit the sick. . . . I had such a sense of, as sisters, belonging to the parish and caring.

Following a retreat at the motherhouse she received the habit on Easter Monday 1932. On Tuesday she found herself teaching at Annunciation parish in Pittsburgh, now as Sister Mary Isabel. A more experienced colleague had to get up early in order to help the newcomer dress in her unaccustomed religious garb. "That's what all communities were doing," she reflected, "dress them up and send them out! Keeping that school was so important." Her canonical year of novitiate was spent at the motherhouse, teaching in the boys' academy there. Spiritual formation was accomplished through summer vow classes, retreat, and the constant rhythm of prayer in convent life.

Sister Isabel, whose life in the convent spans the time of this study, became a community and diocesan school supervisor in her early thirties, and in 1955 earned the first Ph.D. in her congregation, which she served as superior general from 1961 to 1973. She is presently associate vicar for religious in the Pittsburgh diocese. Isabel's initial days in the congregation and parish were rather typical of any sister's in the 1930s except that, entering with a high school diploma, she already formed part of an educated elite. Her obvious vibrance and vitality are witness to the powerful human spirit of those women who flourished in a system where time for a novitiate was secondary to teaching, and primacy had to be given to the need for bodies on the assembly line of the Catholic school.

SISTERS AND THE PARISH

The relationship of sister to parish is difficult to define because of its inherent ambiguities. Sister Mary Isabel's story is illustrative—one had a committed yet strictly regulated and predictably temporary involvement in a given parish to do a work for which one's congregation existed. The sister was indispensable and yet removed, a parish worker but not quite a parishioner. Both aspects of this relationship would weigh heavily in the direction of the future.

Despite sisters' unquestionable contributions to parishes and the prestige they enjoyed there, they remained to a degree outsiders. Sisters had a quasi-clerical image that set them in a niche apart from the rest of parishioners. Sisters' unquestioned dependence on the clerical class was reinforced by their congregations' close canonical and institutional ties with the hierarchy. That, plus the distinctly religious character of their vocation and appearance, tended to assimilate them to the clergy.[32] Actually, sisters' relationship to clergy was not that of colleague, but subordinate, strictly father-daughter.

Acutely aware of their dependence upon the good will of the clergy, Sisters of St. Joseph, whose motherhouse was located about twenty miles from Pittsburgh, needed city housing in order to attend summer school. The superior's admonition in 1939 perfectly expresses an attitude that kept sisters beholden to pastors as their benefactors:

> Since it is through the courtesy of Pastors that we are permitted to use convents during the summer, please be very careful about the use of light and water. Sisters who go to school may remain up until 10 p.m., but the others are to retire at the usual time.[33]

Sisters' apparent similarity and actual subordination to the clerical state placed them at a distance from parishioners and clergy alike, with no real rights in either sphere. It is hard to avoid historian Jay Dolan's conclusion that sisters were "the Catholic serfs."[34]

If outsiders, sisters gave profound and costly commitments to parishes. During the depression, congregations made direct financial contributions by continuing to work in parishes without pay. The financial report of the Sisters of St. Joseph of Baden for 1934 to 1937 reveals unpaid salary in the amount of $12,376, at a time when the community's liability for the motherhouse mortgage and another separate loan stood at $122,064.[35] One Sister of Charity of Nazareth recalls feeding seventy-five people, sometimes as many as one hundred fifty, every morning in Louisville during the depression. The food, prepared by the sisters before going to school, was leftovers donated by a grain company, "Maybe Purina . . . we ate it ourselves . . . we were desperately poor."[36]

In contrast to the monolithic image of sisters confined to the school, congregational records show them participating in numerous parish activities. Most communities taught catechism classes for public school children on weekends or after school hours. Sisters benefited from the

Confraternity of Christian Doctrine's organization and development of systematic programs during the 1930s. Catholic Action, promoted by Pius XI, also drew their support. More than four hundred sisters, brothers, and priests attended a meeting to initiate a program in Catholic Action hosted by the Religious of the Sacred Heart at San Francisco College for Women in 1938. Sisters of the Presentation were there and carried out the proposed plan through classes in Christian social principles and Christian family living. They also established sodalities and the Legion of Mary (highly activist religious clubs) in their high schools, where former students report they imbibed a living sense of social responsibility.[37]

Three of the congregations studied had a strong tradition of visiting homes of parishioners suffering sickness or poverty. Here the influence of historical development is interesting, because the communities who did visiting, Sisters of St. Joseph and both groups of Charities, have roots in seventeenth-century French women's congregations founded specifically to perform the works of mercy outside a convent setting. Both Sisters of Notre Dame de Namur and Sisters of the Presentation had a history of more exacting cloister, which, at least in the early years of the century, restricted their mobility in the parish.

By 1943, however, two Sisters of the Presentation were assigned as parish visitors at St. Agnes, in the Haight-Ashbury district of San Francisco. Their superior thought it important for sisters "to go out to contact public school children and bring them in for catechism."[38] One of the two pioneers, Sister Bernadette Giles, remained at St. Agnes as parish visitor for nearly thirty years. She explained that her community had long staffed the school there, but the pastor in 1943, Msgr. Thomas F. Millet, felt impelled to go beyond "saving the saved." He wanted sisters to reach out to those who fell between the institutional cracks by making a house-to-house census of the entire parish territory. Sister Bernadette, who later served as commissioner for the city of San Francisco in charge of civil rights, sees her work at St. Agnes as anticipating future trends. "I feel that I am the grandmother of parish workers!"[39] She had some rare contemporaries and even predecessors. Historian David O'Brien reports sisters taking census in ethnic parishes in Syracuse as early as the 1920s, and Fichter's study of "St. Luke's" (the fictitious name for a South Bend, Indiana, parish) mentions two sisters assigned there in 1941 who, in addition to supervising catechetical instruction, maintained a current parish census, visited shut-ins, contacted "dormant Catholics," and instructed rural children on Saturdays.[40]

Some parishes had sisters only for a few weeks in the summer, when they arrived to teach vacation schools sponsored by the Rural Life Bureau of the National Catholic Welfare Conference. Sisters of Charity of Leavenworth preserve numerous accounts of their experience in these schools in rural Kansas, Wyoming, Colorado, and Montana. Vacation schools in the diocese of Leavenworth were first organized by Miss Eulalia G. Ehrbacher of St. Mary's, Kansas, then president of the Leavenworth Diocesan Council of Catholic Women. Working with the Jesuits at St. Mary's and Bishop Johannes of Leavenworth, she obtained sisters to staff eight schools in the summer of 1929.[41] Summer sessions, lasting four weeks, were intended for parishes where there were no schools. The curriculum involved sacramental preparation, catechetics for children from primary through high school, recreation and health programs, choir practice, home visitation, and (in practice) adult education. Instruction from the Rural Life Bureau informed pastors in outlying districts that they would be responsible for "housing the teachers comfortably and in the case of sisters of housing them with desired privacy."[42] In fact, sisters occupied church basements, private homes, and abandoned buildings. Letters from Sunburst, Montana (population 309), mention "no water accommodations; coyotes, mice. . . . " Remarking the luxury of having "a bed a piece," one sister reported, "the only disadvantage here is that we have to go from house to house for our meals. Difficult for a person who has a bad stomach." Sisters were oddities to many of the parishioners who had never seen them before, at least at close range:

> One kind and thoughtful elderly lady, in a diplomatic manner, offered to let us have a bath if we wished. We had to travel several miles to her house. . . . We meandered down the dirt road to her house, walked in with a satisfied air to secrecy on her part, only to see around the table a representation of the Ladies' Aid. Secrecy! The whole town knows now that the Sisters take baths—when they can.[43]

Sisters ordinarily taught vacation school without remuneration, except for travel and living expenses. Sometimes they had great success. In 1931, at the end of a three-week course at Annunciation parish in Baldwin, Kansas, the children, at their own request, carried lunch and stayed all day; parents brought supper to be served on the church lawn accompanied by games, recitations, and baseball, in the next field. The pastor arrived from a nearby town to give benediction. The occasion evoked one sister's simple definition of parish: "Cooperation was unanimous; the *parish* was there."[44]

Sisters frequently did extra work in parishes, conducting the choir or playing the organ, counting the collection, or taking care of the sacristy. Just as often, however, these activities were forbidden by rule, either to spare the sisters overwork, or to prevent unacceptable contact with priests or adult parishioners. A fine example of restrictions that kept sisters "in the parish but not of it" is found in the 1914 regulations for the Sisters of Charity of Nazareth:

> 4. Sisters are forbidden to take charge of choirs or preside during the singing of High Mass on Sundays. They may have charge of the children's choir.
> 5. Sisters have no permission to attend to altars in parish churches nor to make Altar breads.
> 6. The Sisters must not attend Lenten or mission sermons given at night.
> 9. In passing through the streets or in other public places, Sisters should strictly observe the rule of silence. Above all, they should never stand and hold conversation with externes [sic] on the street or about the Churches.[45]

These regulations persisted in essence until the 1960s, causing great conflict for sisters, particularly in the matter of holding "conversations with externes on the street or about the Churches." That is precisely where sisters were likely to meet parents of their students or a parishioner who simply needed to talk. The sisters interviewed were virtually unanimous in the opinion that before Vatican II a cloistered mentality quite at odds with engagement in the parish had precluded any extensive involvement with adult parishioners.

LIMITS OF PARISH INVOLVEMENT

The ideal of separation from the world made convent life of the past essentially a closed society, promoting what Sandra Schneiders has called "a certain cultivated distance from the so-called 'secular' members of the Church itself."[46] This distance was achieved by a more or less modified practice of cloister, a form of isolation that lent convents an air of mystery and elitism, and perhaps some of their appeal. While very significant in forming the identity of sisters, cloister and its effects created increasing tensions that, like so much of the Catholic Church's stance toward the world, exploded in the 1960s.

Cloister functioned essentially to isolate sisters from the larger society in order to preserve the total immersion in the ideals, myths, and rituals that sustained religious life and made the sacrifices it demanded worthwhile. In her study of sisters during the 1970s, Helen Rose Fuchs

Ebaugh describes a dominant characteristic of pre–Vatican II religious orders in "the social and psychological totalism of thought, attitudes, and behavior demanded of members."[47] Convents achieved the strict boundary maintenance necessary to their way of life by distinctive modes of dress and behavior, and by careful control of communication with the outside world. Novices underwent a rigorous socialization that prepared them for life in a totally separate social system, dramatically symbolized the transformation effected by the religious habit and the adoption of another name.

Control of what came into convents was a central feature of cloister, which the religious community attempted to prevent from contamination from the outside world and to create a sociology of knowledge that supported its beliefs and goals. Undoubtedly the most drastic form of control was the censorship of sisters' mail. With a few carefully specified exceptions, all letters, both incoming and outgoing, were open to inspection, and sisters had no access to stamps or money to buy them except through superiors. The practice was detested by almost everyone, and indeed it was a federal offense, but tolerated under the rubric of obedience, as part of the package.

The greatest invasion of closed convent culture, and probably a significant cause in its eventual demise, was the introduction of communications' media during the twentieth century. Superiors realized the dangers of telephone and radio (and eventually television) to this way of life and issued repeated restrictions on their use. Mother M. Reginald Leahy of the Presentation sisters was eloquent in her reserve: "Much of the matter transmitted by the radio is neither edifying nor instructive, hence care is needed for its use in the community." Allowing that events of "universal interest . . . educative value . . . and edifying nature" could be allowed, she insisted that the radio should be turned on only with the superior's consent, and was never, except on extraordinary occasions, to interrupt the daily schedule: "Every avenue by which the world may enter our cloisters should be carefully guarded."[48] She seems a paragon of balance when contrasted with the anonymous missionary who in 1931 inveighed in *Sponsa Regis* against the "graphophone, telephone, and radio": "If the devil is not in these contrivances, he at least finds them handy means for promoting worldliness among religious persons, and through that the decay and decline of religious communities."[49]

Sisters did, of course, listen to the radio and were even involved in broadcasts when their pupils performed. On March 2, 1939, the annalist of the Presentation motherhouse recorded with obvious enthusiasm that "Reverend mother and a few of the Sisters who were not in school at the time got the great privilege of receiving our Holy Father's first blessings over the radio."[50] Such a blend of theological naiveté and American exuberance over technology had continually to be tempered by an attitude of rather stringent aloofness toward "the worldliness that is poured out over the radio."[51]

Newspapers were generally banned from convents. Novices experienced a virtual news blackout, like the sister who entered the convent in September 1929 and admitted knowing very little about the crash when it happened. Another woman objected strenuously to the deprivation of information, recalling she had learned nothing of the death of President Harding in August 1923 until about six weeks after the event. The news arrived via a fellow novice who worked in the kitchen and happened to hear of it, "probably from the milk man. . . . I felt it was such a crime."[52]

Regulation of egress from convents was equally important in terms of cloister, and controlled by canon law. It was an area of keen interest to clerical authorities, who considered themselves obliged to supervise sisters' comings and goings. Sisters of St. Joseph of Baden had the rather liberal custom of visiting their families at home for a few days during specified times of the year, although they had to stay in convents overnight. A subject that recurs frequently in the correspondence of major superiors, the home visit became a delicate issue when the clergy were uncommonly unsettled by it. Two letters of Mother Adrian Cushwa, dated November 21 and December 15, 1936, illustrate tension over home visits, as well as the sisters' total dependence on the ideas of male clerical superiors:

> If we abuse this privilege, it may be taken away from us; Father Bryson is evidently questioning it, for he has ordered me to send him a list of all the Sisters who made visits during vacation. A word from him might very easily cause a clause forbidding all visiting to be inserted in our Rule, especially as the Bishop himself is not at all in favor of it. Now, neither you nor I wish to be deprived altogether of this privilege, so it is up to us not to abuse it.

Three weeks later, she relayed the permission from Father Bryson for Christmas visits, with a caveat:

> once again he has requested that the names of all those who visit at that time be sent to him. He made no explanation for this request.
>
> Frankly, Sisters I am worried. . . . I beg each one to be governed by her conscience and thus avoid the whole community being deprived of visiting.[53]

Her concern was not without cause. Sisters simply were not free to govern their own behavior. A faintly intimidating letter from the administrator of the diocese of Kentucky to the superior of the Sisters of Charity of Nazareth in 1922 complains of violations of canon 607 of the new code, which requires a companion for sisters outside their houses. He noted reports of "priests and others" who had seen "sisters of the different communities alone in the most crowded streets of the city . . . in office buildings and department stores, going from room to room and counter to counter unescorted." He concluded:

> I feel that it will be sufficient for me to . . . leave it to the good sense and judgment of the Superioress to correct it where it exists. If this is not done, of course, I will have to proceed further.[54]

Such surveillance was quite common—archives abound with similar letters from bishops and ecclesiastical superiors. As a price of religious status in the church, sisters had to conform to outdated Mediterranean norms for the conduct of women, enshrined in canon law by the men who designed and enforced it.

But sisters also reinforced their own separateness from the rest of the world. Any Sister of Charity of Leavenworth who accompanied another to a doctor or dentist's office was instructed to "remain with her in the room where the examination is made or professional service given."[55] Sisters of Notre Dame de Namur, who pioneered advanced Catholic education for women in this country, were forbidden to teach upper-level boys, and even had to sacrifice parish schools to communities who would teach them.[56] In 1930 young Sisters of Notre Dame were cautioned against too much contact with adults:

> In dealing with parents of children we should keep strictly to business. Do not allow women to tell you their troubles—relate stories of their operations, etc. Such news defiles our minds.[57]

The aspect of convent culture that consciously reinforced "childlike dependence" through vows of poverty and obedience, also aimed at maintaining sisters in childlike innocence by restricting their contact with grown-ups and by distancing them from themselves as women—whether by protection from undesirable knowledge, or through clothing that aimed, as much as possible, to identify them with another era and neuter the appearance of the body. It left them little incentive to identify with other women in the parish and underlined their distinctiveness.

Cloister in its twentieth-century application was part of a rigid milieu control that separated sisters from "worldly" contacts, and gained complete commitment to the religious order and its mission, which included the Catholic school. Evidence of repeated reiterations by superiors and clergy about the importance of cloister are a telling index of how the dichotomy between norm and experience had already begun to strain the fabric of convent life well before Vatican II.

A persistent theme of ill fit recurs in the history of sisters at this period. On the one hand, they operated in an increasingly professional world where, in some instances, they did pioneering work. On the other, they had "left the world"—they were religious. Monastic models dominated all other modes of religious commitment for centuries, so that sisters struggled with ill-defined concepts of religious life and "worldliness." Too often, the desire not to be conformed to the world resulted in conformity to the dictates of a world that was passé.

American Catholic sisters were in fact trying to live in two worlds: the world of the medieval monastery and that of the competitive twentieth-century marketplace. Despite sisters' indubitably religious motivation, the arena of their endeavor—institutional education or health care—had become a commodity demanding increasingly strict quality control and attractive packaging. Due to increasing specialization and an expanding market for the Catholic school, sisters were continually pressured to deliver more services of higher quality, without any basic changes in the convent system that provided for them.

In the fourth decade of this century, however, the strength of institutional Catholicism was more than adequate to hold within its orbit the divergent forces created by what seemed deceptively minor inconsistencies. Certain they were doing what the church wanted of them, sisters identified their service with the corporate works of their community, in which the common effort of the congregation weighed more than the initiative of the individual.

Sisters in the 1930s were products of a Catholic Church aptly described by a contemporary as "so certain and set apart."[58] It was a church strong on no compromise; an age of Catholic culture. Bolstered by the security provided by such a church, and challenged by the continuing demand for Catholic schools, sisters had no need to articulate a sense of mission. It was all too obvious. No crisis threatened their identity, strongly rooted in the institutional church and the congregation. Sisters' environment secured—in fact dictated—the service they would perform. In retrospect, it was a distinctively more cohesive and dependable world, in which even an American woman might find it well worth the high price required in terms of individuality to be part of such a lofty communal endeavor.

8

SUCCESS AND THE
SEEDS OF CHANGE, 1945–1960

The years between World War II and the Second Vatican Council were crucial for the development of sisters' ministerial role in parishes. The entire period was characterized by the apparent cohesion of Catholic culture, startling growth, and the euphoria of success. Between 1940 and 1960, Catholic population in the United States doubled, from 21 million to 42 million.[1] Catholics improved their economic status so rapidly in the postwar years that it was not noticed even by social scientists until the 1960s.[2] This was also the era when Catholics moved en masse to the suburbs, creating unprecedented demands for added classrooms, new schools—*sisters*. For religious congregations, the need to provide sisters for rapidly expanding schools contested with the need to educate them in order to have the schools accredited. There was, furthermore, a growing dissonance between the drive toward professional competence and entrenched practices of convent life. The reasons why sisters would greet Vatican II with such enthusiasm can be found in the developments of this period, and the decade of the 50s is pivotal in accounting for the subsequent revolution in convents.

WORLD WAR II

The upshot of World War II eventually transformed sisters' lives and institutions, but the war itself had relatively little effect on the internal workings of convents. Pearl Harbor did shock the writer of the Presentation motherhouse annals out of her accustomed propriety: "Dec. 7. As if out of a clear blue sky, came the sad news this morning of the surprise bomb attack by the Japs on Pearl Harbor. The thought of war which had always seemed so remote now burst upon us in dreadful reality."[3] Her record of the war years in San Francisco features blackouts, emergency rations as Christmas gifts, and sisters' participation in the war effort through conservation, volunteer work in schools, and donating blood to the Red Cross. She made no mention of Hiroshima, but her account of V-J Day depicts the tenacity of convent order and a unique version of civil religion:

> At four o'clock, while all the sirens and whistles were blowing and bells were ringing to announce V-J Day, Virginia Powers, Sister M. Agnes Perpetua's niece, entered the convent. We were at Holy Hour, and the Te Deum and Magnificat were chanted in thanksgiving for victory.[4]

International congregations like the Sisters of Notre Dame de Namur were inevitably more affected. A letter of the Massachusetts provincial in 1942 reveals her deep anxiety about sisters at the Belgian motherhouse, particularly the two Americans there who could not return home because "the German government has cancelled all visas." She worried over "our Sisters in Japan. Not a word have we heard from these dear Sisters. May God protect them!"[5] When the American Sisters of Notre Dame wound up in Japanese camps, native members of the congregation made day-long trips by train to bring food to their sisters in detention.

In the United States, however, changes in convent life were temporary and minimal. Numerous women's colleges received male students during the war, and unobservable modifications were made in habits because sisters were unable to obtain material from abroad. Generally, the tendency was to maintain the status quo, with a suffocating emphasis on uniformity. In the middle of the war, sisters submitted minutiae to Rome for approval, and directives like those issued for the Sisters of Charity of Leavenworth in 1944 were common. They began, "Bonnets are to be worn from October 1 to May 1 in Montana, Colorado, and Wyoming, and from November 1 to April 1 in other places"—followed by six pages of prohibitions against slang, reading secular books or magazines without permission, attending night devotions in the parish, and wearing glasses with "conspicuous nose pieces or odd shaped lenses."[6] One sister, a postulant in 1941, recalls even then a sense of unease at the pettiness of these restrictions.[7]

POSTWAR EXPANSION: SCHOOLS

Following the war, women's return from the work force and newfound Catholic prosperity combined to produce a surge in population and a rash of building. Between 1944 and 1949 the student population in parish elementary schools alone increased by nearly four hundred fifty thousand. During the next decade it grew to a total of 4,195,781 in 1959—more than double its size at the end of the war. Parishes across the country added over twenty-four hundred new elementary schools. The congregations studied mirror general trends. The San Francisco Sisters of the Presentation opened six schools between 1947 and

1951—as many in four years as they had in the preceding twenty-two.[8] They also extended beyond the state of California for the first time.

Communities experienced a postwar boom in vocations, with the total number of Catholic sisters increasing by more than eleven thousand in the five years before 1950, and over twenty-one thousand during the following decade.[9] This meant a 21 percent increase in the number of sisters, but student population had grown by better than 200 percent during the same period. Growth in convents was not nearly equal to the demand for teachers, and recruitment took on a new urgency. Sisters of Charity of Leavenworth drew up a chart in 1946 showing the number of religious vocations from each of their institutions, and the superior encouraged every sister in contact with girls to cultivate candidates:

> We need more sisters than ever. We are constantly refusing schools and hospitals for lack of sisters. Within the last three months we have had seven requests to take hospitals. We were obliged to refuse them all, and some were grand offers.[10]

Superiors, if they did refuse specific requests, in fact assumed basic responsibility for filling positions that were expanding at a phenomenal rate. Faced with patterns of unprecedented growth, sisters' response was trying harder.

Rapidly rising costs (the bill for public schools grew from $4.7 billion in 1949–50 to $12.3 billion a decade later)[11] made sister-personnel all the more desirable. Congregations embarked on programs of expansion that stretched their resources to the limit. In 1947 the superior of the Sisters of Charity of Nazareth urged the community:

> Unless our branch houses rally to the cause of sacrificing at least one sister for the year 1947–48, we cannot fulfill our obligations to the promised new missions: India; Wakefield; Georgetown, D.C.; Clarksdale, Mississippi; and St. Ladislaus, Columbus. We admit that we have assumed a grave responsibility in attempting to supply these new foundations with even a minimum quota of sisters; but zeal for God's glory led us to be so rash, if rash we were, and despite the pain of facing the consequences of our act, we are still convinced that it is what Almighty God is asking of the community.[12]

The same superior reported she had "refused more than sixty requests for new foundations in twenty-five states and four foreign countries," in the two years since 1945. The story recurs almost verbatim in the correspondence of every major superior during the years following the war.

Sisters took on new commitments not only in the United States but abroad. The American missionary movement, which gained real momentum following World War I, resumed with new vigor after a temporary hiatus during the Second World War. In 1946 Mother Emerentia Snyder requested Sisters of St. Joseph interested in "any works of the community other than teaching" to inform her; the same year a new mission band of six departed for the Hunan province in China (the first had gone in 1926). By 1947 the Sisters of St. Joseph investigated home mission work with Spanish Americans and a hospital in Hot Springs, New Mexico, but nothing came of either. Four of the Baden sisters operated a vacation school in Holly Springs, Mississippi, during the summer of 1949.[13] This expansionist trend on the part of congregations in the late 1940s was really an attempt by sisters to meet new demands in old ways—with one significant exception.

The explosion in Catholic school population after the war led to the first widespread calls for lay teachers. They came from sisters, as they had earlier, but now with more insistence. In 1947 superiors wrote to Sisters of St. Joseph and Sisters of Charity of Nazareth explaining why pastors must be asked to secure lay teachers: "If God's kingdom is to spread, we must use the lay apostolate in our schools."[14] At the NCEA meeting in 1949, Mother Eucharista Galvin set the theme in a national context:

> I believe that educationally speaking, we have behind us, at least in most parts of the country, the crudest of the pioneering period. Many parishes have their church, rectory, schools and convent built and their debts paid. It is to the pastors of such schools we must turn to release sister teachers for training by employing in their stead some prepared lay teachers.[15]

Mother Eucharista wanted lay teachers who were Catholic, with a Catholic education, prepared in the curriculum of the diocese or religious congregation operating the schools. Sisters thought of these institutions, whether they owned them or not, as "our schools," and the hiring of lay teachers as "temporary expedient" or "compromise." If lay teachers came into their own in the Catholic schools by 1957, as Buetow asserts, they did so as second-class citizens: in the minds of religious superiors and Catholics in general, schools still meant *sisters*.[16]

Nonetheless, by the end of the 1940s, the handwriting was on the wall for Catholic schools, though hardly realized at the time. Sisters could no longer supply the schools with sufficient staff; it had become absolutely necessary to hire lay teachers, and with this shift in the balance of supply and demand, the traditional financial base of the Catholic school system in the United States was undercut.

SISTERS' EDUCATION: THE DILEMMA

The availability of higher education following World War II, "one of the great levelling processes in American history," transformed the lives of numerous Catholics, thanks to the so-called G.I. Bill of Rights.[17] Unfortunately, the Catholic Church passed no similar act in behalf of sisters. Pressure for professionalization increased, but sisters were severely handicapped in the search for educational advancement and knew it. "For overlong, many of us had struggled with our academic consciences and put the seal of discretion on our lips over the flagrant *status quo* in Catholic education."[18]

The author of those lines, Sister Madeleva Wolff, president of St. Mary's College at Notre Dame, broke the silence in her famous address delivered to the NCEA in 1949. In "The Education of Our Young Religious Teachers" she issued a ringing challenge to superiors and school superintendents to change the program for sisters' education. Sister Madeleva described a plan whereby "Sister Lucy" would have both religious and professional training to the level of bachelor's degree and license before going into the classroom, and then remarked, "After being Utopian to this extreme of utter abandonment, let us pull ourselves back to the grim realities, things as they are." Superiors found their hands tied by a diminishing ratio of vocations to educational demands. By 1949 they simply could not buy enough time to educate the sisters before sending them into the classroom. In the words of Sister Madeleva:

> The chief and the last, the difficulty before which they [religious superiors] will all be helpless is that of pressure for more schools, more teachers. This pressure can come from our hierarchy, our clergy, our own ambitious selves. Never before have parishes been in a position to build schools before they could staff them. Naturally, there is a clamor for sisters to teach in them.[19]

Wolff insisted that if communities did decide to educate sisters, after two or three years there would be the same number of sister-teachers to send out. The speech sparked a tremendous reaction. It was the vision soon to take flesh in the Sister Formation movement.

Madeleva Wolff was visionary in many ways. Aware of a new moment, she pleaded in behalf of the potential of American women then entering novitiates, recognizing that it meant a departure from the past:

They think and move with the instancies of aviation and television. They think in terms of super-atomic power. They are in spirit and in truth children of God. We must form and educate them in terms of these potencies. We must not frustrate the magnificence of their qualities by our lower-geared Victorian traditions and training.[20]

Sisters in general were trying steadily if slowly to expand their educational horizons. Sisters of Charity of Nazareth introduced two full years of novitiate, effective in 1944; by 1949 they encouraged sisters to take GED tests if necessary, and initiated a B.S. in elementary education at Nazareth College, designed for grade-school teachers.[21]

Sister Madeleva also spearheaded serious theological education for women, opening the graduate school of sacred theology at St. Mary's College in 1943. At the 1949 NCEA meeting she urged congregations with colleges to have their best teachers study for doctorates in order to teach religion. She confronted "heresies" clearly drawn from life, among them, "classes in religion should be taught by priests," and "lay women are not to be thought of as teachers of religion."[22] Some sisters did begin to study theology in summer courses, and the groundwork was laid for women religious even to dream of themselves as competent in matters theological.

The realities of convent life placed serious obstacles to achieving the desired competence. Not the least was a strain of anti-intellectualism, compounded by the unrelenting financial problems sisters had to face. Helen Ebaugh aptly describes the wariness of scholarship: "Sisters lived in an unreal educational world in which college degrees were luxuries and the intellectual life always a little suspect."[23] In the Baden community, where financial distress was a constant theme, a statement by the superior in 1948 implied that college degrees were personal privileges to be paid for. "It would be a sign of appreciation," wrote Mother Emerentia, "if Sisters who are given the opportunity for higher education would give the donations they receive for personal use to help defray these extraordinary expenses."[24]

Sisters' income never matched the professional education demanded by their works. By 1962 a study of sisters' finances presented to the bishops' liaison committee by the CMSW (Conference of Major Superiors of Women) reported that communities could only cover operating expenses; there was nothing left over for education.[25]

Whether professional competence was compatible with religious discipline proved another tension-filled issue. For superiors and hierarchy (who reiterated that it was), the bottom line nevertheless remained keeping the rule. "There is no conflict between religious observance and real progress," said Mother Francesca O'Shea in 1944, "Let us always keep before us the solid religious principle: 'First things first' and trust the rest to Divine Providence."[26] It was what Mary Schneider has termed an *ex opere operato* mentality, by which religious profession made all things possible.[27] But it became increasingly clear that there were not enough hours in the convent day for serious study. The convent horarium simply had to give, and small changes were cautiously introduced. Mother Olivia Hargadon, first American-born superior of the Presentation sisters in San Francisco, modified the sisters' schedule at least twice during her first year in office (1949), and each time the issue was study. A woman who entered the congregation during that year saw it as "the beginning of the beginning."[28]

THE ROMAN CATALYST

In 1950 Pope Pius XII added the voice of ecclesiastical authority to the mounting pressures for change in women's communities. This had been a point of discussion in Europe for some time, where it was recognized that postwar circumstances required alteration in at least some aspects of religious life.

In 1949 translations of articles written for European religious communities appeared in *Sponsa Regis* and *Review for Religious,* calling for "adaptation." An essay by Albert Plé, Dominican director of *La Vie Spirituelle,* was given originally to French religious superiors in 1947. It dealt with the spiritual and religious formation required by candidates who were questioning Christians and budding feminists. The double crisis of a critical modern-day mentality and feminine emancipation meant that candidates would require substantial theological formation—Bible, liturgy, fathers of the church, and the mystical body of Christ. Women presented a particular problem. Allowing that "feminine psychology has a greater need of a precise and firm framework than the masculine," in order to "neutralize an excess of sensibility," Plé argued that the more rigid control appropriate for women "must not be to such an extent that the letter stifles the spirit."[29]

J. Cruesen, S. J., explored the theme of professional competence in the 1949 *Review for Religious,* a translation from the French *Revue des Communautés Religieuses.*[30] Introducing a historical perspective, Creusen spelled out causes for change in religious communities: alteration in ecclesiastical legislation, growth in the order beyond its original cultural matrix, rapid change in ideas and customs, special local circumstances, technical progress (religious *should* be allowed the use of a typewriter), and the demands of teaching. The latter, he insisted, necessitated changes in horarium in order to provide for prolonged study.

During the last decade of his pontificate, Pius XII took insistent and long-reaching action in view of promoting change within religious communities. Beginning in 1950, a series of congresses was held in Rome to which heads of orders were invited; similar meetings were encouraged on a national level. These Roman assemblies (there were three: for members of the states of perfection, 1950; for religious educators, 1951; and for superiors of women religious, 1952) had a common theme: radically new circumstances demanded a renewal of religious life. In November 1950 Pius XII outlined basic principles of renewal in a letter to Cardinal Micara, prefect of the Congregation of Religious. The pope urged reform of religious orders "so as to be able to face up to the new manner of life in our day and to the spiritual distress of the period," and added:

> [renewal] consists in not growing numb with inertia, [but] in translating into life the great examples of the founders . . . so that the holy laws of each institute will not degenerate into an assemblage of exterior regulations uselessly imposed, whose letter, in the absence of the spirit, kills.[31]

This twofold principle of reform, return to the spirit of the founders and adaptation to contemporary conditions, would be enshrined in *Perfectae Caritatis,* the Second Vatican Council decree on religious life.

Pius XII maintained a strictly hierarchical interpretation of church, religious life, and apostolate. In language reminiscent of his predecessor's definition of Catholic Action, the pope spoke to the assembled religious in 1950 of "the urgent necessities of the apostolate, of which you take upon yourselves with so much eagerness so large a share." He defined religious life as a state inserted between the two degrees of clergy and laity, whose members followed the common call of Christian perfection through a special and "more elevated" means. Nonetheless, while holding the line on "essentials" in religious life, Pius XII announced plainly, "there are many accessory things in which you can and you should conform to the mentality of the men and the needs of the times."[32] While criteria for change were left in extremely generalized terms, the idea that religious needed to bring their institutes into line with the world of the 1950s was clear.

The compatibility of religious and professional obligations and the need for vocations occupied the congresses for religious educators held in Rome in September 1951, and superiors general of orders and congregations of women a year later. In his address to teaching sisters,

Pius XII hinted that some religious habits were in need of revamping: "Choose one which will be the expression of interior unaffectedness, of simplicity, of religious modesty; then it will serve to edify all, even modern youth." Contemporary innovations, the pope said, were consistent with religious life—it was acceptable for sisters to use a motorcycle! In the interests of teaching, features of the horarium and customs that "correspond, perhaps to the conditions of another period . . . ought to be adapted to new circumstances."[33]

The pope's insistence on the congeniality of religious life and professional competence struck a deep chord in the United States, corresponding as it did to currents already in motion on this side of the Atlantic. Professional preparation of teachers and the shortage of vocations touched points of urgent concern for American sisters. In 1952 the total number of sisters in the United States had risen to 158,946, and Americans then represented 15 to 20 percent of all religious in the world—the largest single national group working within the Catholic Church.[34] Despite these numbers, vocations were critically needed in the United States, in order to staff the Catholic schools then bursting at the seams. Estimates of the numbers required to take care of even 50 percent of Catholic children in the parochial school system ranged from twenty-five thousand new vocations in the ten years between 1950 and 1960, to sixty thousand for the following decade.[35] Sisters, taking heart from their growing novitiates and the popular demand for their schools, undertook campaigns of prayer, penance, and public relations in order to recruit new membership: "We must keep the vocations coming to fit the work to be done."[36]

At the same time, government requisites for teacher and principal certification continued a steady rise; by 1955 twenty-five states and the District of Columbia demanded a bachelor's degree for a basic elementary license.[37] The confluence of American experience and the authority of papal pronouncements sparked the movement called Sister Formation, aimed at a systematic, nationwide program for the education of sister-teachers.

THE SISTER FORMATION MOVEMENT

The origins of the Sister Formation movement are usually identified with the April 1952 NCEA meeting in Kansas City.[38] A panel in the teacher education section of the college and university department addressed the implications for American sisters of Pope Pius XII's discourse to teaching sisters the preceding year. The remarks of Sister Mary Emil Penet, I.H.M., electrified the audience, and prompted a meeting the next day to strategize for action. One woman who was present remembers emerging from that session feeling a "tremendous sense of pride" at being a sister.[39] It was an event full of vision and determination: American sisters were convinced they themselves could do something to better their own situation and that of the schools. In so doing, moreover, they knew they acted in accord with "the mind of the church."

The NCEA panel had isolated three major obstacles that prevented American sisters' implementing the pope's exhortation that sisters be "masters of the subjects they expound . . . that they are well trained and that their education corresponds in quality and academic degrees to that demanded by the State."[40] These were the major problems: sisters lacked time to complete degrees; they needed resources to pay for prolonged schooling; and there was generalized misunderstanding of what was actually required for the formation of teaching sisters. The panel suggested a threefold remedy: (1) a generalized policy of hiring lay teachers to supplement sisters in schools; (2) a study to determine the exact situation with regard to sisters' education and resources; and (3) an institutionalized opportunity for exchange of information among motherhouses and colleges engaged in the formation of sisters. Sisters had begun the revolutionary process of sharing experience and organizing resources.

Following the eventful NCEA meeting of 1949, Sister Madeleva had been invited by Sister Patrick, I.H.M., to the Monroe motherhouse for future planning, and there they involved Sister Mary Emil.[41] These three figured in the decisive events of 1952, Sister Mary Emil at the NCEA meeting, and the other two at the first national meeting of American religious orders, held at Notre Dame University, August 9–13. There Sister Madeleva addressed the assembly, again presenting the case for professional training for sisters before beginning teaching, and Sister Patrick outlined the dilemma created by the simultaneous increase of demands for sisters in the schools and for more rigorous academic training.

In her "Share the Sisters" speech, Sister Patrick called for a nationwide policy of redistributing sisters so that every Catholic school would have a uniform ratio of four sisters to one lay teacher. In 1952 that meant hiring more lay teachers at salaries that, while still inadequate, were far beyond those of sisters. The necessity of such a costly move was supported by the speaker's frank picture of sisters severely overworked—sisters who, in her estimation, were little likely to inspire needed vocations:

> You bring with you to this Congress mental pictures of overcrowded classrooms, of schools operating on half-day sessions, of old sisters

and half-sick sisters standing before large classes ... of sister after sister whose preparation is seriously sub-standard, who is having discipline problems because she is not well enough versed in her work, who meets every new school day with fear and who welcomes every dismissal bell with a joy that means there is no joy in her work.[42]

Commenting on this rather grim portrait of ill-prepared and exhausted sisters thrown into classrooms, Sister Madeleva later wrote: "The facts of sister-shortage, sisters' education, sisters' salaries were emerging. We were coming at this late hour to the use of reason."[43]

Two surveys resulting from the NCEA meeting in 1952 revealed that only thirteen communities of the 255 responding had a full bachelor's degree program in place for preservice training of sisters. Nearly all congregations relied on in-service education, which required from ten to twenty years for a sister to earn her basic degree.[44] Numerous data, moreover, support Sister Patrick's assertion that sisters in the 50s were overworked and exhausted. Records of communities contain repeated rebukes from superiors for the use of corporal punishment. Universally proscribed, and referred to by one Sister of St. Joseph as "cruel and a relic of medieval times," the fact that the issue of corporal punishment appears at all betrays that some women were in situations where they found no adequate way to cope.[45]

One must ask why sisters did not refuse this overextension of their resources. In 1958 a superior, upset by repeated statements in *Review for Religious* that sisters were overworked, wrote to the editors:

> What can the superiors do? Are they to blame for the number of Catholic children to be educated? for the opening of new schools? for the vacation schools? for the added demands of modern education?[46]

If superiors like this one failed to draw the line, perhaps the reason can be found in the mark of success it was for communities to take on more schools, the disadvantage in not being able to supply enough sisters. Although their motivations were religious, sisters had internalized the definition of themselves as the Catholic Church's indispensable labor force.

THE SISTER FORMATION PLAN

The Sister Formation Conference, a grass-roots organization, developed from the Sisters Educational and Professional Standards Commission, formed as a result of the NCEA meeting in 1952 and renamed in 1954. Sister Mary Emil was the first chairperson and executive director. The SFC aimed toward a comprehensive five-year preparation for sisters, which would include college and the canonical year of novitiate. A $50,000 grant from the Ford Foundation permitted extensive research of the educational needs of sisters and the development of a curriculum (*The Everett Curriculum Report*) to be taught at Sister Formation colleges.

The conference used a many-pronged plan to implement its goals, including regional meetings, a bulletin issued quarterly, workshops for superiors and formation personnel, and the annual publication of a volume of proceedings. Although in some ways the focus of Sister Formation was insular, seeking to educate sisters "as sisters," the ability of sisters to plan such a program and carry it off was a mark of the maturity of Roman Catholicism in the United States. Sister Formation was essentially an intellectual critique of American sisters, which paralleled the Catholic intellectualism furor of the mid-50s. Sparked by the article of John Tracy Ellis, "American Catholics and the Intellectual Life" published in *Thought* in the fall of 1955, the dialogue was an instance of Catholics come of age taking stock of themselves, including their schools.[47]

As women's communities became cognizant of the critical need for preservice education, they tried various means to expand the duration of formation programs, from increasing the postulancy from six to nine or twelve months to providing young sisters with extra years of study before sending them out to teach. Directly inspired by the Sister Formation Conference, both Sisters of Charity of Nazareth and Leavenworth decided to keep sisters back in 1959 for two years after first vows in order to complete their degrees.[48] In each case, superiors expressed concern over this controversial step, which would require patience and forbearance on the part of overburdened sisters in the schools who could look for no relief, and diplomacy with pastors.

Many (probably most) congregations were unable to implement such plans. Sister Loretto Julia, Massachusetts provincial of the Sisters of Notre Dame de Namur, regretfully informed the community in August 1959, "we have had to send *all* out to duty in the schools so that for the present we have no scholastics. . . . This gives evidence that *no Sister* is available."[49] But they were expecting fifty-four postulants in August, and more in February—the race was on.

Through the programs offered for the education of superiors and formation personnel, a small but significant pool of sisters took shape in each community who were exposed to developments in theology and psychology, with heavy emphasis on the future. The entire content of the Sister Formation Conferences for 1956 and 1957, for example, was geared toward planning for the future of schools. Continued pursuit of such themes had the inevitable effect of producing a new level of historical consciousness, and a keen awareness of development, flux, and change. Sister Ursula Grimes, who had attended the Sister Formation Institutes since the late 1950s, commented, "I was fortunate; when the changes came, I was ready."[50]

The *Sister Formation Bulletin,* which began publication in October 1954, was immensely influential in disseminating broad-based facts regarding Catholic schools and teacher training, as well as current theological topics of extraordinary value. Subscribed by local convents, it made information otherwise confined to a select group of superiors and formation directors available at the grass roots, where it was eagerly consumed. A sister of St. Joseph relates how important reading the *Bulletin* was during her late twenties and early thirties: "I remember watching the mail . . . so eager to see what was happening."[51] Publications like the *Bulletin,* and later *Envoy* (by the Institute of Man at Duquesne University), and *The Nun in the World* introduced sisters to new ways of thinking about themselves, and seriously challenged long-established patterns. The woman quoted above related that such reading provoked her "first level of awareness that there was another part of life that had not been nourished at all."

As a result of Sister Formation, an increased number of sisters were encouraged to do doctoral studies, either to teach in their own colleges or to train young sisters. While the first sister in the Baden congregation started studies for a Ph.D. at St. Louis University in 1951, by the end of the decade four more were working toward advanced degrees in the fields of history, education, and English.[52] These women would supply important leadership for the congregation throughout the next two decades, two serving as superior general from 1961 to 1973 and 1973 to 1983, respectively. All were involved in key positions relative to formation or administration within the congregation. The Baden example merely confirms Helen Ebaugh's perception that educated sisters exercised an influence on their orders far in excess of their numbers. They brought ideas and shared an evaluative framework with members of the community who had not had the direct educational experience. More educated members also tended to hold positions of administration and policy-making,[53] with the result that their communities were structurally more open to change.

Sister Formation gave communities of women in the United States crucial elements for the potential to change: self-awareness, communication with like-minded individuals, educated leadership, and general membership exposed to secular knowledge and critical thinking. In her study of Sister Formation, Mary Schneider concludes that, during the late fifties, Sisters Emil Penet and Ritamary Bradley, executive secretary and editor of the *Sister Formation Bulletin*, respectively, were "the most influential women religious in the American church." She was sincerely echoed in the words of one sister interviewed who declared, "Sister Mary Emil had more influence on sisters than Vatican II!"[54]

Further components of change were added when the Conference of Major Superiors of Women (CMSW) was established in 1956, along with numerous federations of congregations with common historical roots. These provided forums in which common problems were aired, new solutions given credibility, and an alliance previously unknown was forged among American sisters. CMSW effected a conscientization of American women religious, who developed the self-understanding that occurs when formerly isolated persons congregate and engage in disciplined reflection on their condition.

Good theology also became available to sisters through college and university programs and new publications. Sisters were actively encouraged to take advantage of these opportunities in light of their teaching duties. When the archdiocese sponsored a series of theology lectures at Boston College for sisters in 1952, attendance was mandatory for the sisters of Notre Dame. Sisters of the Presentation heard Johannes Hoffinger lecture at Sister Formation meetings and the University of San Francisco on the "kerygmatic" method in catechetics, which stressed biblical and experiential themes. By 1959 reading lists for Sisters of Charity of Leavenworth included works of contemporary theologians like Guardini, Desplanques, de Guibert, and Kelly.[55] Articles by Thomas Merton and Karl Rahner appeared in *Sponsa Regis,* and the *Sister Formation Bulletin,* edited by Sister Ritamary Bradley, carried judicious suggestions for updated theological fare. In sum, a "biblically and theologically literate population"[56] was developed, as the education of sisters began to partake of the same theological influence that would shape Vatican II.

Still, there seemed little awareness of the profundity of the potential for change thus being created. Reminding the community that Pius XII and the Sacred Congregation of Religious had called congregations to "renew their interior spirit and adapt to the urgent needs of the present day," Mother Benigna Kirkpatrick, superior of the Sisters of St. Joseph of Baden, identified renewal of spirit with "love for our holy habit," which in this case meant not neglecting to have it blessed.[57] Both church officials and religious communities envisioned no basic change in religious life or sisters' occupations. While deep spiritual renewal was desired, it really seems to have meant trying harder; in the case of externals, renewal meant tinkering—whether in ways small, as with details of the habit, or large, as in the massive reorganization of sisters' education.

PARISH

The fifties were the heyday of the American Catholic parish. Prosperity, better education, religious certitude, and up-to-date buildings justified Catholics' sense of well being—"proud of their church and of their priests and of their schools."[58] The center of gravity shifted from city to suburbs. Reflecting on the phenomenon of suburbanization, Jay Dolan observed that the suburban parish simply reproduced the city model—a "parish plant" with church and elementary school.[59] Conspicuously child-centered, the parish invested an enormous share of its resources in the school. With continually rising costs, by 1969 schools would consume as much as 75 percent of the parish budget.[60] In return, the school served to focus a sense of parish solidarity by uniting church and family in a cooperative effort for the sake of the child.

Beyond the socialization of children as Americans and Catholics, the parish school performed vital functions in supporting communal identity: it was a symbol of Catholic subculture to which the entire parish contributed and in some way benefited.[61] Children themselves were drawn at an early age into a sense of closeness and loyalty to the parish through acquaintance with significant adults, their teachers, and clergy, and through the intense liturgical participation provided through the parish school. Adults who may not otherwise have had any communication joined forces through the school with its variety of educational, cultural, or athletic activities, or perhaps through serving in the school cafeteria or library. In 1957 Joseph Fichter concluded that the school brought together "in cooperative action more lay parishioners in a more intimate and functional way than any other program, agency, or group in the parish."[62]

Schools were supported by parishes primarily to inculcate religious values and knowledge, and this was seen (all too much in retrospect) as the task of professional religious—priests, brothers, and sisters. Parents did indeed contribute finances and service toward the operation of the school, but they had essentially no say in what went on there.[63] The Catholic's proverbial "if you caught it in school, you'd get it at home," betrays the truth that church (school) authority was seen as an extension, if not substitute, of parental authority. And schools were in many ways extensions, not so much of the home, as of the religious communities that ran them.

The religious atmosphere of a Catholic school partook of the rarefied convent milieu—a world suffused by religion even in decor, orderly, devotional, highly moral, and operating according to the rhythms of the liturgical year. Catholic schools also kept producing vocations for the religious life and priesthood. Catholics esteemed and even idealized sisters in their sacrificial and "higher" calling, and generally respected the service they gave. In fact, the all-embracing Catholicism of the laity before the council was not so different from that in convents. When he writes of "the intense devotionalism, the piety, the drive of personal sanctity—all coupled with deep loyalty to the church—that was so conspicuous a feature of Catholic life,"[64] Philip Gleason is describing *lay* piety. Such Catholicism was a nursery for religious life, as seen clearly in the numbers that crowded the facilities of novitiates across the country in the 1950s and early 60s.

Sisters took on new schools in greater numbers than ever before and did their best to cope with an enrollment increasing more rapidly than the national average. While the elementary public schools showed a growth of 30 percent in student population between 1950 and 1956, sisters' schools were eight points higher. Catholic elementary schools sustained an increase of nearly one million students, from 2,560,626 in 1950 to 3,544,598 in 1956. During the same period, the average teacher-student ratio in elementary Catholic schools rose from 1:39 to 1:42. Although the number of sisters teaching in elementary schools increased almost 10 percent in the same period, the number of lay teachers nearly tripled.[65] Despite, or perhaps because of, the challenge, it was a time of euphoria and tremendous energy in regard to the schools.

Sister Clare Reese, who began her teaching career in 1951 at twenty years of age in a Pittsburgh suburban parish with nearly two thousand students and four to five classrooms of each grade, described the situation.[66] In addition to a well-built three-story building, the school consisted of the parish's large and deliberately unfinished "upper church." There twelve classrooms with fifty students each were divided by beaverboard partitions about seven feet high. Blackboards, desks, books, and "walls" were packed away every weekend for Sunday Mass. Despite conditions ripe for chaos, Sister Clare recalls, "it was more than survival; we really taught!"—a claim to which the author can attest, having been a fourth-grade pupil in her classroom in 1952 to 1953.

After St. Bernard's, Sister Clare was transferred to Holy Name in the mountain town of Ebensburg, Pennsylvania, where the convent and school were much smaller, but expediency was still the norm. Being "low person on the totem pole," she taught alternately first, fifth, and first grade: "No questions—you did what you were asked." She spoke of the dedication of the sisters, and the mentor system within the convent, "we were training to be a teacher our whole life." The strength of the institution supported identity: "Without verbalizing it, we were imbued with the idea that this was what the church was asking of us. . . . In the early days, I was so caught up with the common task, there was no room for my own vision." Like the rest of the church in those exuberant days, "we were on a roll!"

When Sister Clare arrived at St. Bernard's in 1951, the thirty or so sisters assigned to the school had recently moved into a newly constructed convent, having lived for almost thirty years in two old houses on the parish property where ice formed on the inside of the bedroom walls, and one sister's mother used to call after each severe storm to ask if "that shack" was still standing. Survivors report the new building provided more shelter from the elements, but less from the observant eye of the superior. Within convent buildings, new or old, sisters experienced a great degree of cultural restraint, which in a certain sense paralleled the domestic situation of other women in the 1950s.

The "feminine mystique" in convents was a combination of a child-centered world and a pedestal image. In June 1958 the Massachusetts province of the Sisters of Notre Dame received a copy of a letter sent to the provincial by a woman lately arrived in a New England parish. Anxious about getting her children registered in Catholic schools, the mother of five had written to express both her dismay at crowded conditions, which she described as "dreadful," and her appreciation for the sisters' generous equanimity (they had admitted her child):

> In the midst of all these pressures you Sisters stand out the way Sisters should stand out. In my Protestant husband's eyes, *you* are the Church. He had been almost scandalized by the manners of some religious . . . but you Sisters act the way we expect sisters to act. We know that you sacrifice everything for us and our children, and so we demand more of you. We do not expect you to act or talk the way we do. We watch you so closely.[67]

If sisters internalized this praise with its questionable assumptions about larger-than-life humanity, it was not unlike the expectations for a suburban wife to be well groomed and charming, putting on a good face to soothe her husband, no matter what had gone on with the children that day. For sisters, the feminine stereotype was compounded by religious overtones. "It goes to show how we are all on pedestals," the

Notre Dame superior admonished, "and silently the world looks on to watch how we conduct ourselves." Exalted status for Catholic sisters as idealized models of virtue, however, carried the price tag of remaining dependent, underpaid hired help. If nothing new, it was more pronounced and regulated during the 1950s than ever before.

Sisters maintained continued reserve and apartness from the rest of the parish and all other adults—whether parents of students or lay faculty. A Sister of St. Joseph who entered in 1957 described the school operating as a separate entity—the only meeting point for the average sister with parishioners outside of school was the annual football banquet. As for clergy, "you could never have guessed we were working *together* with the priests." The only other contact came from asking parishioners for rides, for the sisters had no car.[68]

Convent orthodoxy reached its peak in the 1950s. Education was standardized (in theory at least) and formation regulated. Novice mistresses were abreast of canon law for religious, and fewer sisters in parishes lived in virtual shanties. Norms were clear; there was little room and apparently little reason for deviation. It seemed that sisters had finally arrived.

A DECEPTIVE UNITY

The collapse of the Catholic subculture in the 1960s may suggest that underneath the unruffled success of the 50s, all was not well.[69] There were serious problems with the schools by the 50s. James W. Sanders's evaluation of Catholic education in Chicago is valid for the entire country: the school system was a victim of its own success.[70] The "astronomical" numbers of students and the sudden demand for suburban schools led to overcrowding and a critical shortage of religious teachers. Academic standards in the public schools of suburbia were hard to match, and spiraling costs of operating a competitive institution proved enormous when increased salaries for lay teachers were added into the bill. Catholics' agitation for federal aid led to bitter controversy and in the end proved futile. Schools came in for criticism as part of the Catholic intellectualism debate, and from some quarters questions began to surface as to whether such an investment was worth it.

The introduction of new professional demands and educational exposure, without fundamental alteration to the convent system or its interpretive framework, created steadily increasing tensions for sisters. At the same time, communities assumed responsibility for schools in the dioceses where they were and took on works in farther fields— Sisters of the Presentation, for example, extended beyond California, opening houses in Pecos, Albuquerque, and Seattle. Sisters of St. Joseph from Baden went to Georgetown Hospital in Washington, D.C., opened two schools in Florida, and one "missionary" venture (a black parish school in Atlanta, Georgia)—despite thinly veiled objections from the bishop of Pittsburgh.[71] Archives reflect continual anxiety on the part of sisters to meet demands in schools. In 1959 Mother Ursula Lowe wrote to a pastor explaining her inability to supply sisters for his parish in Norco, Louisiana: "At the present time, we are slowly completing the faculties of our schools opened since 1952, which have doubled almost overnight and yet are not adequate to fill the needs."[72] It was a system on overload.

Communities attempted feats worthy of Houdini to keep up with the need for more vocations and to balance their precarious finances. This created a vicious circle, exemplified in the statement of Mother Olivia Hargadon in 1954, explaining the new commitment of the Presentation sisters to staff a high school in Seattle: "This is something we must do so that we may get more vocations."[73] But the fact that there were never enough vocations to carry on staffing remained an unrecognized harbinger of institutional crisis.

Finance was equally uncertain. Parishioners' support of Catholic schools included uncommon generosity to sisters, hauling them about in their cars, supporting benefits for their orders, supplying donations of food and money. This system of largesse compensated for and largely hid the fact that communities were increasingly straitened by trying to meet the cost of professional education on a completely inadequate salary. In 1955–56 the Sisters of Charity of Leavenworth working in schools received between $450 and $720 yearly, depending on the diocese, while school income for Sisters of Charity of Nazareth ranged between $500 and $850, the average being about $700 per year in 1959.[74]

The cost of Catholic schools had tragicomical results for the lives of sisters. In her financial report to the Baden congregation in 1950, Mother Mary Grace Gilboy announced that the community had accumulated $295 interest in the building fund, which she thought could be augmented "by 'hugging' each dollar and putting it to the fund to draw interest." In order to pay off the debt on a new addition to the motherhouse, the Sisters of St. Joseph were asked to raise $100 each during 1957. While "private enterprise, such as selling hand-made articles," was forbidden, the sale of Avon products to relatives and friends was undertaken as a community project.[75] Lists were sent out to the community detailing who had reached the $100 quota. Sisters were reminded repeatedly to moderate their personal requests (such as "unnecessary" street car and bus fares), and income from music lessons was crucial to meeting expenses. The nickel-and-dime ventures of sisters came in for much criticism, but the causes are readily recognized. The two basic problems that gave rise to Sister Formation in the early 1950s remained unsolved at the end of the decade: the shortage of sisters' education and the financial condition of teaching communities.[76]

The upshot of rapid development during the fifteen years following the Second World War was that the Catholic schools had become a system with needs fundamentally beyond the capacity of sisters' congregations to meet. In addition to an institutional crisis of schools not yet fully comprehended, the as yet unforeseen consequences of education were changing the institutional underpinnings of women's religious life.

The original goals of Sister Formation, while essentially conservative in that they sought to meet the institutional needs of the Catholic Church, envisioned genuine personal development for all sisters. According to Sister Mary Emil, Sister Formation aimed at the total education of a sister "to make her a better religious and a better professional person," to prepare her to exercise effective influence "in the spiritual, intellectual, and apostolic life of the church and of our nation."[77] Extensive education, however, resulted inevitably in questioning of the institutions. In *Out of the Cloister*, Helen Ebaugh speaks of this situation as an organizational dilemma. Qualified membership was a necessity for communities to operate accredited institutions; at the same time:

> in the process of preparing professional women for adequate service, many women became exposed to ideas and experiences which were an impetus for changes within the order and to increased numbers of women who ... asked for dispensations from their religious commitment.[78]

Education served to undermine the closed and all-embracing system formerly characteristic of convents and precipitated sisters into the necessity of developing a new integrative framework for their lives. It made them competent and therefore questioning.

The bishop who informed the late Sister Emily George "where it went wrong for sisters" undoubtedly had a point: "When those sisters were educated, they no longer were docile."[79] But education alone is not sufficient to explain what would happen in the 1960s. Equally important is the fact that Sister Formation and its antecedents succeeded in giving sisters splendid preparation for institutions just at the moment when those institutions themselves were on the brink of severe crisis.

As a result of precipitous developments during the 1950s, tensions arose over the conflict between professional demands in schools and an outdated conventual spirituality. By the end of the decade, that conflict had grown, as one sister put it, "almost . . . to the point of absurdity."[80] Familial ways of handling personnel failed to cope with the professional school situation, and, while education was promoted, there was often an unspoken but operative assumption in convents that humility was incompatible with intellect. The internal disparity between professional and religious development became a powerful force moving sisters toward the upheaval of the 60s.

In the face of an unnamed but dimly perceived shift in terrain, valiant attempts were made on the part of administrators to keep the lid on. Officially, for example, superiors strove to reinforce silence and to govern the use of television—on which regulations were sent out by the Vatican in 1957 binding superiors *graviter onerata eorum conscientia* (under serious obligation of conscience).[81] Such efforts at control, if they failed to prevent it, underlined the power of technological culture to make inroads into a cloistered convent milieu. Although actual dimensions of the crisis remained unperceived, far-sighted women realized they were already in a new situation that challenged former solutions. "To use things as we should," wrote one superior in 1958, "to take advantage, *in reason,* of all the modern discoveries which make work so much more effective . . . yet not depart from the spirit of religious Poverty, is a much greater problem now than in more simple days."[82] Although the 50s canonized regularization and professional respectability for sisters, this very process put forces in place that would end the "more simple days" of convent life.

Not only sisters but all Catholics were subject to profound cultural and educational transitions during the postwar period. Only what David O'Brien has called a "superficial unity" masked the tendency to diversity that had been early sown and steadily nurtured in the Catholic community.[83] The 1960s could not have happened without the 1950s. By the end of the decade there were clues—whether a convent schedule adjusted to allow more study time, or three new lay teachers hired in the school—that signaled the evolution already underway that would soon make it impossible to maintain sisters' life and work in parishes as they had been to that time.

9

A TUMULTUOUS DECADE, 1960–1970

In December 1961 Sisters of St. Joseph of Baden received notice that diocesan officials wanted them off the streets at night. The vicar for religious complained that "some members of religious communities" were "repeatedly violating the regulation of being in the convent . . . by seven o'clock."[1] Archbishop Montini of Milan, on the other hand, exhorted sisters in his diocese to break out of their accustomed seclusion:

> In the past it was enough for you to remain within your monasteries, within the convents. Today, you must give up this comfort, this tranquility. Now you will be plunged into the midst of the life of the citizens of the cities of the world.[2]

The contrasting emphases of future pope and Pittsburgh vicar quite accurately capture the situation of Catholic sisters at the beginning of the 1960s. They were perched between two worlds—between the fast-fading seclusion of the past and a future open to the impact of a highly secularized and complex environment.

Although Vatican II catalyzed massive changes in convent life during the 1960s, a central factor in promoting them was the cumulative effect of Sister Formation, CMSW, and the educational emphasis of the preceding decade in preparing a key group of sisters ready to move quickly on the council's call to renewal.[3] Because those sisters were almost unique in their readiness for the council (the only others so prepared were the small number who attended liturgical conferences), the progressive reforms they advocated were costly in terms of painful self-examination in religious communities and widespread dismay and misunderstanding on the part of many Catholics.

What Philip Gleason has aptly called the "seismic" upheaval of the 1960s[4] resulted from the convergence of several streams of change—religious, political, and cultural. Historian David O'Brien isolates three particular movements that coincided during the 1960s to affect the Catholic Church in the United States: the americanization of Catholics, who no longer identified themselves as a religious minority; the

Second Vatican Council, which reversed the Catholic Church's nineteenth-century stance of hostility to modernity; and mammoth disruptions in the social fabric of the United States.[5] All three trends are discernible in the story of sisters during this tumultuous decade.

AMERICANIZATION ACHIEVED

The long struggle for professional competence, so congenial to American values, produced new levels of self-confidence on the part of sisters, and a willingness to question existing custom. Well in advance of the council, superiors and chapters began to initiate changes that, however minuscule, indicated that communities had begun seriously if cautiously to chart their own course. Sisters of Charity of Leavenworth, for example, discontinued wearing large removable sleeves, and Sisters of St. Joseph were finally allowed to wear wristwatches.[6] These innovations were only the tip of an iceberg of growing intolerance for the more extreme restrictions of convent life.

Sister Bette Moslander, who joined the Sisters of St. Joseph of Concordia, Kansas, in 1957 at the age of thirty-five with a Ph.D. in theology, knew from the day she arrived, that "some things had to change . . . they were not humanly defensible." Local superiors and sisters in charge of formation found it increasingly difficult to maintain the convent status quo; it had become too incongruous with the rest of sisters' lives. "If Vatican II had not come along, I'd have invented it!" Sister Katharine Hanrahan, speaking of her days as superior and principal during the early 1960s at St. Joseph's in Bowling Green, Kentucky[7] expressed the sentiments of many sisters at the time.

The dichotomy between professionalization and religious community life was a prime source of strain. Michelle Bernstein's comment that "nuns were trying to do modern jobs under medieval systems"[8] exaggerates only a little. Frustration mounted at what appeared mere formalism: "Week after week we asked permission to do what we could not possibly *not* do. . . . Every day life got smaller. Religious life had become a celebration of the trivial."[9] Records of the Sisters of St. Joseph in 1965 make it clear that part of the difficulty was conflict with American ways. Reasoning that "the custom of kneeling as symbolic of respect and submission has little relevance in our American culture," the general council eliminated it as a requirement on numerous occasions, including asking penances or permissions from a superior.[10] Women in convents reflected the more americanized attitude of Catholics in the post-1930 generation, who simply did not see themselves as separate from the American mainstream. Sisters shared the sense of having arrived felt by many Catholics at the election of John F.

Kennedy. Educated and professionally come of age, they believed that even convent life could at last become American.

Sisters continued to pursue professional accreditation—"our personal responsibility to Holy Mother Church"—still in the face of tremendous odds. In 1962 Sisters of Charity of Nazareth made plans to complete education for the 73.6 percent of their sisters in elementary schools who still lacked degrees (the story of a talented woman who earned a bachelor's degree in 1963 after nineteen years and 228 credits is not an isolated case). At the same time, the congregation faced requisites for high school personnel equipped with masters' degrees, and needed three-fourths sister staff with Ph.D.s if its two colleges were to survive financially.[11] Sisters of Charity of Leavenworth targeted 1973 as the year when all their elementary teachers would have degrees.[12]

During the 60s the nature and quality of education for sisters took a quantum leap forward, particularly in areas theological. Sisters of the Presentation began a program of collaboration with the Jesuits for education and spiritual formation that would have been unthinkable a decade earlier. The location of their motherhouse next to San Francisco University provided ready exposure to scholars of outstanding quality. Among those mentioned in the community annals are Hans Küng, Raymond Brown, Ignatius Hunt, Roland Murphy, Gerald Sloyan, Alfonso Nebreda, Godfrey Dieckmann, Joachim Jeremias, Daniel Berrigan, Karl Stern, Bernard Cook, Bernard Häring, John Tracy Ellis, Victor Francoeur, Charles Curran, Joseph Gelineau, and others. The sisters also attended local institutes covering subjects from liturgy to Marxist-Leninist studies. Reading lists for novices and sisters with temporary vows reflected the new training available to sisters in charge of formation. Authors like Rahner, Schillebeeckx, von Balthasar, Durwell, Ahearn, Davis, and Houtart began to replace Rodríguez and devotional writers.[13]

Intercommunity contacts expanded sisters' horizons. Sister Virginia Mulhern, who studied for a master's degree in mathematics in summers between 1959 and 1964 at the University of Notre Dame, remembers her "consciousness of moving out." In the hootenanies she found herself rubbing shoulders with lay people; exposure to midwest Catholicism and discussions with sisters of other communities provoked a critique of her previous assumptions; professors like Goldbrunner and Häring stimulated new ways of thinking. Returning to her convent in New England, she realized she had learned a foreign language.[14] Her experience could have been described by countless sisters at the beginning of the Second Vatican Council.

VATICAN II

In a striking letter to the Massachusetts province in 1964, Sister Eleanor Joseph of the Sisters of Notre Dame de Namur applied insights of history and biblical theology to community life:

> We religious of the Bible are of today. Hence, we shall always be close to the social problems and challenges of our decade because we are close to God who is using this specific time and place to open upon eternity.[15]

In a challenge to isolationist tendencies, she insisted on the "love of man and of God—in this order, my dear sisters. . . . We biblical religious must become socially responsible for this decade." Sister Eleanor Joseph's emphasis on Bible, gospel values, social responsibility, and human love as a prerequisite to divine represent a decided shift in theological perspective. Her concerns echoed the call for aggiornamento issued from Pope John XXIII and then taking shape in the deliberations and decrees of the Second Vatican Council.

Discussing the revolutionary nature of aggiornamento as a principle of reform, church historian John O'Malley claimed:

> Of all the affective needs felt by Catholics at the time the Council opened in 1962, few were more urgent among Europeans and Americans than the recognition that the Catholic culture ghetto had to be terminated, a new attitude towards the "world" had to be assumed.[16]

While these sentiments may not have been pervasive at the grass roots, they were keen among many religious professionals. Thus, when *The Nun in the World* by Cardinal Suenens, archbishop of Malines-Brussels, appeared in an American edition in 1963, it was devoured by sisters. Its message vibrated in their experience: a "world on the move," a "planetary unit," demanded new response, and that response required new structures. In light of a reformed ecclesiology, distance from the world was no longer seen as an ideal for sisters, and cloister for active communities was called into question: "The chief obstacle to the apostolic advancement of nuns seems to be the conception of enclosure and what it entails."[17] *The Sister Apostle,* which appeared in 1964, expressed many of the same themes as Suenens—this time by a sister, in an American idiom. In the preface, Sister Charles Borromeo Muckenhirn announced, "Contemporary Christians need a new spirituality in view of their relation to the world. The era of private and isolated piety is over."[18]

It would be misleading to suggest that the piety of sisters or of Catholics in general was merely "private and isolated." Sisters had "left the world" *for* the world—service was essential to their vocation. But so was separation. An inherent dualism separated religious and secular, sacred and profane. Church, and therefore sisters, stood firmly with the former. When the Catholic Church abandoned its adversarial stance toward modernity and said the world must be embraced, sisters had to reevaluate their lives.

The most profound influence exerted by Vatican II on religious life was not, as Sandra Schneiders rightly asserts, through its explicit statements on that subject, but in what it said about the church.[19] In "The Call of the Whole Church to Holiness" (chapter 5 of *Lumen Gentium*), the council strongly affirmed the invitation to holiness as universal:

> Thus it is evident to everyone that all the faithful of Christ of whatever rank or status are called to the fullness of Christian life and to the perfection of charity. By this holiness a more human way of life is promoted even in this earthly society.[20]

The council thus spelled the end of two-story Christianity, of a theology that supported a privileged status for vowed religious. The strong social content of the Pastoral Constitution on the Church in the Modern World was perhaps even more influential, pursuing themes familiar from the encyclicals *Ad Petri Cathedram* (1959), *Mater et Magistra* (1961), and *Pacem in Terris* (1963), which sisters had already begun to study.[21] Women with a strongly ecclesial identity, whose experience and training inclined them toward altrium, sisters could hardly ignore the opening words of *Gaudium et Spes:*

> The joys and the hopes, the griefs and the anxieties of the men of this age, especially those who are poor or in any way afflicted, these too are the joys and hopes, the griefs and anxieties of the followers of Christ. Indeed, nothing genuinely human fails to raise an echo in their hearts.[22]

In the face of such evangelical summons, the observance of convent minutiae—being in by seven o'clock, not speaking to parishioners around church doors—seemed a paltry, even contradictory, response.

Sisters made changes in their community life during the 1960s for explicitly religious reasons: "The Church asks of us dynamic thinking; she reminds us that clinging to the status quo, the way we used to do it, may be a form of pride."[23] Superiors mandated prayer for openness to the council and general chapters exhorted sisters to undertake renewal as a matter of obedience to the church. New works were undertaken "as a response of the Congregation to the need to seek out new forms of service to the People of God."[24] The revolution, which seemed so sudden in the mid-1960s, had been in preparation at least since the late 1940s and early 50s, when sisters had heard a call to renewal. They had worked hard to promote it but had been hampered by the needs of the church and attitudes of bishops and priests. They could now call on the council for a mandate.

It may still be asked why change happened so quickly, and why it took the direction it did—departing from structures that had been the hallmark of convent life to that time. The causes are numerous and complex, among them explicit directives of the church to implement renewal, the concerted effort of American congregations supported by national organizations, a massive program of reeducation for sisters at the grass roots, and a simultaneous awakening of the American social conscience.

Ecclesiae sanctae, the 1966 papal directive for implementing the council's decree on religious life, ordered congregations to convoke a special general chapter within three years, "in order to put renewal and adaptation into effect," and also required the revision of constitutions.[25] In the United States, the CMSW supplied a determined effort on the national level to help sisters to prepare for the mandated renewal.

Subsequent chapters and constitutional revisions set the course for radical change in all aspects of sisters' lives, including the expansion of works in order to meet newly perceived needs. For many communities, chapters that were held during the 1960s were the first time there had been systematic community involvement in their preparation. Sisters undertook renewal from the ground up, in that all sisters were called to participate—through study, discussion groups, and recommendations to the chapter. They could not do that without asking questions about their own vocation and that of the community. In a sense, they had to face head-on what challenged the whole church: confronting their own faith in view of the collapse of a supportive substructure. For some sisters, this led ultimately to a decision to leave their communities; for nearly all it meant a radical personalization of the meaning of their lives and ministry.

The process itself was transforming, although it is true that chapter delegates were affected in a way not possible for the entire community.[26] The resulting disparity produced a difficult period of polarization and misunderstanding. It was a time of excruciating pain for congregations when, for the first time in their remembered history, conflicting mentalities had to battle it out over new terrain, with no authoritative formulation ready at hand to settle disputes.

A major effort of the CMSW to aid renewal was the project hatched during the summer of 1964, to do an extensive study of women's religious communities in order to determine what resources they had to respond to the council's document on religious life, then in preparation. The Religious Community Survey, the "Sisters Survey," was mandated by the CMSW in the fall of 1965, coincident with the release of *Perfectae Caritatis*, and entrusted to a committee under the direction of Sister Marie Augusta Neal of Emmanuel College in Boston. The survey, conducted in two parts during 1966 and 1967, included 139,000 individual sisters and covered 88 percent of all the women's congregations in the United States. The survey was immensely significant, not only because of the wealth of information collected but because the questions asked stimulated the minds of sisters participating, particularly a section designed to assess the effect of religious belief on structural change.[27] With extensive questions about reading materials, it forced sisters to reflect on the issue of their own theological perspective and religious formation.

A flood of publications also served to create a massive change within collective mentalities of congregations. The literary market was inundated with books on renewal, some of which show early awareness of many issues that would highlight development for the next twenty years. *The Changing Sister*, published in 1965, included an essay by Sister Marie Augusta Neal, "Sociology and Community Change," which pointed to problems related to demographic shifts, the contemporary search for community, and service organizations hampered by old structures irrelevant to new needs.[28] Other contributors, all sisters, dealt with psychological issues, secularization, and the question of religious life in the American context. The new *National Catholic Reporter* ran a column entitled "Sister's Forum," where women religious could express their views and share experience.

Catholic sisters and their revolution became topics in *The Christian Century*, *The Saturday Evening Post*, and *America*.[29] The cover of the Christmas issue of *Newsweek* in 1967 portrayed Sister Corita Kent before and after her change of habit, and a feature article, entitled "The Nun, A Joyous Revolution," spoke of sisters' "desire to be creative neighbors to those in need outside church walls."

Sisters were forming a new understanding of church—derived from the council itself, and from their own sustained efforts to gain competence in theology. Commenting on the difficulty of figuring out what it meant to be a formation director between 1966 and 1970, Sister

Katharine Hanrahan recalled, "My little red Vatican II book was my treasure." In all the congregations studied, at both administrative and grass-roots levels, the determination of sisters to unlock the contents of that treasure for themselves is evident. In 1968 the general chapter at Leavenworth identified one of the congregation's greatest needs as education in "Scripture, sacramental life and liturgy, theology, the social doctrine and mission of the Church, missology and ecumenism." The assembly decreed "that as soon as possible sisters be prepared in the above areas of study as teachers or resource people for the community." By fall 1969, three sisters were studying full-time for master's degrees in theology at Fordham and the University of San Francisco. One of them, Sister Mary Cele Breen, reported that she spent the entire academic year of 1971–72 sharing what she had learned with local communities of the congregation.[30]

Communities also discovered that their new candidates suddenly "didn't buy it" any more: "They did the unbelievable. They asked 'Why?'"[31] The postwar generation proved a different breed. They had been raised in the increasingly independent, motorized atmosphere of the 1950s and some had experienced the social tensions of the 60s firsthand. They wanted answers; and if answers were lacking, they refused to cooperate. Young persons introduced a rebellious element into communities whose older members had already begun seriously to question the status quo.

Wary of formalism, seeking closer relationship to the people they felt called to serve, some sisters moved into small communities where they hoped to recover the more simple and charismatic experience of their origins. In her anthropological study of nuns in the 70s Suzanne Campbell-Jones compared their responses to that of hippies, critical and disillusioned with society:

> They took up their folk guitars, asked for greater poverty in their daily lives and celebrated their small communities as a social fellowship—with the church's sacrament of the Eucharist as their principal ritual. Further . . . they idealized their world to create a "kingdom on earth" like so many other communitarians before them.[32]

By the end of the 60s the key issue for sisters was no longer professionalism for the specific works of the congregation, but rather how to understand themselves as community, and how to deal with a new world. The process of transformation in convents was at first internal, directed toward outdated customs and practices that impeded efficiency in apostolic occupations. Soon, however, it involved a radical redefinition of mission, stemming in part from awareness of the urgent social issues that captured the attention of Americans during the 60s.

SOCIAL REVOLUTION

The revolutionary social situation that sisters experienced during the 1960s, both in Latin America and in the United States, contributed significantly to the reversal of their previous mind-set.

Pope John XXIII had requested American congregations to send 10 percent of their personnel south of the border. Although that quota was never reached, sisters' eager response is evident in the fact that congregations researched opened at least one mission in South or Central America during the 1960s or early 70s. The overseas service of some members would impact the overall communities in enormously significant ways. Experts in education or health care set off, realizing they would be neophytes in language studies. They soon discovered they had much more than that to learn.

Letters of the three teachers and two nurses who left Leavenworth for Talara, Peru, in 1963 allow us a glimpse of the Latin American experience. The new missionaries found their way of life did not work in Peru. First, it was the habit—too hot, impossible to keep clean, and veils blew off in the strong winds. Gradually, the American sisters discovered their mentality needed to change as well. The five related their awakening to the social and political realities of their new country when their first trip through a Lima *barriada* brought them face to face with the harsh poverty they had only observed at a distance:

> Wouldn't the promise of Communism look good. . . . Suddenly we saw the countless numbers who sold oranges, tortillas, granadillas, bananas, candy, sweet drinks, cakes, all along every sidewalk. And we saw the man selling air mail envelopes through the mercado. And we saw them in an entirely different light. What must it be to have spent the day extolling fruit that no one wanted and go home to a hovel in a barriada one penny richer.[33]

The sisters' previous views on religious "poverty" were also quickly disabused. They told of a man who brought them the gift of a large live crab to thank them for saving the life of his sick child:

> Just this little display of gratitude is very rewarding for the fact that it is so rare. This is not to say that the people are not grateful; the

problem is very simple. "The rich gringo sisters have things they don't need; why shouldn't they give them to us?"[34]

In the face of such overwhelming need, the artificial confines of conventual life seemed suddenly meaningless. The experience was radicalizing.

Sisters had arrived in Latin America, moreover, at the moment when Vatican II, the Medellín Conference, and growing revolutionary awareness created drastic demands on a church formerly connected with the political establishment. In a sobering review of North Americans' first decade in Latin America, church leaders from both continents agreed that their continued presence would be useful only if they would help to form laity for leadership in the local church, identify with the poor, and be open to new forms of religious life.[35] The Latin American experience served in the long run to reshape communities' self-understanding, and the result became institutionalized when they incorporated service of the poor and work for social justice in their revised constitutions and criteria for corporate commitments.

At home, the 60s in the United States also proved revolutionary, with the tumultuous unrest of racial violence, Vietnam, campus protests, and the abandonment of traditional sexual mores. For many sisters, a heightened level of social awareness began, as did so much in contemporary American history, with the civil rights movement. Sisters frequently had their first encounter with civil rights through inner-city schools or summer programs. Violence over school integration in the south during the late 50s and the Civil Rights Act of 1960 brought issues of racial discrimination to the fore. As early as 1961, several religious communities in Chicago city schools had begun to plan a cooperative effort that became the Urban Apostolate of Sisters. Its program of education, communication, and action included visits to homes of students and cooperation with civil and religious leaders.[36]

By the mid-1960s it had become common for sisters to watch television and read newspapers, and the media exercised a profound affect on their social consciousness. In March 1965 nearly fifty sisters marched in Selma, recruited in response to televised beatings of marchers by police earlier that month.[37] When sisters viewed television pictures of their own members directly involved in the civil rights movement, many wondered how, in the light of gospel, it was possible for them to stay home.

Sisters who became social activists in the 60s often had their basic training in schools, or in the Catholic church's program for racial justice. Sister Margaret Cafferty's began at home, where she learned as a child that her family never crossed a picket line.[38] As a sister, she taught social sciences at Presentation schools, with an educational background in political science and economics, including an eye-opening eight weeks in a race relations class at U.C. Berkeley during the summer of 1965. The following year, as part of the diocesan social justice program, she visited over fifty San Francisco parishes, speaking on "Sociological Foundations of Racial Prejudice." It provided her first exposure to hostile audiences.

The racist reactions of some Catholics and the de facto segregation of most Catholic schools began to raise questions about the effectiveness of Catholic schools at educating Christians. Civil rights was also important in awakening participants to the religious meaning of the secular. Recounting the New York rent strike of 1965, Mother Patricia Barret observed that it "led nuns and priests who had hitherto remained pretty exclusively in their churches to broaden their concept of the people of God."[39] The whole inner-city experience brought together the three streams of mature American identity, new ecclesiastical orientations, and current social conditions that precipitated the explosive changes of the 1960s.[40]

For sisters like Margaret Cafferty, reading the signs of the times and the gospel led to direct social action. She was one of the eight sisters in the grape pickers' march from Delano to Sacramento led by Cesar Chavez and the National Farm Workers of America in April 1966. In October 1968, when she heard the noise of the first race riots in San Francisco, secure on the balcony of Presentation convent where she was saying the rosary, the experience left her with a need to be much closer, to have direct involvement in social change. As a beginning, she moved into an apartment in a condemned building in Sacred Heart parish with sisters from two other communities.

In January 1966 the mayor of San Francisco appointed to the Human Rights Commission Sister Mary Bernadette Giles, whom we met as a pioneer parish visitor at St. Agnes in the Haight-Ashbury district in 1943. She was still there in 1966. Her practice for city commissioner came from parish experience, where her combination of catechetical and social work involved her in multiple civic contacts, including the housing commission and the local public school. In 1967 she originated the highly successful "Summer of Love," a program which eventually involved twelve San Francisco parishes and reached over three thousand children of various racial and religious origins. "It started as a CCD project in St. Agnes Parish, a Bible school open to all the children of the neighborhood in 1966," Sister Bernadette explained: "Then in 1967 the Bible School became a Summer of Love at the height of the 'Flower children' invasion of the Haight-Ashbury." Sister

Bernadette's activities have also included supervising a government-funded program for teaching reading to inner-city children, advocacy on behalf of Soviet Jewry, and serving on a city commission for the aging—a marvelous diversity of interests, all rooted in concern for the parish. "It started with a CCD program."[41]

Sister Bernadette's involvement in the parish outside the school represents a movement, encouraged by Rome particularly from the 1930s on, to attend to the religious education of nonparochial school children. CCD work in parishes was pioneered by lay people in this country, but sisters frequently taught catechism after school and on weekends, both in their own parishes and in outlying districts that had no school. Various congregations, like the Trinitarians and Mission Helpers of the Sacred Heart, worked specifically outside the Catholic school system. Lacking the strong institutional base provided by school, perhaps those sisters were more directly exposed to the social problems of parishioners, and more sensitized to the need for political structures to address them.

The social agenda of the 60s, providing funds as well as motivation, paralleled sisters' religious values and moved them (not only veteran organizers like Sister Bernadette) into contact with the secular environment. Sister Judy Raley, who became a student at Kent State in 1968, related that for her events there "blew open a secure world."[42] Step by step, sisters entered a wider universe, and to a very significant degree, this happened through individual members whose experience gradually became part of the community's self-understanding.

Exposure to issues obviously of more moment than some point of convent custom began to effect a radical shift in the focus of authority. Sisters who were refused permission to march in Selma and other civil demonstrations began to question the validity of that kind of obedience. One woman said emphatically, "Even without permission I would have gone."[43] In a wider perspective, it is clear that convent authority structures came under the same scrutiny as the ecclesiastical, when Catholics had to deal with *Humanae Vitae* in 1968, or those of the American government, when citizens opposed its policy in Vietnam. Some sisters did participate in antiwar protest and civil disobedience—Marjorie Melville of Maryknoll, for example, was sentenced to jail in 1970 for her role in the Catonsville 9, along with the more famous Berrigans.

OUT OF THE CLOISTER

What did it mean that sisters had gone from the narrow, if significantly perforated, confines of convent life in 1960 to living in apartments and questioning the morality of obeying a superior's command?

When the sustaining myth of religious life as a better, upper-story Christianity dissolved in light of an ecclesiology of the entire people of God called to holiness, there was no longer any reason for sisters actively involved in the needs of society to maintain the apparatus of cloister, which signaled a sharp distinction between the sacred world of the convent and the secular realm outside. When Vatican II spelled the end of the separation of church and world, the convent-world dichotomy came to an end as well.

Sisters' change of habit (itself a kind of portable cloister) was highly symbolic of a new relationship with the world. Women who for years had accepted the inconvenience of starch, pleats, long skirts, and layer upon layer of material simply stopped doing so. There was no longer any need to place such distance between "virtuoso" Christianity and contemporary life. Abandonment of the habit raised a howl of protest within convents and outside; some orders attempted delicate public relations strategy to push their new look.[44] The fact that sisters were allowed to drive cars, visit their families, read what they wished, and go to movies all related to the end of the censorship, restrictions on mobility, and contact with other adults, which were formerly used to ensure cloister. The elimination of cloister was, sociologically, a radical change. Its demise collapsed a whole symbolic pattern that to a large extent had provided sisters with identity and secured them a recognized place in the ecclesiastical regime.

Loss of cloister ended the previous closed society of convent life and made sisters reevaluate a long tradition in which *contemptus mundi* had meant separation. Inevitable questions were raised about "the most ecclesial becoming worldly." Communities appealed to their founding experience and legitimated agonizing change in the name of fidelity to gospel and charism.[45] Often this reformulation of basic beliefs resulted in behaviors directly opposed to previous norms: conversation with parishioners, for example, was now considered holy, part of witnessing to Jesus Christ in the world.[46]

Sisters in mufti, moreover, signaled the destruction of an elitist understanding of religious life. Like the Catholic Church in the French Revolution, with loss of privilege, sisters were faced with the enormous challenge of working out a new relationship with the larger society. Unprotected status was at times tied to sisters' new ministries, as when Margaret Cafferty faced hostile response from Catholics for the first time when she dared to articulate the facts of racism. Whether perceived as capitulation or commitment, a new orientation toward the world was the most profound reality underlying all change in convent life during the 60s and it had concrete effects in the works sisters chose to do.

NEW WORKS FOR SISTERS

The 1968 publication *New Works of New Nuns*[47] signaled a situation already widespread—sisters had begun to move beyond their traditional occupations of health care and teaching in Catholic institutions. In 1967 Sister Mary Luke Tobin, president of CMSW, who had been one of the four nonclerical American observers at the council, wrote an essay, "The Mission of the Religious in the Twentieth Century." She spoke of the "ardent desire on the part of religious everywhere to be where the Church is." This, she said, would call for a profound renewal of faith, accompanied by a second level of conversion: "The Christian today must vitally concern himself with the world of today. It is no longer permitted to avoid it, to ignore it, or merely to tolerate it." The contemporary world continued to require sisters' traditional works, but, in her estimation, it also begged concern for "the ever larger number of Catholics who are not reached by the present commitments of Orders and Congregations."[48]

By 1967 sisters could already be found in a plethora of ministries: urban parochial and civic programs, educational and advocacy work with migrants and in Appalachia, alcoholism counseling, university and seminary teaching, campus chaplaincy with Newman clubs, and government posts funded through agencies for the "Great Society"—sisters worked with Head Start, Job Corps, and VISTA. All this received an upbeat review from Michael Novak in his 1966 essay for the *Saturday Evening Post*, "The New Nuns," in which he depicted sisters as "the vanguard of all Americans who believe in God."[49]

Innovative experiments resulted from two evolutionary developments within religious communities: a new sociological perception of societal needs and the replacement of a pyramidal mode of governance by a consensual, inclusive pattern of decision-making. Taking seriously the conciliar principles of collegiality and subsidiarity, sisters tried to remodel their communities. An instruction from the superior of the Sisters of St. Joseph in 1965 indicates it was uncharted territory:

> The inspiration for the procedure we are following in regard to Chapter preparations lies in the principle of collegiality which contains, of course, the concept of shared authority. Since this principle, so forcibly enunciated and demonstrated by Vatican II, can provide at best only the most general guidelines for our present endeavor, we are constantly facing problems for which there are no ready-made answers, nor simple solutions, nor even written canons to serve as norms.[50]

In the name of collegiality, communities began to adopt policies whereby no sister would be given an assignment without her participation in the decision. Very quickly many asked to do work other than teaching school.

Discussing the sociological implications of this change, Helen Ebaugh identified it as a further collapse of the closed society through the introduction of personalist values into a totalist system. The inevitable result was erosion of the former absolute commitment of members to the institutional work of the community.[51] Personal development is certainly cited by numerous sisters as a significant factor in their change of occupation. Reflecting on the frequently expressed desire to work with adults, one personnel director said she believed sisters suddenly realized that they "could relate to people outside the community—adults!. . . . They discovered they were competent, bright. . . . Not that we thought less of teaching; we found a new dimension within ourselves [which was] highly relational."[52]

The issue of growing up emotionally as well as professionally is mentioned over and over by sisters as an undeniable factor in the choice of some to move out of institutional, technical structures. That such a motive was heard at all reflects the distance communities had come in the few short years since school assignments for September were delivered unilaterally on August 15.

A choice of different work, closely related as it was to the restructuring of convent government, was not simply an issue of personal preference. The abolition of absolute monarchy in convents reflected the reality of a complex world in which no one person was any longer able to control all the facets of a community's life and work. The Sister Formation Conference warned superiors in 1965 that sisters were in danger of being discounted for government grants because, when awarded, they were too often unable to accept them because of permission withheld.[53] The old way had run so much on its own steam that superiors could command and achieve as they saw fit. That was a bygone day.

Numerous sisters began to doubt that schools were enough, and sought ways of reaching adults and children not included in the school system. It was not a unique idea. Cardinal Ritter, at the Second Vatican Council, had intervened before the vote on the *Declaration on Christian Education* to insist that schools must not be the church's only concern, since in fact most Catholic children in the world were in state schools. Similarly, in 1968 the NCEA changed its constitution to encompass a broader goal, stating that the organization was at the service of society, rather than only the Catholic schools.[54] All these developments, supported by a theology of "living the gospel in the world," were part of the phenomenon of the Catholic Church's moving out of the ghetto, of which its institutions had been a bulwark.

Sometimes a sister's move from school happened precisely in the context of a deeper realization of the intimate connection between school and parish. For Sister Michelle Prah that insight "changed school from a learning institution to a community," and opened her eyes to the need for cooperation at other levels of parish if the school were to be genuinely effective. Her consequent desire to be more closely involved with the larger parish led to a history of almost twenty years in catechetics and parish ministry.[55]

Behind this new approach to apostolic work lay a very significant change in sisters' understanding of their mission. From viewing it as a collective responsibility for institutional work, always with a supernatural end in view, mission came to be seen as a personal response to the gospel, made within the historical commitments and charismatic orientations of one's community. Individuals were expected to observe and assess the way they could best serve the needs of society.

Issuing assignments for the first time as superior of the Sisters of the Presentation in 1964, Mother M. William [Joan] Murphy appealed to the section of their rule which affirmed that "all sisters, however occupied, shared in the apostolate of the congregation."[56] Her comment underlines the transformation of apostolate (or mission) from a specific institutional task to a more abstract, flexible notion having to do with the charism of the community. It signaled the reversal of the earlier twentieth-century development, which, in light of a rigidly hierarchical notion of church and institutional needs, had defined apostolate as a specific function delegated by the hierarchy and performed by communities under their direction. In Weberian terms, it was the routinization of charism; in practice, a completely functional approach to the meaning of religious orders within the church. Where the idea of church changed, works of sisters began to diversify.

One Presentation sister was assigned to full-time Newman work at San Jose State College for the fall of 1966, and during the same year plans were made to have four sisters trained for parish ministry—an administrative decision that produced considerable criticism within the Presentation community because it meant four fewer sisters in school. Similar patterns appear after 1965 in all the congregations studied. Sisters of St. Joseph, for example, had opened a new parish catechetical center in 1963 and started Newman work in 1965. Sisters of Charity of Nazareth adopted an urban and Appalachian focus, consciously reclaiming an older congregational tradition of strong investment in social work. Sisters of Charity of Leavenworth closed a children's home in Helena, Montana, because of the transitions to foster care, marking the general societal trend toward deinstitutionalization.[57] Simultaneously, the ecclesiastical voice called for a new focus, and communities tried earnestly to answer the question put to them in *Evangelica Testificatio* by Paul VI in such poignant and challenging terms: "How . . . will the cry of the poor find an echo in your lives?"[58]

By 1969 major diversification of sisters' employment was already a fact, even in congregations previously confined to schools. The trend affected parishes and moved a number of sisters into activities organized at the diocesan level or by secular agencies. Seven Sisters of the Presentation were appointed to parishes in 1969–70 for work that was not school-related. Sisters of Notre Dame de Namur, founded as a teaching congregation, interpreted their foundress's nineteenth-century directive toward the "most neglected places" as a mission in 1969 "to bring the good news to the poor." In light of that decision, the Massachusetts provincial asked for volunteers for service in rural Maine, which would involve extensive travel and mean living most of the time in a trailer.[59]

If sisters' taking on works other than school in the late 1960s was consistent with religious priorities, it posed a ministerial dilemma, for Catholic schools were already facing a critical shortage of sister-teachers. Sisters' decisions were incomprehensible to many Catholics, who often blamed them for the decline in the parochial school system. It is certainly true that congregations ceased to concentrate all their personnel in the schools. It is also true that sisters could not have changed the balance in favor of Catholic schools—that problem was the result of runaway growth in process since the end of the 1940s. But the issue is so important for the history of parishes it must be examined.

THE SCHOOL CRISIS

In October 1963 *Look* ran an article entitled "Trouble Ahead for the Catholic Schools," accompanied by a photo essay on "The Vanishing Nun."[60] The "vanishing" epithet proved prophetic, but in 1963 it was hardly true. In 1963 there were more sisters than ever, 104,441 of them, teaching in Catholic educational institutions.[61] Noting a 129 percent increase in enrollment in Catholic schools since 1940 (compared to 53 percent in public schools) the author, Jack Starr, pointed to a shortage of sisters and lack of funds for lay teachers as creating a dilemma in the schools, which had become the source of much critical attention due to overcrowding and fear of inferior educational standards. One unnamed superior said sisters were "in the middle of it," finding it hard to keep a limit of fifty students for each classroom—some women in her community were dealing with numbers as high as ninety.

Predictions then suggested 1970 for the year lay teachers would outnumber sisters in the schools (it actually came in 1968).[62] Still communities scrambled to fill slots. A revealing example of the strain on congregations and the lengths they took to provide school personnel is found in Mother Mary Isabel's letter to the Sisters of St. Joseph in July 1961:

> Sisters, the bulletin could have gone out last week; the delay was the inexorable task of finding, of "creating" sisters. Generously, Sisters who are scarcely able for duty expressed their willingness to serve for another year. Willingly (or reluctantly) pastors released a faculty member where we thought such action would not work a severe hardship on the school. . . . Several sisters accepted our decision to interrupt their educational programs. . . . The Hospital released to the schools on a temporary basis three members of their staff.[63]

Despite this tour de force of robbing Peter to pay Paul, new schools stood empty, waiting only for teachers.[64] Sisters simply could not begin to meet the needs, a reality only partially understood by the clergy and laity, and possibly by the sisters themselves. "Many bishops and priests have realized that this is so," wrote Mother Lucille to the Sisters of Charity of Nazareth in 1962; "others have not yet come to this realization." Four years later the congregation's general chapter still strove to impress the facts of the school situation clearly upon sisters, and enlisted their aid in making them understood.[65]

During this period, criticism of the schools escalated. In 1960 Myron Liebermann, in view of what he judged low performance, challenged the superintendent's department of the NCEA to do scientific research on Catholic schools. Mary Perkins Ryan questioned the advisability of a Catholic school system in her 1964 *Are Parochial Schools the Answer?* By 1967 church officials, as well as the *New York Times,* were debating the morality of schools "increasingly serving a middle-class and upper-middle-class . . . population." The president of the NCEA, Bishop Ernest J. Primaeau of Manchester, New Hampshire, admitted that Catholic education had been "smug, content—and badly out of touch."[66] Overall problems of finance and personnel were immense. Yet the worst of the crisis lay hidden, just beyond the horizon. Responding to an NCEA study in April 1966, the Sisters of Charity of

Leavenworth reported 43 percent or 400 sisters of 932 active members, involved in elementary education, and another 15.4 percent in secondary. They anticipated no appreciable change in this pattern during the next five years.[67]

Five years later, in 1973, the Leavenworth community's contingent in elementary schools had shrunk by nearly one-half; they then counted only 205 sisters employed at that level.[68] Nationally, the picture for Catholic schools in the second half of the 1960s is catastrophic. Between 1964, when parish elementary schools peaked at 4,476,881 students, and 1969, they lost nearly 880,000 students in a slide beginning in 1965. As far as teachers were concerned, the number of sisters in schools started a steady decline from the high point in 1963 (when they numbered 104,441), to 85,616 teaching sisters in 1969. Numbers of lay teachers, on the other hand, more than doubled during the 1960s from 45,506 in 1959 to 98,001 in 1969. Lay teachers outnumbered sisters by 1968.[69] What happened?

Fundamentally, there was a dramatic and unforeseen decline in numbers of Catholic sisters, which began with severely falling entrance rates after 1963, accompanied by a simultaneous rise in the rate of sisters who left communities. From 765 sisters leaving in 1960, the number rose to 1,562 in 1965, and jumped drastically to 2,015 in 1967. In 1970, the peak year for departures, 4,337 sisters left their orders.[70] The years between 1967 and 1970 produced a hemorrhage in convent life, which seriously debilitated a congregation's capacity to provide personnel for institutional commitments.

The baby boom had come into the schools, but very few of their number ever entered convents. Signs of decline in candidates began in 1963, the year when women born after World War II would have been ready for convents. A 1961 study showed that, while Catholics revered sisters, they preferred someone else's daughter to make the sacrifice.[71] The reason why sisters left is extremely complex, and perhaps not yet fully understood. Structural changes in convents during the 1960s allowed for questioning previously precluded by the mechanisms of a closed society, and to some extent lessened personal commitment to the community on the part of many members. Education, furthermore, provided sisters with contacts in other ways of life as well as marketable skills. Leaving, in other words, had become a psychological and economic possibility for anyone who desired it. With the abandonment of cloister and the end of split-level Catholicism, a way of life whose rewards were largely symbolic became in a sense more costly.[72] The question of religious vocation was brought into radical focus, and in fact every thinking member of a congregation was forced either to leave or to redefine what was meant by religious life.

Assessing the cause for the decline in Catholic schools after 1965, James W. Sanders proposed the end of Catholic alienation in American society and huge costs, but mainly a certain disenchantment that made Catholics less willing to pay the bill for schools. This he ascribes on the one hand to the massive replacement of religious by lay teachers, thereby making the schools seem less "Catholic," and on the other, to the new teachings of Vatican II, which presented values in the schools not recognized as familiar. As a result, "the more conventional began to find the Catholic school too liberal, while the more liberal found it unnecessary."[73]

The dream of "every Catholic child in a Catholic school" remained unrealized; by the end of the 1960s it was fading fast. Even the American bishops, longtime champions of the schools, opted for realism:

> Like our colleagues in the teaching apostolate, we do not wish to go beyond our means, not to dilute quality for the sake of quantity, nor to expend excessive resources on one kind of education with consequent neglect of other forms.[74]

By the end of the decade Catholics—parishioners, priests, bishops, sisters—still highly valued the Catholic school, but they were much more inclined to view it as one way of many to educate youth, and seemed less willing to sacrifice everything for its survival.

If the diminished number of sisters available to teach made the viability of Catholic schools more precarious, this was due less to planned change for moving into other works, than to the unforeseen trauma of a net loss of nearly twenty-eight thousand sisters between 1965 and 1970. The decrease of sisters in schools during this period was actually less than the total—25,461. As the years went on, of course the cumulative impact in schools was even greater, because those who had left convents were chiefly of working age, and were never replaced by comparable numbers entering: whereas between 1958 and 1962, there had been 32,433 new candidates for sisterhoods, the number for 1971–75 was only 2,590.[75]

To make this picture concrete, we may look at the Sisters of St. Joseph of Baden, who in 1965 numbered 636 professed sisters, plus 93 novices and postulants. Their membership in 1988 includes 400 professed sisters, of whom approximately one-third are over seventy years of age, eight novices and postulants. Of the entire community, 30.4 percent are still involved in education in 1988, of whom 22.3 percent are in elementary schools. It is the second largest single category of "apostolic labors," exceeded only by "ministry of prayer" (23.5 percent), which essentially represents retired sisters.[76]

When communities espoused new works in the 60s, they were not indifferent to existing institutional commitments. Citing their constitutions, Sisters of Charity of Nazareth argued: "we are not free to withdraw from established schools, hospitals, or orphanages in order to take up some other work which may seem to offer greater apostolic opportunities."[77] That was in 1965, before the impact of small novitiates and large numbers leaving had begun to affect the work force. By the early 1970s the whole system had broken down at the level of personnel, and then it seemed somewhat ridiculous to insist that individual sisters remain in institutions against their better judgment, when what was needed was an army.

In the parish, vocational crisis was felt primarily in the schools where, by 1970, large-scale withdrawals had begun on the part of congregations studied. In some places communities were unable to provide even a skeleton crew. The reality of the situation was so unpalatable to all concerned that parish, diocese, and religious community frequently indulged in a game of "pass the buck," with no one taking responsibility for action. Some dioceses or local school boards and parish councils did take initiative, however, as with the 1969 closing of elementary and secondary schools by local authorities in Butte and Helena, who cited financial problems resulting from the acute shortage of religious.[78] Individual sisters found themselves faced with painful decisions. Sister Kathleen Healy eventually chose to leave a progressive school that had been her brainchild, St. Teresa in San Francisco, because of her conviction that the school system promoted inevitable injustice, due to its inability to meet the individual needs of children, and in particular because it could no longer be afforded by the poor.[79]

Sisters' migration from standard schools to alternate works created tension within communities about "apostolic priorities" and provoked clashes with clergy over congregational works and internal discipline. Two notorious cases are the disputes of the Glenmary Sisters with Archbishop Karl Alter of Cincinnati, and the Sisters of the Immaculate Heart of Mary with Cardinal McIntyre of Los Angeles. In both cases, episcopal ultimatums resulted in a decision by the majority of each community to elect noncanonical status.

Numerous congregations did attempt dialogue with clergy and parishioners over their service in the schools, which in some cases proved fruitful for future planning.[80] Sisters of St. Joseph, for example, invited parish representatives to be part of their self-study during the early 70s, and in the last part of the decade attempted to work out a "parish plan" with pastors and parishioners in every place where they staffed schools.[81] There was great resistance to accepting the reality of communities' real inability to provide teachers, and many parish schools simply lost sisters year after year through gradual attrition, without any serious programs for change.

CONSEQUENCES

Between 1960 and 1970, not only sisters, but all Catholics suffered the disappearance of a symbolic cultural milieu, a loss exaggerated in convents because there it had been so rich and comprehensive. In religious communities, the supernatural referent and religious values remained intact, but the symbol system that embodied them was in large part transformed. Change was legitimated by appeal to the gospel, to the charismatic origins of the congregation, and fidelity to the Holy Spirit working in the present. Theologically, there had been a shift of emphasis from an eschatological interpretation of religious life as a foretaste of eternity, to an incarnational focus on cooperation with the action of God in the world.[82] Sisters, who had represented the "old church" to the utmost, painfully embodied the postconciliar crisis of that church—in them it was acute.[83]

The exhilarating feelings of the early 60s, of being stretched and reaching beyond—all at the behest of the *church*—had produced tremendous energy and optimism, as voiced by one woman: "I was proud to be a daughter of the church."[84] In the long process of change, sisters relinquished the pedestals they had occupied in 1950 Catholicism, and found their chief product, the schools, no longer secure. Diminished numbers meant sisters could no longer run the schools on their own resources. When congregations lost institutional control of schools, hospitals, and other facilities, they lost the corporate works that had formed so much of their identity in the past. No longer upper-class Christians, neither were religious the backbone of the church's institutional labor force.

Sisters had undertaken the risky venture of trying to reform a highly authoritarian way of life, and found that it demanded nothing less than reformulation of their identity and sense of mission. The significance of this painful yet exciting period is that what happened to sisters during the 1960s would and did happen to the church at large, and to the parish. Questions about institution, purpose, or mission, and relation to the world were dilemmas posed for the entire church, and Catholics, knowingly or not, were forced to ask: What is the church, and what purpose does it serve?

10

DIMINISHMENT, DISILLUSION, DISCOVERY, 1970–

The 1970s were costly for the nation, for Catholics, for sisters. During this decade, the country went through Richard M. Nixon, Watergate, the dreary end of American involvement in Vietnam, and the "me" generation. A spirit of passivity and withdrawal prevailed when, after so much action and involvement, the 1960s had failed to change the world. Catholicism had consented, in Langdon Gilkey's phrase, to "confront modernity," but the price was high: the blurring of hard and fast boundaries meant it was no longer so clear what it meant to be Catholic.[1] Church attendance in general declined. Many Catholics came into the 70s confused and disillusioned about both church and country. Sisters, in hopes of a new creation, had risked the most radical changes in their remembered history—and suffered massive decline in membership and the possible demise of their greatest single contribution to the church in America, the parochial school.

Yet potential for real gain lay beneath the surface and, as Jay Dolan points out in his history of American Catholics, that gain was spiritual—a heritage from the 60s. American society was "substantially changed" in its concern for social justice, and new values emerged as accepted moral priorities: "Women's rights, concern for the environment, racial justice, political accountability, and a desire for peace in a nuclear age had become part of the American mainstream."[2] Similar concerns were alive in the church, where papal encyclicals, a Roman synod, and pastoral letters of American bishops sounded themes of world peace, racial equality, and global justice.

Women's religious communities were deeply affected by the social and religious trends. Looking at congregational records for the 70s, one's first impression is continued loss in terms of numbers, institutional works, and finances. The exodus from convents did ebb sharply in 1971, when 1,191 sisters left communities, a drop of more than three thousand from 1970, the peak year for departures. After 1975 there was a slight upturn in the numbers of women entering communities, but the small gains represented in these figures in no way compensated the loss of the preceding ten years. Marie Augusta Neal points out "the stark contrast of 34,448 entering and making vows in the nine-year period from 1948 through 1957 and only 6,349 in the nine-year period 1966 through 1975 . . . a drop of 81 percent."[3] The numerical balance in communities had been permanently altered.

The trauma of such sudden decrease inflicted immense grief and shock on those who remained. Sister Rosalie Curtin remembers dreading the arrival of community letters, bound to contain news of the latest departures. She experienced the loss of good friends, feelings of rejection, and the nagging question: "What do they know that I don't?"[4] The median age in communities rose; for Sisters of the Presentation it was 52 in 1976, ten years later it would be 62.[5] Youth in congregations shifted from North America to developing countries. Whereas Sisters of Notre Dame de Namur in 1967 had by far their greatest percentage of sisters in formation in the United States, by 1986 it was in Zaire.[6] Sisters of Charity of Nazareth counted their largest numbers of novices in India. Although vocations continued to trickle in to American communities by the 1980s, current statistics locate the future of traditional women's congregations in Africa, Asia, and South America.

Religious communities also suffered the loss of corporate works, which in this country had been the hallmark of women's congregations. As a result of the drastic loss of sisters, communities could no longer control their works as they had, through the relatively independent regulation of institutional personnel. Sisters of the Presentation acknowledged the new situation in their 1986 chapter report: "Realistically, the congregation is not the only factor making decisions about ministry." They admitted that diversity in works had posed problems about identity:

> The congregation faces the challenge then of identifying a common focus in our diversity, of helping sisters to integrate that focus into their own choices so that they feel they "belong" within the Presentation mission.[7]

The process of grappling with identity held the possibility of radical renewal for communities. Sisters began to ask penetrating questions about their charism, mission, and role in the church. Justice emerged as an urgent contemporary issue, and historical research revealed to many communities that they had been founded specifically to help the poor. But solutions to the problems of identity and mission were riddled with a new sense of collective diminishment, voiced pointedly by

Sisters of the Presentation. What does it mean, they asked, to follow the footsteps of an Irish foundress who risked everything to assist the indigent of her day, "when we find that often we are not where the poor are, nor do we speak their language, nor have the skills for the ministry they need, nor the energy to begin again?"[8] Rediscovering the founding spirit was not the same as making it live. One sister's trenchant comment described the irony of the 70s: "At the highest sense of mission, least ability to deliver."[9] The cumulative effects of change in society, the church, and congregations had tremendously impacted on sister's lives and works.

COMMUNITY LIFE RADICALLY ALTERED

"Ministry has changed our way of living together." That simple statement of a sister who entered her community in 1940 sums up what happened to religious congregations after 1965. With diversification in works, all aspects of life changed: schedules, housing, finances, institutional involvement, spiritual development, and relationship to the church.

In the first place, sisters had to cope with a new disparity of timetables, which meant that they could no longer rely on uniformity to protect a sense of shared life. Community structure was more relaxed ("much less standard; haphazard") and proved a challenge—in some cases a disappointment—to women used to an intensely regulated and orderly life. Sisters had to devise new ways of relating to each other, or as some thought, to relate on a truly personal level for the first time. Their houses began to look more like the homes of lay people, less institutional and specialized than before, when there had been areas of strict cloister and parlors for outsiders next to the door.

Housing became a critical issue for sisters. Previously, they lived in their own institutional establishments or in parish-owned convents. In 1966 only 1.2 percent of all sisters lived in rented housing, but by 1982 it was the residence for 10 percent of all sisters in the United States.[10] Financially, communities have never commanded a common salary equal to sustaining many members who have to pay standard prices for housing. Congregations now find they have to rent parish convents where they may have served for decades in order to house a growing number of older sisters no longer able for full-time work.

The loss of corporately controlled works was a source of keen emotional pain. While congregations struggled to maintain institutions, the choice of other work created strain, and at times "Sisters' moving out was seen as a betrayal." Some found they simply could not adapt to a less institutional style of ministry, and other did not want to. Because new models emerged in tension with the old, the human cost was great.[11]

Dissension and criticism went deeper than issues of sisters' personal preference about work and living arrangements. Some believed that the very nature of religious life was at stake. Divisions appeared nationally when the Consortium Perfectae Caritatis was established in 1971 by a group of communities that sought a more traditional interpretation of religious life than was general among the membership of CMSW at the time. According to sociologist Helen Ebaugh, an essential change had taken place in religious orders: "The process of greater individualization and personal decision-making led to a deemphasis on group values and finally to a total transformation of group identity."[12] Communities that resisted change initially lost fewer members and maintained higher entrance rates than others, but they did not thereby escape internal strife, for some members thought their conservative leadership had held the lines for far too long.

Much dissent hinged on ecclesiological perspective. Change within congregations in regard to authority structures and relationship to the world generally paralleled sisters' idea of the church. Where emphasis on the institutional aspect of church was downplayed, and religious life seen more in terms of relationship, community, and charism, the definition of sisters' role in the church became much less clear than previously.

Theologian Johannes B. Metz identified this phenomenon as a "crisis of function, caused by the absence of major specific tasks in the Church, tasks that to a certain extent cannot be handed over to others."[13] Sisters have discovered that the institutional tasks that were theirs in the past can be, have been, and maybe should be handed over to others. Although the totalist, supremely functional model for congregations proved inadequate, with it sisters lost both bad and good:

> The beauty of this expression of corporateness lay in its capacity to integrate all talents into a common thrust and the strong sense of corporate identity which it gave to each member; its weakness lay in the narrowing of perspectives, fostering dependency, and violence to certain talents and charisms which often accompanied it.[14]

Loss of the old symbolic corporateness propelled many women religious into a search for self-understanding precisely because institutional structures had carried even personal identity for so many of them. The failure of those structures caused sisters, in the words of one, "to peek around the other side of external realities," to discover who they were, and what relationship they had to God, to the religious community, to the church.

Congregations provided intensive programs of spiritual renewal during the 70s, including workshops and lectures, directed and thirty-day retreats, often based on the *Spiritual Exercises* of St. Ignatius Loyola. Great value was given to reading scripture and individual prayer. Many sisters realized a sense of personal liberation through religious experience, which gave them a new confidence in God—hence, a new realization of personal authority. As a result, sisters strongly internalized religious values and assumed personal responsibility for ministry. A number of those interviewed spoke of a choice either to change or remain in a given work as directly affected by a retreat.

The conditions of ministry and of religious experience are closely related. "Even my concept of God changed dramatically," Sister Patricia Halliday, a New Englander, said of her work in the south. She affectionately described a woman in a nursing home there who used to tell her, "You'd be great if you let yourself go!" She found family- and community-reinforced impressions that "God loves you for what you do" gradually giving way to an understanding of God "Who came down from the remote region; He walks beside me." Work in a parish where the laity were highly involved also transformed her image of church—"from a holy place to *people*."[15] Her story beautifully depicts an event common for contemporary sisters. Their world, fundamentally religious, depends for its meaning on relationship with God. When institutional confusion multiplied, sisters sought a more direct approach to God than they had needed in the former orderly paradigm, where system and ritual were more likely to provide contact with the divine. It is a theme familiar to students of religious history and anthropology,[16] and part of the spiritual gain of the 1970s.

Within a theological horizon that was highly incarnational and personal, ministry also began to be seen as something deeply personal and fundamentally relational. Sister Michelle Prah described her renewed understanding of mission as "not so much work" but rather "to be a model of church in our [community] life." For her, ministry became "*Linkage* . . . it used to be supply and demand. Now—we're all in a common struggle."[17] The common struggle of Catholics to define themselves in the postconciliar age was played out to a heightened degree in the ministry of religious women.

A NEW UNDERSTANDING OF MINISTRY

Any sister who has lived in a community before 1965 can relate to the observation of Sister James Maria Spillane that when assignments were handed out by a superior, "it was cut and dry—God's will was very clear." Already convinced of the need to change many things in convent life considerably before Vatican II, she nevertheless appreciated the positive side of the older way: "I learned so much ... many of the things I've done, I wouldn't have if I had not been told—it brought out many qualities in me I would never have. . . . I thought God was asking me to do it."[18]

Religious obedience and a superior who could assign sisters to congregational works had ensured the connection between the will of God and one's occupation. A changed theology of obedience tended to replace the superior by the sister herself as the primary source of discerning God's will, but it was undoubtedly diminished personnel which most seriously altered the former secure, if exigent, pattern.

Retrenchment of school staffing, already necessary by 1970, continued. In 1975 Sister Mary Kevin Hollow, community director of the Sisters of Charity of Leavenworth, announced to pastors and other concerned parties that "all schools must be prepared to share in the impact of the probable decrease in sister personnel."[19] While the school crisis persisted and community membership continued to drop, sisters moved into a variety of occupations unprecedented in their history.

A special section on sisters in the San Francisco *Monitor* for April 2, 1981, counted more than five hundred of them in the colleges, elementary, and high schools of the archdiocese, but also catalogued a host of other occupations:

> psychiatrists, attorneys, lecturers, hospital chaplains, youth ministers, writers, television and radio specialists, spiritual and retreat directors. . . . Parish sisters, pastoral ministers, and directors of religious education . . . secretaries, clerks, bookkeepers. . . . Social work . . . seminary housekeepers . . . campus ministers, or child workers.[20]

Sisters began to occupy positions in professional and service fields nearly as diverse as those of the larger population of women in the United States.

Geographical diffusion resulted from the new occupational diversity, often because an individual worked alone or with one other sister far from the congregation's institutions. Search for employment prompted some moves, as when a sister's specialized skill required a job not available in her community. Sisters also took on distant work because it seemed more urgent. Sister Clare Reese, the young teacher in the suburban parish of the 50s, had served as principal of a new and growing school, then completed a master's degree in social work. When she saw a brochure counting three thousand sisters in the Pittsburgh diocese, her reaction was: "They don't need *me!*" It led her and another Sister of St. Joseph to start work in Martin County, Kentucky, an area of few Catholics and much mountain poverty.

It seemed to many observers that change from a highly regulated way of life had been taken to extremes, with sisters "free to work where and as they wish, as unconfined and liberated as any western career woman."[21] What had happened was basically the end of a monastic model of ministry, where religious orders offered service within their own structures, structures radically distinct from the secular "world." An insightful essay by James L. Connor, S.J., describes the change:

> We no longer conceive ourselves as bringing students, patients, parishioners, retreatants, and the like into *our* world to share *our* experience. Rather, we conceive ourselves as entering into *their* world, to share *their* experience . . . in a sense, the emphasis has shifted inside out.[22]

Such change in the focus of ministry was not easy to accomplish. It meant a shift toward listening, empowerment, and service, when religious life had been legitimized as offering the rest of the church something (either spiritual perfection or material assistance) it could not provide for itself. It also highlighted the ambiguity of the relationship of religious community to local church—parish and diocese.

When ministry moved from an institutional base, religious communities were forced to develop criteria for the apostolic placement of sisters, or else to relinquish any connection between the congregation's corporate goals and what its members actually did. A combination of common sense and idealism, those criteria usually included service of the gospel, the community's charism, concern for the poor, urgency of need, social justice, community demands, and the capacity of the individual.[23] Notably missing was any specific objective, such as school, church, or parish. Rather than prescribing a specific area of common endeavor, congregational mission statements began to reflect the actual diversity of sisters' works. Sisters of Charity of Nazareth, whose 1966 constitutions had spelled out sisters' occupations as "(1) Christian education; (2) care of the sick; (3) social service," spoke instead in the 1980 version of "multiple ministries in accord with community priorities."[24]

Although every community, under the rubric of obedience, insisted upon the confirmation of apostolic works by the major superior, the decisions of individuals took on more and more importance and were validated by the congregation. Recognizing that over the years they had changed "from organized communal attention to school and hospitals" to "a wide variety of pastoral work," Sisters of St. Joseph of Concordia, Kansas, took the monumental step of divesting themselves of congregationally-owned health care institutions. It was done, they said:

> Not out of a whim to "get rid" of the hospitals, or out of the disability to learn how to own and sponsor hospitals, nor out of a desire to get out from the onus of a businesslike approach to a multifaceted industry. We are, at this time, facing the question of change from hospital ownership and sponsorship which means institutional change because the members themselves have changed.[25]

The Concordia congregation provides an outstanding example of revolution in religious life, in the recognition that cumulative decisions of individuals could legitimately shape the direction of an entire community.

Ministry, although still understood within a corporate context, became in its concrete conditions more and more individualized. It seemed a long distant day when congregations could specify, as did the Sisters of Notre Dame de Namur in 1963, "it is the community which undertakes the works and not the individuals."[26] The price was high. Various documents relating to mission or ministry reveal the crucible of pain that marked such transitions for all congregations. In 1973 Mother Leo Frances wrote the Sisters of Charity of Leavenworth to inform them of progress in preparation for the upcoming chapter:

> The "cry of the poor" and the many urgent needs of our global community were not ignored in the Commission sessions, but they admitted that our responsibility to "help heal the ills of our times" bids us emphasize the healing that must take place within ourselves before we dare speak to men about the ills of society.[27]

Sisters could no longer view themselves as "the church's front lines," prepared to meet any emergency. They knew they were limping and had to address problems of internal cohesion.

As early as 1968 Sisters of Charity of Leavenworth had honestly identified as a problem "the question of whether or not we have a common vision which can admit of, and even foster, diverse responses to that mission."[28] Communities now spoke of common vision, common mission, rather than a common task. Definitions of mission were statements of universal value to which every member could subscribe and theoretically encompassed almost any occupation. The paradigm shift was not unique to religious congregations; parallels can be found in mission statements of numerous institutions during the 1970s. Use of broad and general language in restating the nature and purpose of the church (community, institution), while it allows diversity and avoids splits, at the same time makes difficult the clear identification of institutional purpose, recruitment, and mobilization of resources.

Congregations tried, however, to implement their stated priorities in specific apostolic decisions. In line with convictions about responsibility for the socially disenfranchised, congregations made decisions sometimes incomprehensible to suburban parishioners. Sisters of St. Joseph of Baden, for example, reaffirmed their commitment to poor urban parishes in Pittsburgh, urged sisters to work in these schools (where the student population was largely non-Catholic), and established their novitiate at Holy Rosary Convent, in the heart of an "inner-city" neighborhood.

SOCIAL JUSTICE AGENDA

Sisters shared the emerging national and ecclesiastical consciousness about the priority of social justice as a moral imperative. The Vatican II documents, their own experience with urban and rural poverty at home and in developing countries, and the 1971 Synod of Bishops all called for increased attention to social realities as the arena of divine action and the focus of Christian responsibility. In 1971 Sisters of Charity of Nazareth committed themselves to "alleviation of poverty; combating racism; effecting peace; and humanization of values."[29] As major superior, Sister Barbara Thomas addressed the same community in 1974:

> Until recent years we did not experience a clear call from the Church around social issues. Of late, however, we as a Community have known confirmation and support from the Church not only in the definition of our priorities, but also in our struggle to embrace them as a corporate body.[30]

She was president of LCWR (the former CMSW, renamed Leadership Conference of Women Religious in 1972) in 1976 when for the first time it defined a common goal: "A gospel way of justice: faith-service directed toward empowerment."[31]

Citing *Justice in the World*, the pastoral of the 1971 Synod of Bishops, the general chapter of the Sisters of Notre Dame de Namur in 1975 declared: "We cannot remain unaware, indifferent, or uninvolved in our world, since 'action on behalf of justice is a constitutive dimension of preaching the Gospel.' "[32] Serious historical research contributed to the understanding of mission that appeared in revised constitutions. Sisters of Charity, who trace their tradition to Saints Vincent de Paul and Louise de Marillac, in 1981 adopted a clear self-definition as "servants of the poor."[33] Similar elements, with varying degrees of emphasis, appear in nearly all constitutions where the congregation's historical roots grew from a situation specifically addressed to the issue of poverty. The ideals proved difficult of application, particularly when material support of the congregation depended largely on earned income, therefore on selling its product. "Perhaps one of the most painful dilemmas the congregation now faces," wrote Sisters of the Presentation in 1986, "is balancing our commitment to serve the poor with our responsibility to meet our own expenses."

The LCWR commitment to social justice coincided with the 1976 Detroit Call to Action, a benchmark in collaborative effort on the part of Roman Catholics in America. The meeting of more than thirteen hundred delegates had been preceded by preliminary regional hearings all over the country. Sister Margaret Cafferty, who had experience recruiting and organizing people for hearings in San Francisco on unemployment, was invited to Washington to help every diocese in the country to organize for participation in the Call to Action, and to give training sessions for the delegates.

As a direct response to the Call to Action, the newly-formed Boston province of the Sisters of Notre Dame de Namur wrote to twelve bishops and the Glenmary Research Center offering services of "one or two small ministry teams . . . interested in living and working among the materially poor in a simple way in a diocese with need." In September 1977 seven sisters began work in the diocese of Charleston, South Carolina. They did "hospital ministry in Spartansburg, legislative work in Columbia, the state capital, and pastoral ministry in Cheraw, and other areas from Moncks Corner."[34] It was a region only 2 percent Catholic, and sisters went with the aim, not of conversion but of presence.

Sisters associate their sense of ministry with a profoundly transformed understanding of church. One woman contrasted her preconciliar experience as a Catholic and a sister, when "we never had to think . . . or make decisions," with her present sense of personal responsibility for the religious community as a whole and for the church, simply "because we are the church."[35]

For Sister Clare Reese, Appalachia served to challenge and shape her understanding of both ministry and church. "If I went with a 'do-good' attitude," she said, "it dropped off in about twenty minutes."[36] Her work in a Kentucky mental health clinic quickly revealed that the benefits of ministry were in reality mutual. The context of church had been considerably other in heavily Catholic Pittsburgh from what it was in Appalachia; "It was kind of different to be a Catholic in some of those areas." Appalachian culture, with its ethic of religious rigorism, provoked her to rethink the effects of religion and its true meaning: "I didn't care whether they became Catholic, but to let them know that God really loves them."

The mountain situation, where there was no Mass except on Sundays, left her hungry to talk about God with other people, so, while maintaining her professional job, she started to work in rural parishes, simply sharing with other women their prayer, life, and faith. This dialogue gradually changed her perception of both ministry and church. In the Kentucky setting, with people whose daily lives were constituted in poverty and hardship, she discovered "the old spirituality of 'what's harder is better' did not make sense, if God calls us in joy. God does call us in *joy* . . . that is ministry." Rules and regulations seemed of relative importance, particularly when she saw them used destructively in a fundamentalist context: "the *only* real thing is that God loves."

For sisters, and for the American church, direct work with economically oppressed people proved a school of faith, and experience similar to Clare's can be found in *This Land Is Home to Me*, the 1975 pastoral issued by bishops of the thirteen states of Appalachia. Some sisters also began to work with migrant farm workers, through summer programs like the East Coast Migrant project or in California with Cesar Chavez.

Catholics sometimes found it hard to swallow when sisters became involved in public protest and civil disobedience, like those who prostrated themselves in the center aisle of St. Patrick's Cathedral to protest Catholic apathy about Vietnam in 1972 during Cardinal Cooke's Mass or Sister Ann Montgomery, R.S.C.J., one of the "Plowshares 8" who scattered ashes and splashed human blood in the General Electric plant at King of Prussia, Pennsylvania, on September 9, 1980. The group earned its title from banging dents into two nosecones of Minutemen 3 intercontinental ballistic missiles, figuratively "beating swords into plowshares."[37] More common, but not necessarily more palatable, were communities' concerted efforts to introduce teachings on social justice at every level of their work, particularly in school curricula.

Congregations have been less than completely successful in a consistent application of social justice criteria, their energies consumed in maintenance. They remain in some cases spread thin in institutional commitments made when novitiates were bursting. Sisters, for example, have not been able to provide the new immigrants service equal to that given by their congregations when American immigration was mostly European. Then, it was largely a matter of taking care of one's own ethnic group, but the present-day situation poses the added challenge of crossing cultural barriers. Since the end of the previous quota system in 1965, American immigrants have been chiefly Filipino, Italian, Portuguese, Hispanic, together with the more recent Asian arrivals from Vietnam and Cambodia.[38] In 1986 Sisters of Charity of Leavenworth cited as a number one trend in the American church the need "to work for and with Hispanics," but questioned, "How many can do this with our decreasing membership and increasing age?"[39]

An appraisal based on impressions suggests that perhaps religious communities who have remained more institutionalized, less assimilated to the American mainstream, have been more accessible to the new immigrants. Many preserved a bilingual tradition longer than other communities, adapting them for the need to learn a new language. Their sisters were in institutions, where they could easily be found, and they presented an image, wearing habits and living in convents, which was readily recognized by newcomers and therefore deemed worthy of trust.[40]

THE WOMEN'S MOVEMENT

It is impossible to raise issues of justice without taking a hard look at the status of women. Sisters found themselves in the double bind of being what Mary Jo Weaver has called "inside outsiders." "Their problems," she declares, "are exacerbated by their history of isolation, as well as by a tradition of superiority and an illusion of power."[41] Actually exercising very little power in the institutional church, sisters have nevertheless been perceived as officials; defined as lay people, they were seen by many parishioners as part of the clerical caste: "They were outsiders with an insider's profile."[42] Traditional Catholic teaching has consistently identified women with the roles of wife or nun, each defined in terms of function. For married women, it was reproduction and child rearing, for sisters it was education (child rearing) and care for the sick. The feminist agenda therefore held rich insight for sisters—that being defined as functional was being oppressed; that functionaries receive validation from the outside, from the patriarchal world.[43]

Sisters' understanding of the feminist perspective had been slowly developing since the early 1960s. In *The Nun in the World,* written in 1962, Cardinal Suenens devoted a chapter to "Women Today," in which he allowed that countries with a Catholic tradition often showed the least understanding for women and their needs. But the day of "Kirche, Küche, Kinder" was past:

> The classical picture in which initiative lies with the man, and woman's part is submission, is no longer current. Penelope at her weaving, Marguerite at her spinning wheel, Juliet on her balcony, Sister Anne shut up in her tower living on expectation . . . nowadays they all smack of folklore.

The cardinal did not omit a caveat about the "awe-ful choice of being Eve or Mary," but he did insist that the changing status of women brought "new dimensions to the apostolic work of contemporary religious."[44]

Sisters themselves began to critique their appallingly dependent status. In 1966 *Sisters Today* carried an article calling for women theologians in the church. The author, Sister Teresa Mary Deferrari, declared that the repression of women was "even more true in the church" than in civil life:

> The prejudice against women is tied more to the kind of general authoritarianism that has been the bane of the Church's existence in the last few centuries and has made itself felt frequently toward any progressive person, lay or cleric.[45]

Sister Mary Aloysius Schaldenbrand's essay "Freud and Sisters" (1967) recognized and deplored sisters' childish dependency on ecclesiastical authority, and displayed a vivid awareness of their need to assume adult status.[46]

The process of renewal begun in the 50s, with its stress on education and self-examination, led inevitably to sisters' waking up to their own condition in the church and their solidarity with the situation of other women. Throughout the 70s communities began seriously to study the ecclesial role of women, a direction promoted through LCWR.[47] The Women's Ordination Conference held in Detroit in November 1975 was a watershed for feminist consciousness among American sisters, who numbered among the twelve hundred registrants.[48] At the end of the decade growing awareness was reinforced by the memorable event of Sister Teresa Kane's address to Pope John Paul II during the course of his 1979 visit to the United States. With its restrained allusion to women and church order, it nevertheless created a sensation:

> Our contemplation leads us to state that the Church in its struggle to be faithful to its call for reverence and dignity for all persons must respond by providing the possibility of women as persons being included in all ministries of our Church. I urge you, Your Holiness, to be open and to respond to the voices coming from the women of this country who are desirous of serving in and through the Church as fully participating members.[49]

Among many sisters present in the Washington cathedral, in the dynamic of that moment—the pontiff's apparent reaction no less than the woman's utterance—a new generation of feminists was born.

The genuine pain of the present lay-clergy dualism is exquisite for women who are, historically and by vocation, intimately connected with a public manifestation of church. Although their experience has brought many to vow, in the words of one sister interviewed, "the control of women—never again!," American sisters maintain deep affective as well as structural bonds with the Roman Catholic Church. In her address to the LCWR in Kansas City, Missouri, in August 1984, Margaret Cafferty, the newly elected president, spoke in the name of women religious, "we have been and will continue to be faithful to the church."[50]

Feminist insight has also shaped ministerial choice for sisters—as women to women. Sister Virginia Scally relates that working with CCD teachers, all women, in a Massachusetts parish, "sensitized me to a lack of nourishment for these women from the church." It rankled: "I knew I reached them, but had no access to pulpit, to pastoral work." This led to a master's degree in applied theology, and eventually to her present position in campus ministry at two secular colleges in Boston, where much of her time is spent with women, "who want to know what the Church is teaching and *why*; who do not agree with everything, who feel alienated and yet not satisfied."[51] The women's issue is also an inescapable fact of life for the many sisters who, like their predecessors, continue to work in Catholic parishes.

THE PARISH

The overall number of sisters in parishes has declined, and their work there has become highly diversified since the 1930s, when parish for sisters meant school. A careful look at personnel trends from the communities studied reveals continued priority given to service in parishes and bears out the statement of the 1986 chapter report of the San Francisco Sisters of the Presentation: "While the number of Presentation Sisters in some other areas of ministry has declined, sisters continue to maintain a strong presence in parish ministry."[52] It is true that the massive change in religious communities by the end of the 1970s does not lend itself to an easy fit in a traditionally structured parish, but sisters have not abandoned parishes.

The role of women in the local church has evolved considerably since Vatican II. The Notre Dame Study of Catholic Parish Life estimates that 55 percent of all parish leadership is female, with a heavy concentration in spiritual renewal, religious rites, ministries to the sick, grieving, handicapped, and poor, but also in parish organization, where women represent 52 percent of membership in parish councils. Sisters, however, do not emerge in the profile of perceived female parish leadership, except where they are in charge of schools. Pastors and parishioners still associate sisters, and women generally, with education: "Women educators are in positions that have had long standing in the parish; their roles are crystallized; people know what to expect of them and how to treat them."[53] The parochial school, according to studies of sociologist Andrew Greely, maintained strong support from three quarters of the Catholics in the United States in 1977.[54] But simple numerical facts have altered sisters' accustomed role in parish schools.

For sisters, the question became whom to educate, and how. The number of lay faculty and principals in Catholic schools increased dramatically during the 70s, and costs continued a steady upward climb. Decreased funding forced the closing of more inner-city schools, while affluent parishes contemplated opening new ones. Day care became a correlative of school for the American child.[55] Sisters who chose to remain in parish schools have had to explain to themselves why, just as those who opted for different work. After finishing two terms as major superior of the Sisters of Charity of Leavenworth, Sister Mary Kevin Hollow, with extensive credentials in education, chose to return to a Topeka elementary school, as she said, "to make a statement: education is the way to break the cycle of poverty."[56]

Sister Marie Francette Holes has been an elementary school teacher and principal for almost thirty years. Like Andrew Greely, she does not see anything else accomplishing what the Catholic schools are now doing in parishes. She believes the school system is "an institution in place where we can do what we're *trying* to do other places." Sister Francette sees school administration as a difficult but meaningful job, "education is my gift, my call. . . . Forming, educating children's lives—

there is no better way to serve." She is part of the parish team, attends monthly staff meetings, and all parish functions, such as women's guild and parish council. For her, contact with persons is greater through a parish school than in her congregation's private academy. She sees the school as vital to parish, and cites personal experience in one parish where the elementary school offered "the only source of life, the only avenue of self-expression, of spiritual life—through prayer experience provided in school activities."[57]

Through the 70s, communities strove to maintain at least a sister-principal in parish schools. Although teaching personnel decreased drastically, the number of administrators provided by communities remained relatively constant. The unmistakable trend, however, is toward lay faculty and administration. Sisters now hold numerous pastorally oriented occupations in the parish. While formal education is by nature conservative, parishes are laboratories of ecclesiology and have served to change an understanding of ministry in both education and newer forms of service. Outside the schools, sisters figure chiefly in religious education and parish ministry. Records of Sisters of Charity of Leavenworth and Sisters of the Presentation for 1986 show a greater number of sisters relative to their total active membership involved in parish ministry than ten years previously. "Parish ministry" as a single heading covers a variety of realities.

In a San Francisco parish, Sister Kathleen Healy is part of a parish team where formerly she was the principal of a school, which closed in 1972 for financial reasons. The model for ministry in the parish is garnered from the *comunidades de base* in Brazil. Numerous small communities meet twice monthly and hold two series yearly of night classes. Each group has a goal of three prongs: to grow personally, to be educated, to have a task. The philosophy guiding the parish staff has been to prepare the people to take over. In 1982 the eighty-two thousand refugees in San Francisco posed "a moral problem which could have split the parish." Through a process of reflection, however, the resolution was adopted by a vote of 81 percent for the parish to become a public sanctuary. Sister Kathleen observes, "There are not many parishes where I could do the work I'm doing now." Sister Kathleen considers her new role in the parish an occasion of conversion. The impossibility of doing everything has left her with "powerless feelings," which serve to create a profound sense of "identification with the people."[58]

Where team ministry becomes genuinely collegial, sisters have realized a radically new sense of church. Speaking of her work in a mill town near Pittsburgh between 1972 and 1986, Sister Michelle Prah described the parish community:

> My varied work was a means of being involved with the people, a means of mutual sharing of OUR gifts, talents, time, energy, dreams, struggles, etc. For the first time I felt a mutuality in ministry—it was a real being with the Church—Fr. Farina, the people, the Sisters . . . we lived, prayed, worked and grew TOGETHER. [I] didn't feel like a vendor giving out my service—it was a cooperative life.[59]

Whether through shortage of priests, or through validation of persons who affirmed their activity and presence, sisters took on ownership vis-à-vis the church and ministry: "I found out I could be a presence of church," said one, "I could be a minister."

Sisters in parish team ministry are designated by a variety of titles, from "parish sister" to "associate pastor," describing the arc of tolerance for women in roles that suggest some relationship to ordained ministry. In a parish team between 1970 and 1979 at Sacred Heart Cathedral, Raleigh, North Carolina, Sister Katharine Hanrahan's job description was basically to "help in everything except sacraments." As a member of the finance committee, she was in charge of parish grounds; her work on the Christian education committee involved adult education and sacramental preparation at all levels; her general parish responsibilities covered parish council, the elderly, and ecumenical group, hospital visitation, communion calls, funerals, wakes, preparing the parish bulletin, and regular turns on duty in the rectory office.[60] The diversity of parish ministry for sisters could be endlessly multiplied and is nuanced in various types of parishes, such as rural areas where there is a shortage of priests: "I am the local pastor," said a sister in one such parish.

Experience outside the United States has also broadened sisters' experience. Sister Judy Raley's work in Belize between 1976 and 1982, for example, consisted of parish ministry. The parish team, which really functioned as equals, challenged a strictly hierarchical interpretation of church. Because of the scarcity of priests, the focus of ministry necessarily shifted from the narrowly sacramental to one that emphasized the laity. "Don't do anything you can get someone else to do," became the rule of thumb for clerical and religious personnel. The result was the formation of a highly communitarian, grass-roots, predominantly lay-oriented sense of church.[61]

Within the parish, sisters offer many different kinds of service. Sister Ursula Grimes presently does adult education in a Pittsburgh suburban parish, where her work entails scripture classes, scripture sharing, involvement with divorced and separated Catholics, and widowed parishioners. Sister Ursula holds a Ph.D. in education and once served as school principal, but believes her present work is equally important. "Adults," she says, "have no way of getting their questions answered."[62]

The changing composition of a given parish has also propelled sisters into new areas of ministry. Sister Cleta Herold's work in Holy Redeemer parish in the Castro district of San Francisco is primarily with older parishioners who remain, and with the recently arrived gay population, through whom she has been plunged into the suffering of AIDS with patients and their loved ones. Sister Edna Malloy works in St. Mary's parish in Cambridge, Massachusetts, which now has no child in a school where previously there were more than fifteen hundred students. Sister Edna is there for the parish's aging population, whose faith sustains her, and for whom in turn she provides trips to doctor's offices, arranges social security benefits, and visits three nursing homes, three hospitals, and the parish shut-ins. "I love dealing with the elderly," she says, "and they're forgotten." Sister Herman Joseph Koch has herself gone through three careers—till 1968 a nurse, then ten years in Catholic social service, and working since 1978 in a cathedral parish, where she helps the aged, takes care of the church "for *every* Sunday Mass," and provides support and sponsorship for the catechumen group.[63]

Diocesan administration provides another avenue of ministry for parishes, and is a likely outlet for sisters whose extensive education suits them for such positions. Others put their own parish experience to work to help facilitate ministry for others. Sister Patricia Johnson, chemistry teacher, supervisor for clinical pastoral education (the first sister so certified in CPE), and city parish minister, has developed a program at Boston's Emmanuel College for training in urban ministry.[64]

Two strong themes emerge from the newer service of sisters in parishes: the role of the laity and the position of women in ministry. Sisters interviewed, realistic about their diminished numbers and convinced that church includes all the people, repeated over and over the importance of an emerging laity for the church. Sister Ann Victoria Cruz saw the most important facet of her present work in Renew as "development of lay leadership—there are people with potential but with fear, who need support and affirmation." Looking back on a career of service approaching its fiftieth year, she remarked with optimistic equanimity, "change is a hallmark of living things."[65]

The new roles of sisters are a key place where the question of woman as minister is being hammered out in the Catholic Church.

One sister told the story of the first time she conducted a communion service, when the priest could not make it for a Lenten Mass. As an older parishioner approached her afterward, she feared the worst, but the woman's only comment was an enthusiastic "Thank God for Vatican II!" The issue, however, is fraught with tension. One sister, present at a regional diocesan meeting in 1986 as part of the parish team, was invited out by the archbishop, a humiliating instance of the conflict generated by the emergence of new roles within the Catholic Church.

Rocky relationships with the clergy have become an uncomfortable commonplace for sisters and for religious congregations. Numerous sisters spoke of parish programs that fell apart when a new pastor arrived, simply because they depended on initiative to which he was not sympathetic. Without the ballast provided by institutional structure, sisters found themselves and their work even more vulnerable to the control of pastors. Sisters therefore have a high stake in developing structures of shared responsibility, and tend to be more progressive in their ideas about church order, at least generally, than the clergy. Conflict with clergy is also one of the key factors in sisters' seeking work outside a parish situation. Others include lack of scope in parish jobs for the specialized education of many women religious, and community finances. At a time when congregations' economic survival hangs in the balance, elementary education and parish ministry provide some of the lowest percentages per capita of congregational income.[66] Nevertheless, many sisters prefer to work in parishes, recognizing it as the basic unit of church structure, and the place where most Catholics live out their lives.

The story of Sister Ursula Grimes, a Sister of St. Joseph, in many ways dramatizes devotion to parish. Her varied and interesting life history has been a journey from a parish back to parish. As a high school student, she taught CCD in her home parish of St. Titus, Alipquippa, Pennsylvania, and from her entrance into the convent, she said, "I always wanted to work in a parish . . . always, always liked working with lay people." As a young woman, she taught and was principal in Pittsburgh schools, but after completing her doctorate in education, she was assigned to the community's novitiate, and spent the next twenty-two years of her life in congregational formation and administration. Completing her second term as assistant superior, Sister Ursula spent a year brushing up her theology so she could go back to parish work, where we met her in her present ministry of adult education. She believes that communities in the future "are going to move into areas of greater need," such as the elderly and the poor, but envisions this in a parish context: "Those parishes are a part of us!"[67]

FUTURE

The question of sisters' ministry in the future remains open. General trends indicate that sisters' works are headed in the direction of more diversity and professional specialization, more cooperation with laity and clergy, and even less in institutions. Schools face the challenge of financial pressure, a changing ethnic population, and the new need for child care created by social breakdown in the United States.[68] Membership, of course, is the crucial issue if religious communities are to have any future at all. The picture on that score is not very encouraging, if one thinks in terms of past numbers. According to Donna Markham, a Dominican psychologist: "All the data suggest that if present factors remain constant, the women's congregations will continue to lose members and won't gain enough new ones to replace them." She cites a discrepancy between single lay women's perceptions of religious communities and their own, which bodes ill for recruitment ("women religious think religious life is viable and dynamic; most lay women do not"). She also comments on communities' corporate depression and confusion in regard to task.[69] It is possible that Andrew Greely's prediction of a "vanishing species" will come true for sisters' communities.[70] Religious life is always vulnerable to the socio-economic status of convents in a society as well as to religious factors. Like the Beguines, who flourished in the late Middle Ages and then died out, active congregations of women may be a time-bound phenomenon.

Whether or not sisters are burying their heads in the sand in regard to the future, those who are around—including the few younger members who do continue to enter—still carry on with great determination. The results of a survey of major superiors in the LCWR done by the School Sisters of St. Francis, Milwaukee, in 1985 suggests some present directions in sisters' ministry: (1) traditional works of health care and education have changed places with social and pastoral works; (2) superiors see a geographical shift from urban-middle and upperclass ministries to urban and rural poor; (3) the highest area of correlation between perceived need and community commitment is in the area of pastoral ministry, including retreat work, counseling, and parish ministry.[71] The future of sisters' ministry may be in question, but there is no indication that it is headed away from the parish. Sisters remain very connected with parish, but in much fewer numbers and less highly visible form. Because their presence has changed, it is harder to recognize, and perhaps tends to be overlooked.

For all religious women it has been a long journey from the days of 1930, when their identity in parishes was equivalent to their role in school. If their identity is less clear today than it was then—to themselves and parishioners alike—it is due perhaps to the nature of their vocation, distinct from official structures, yet very close to the heart of the church. Just as they stood in previous times for a church characterized by James Hitchcock as "one of the most solid, self-confident, and enduring institutions in the history of the world,"[72] sisters have experienced and perhaps personified all the shocks of change felt by a church undergoing profound evolution, of which it is now, to quote one sister, "in the molting stage."

CONCLUSION

In the five decades between 1930 and 1980, sisters have undergone a metamorphosis as dramatic as that following the Council of Trent, when they emerged (church law notwithstanding) as groups without strict cloister, actively engaged in the pastoral work of the church. Historians assert the aptness of the post-Tridentine women's congregations to deal with the needs of a preindustrial European society, and later, in the United States, with the immigrant church of the nineteenth century. The apex of what could be called the nineteenth-century style for sisters was the result of the canonical and professional regulation following World War I, combined with congregations' accelerating drive, right into the mid-1960s, to keep abreast of a rapidly expanding institutional system of schools and hospitals. The former conventual mode, like American industrial society, peaked during the 1950s, and the scientific and critical advance achieved in that period catapulted both America and American sisters into a new era. The crucial decade, therefore, in terms of understanding long-range changes in sisters' ministry is really the 1950s, although it was not obvious until the 1960s. The cultural and ecclesial movements impinging on the lives of sisters clearly antedate the Second Vatican Council, and have to be understood in terms of the social and demographic development of American Catholics as a whole.

What is not yet clear is the form of religious life appropriate for the First World technological society of the late twentieth century. The success of institutional Catholicism was largely the result of sisters' ability, through concerted effort and fierce labor, to keep one step ahead of the needs of the people they served, and in so doing either to provide what was lacking or to compete successfully with a secular system of education and welfare. One woman with a long and outstanding career in an educational congregation has suggested that it has now become impossible for sisters to stay in competition with the pace and complexity of this newly emerged world. It is time, she argues, to stop competing and consider a completely different stance.[73]

Issues of world poverty and justice figure more and more in the conscious decisions of sisters in regard to ministry. They feel called by the church and the times to address the agenda of human suffering in a world where 20 percent of the population controls 80 percent of the world's resources. Yet sisters themselves, their neighbors and relatives, are among the "have's." Global consciousness wars on what Elizabeth Carroll has called a "bourgeois" mentality, and there is undeniable tension between professionalism and poverty. Professional development for the sake of institutions actually distanced sisters and many of their works from material poverty, as European immigrants entered the American mainstream.

The traditional tasks assumed by religious orders still remain: there are new ethnic groups to be assimilated, and poverty is an increasing concern. But older religious communities in the United States have also gone through the long process of americanization. They find themselves removed culturally and even geographically from the new immigrants. Complex economic developments, moreover, have spelled the end of private charity's ability to deal effectively with social ills, and religious organizations may question concentrating their efforts on what seems a band-aid approach to social pathology.

Congregations, furthermore, continue to struggle with institutional commitments that they are yearly less able to meet. In addition, they often face increasing financial debility in caring for their own aging membership, a result of the depopulation of convents since the late 1960s. The history of most women's communities as teachers in parish schools has left them with no reserves adequate to meet the crisis.

Still, attention to "the cry of the poor" is felt to hold the seeds of their future. Because the problems of the present are so overwhelming, and the collapse of what was a masterpiece of institutionalization so stunning, it is difficult for congregations to give adequate attention to the sprouts of newness that signal life.

The changing role of women religious in parishes since the late 1960s raises questions about the very meaning of the vocation of the sister. Modern congregations have always legitimized themselves societally by their usefulness. In the nineteenth century this meant adapting to the institutional framework of an industrial society. Sisters came to be seen, and to see themselves, as a work force to run the church's institutions, which in the United States took the shape primarily of the Catholic school system.

When Pope Pius XII expressed concern in 1950 over the inadequate number of religious vocations, and sisters in this country set themselves quotas ("one hundred for the Marian Year"), they were not thinking so much in terms of the divine call of an individual, which was assumed, but of recruiting workers for the institutions. It is striking that since women's congregations no longer provide the bulk of staff for parish schools, little if anything is heard about "vocations" from the pulpit or elsewhere.

It would seem, however, that there is an inherent conflict between the idea of vocation as a charismatic gift and as a mass labor force. The demands of religious life, its particular spiritual and psychological appeal, cannot be expected to attract the many, but a few. Overshadowed in its origins by the prevailing norms of cloister, and more recently by the industrial-age demand for labor, it is possible that the vocation of the *sister* in the church has not yet been fully understood.

In Catholic schools, once the backbone of sisters' ministry in parishes, the original social task of integrating European ethnic groups has been fulfilled. The religious function of transmitting faith is perennial, and indeed primary, but without the buttress of social and economic motivation, it is questionable whether even affluent Catholics are willing to assume the extraordinary financial burden entailed in maintaining a separate system of education for primarily religious reasons. The cost of Catholic schools puts them out of reach of most of the less fortunate.

The church's mission of educating has become even more complex, more urgent, in a situation where Roman Catholics face the dual problem of assimilating Vatican II and forging a religious identity no longer tied to cultural separatism from the rest of Americans. Whether these urgent needs of the Catholic community can be met by assigning them to any subgroup, such as religious communities, is seriously questioned. The integration of Catholic values in a rapidly changing secular and ecclesiastical culture has become a matter not only of educating youth, but of reeducating adults, and demand a concerted, systematized effort of the entire Catholic community from top to bottom.

The future of religious communities and their role in the parish is deeply connected to larger and still unresolved ecclesiological issues. Religious communities are ecclesial communities. How the wider church understands itself and its relationship to the world, and how that church functions are crucial to the role of religious communities. Women religious must ask their own particular questions about the traditional history of separation from the world and what that means in terms of contemporary society and ecclesiology; they must also reevaluate the status of women and its implications for their role in ministry.

Sisters, essentially, are products of the parish. They have come, for the most part, from practicing Catholic families. Their history as parish helpers with an extraparochial base, closely subject to the authority of the pastor, has evolved a rather complex relationship with parish in the present. Diminishing numbers make them unable to provide the kind of help to which parishes are accustomed; loyalties rooted in both parish and religious community structures can conflict, and uncomfortable issues in regard to women's relationship to local ecclesiastical authority at times plague interaction with the pastor.

The future of sisters in parishes to a great extent depends upon the development of parishes as faith communities, as expressions of local church. Religious vocations come from parishes, and the service of sisters in parishes is a matter not only of what they are able to offer, but also of what parishioners can envision them to do. If sisters' realization is accurate, that ministry is a mutual reality, then so will be the creation of a new role for sisters in parishes.

APPENDIX
Constitutions of the Sisters of Charity of Nazareth

1878

The object of the institution of the Sisters of Charity in the State of Kentucky, according to the plan laid down by St. Vincent of Paul, being: first, to honor our Lord Jesus Christ, as the source and model of all charity, by rendering to him every temporal and spiritual service in their power, in the person of the poor, either sick, or children, prisoners, or others; secondly, to honor the sacred infancy of Jesus, in the young persons of their sex, whom they are called upon to form to virtue, whilst they sow in their minds the seed of useful knowledge: Accordingly, the care of poor, of all descriptions and ages, sick, prisoners, invalids, foundlings, orphans, and even insane, in Hospitals and private houses, shall be the objects of the solicitude of the Sisters of Nazareth. . . . Thirdly, The next object of their zeal, no less important at this time, will be the education of young persons of their sex, of all description, in virtue, piety, and all the branches of useful learning, which they will endeavor to extend gratis to poor orphans, as far as their circumstances will permit them.

(chap. 1, art. 3)

1922

1. The object of the Congregation is twofold:

First, the sanctification of its members by the observance of the three simple vows of Poverty, Chastity, and Obedience, and of the Constitutions.

Secondly, the welfare of the neighbor, the suffering poor, the sick, the insane, the orphan in Hospitals and Asylums; and the Christian education of ["female" crossed out] youth in Parochial Schools, Academies and institutions of Higher Education.

2. The Sisters shall endeavor to honor Our Lord Jesus Christ, the Source and Model of all charity, manifesting in their lives the love of Christ for mankind. The name they bear shall remind them of this obligation.

(part 1, chap. 1, art. 1–2)

· PART III ·

The Struggle to Serve: From the Lay Apostolate to the Ministry Explosion

INTRODUCTION

The 1970s began a distinctly new era in the history of the Catholic Church in the United States. In the wake of the spiritual renewal catalyzed by Vatican II and the social and political turbulence of the 1960s, American Catholics entered the 1970s with a new vision, and a new set of questions and priorities. Central to this new vision was a radically changed perspective on the role and status of the laity in the church. While the vast majority of American Catholics were aware of these changes, they were far from reaching a consensus on what the role of the laity should be in the post–Vatican II church. The contemporary debate concerning the present and future prospects of the laity in the American Catholic Church has its roots in the uncertainties that surfaced in the 1960s. If one were to isolate a single phrase that has served as the lightning rod for the heated discussions concerning the laity that have continued unabated throughout the 1970s and 80s, that phrase would have to be lay ministry.

The term "lay ministry" is used to refer to a wide spectrum of contributions made by the laity both within the church and in society at large under the auspices of the church. There have been attempts to clarify and restrict its meaning, in part because the broad use of the word "ministry," formerly considered the Protestant counterpart to the Catholic priesthood, has created misunderstandings and considerable anxiety within the Catholic community. New definitions do not necessarily alleviate the anxiety accompanying the contemporary ministry explosion, however. The inclusive definitions of ministry that have emerged out of the post–Vatican II Catholic experience reinforce the growing conviction that lay ministry is not a discrete byproduct of past renewal but an everpresent mandate for future changes that could ultimately bring about a radical restructuring of the church.

In *Theology of Ministry* (1983), theologian Thomas Franklin O'Meara defines Christian ministry as "the public activity of a baptized follower of Jesus Christ flowing from the Spirit's charism and an individual personality on behalf of a Christian community to witness to, serve, and realize the kingdom of God." This definition explicitly rejects the notion that ministry is, generally speaking, what ordained men do for a living. It also rejects the popular use of the term "ministry" to refer to anything that a good Christian does for anybody under any circumstances. O'Meara reiterates the sacramental grounding of ministry in baptism rather than ordination, and in the process, undercuts the exclusion of nonordained women and men from ministry simply on the basis of their status (or lack of status) within the institutional church. In fact, according to O'Meara, ministry cannot be confined to the institutional church; rather, it should "[expand] the community" from which it emerges.[1]

American Catholic women, who have a long tradition of voluntary, unacknowledged service to the church, have welcomed the broad application of the term "lay ministry" to the kind of work that women have done for the church for at least a century. A study of women in ministry sponsored by the Leadership Conference of Women Religious in the early 1980s rejected the traditional association of ministry with ordained clergy, while attempting to delineate what kinds of activities should be considered ministries. Using data on the ministries of four thousand women, the study proposed nine classifications of ministry based upon the actual work being done by women in the church. It divided women's ministries into the following categories:

1. liturgical: including lectors and eucharistic ministers, along with musicians and altar decorators.
2. general pastoral: including youth ministers, as well as participants in pre-Cana, parish renewal, evangelization, and special outreach programs.
3. spiritual: including charismatics, prayer groups, Cursillo, Third Orders, and sodalities.
4. education: including CCD, teaching or library work in Catholic schools or adult and special education programs, and those serving on education boards or as school administrators.
5. health: including nurses, doctors, aids, and administrators in health care facilities.
6. social services: including social workers, counselors, and workers in community centers and Catholic social service agencies.
7. recreation: including those engaged in social and recreational work, e.g., in CYO, scouting, arts and crafts, and in programs for senior citizens.
8. social activist: including activists lobbying for a variety of causes, as well as those in ecumenical activities.

9. administrative/support: including secretaries, fund-raisers, those who work in church maintenance communications, on parish councils, on diocesan and national boards, and in Catholic organizations.[2]

These nine classifications underscore the problem inherent in an expanding, inclusive concept of ministry. They would appear to suggest that anyone who does maintenance work at a parish, decorates the altar, or acts in a leadership capacity in a Catholic organization is engaged in ministry. And indeed the term is increasingly used in this nebulous sense. While some Catholics of the 1970s and 80s emphasize the new opportunities for service and spiritual growth in the "ecclesial lay ministries" that emerged in the 1970s, others who use the term "lay ministry" more broadly deny that the recent ministry explosion represents a dramatic change. As Dennis Geaney maintained in 1979, "today is not an age of lay ministry any more than was yesterday. The difference is that we are lifting up and giving a name to the glue that has held every community together."[3] From Geaney's comment one might at least infer that what makes the lay ministries of the 1970s and 80s stand out from the lay organizations, apostolates, and committees of the pre–Vatican II era was, in large part, the new level of lay self-consciousness that accompanied them.

A vocal segment of the American Catholic community rejects the popular position articulated by Geaney. In 1981 the Committee on Doctrine of the National Conference of Catholic Bishops decided to reserve the term "ministry" for two specific cases: "ordained ministry" ("official work . . . in the orders of bishop, priest, and deacon") and "designated lay ministry" ("the official work of acolyte or reader . . . carried out by people commissioned in those two canonical offices"). The committee chose to call all other work done by unordained, baptized persons under the auspices of the church "Christian service."[4] This committee was not alone. Pope John Paul II himself eschewed the term "lay ministry" in his 1987 visit to the United States. And a conspicuous coalition of laity and clergy associated with the National Center for the Laity in Chicago have likewise rejected the broad use of the term "lay ministry." They do so to call attention to the distinction between Christian service in the family, neighborhood, and workplace, which they consider the laity's primary responsibility, and the growing involvement of the laity in ecclesial ministries within the parish and the diocese. Affiliates of the National Center for the Laity reserve the term "lay ministry" for the ecclesial ministries which they fear are diverting the attention of the laity away from the home and the marketplace where they can make their most substantial contributions.[5]

These disputes over the term "lay ministry" are not merely arguments over semantics. Both the growing popularity of lay ministries and the consistent efforts to restrict or clarify the use and meaning of the term bear witness to the urgency of two underlying questions that are inextricable from the lay ministry debate. The first question concerns the future prospects of the parish system in the American Catholic Church. A second, closely related question concerns the proper understanding of the distinction between the clergy and the laity in the post–Vatican II church. The necessity of the parish system, in which priest-led parishes form the basic component of bishop-led dioceses, and of the fundamental distinction between the ordained and the unordained, upon which the parish system rests, have long been considered axiomatic in the Catholic community. And the emergence of lay ministry, whether viewed as a foray of the laity into the formerly clerical arena of parish and diocesan leadership, or as a reinterpretation of the mandate for Christian service contained in the sacrament of baptism, represents an increasingly visible reminder that the parish and the priesthood must change with changing times.

Viewed from a wider historical perspective, the appearance of lay ministries in the 1970s was part of a twofold change: a shift in the laity's attitude toward the work that it had long been doing within the Catholic community and an expansion of lay responsibility, which became a mandate for further theological and ecclesiological change. In order to understand these two related changes, however, it is necessary to take a closer look at the roots of lay self-consciousness and at the kinds of contributions made by the laity in the decades preceding Vatican II.

In order to underscore the changing consciousness and expanding role of the laity in the American Catholic community, it is helpful to focus upon four distinct periods. The first period (1889–1928) witnessed the establishment of patterns of lay leadership and activism under the aegis of clerical "organization men" such as Cardinal William O'Connell of Boston (archbishop 1907–44) and Cardinal George William Mundelein of Chicago (1915–39), as well as under the influence of clerical "midwives" such as Thomas Augustine Judge and Peter Dietz, who nurtured alternative visions of lay responsibility and service. The second period (1929–59) represented the heyday of the lay apostolates stimulated by papal encouragement and European Catholic models, as well as by indigenous developments within American society and the American Catholic community. The third period (1960–69) was the age of aggiornamento in which the American Catholic laity struggled with the implications of Vatican II. The fourth and final period (1970–80) saw the debates about the role and status of the laity focus increasingly on the question of lay ministry.

Each of these four periods, examined in the chapters that follow, represents a distinct stage in the evolution of the commitments and self-consciousness of the American Catholic laity. Despite the fact that the history of the laity remains largely unexamined by scholars, it will be necessary to venture some speculations concerning the relationship between the individual stages, even without the safety net of a sense of consensus on the history of the laity. For only in so doing can we begin to answer the question of whether the current explosion of lay ministries is indeed a radical departure that threatens to dismantle *the* established pattern of parish and diocesan life and of lay-clergy relations. For it is also possible that we might find alternative patterns, a more flexible vision of lay activism, and a more expansive concept of lay identity within the raw materials for the yet unwritten history of the American Catholic laity.

11

LAY ORGANIZATION
AND ACTIVISM, 1889–1928

It would be anachronistic to speak of lay ministries in the immigrant church of the late nineteenth and early twentieth century. During this period, even the term "lay apostolate," just coming into vogue, suggested novelty and innovation. Nevertheless, it is accurate to describe the 1880s as a turning point in the history of the American Catholic laity. The closing decades of the nineteenth century witnessed new patterns of lay leadership and activism, not only in the labor unions but also within a whole spectrum of Catholic organizations and movements that sought to meet the spiritual and material needs of the immigrant church. In 1889, when the prophets of doom lamented the "leakage" of a hefty proportion of the Catholic immigrant population from the fold, Archbishop Ireland urged the laity to counter the trend by forming " 'salvation armies' . . . [to] bring God's word to the ear of the most vile, the most ignorant and the most godless."[1] A select minority of lay persons rose to Ireland's challenge, assumed responsibility for the bodies and souls of their less fortunate neighbors, and in the process, raised new questions about the laity's proper role in the church and in social reform movements.

Despite the exhortations of Ireland and other liberals in the hierarchy, Catholic lay persons were slow to enter the competition for the souls of the unchurched. With the notable exception of the convert David Goldstein who self-consciously emulated the Salvationists in his street apostolate to the unchurched beginning in 1917, Catholic lay people remained aloof. They cringed at the thought of stooping to the level of the Salvation Army, and were even slow to adopt the methods of the real competition: professional social workers and settlement workers. The years between 1889 and 1928 witnessed the burgeoning of organizations for the laity on the parish, diocesan, and national level; much of this growth was due to the expansion of traditional Catholic lay societies under clerical supervision. These established lay societies became the training ground for future lay apostles. And on rare occasions, sometimes with the help of forward-looking clergy, new movements for the laity were born within the framework of the old established organizations. These new movements both reflected and catalyzed the changing self-perceptions of lay leaders, and laid the foundations for the age of the lay apostolate, which began in the United States in the 1930s.

Members of an urban parish at the turn of the century had the opportunity to join a wide variety of voluntary societies. In *The People of Our Parish* (1900), Lelia Hardin Bugg called attention to the emphasis that was placed upon lay organizations in a typical upwardly mobile urban parish. "This parish is being 'clubbed' into model behavior if not into premature translation to glory," one of Bugg's young female characters dryly observes. "Father Ryan believes that in union there is strength, . . . and he evidently wants all the kinds of strength that he can get." The repertoire of societies enumerated by Bugg includes a vast array of clubs, sodalities, social groups, and reading circles divided by age and gender. The impression given is that the parish sought to be a self-contained world that provided not only spiritual sustenence but the opportunity for self-improvement (e.g., the Father Mathew Temperance Society, the Shakespeare class, and the university extension club), outreach to the less fortunate (e.g., the St. Vincent de Paul Society and the St. Catherine's Industrial Club), and socializing within an exclusively Catholic environment. At least some of the parish societies appear to have been attempts to provide Catholic alternatives to popular Protestant service organizations. For example, Bugg includes the Queen's Daughters, which provided lodging for working women, and religious and domestic training for the poor. The original chapter of the Queen's Daughters, established in St. Louis in the late 1880s by Mary Hoxsey, bore a strong resemblance to King's Daughters, a Protestant women's society.[2]

One could divide late nineteenth-century parish organizations into roughly four types: devotional, mutual aid, charitable, and educational societies. Within the day-to-day life of a parish, however, these neat functional classifications broke down and it became increasingly likely that every society would serve more than one purpose. Mutual aid societies such as the Catholic Central Verein (1855) or the Knights of Columbus (1882) launched educational programs to popularize Catholic social teachings or fight anti-Catholic prejudice stemming from false stereotypes of the church.[3] Devotional societies organized bazaars to help fill parish coffers, or sought to expand their activities into the surrounding neighborhood, as in the case of the antismut campaigns sponsored by Holy Name Societies. And virtually all types of parish societies had some devotional or sacramental component, such as group adoration before the Blessed Sacrament, recitation of the rosary, or monthly communion received together as a body.

Until the 1880s devotional societies, sodalities, and confraternities constituted the vast majority of all Catholic parish organizations. Prior to 1860 it is estimated that 70 percent of all parish societies fell into this category. Even during the period between 1860 and 1900, an era marked by the increasing diversification of parish organizations, as many as 60 percent were primarily for devotional purposes.[4] The volunteers active within these parish societies were largely female. Leslie Tentler's research on the archdiocese of Detroit calls attention to the disproportionate participation of women in parish societies during this period. Tentler portrays the typical Detroit parish at the turn of the century as essentially a women's world with female parishioners "more directly involved in the day to day life of the parish" than their male counterparts. She suggests that this fact helps to explain Detroit Bishop Foley's decision not to implement Pope Pius X's motu proprio issued in 1903 which called for the removal of women from parish choirs. Had Foley opted for implementation, he would have called attention to one of the awkward facts of parish life in the opening decades of the twentieth century.[5]

Tentler's research is reinforced by a popular seminary textbook published in 1896, William Stang's *Pastoral Theology*. Stang openly acknowledged the other side of women's disproportionate participation in parish activities: men's conspicuous absence. He even suggested that women's frequent recourse to the sacrament of penance is not an unmitigated blessing. According to Stang, if men were ever to consider the church more than a women's society, women would have to stop "[pushing] themselves forward in the church as if they owned it."[6]

At the turn of the century the enthusiasm for voluntary organizations spread to the diocesan and even the national level. This organization process might be viewed as three separate, but closely related, developments. The first is the drive to establish Catholic versions of a whole spectrum of essentially nonreligious societies—for example, the Catholic Daughters of America (1903) as an exclusively Catholic equivalent to the Daughters of the American Revolution (1890), the National Catholic Educational Association (1904) as a Catholic alternative to the National Education Association (1857, 1870), and the Catholic Press Association of the United States, Inc. (1911) as the Catholic counterpart of the National Press Club (1908).[7] Like voluntary societies within the parish, but to an even greater extent, these national organizations (and their diocesan subgroups) became the training ground for lay leaders of both genders.

The emergence of a cadre of lay leaders on the regional and national level contributed to a second development, a movement advocating the organization of the laity along national lines for service to the church. Among the major milestones in this movement were the lay Catholic congresses held in Baltimore in 1889 and in Chicago in 1893, and a parallel series of five congresses for black Catholics that met between 1889 and 1894. These congresses encouraged lay people to consider the running of the church to be at least partly their responsibility. The black congresses, spearheaded by Daniel A. Rudd, a black Catholic editor from Cincinnati, were especially forthright in identifying and protesting discrimination against blacks not only in society at large but also within the institutional church.

At the first lay Catholic congress held in Baltimore in 1889 in conjunction with the celebration of the centennial of the American hierarchy, Archbishop John Ireland encouraged the lay leaders present to be more self-conscious about "the power existing in the midst of the laity," and he promised to do what he could to unleash that power. Ireland exhorted the assembled lay leaders to consider themselves soldiers of the church under the leadership of clerical officers. He opened the door to independent lay initiative when he reminded the laity that "in wartime against error and sin, the soldier is not always near the officer and he must be ready to strike without waiting for command." Ireland explicitly rejected the notion that confirmed lay people had no responsibility to the church beyond "[saving] their souls and [paying] their pew rent," and urged them to "think, work, organize, read, speak, act as circumstances demand." The arena in which lay activism should take place remained unspecified, although Ireland's intimation that lay soldiers would be working far from the officers suggests that he was not thinking specifically of the institutional church proper.[8]

When the lay congress movement died in the 1890s, in large part because its friends in the hierarchy withdrew their support, the hopes of lay leaders were concentrated on the effort to establish the American Federation of Catholic Societies, founded in 1901. The federation, a coalition of national Catholic organizations engaged in a wide array of activities including social and charitable work, education, and journalism, grew to a membership of about three million by 1912. Under the influence of Peter Dietz, a labor priest who had been active in the Catholic Central Verein, the federation became increasingly involved in lobbying for labor legislation and other social reforms. In a sense, the federation was replaced after the First World War by an even more ambitious example of the organizational impulse in the American

Catholic Church: the National Catholic Welfare Conference and its single-sex subdivisions, the National Council of Catholic Men (NCCM) and the National Council of Catholic Women (NCCW). In another sense, however, the latter organization, firmly under hierarchical control, represents the bishops' decision to dispense with massive, free-standing lay organizations in favor of lay movements with an official tie to the hierarchy.

This trend toward firmer hierarchical control of lay organizations, which became evident during the early twentieth century, represents the third major development within the effort to organize the laity during the immigrant era. It was epitomized and institutionalized by a new breed of bishops, the ecclesiastical organization men who came to power during the first two decades of this century. The careers of two men, Cardinal William O'Connell of Boston and Cardinal George William Mundelein of Chicago, serve as an especially good introduction to the world of this generation of bishops, aptly described by historian Edward Kantowicz as "builders, administrators, politicoes, anti-intellectuals, and chauvinist patriots."[9] Both O'Connell and Mundelein were ecclesiastical corporation men whose concern for efficiency and centralization strongly colored their vision of the role of the laity in church and society. And both men encouraged—even orchestrated—the development of a cohesive network of lay organizations on the diocesan and parish level under the supervision of priests whom they had appointed.

During his first year as archbishop, Mundelein made his priorities known. He sought to institutionalize uniformity of worship in the churches and uniformity of education in the parish schools. When he announced his uniform sermon plan in December 1916, he explained that it was part of his strategy to develop "a well-instructed, watchful, active Catholic laity." He insisted: "This is the day and the hour of the layman's apostolate." While he had free rein with his diocesan priests and could demand instant reform of their behavior—for example, curfews and a moratorium on theater attendance, Mundelein had to be a bit more subtle with the laity. He personally met with most of the major Catholic organizations in the archdiocese during his inaugural year, and, in the interests of preventing "dry rot" within lay societies, recommended a pet project to each group. To the Knights of Columbus, he proposed a reform school for boys; to the Holy Name Society, a Big Brother program. He urged the Order of Catholic Women Foresters to start a downtown club for Catholic working girls, an alternative to the temptations of the YWCA. He went to the Catholic Women's League for support for a new day college for women. Mundelein admitted that he could probably launch such projects on his own, but he wanted the help of the Chicago Catholic community. He assured the laity: "I would not deprive you of the opportunity of doing great good." Nevertheless, he would deprive them of responsibilities that he believed might be more efficiently undertaken by the clergy, as he did in 1920 when the lay leaders of Associated Catholic Charities of Chicago showed themselves unable to solicit adequate donations from everyday Catholics within the parishes.[10]

O'Connell, too, emphasized uniformity and discipline. Like Mundelein, he sought to unify the vast array of existing Catholic organizations within his jurisdiction under his strong leadership and in the service of his agenda. O'Connell, the son of Irish immigrants who had fled the potato famine, believed that Boston Catholics had lived too long in the shadow of the Brahmins. He was convinced that the time was ripe for American to be transformed by the growing Catholic presence, under the leadership of the bishops, but primarily by the people in the parishes. In an address commemorating the centennial of the archdiocese of Boston in 1908, O'Connell reminded his constituency that "the child of the immigrant is called to fill the place which the Puritan has left. He must learn to fill it worthily and well." O'Connell proceeded to admonish his flock not to forget the lessons that their immigrant parents had taught them: "to keep [their] faith undimmed and [their] charity unquenched."[11]

O'Connell delighted in massive public displays of that faith and charity. During the centennial celebration he stood at the reviewing stand with Boston's Mayor Hibbard for almost five hours to watch a parade of forty thousand Holy Name Society members drawn from every parish in the archdiocese. He coordinated the charitable activities of St. Vincent de Paul Societies and assorted institutions for the poor and orphans into an umbrella organization, the Catholic Charitable Bureau (1903). He wanted Catholic charitable workers to operate in sufficiently close proximity to non-Catholics to display their training, and the superiority of the distinctly spiritual emphasis of Catholic poor relief. Still, he remained uneasy about the cooperation between Catholic and non-Catholic charitable organizations that became increasingly common in Boston and in other urban centers by the First World War.[12]

The style epitomized by O'Connell and Mundelein spread throughout the ranks of the episcopacy and the clergy, partly by design and partly by osmosis. Both O'Connell and Mundelein made the establishment of the Holy Name Society in all of the parishes of their archdioceses an episcopal priority. The Holy Name Society represented a way to organize the men in the parishes so that their services would be accessible to the diocese. It also served as an antidote to the feminization of the early twentieth-century parish by providing a specifically masculine way to be a faithful and devout Catholic. The episcopal priorities of uniformity and discipline were spread not only by the explicit policies of archbishops like O'Connell and Mundelein. The pervasive influence of the corporate mentality, which informed the values of government, industry, and church alike, also found its way into the sermons preached by pastors. Historian Donna Merwick has uncovered sermons delivered in the Boston archdiocese that extolled the virtues shared by the three great consolidators: Theodore Roosevelt, J. P. Morgan, and Pope Leo XIII.[13]

This same spirit of centralized organization characterized the National Catholic Welfare Conference, which emerged as heir to the National Catholic War Council formed during the First World War. The NCWC approach to the mobilization of the laity was that of O'Connell and Mundelein writ large. The NCCW and the NCCM were formed as federations comprising members of Catholic organizations on the parish and diocesan level. The sheer size and visibility of the NCCW and the NCCM might be seen as a two-edged sword. The councils were established to provide the laity with a voice and an opportunity to influence national opinion, as well as to stimulate Catholic organizations on the parish and diocesan level to greater service. The close relationship between the two councils and the hierarchy both helped and hindered these goals. And as one delegate to the founding meeting of the NCCW in Washington, D. C., in 1920 observed: "[those] who have tried to do any organizing of Catholic women, outside of simply parish organizations, find that we . . . need to educate a great many of the priests."[14] Of course, there were clergymen who understood the problems inherent in this hierarchical vision of the organization of the laity. In 1906 Father John Burke, C.S.C., who would later become an important figure in the NCWC, described the lay person as "an extern" in the church,[15] and the launching of new Catholic societies, even massive federations of Catholic societies, did not significantly change this situation.

Alongside the "organizational approach" to clarifying the role of the laity, exhibited by the proliferation of parish societies in the immigrant era, the drive for a national forum in the lay congresses and the American Federation of Catholic Societies, and the policies of O'Connell, Mundelein, and their fellow bishops in the NCWC, there emerged a totally different approach to the problem. This second approach sought to develop the unfulfilled potential within Catholic societies and the lay leaders themselves. Like the organizational model, this second position had its clerical supporters, but these priests tended to be mission preachers and "freelancers" whose sphere of influence extended beyond the confines of a given parish or diocese. While O'Connell and Mundelein might be described as *boosters* of lay activities who used their administrative talents and position to encourage the growth of Catholic organizations, clergy in the second category served as *midwives* of lay potential and precursors of the lay apostolates born in the 1930s.

These clerical midwives were few and far between during the opening years of this century. Their vision of the expanding role of the laity and the changing relationship between the laity and the clergy set them apart from most of their contemporaries, ordained and unordained. Nothing in their seminary education explicitly prepared them for their futuristic vision of the role of the laity in the church. Clerical midwives were innovators in an age in which the word "innovation" had negative connotations for the Catholic hierarchy. In some sense, they deserved to be considered anomalies in the American Catholic community. In another sense, however, they were groping toward a consensus on the need to change existing perceptions of the laity and the way to begin to implement this kind of change. A brief look at two clerical midwives active during the opening decades of the twentieth century should serve to suggest both the originality of the individual men and the kind of consensus they appear to have been forging, at least among a tiny minority of priests and lay pioneers.

The first example, Thomas Augustine Judge (1868–1933), a Vincentian mission preacher, Brooklyn pastor, and missionary in Alabama during the critical years between 1899 and 1929, experienced firsthand the inadequacies of the clergy in meeting the needs of the urban Italian immigrant population and the unchurched in the rural south. Nor could sisters fill the gap, for they were overburdened in the urban centers and held in suspicion by the natives in the Alabama mission territory. Through his experience as a mission preacher and popularizer of the Archconfraternity of the Holy Agony, Judge became aware that neither the laity's spiritual needs nor their leadership potential were being acknowledged within the parishes that he visited.

During his brief sojourn as assistant pastor at St. John the Baptist Church in Brooklyn (1909–10), Judge, in good Vincentian tradition, encouraged the (primarily female) membership of the parish branch of the Archconfraternity of the Holy Agony to visit the homes of the Italian immigrants in the surrounding neighborhood. Judge shared with this group his special devotion to the Holy Spirit and his belief in the importance of daily communion (even before Pius X had officially encouraged it). He explained that the archconfraternity must live up to its responsibility "to fill up what is lacking in the sufferings of Christ." And he put this in concrete terms, urging members to "think of abandoned children who have never gazed into the crib with Catholic thought and love." The care of "the dirty-faced child," the "spiritual derelict" of the age, represented both a material and a spiritual challenge to the Catholic community. And Judge insisted that it was an obligation that could not be fulfilled by priests.[16]

Had Judge simply urged his parishioners to care for the needs of the poor immigrant, he would have been functioning in much the same way as the clerical boosters of the laity, Mundelein and O'Connell, did, only on a smaller scale. But Judge was responding to the needs of the church, the immigrants, *and the laity* when he proceeded to bring to fruition a lay-led movement, the Missionary Cenacle Apostolate, in which the spiritual renewal of the members might be achieved through their consistent attention to the spiritual and material needs of the poor and the unchurched. When Judge convened the first meeting of the five pioneer members of the Missionary Cenacle Apostolate in the St. John Gabriel Perboyre Chapel in Brooklyn in 1910, he did so with the hope that the laity would lead the movement. As he explained in response to an inquiry from Cardinal O'Connell in 1913:

> There are in every locality many hidden saints who need but a word of encouragement to do and suffer much for souls. There are, even, those who are tempted to worldliness, pleasure loving spirits, but who have good hearts and generous dispositions . . . ; these, interested and persuaded to sanctify themselves . . . become fervent and zealous, and God seems to favor in them remarkable conversions.

Because of this hidden potential for sanctity and service that he found buried within the hearts of a wide variety of lay people, Judge referred to the laity as "a sleeping giant" whose awakening might radically transform the situation of the Catholic Church in the United States.[17]

Judge sought out and encouraged lay people whom he met in his capacity as mission preacher, confessor, and retreatmaster, persons who appeared to be seeking a deeper commitment, a more strenuous form of sanctity and Christian service. These lay leaders not only organized visitations to the homes of the poor, "picture classes" to instruct the poor in the doctrines of the church, sewing classes and other efforts at vocational training, and biweekly meetings in which lay people reflected upon the spiritual significance of their experiences with the unchurched. They were also encouraged to nurture—quietly and discreetly—similar vocations among lay people of their acquaintance.

The Cenacle ideal spread, in part through Judge's expanding network of prospective lay apostles, but in large part through the efforts of the first generation of Cenacle members. Amy Marie Croke, a stenographer and business school instructor, was the primary leader of the movement during its first few decades; she helped it to achieve unity even as it quickly spread to parishes in Baltimore (1910), Boston (1911), Bridgeport, Conn. (1914), Bronx, N. Y. (1910–11), Lyons, N. Y. (1911), Meriden, Conn. (1911), New Britain, Conn. (1911–12), Newport, R. I. (1911), Philadelphia (1910–14), Pittsfield, Mass. (1912–13), Hartford (1912), Syracuse (1913), Worcester, Mass. (1912), Wheeling, W. Va. (1913–14), Brattleboro, Vt. (1911), and Orange, N. J. (1915). The year 1912 witnessed the creation of two new structures that facilitated the development of lay leadership in the movement. The first was the self-governing body known as the Inner Council composed of the leaders of the individual Cenacle branches. The second was Mission House in Baltimore, which served the dual purpose of providing a shelter for working women and a "nursery" for prospective full-time members.

After five years of traveling with a mission band, Judge was transferred in 1915 to the Vincentians' Alabama mission. He immediately sensed that "the cooperation and good will of a highly spiritualized laity" might achieve what priests had been unable to do in four years of sustained but fruitless effort. During the next few years, Judge and Croke persuaded an expanding circle of women, and a handful of men, to come to Alabama to join a full-time community of lay apostles engaged in teaching, health care, catechetical training, and home visiting in Alabama. Cenacle members were doing similar full-time work in Roselle and Orange, New Jersey, and Brooklyn during the same period. Although some of these lay volunteers eventually evolved into a community of sisters and another of priests and brothers, Judge continued to promote the lay apostolate until his death in 1933. Writing in 1918 in the heyday of the Cenacle lay apostolate in Alabama, Judge maintained that "many children [were] being saved from fatal dangers, and a very large volume of sacramental reconciliation [had] taken place, and many probably . . . [would] owe their eternity of blessedness to [the lay volunteers of the Alabama mission]."[18]

The work of Father Peter Dietz (1878–1947), provides another example of a priest who served as midwife to an experimental lay movement during the opening decades of the twentieth century. As a friend and advisor to the Catholic Central Verein and the American Federation of Catholic Societies, as well as to the Catholic constituency within the American Federation of Labor, Dietz can truly be labeled a collaborator with lay leaders in the fight for social justice and against socialist infiltration into the unions. In this capacity, he helped to establish the Militia of Christ for Social Service (1910), an organization for Catholic union members who sought to forge a link between the church and labor activism. This kind of cooperation between a minority of labor priests and lay people remained the normal pattern for clergy who sought to participate in the struggle for social justice prior to the First World War.[19]

Dietz also sought to create new structures within the Catholic community in which lay people might develop their capacity for sanctity and service. Before he was ordained, Dietz had worked as a lay street evangelist in North Carolina in 1904 under the influence of Father Thomas Frederick Price, future founder of the Maryknoll Missionaries. As a layman, Dietz had functioned as a one-man mission team, playing his cornet to attract a crowd to which he would then lecture on Catholic doctrine. As a priest, he saw the need to create a communal framework for lay people wishing to serve the church and society in the struggle for social justice.

While the Militia of Christ nurtured a sense of community for Catholics within the labor movement, Dietz's American Academy of Christian Democracy for Women, established in Hot Springs, North Carolina, in 1915, was a residential community that sought to provide a "social service novitiate" for women. The all-female student body, composed chiefly of women in their late teens and twenties with a smattering of older women, was organized into an association called the White Cross Nurses (the word "nurse" was carefully chosen to signify one who "nourishes, fosters, and manages with care and economy"). The White Cross Nurses were daily communicants who shared with Dietz, their spiritual director, a special devotion to the Holy Spirit. Their days were rigorously scheduled, and they were encouraged to spend what little free time they had in meditation and spiritual reading. The training was not specifically vocational, but rather, a general course in "the Christian philosophy . . . [its] principles, and there [sic] application to church, state, family, and associations of every kind," supplemented by some courses in health care, charity, correction, "state and social agencies," the collection of statistics, public speaking, writing, and "parliamentary practice and organization."

Apparently, the White Cross Nurses incorporated an idea whose time had come. Between 1915 and 1918, over two hundred women from thirty-two states and Canada responded to Dietz's advertisements in the Catholic press and letters informing bishops, women's leagues, academies, and convents about the project.[20] By the First World War, Catholic colleges and universities began to offer courses and programs in social services, and the academy died a natural death. Nevertheless, the popularity of the short-lived program, despite its isolated location and demanding schedule, attests to the growing hunger—especially among Catholic women—for alternative arenas in which lay people might propagate the faith and reform society.

Judge and Dietz explored new possibilities inherent in the relationship between the clergy and the laity. They were both administrators and spiritual directors. They arrived at their vision of the laity's potential in the church by listening to the laity's own concerns in the relative informality of the confessional, the private spiritual conference, and the union hall. They found their collaborative models for the clergy-lay relationship outside the parish and the diocese, as well as within it. Judge and Dietz were part of a fringe movement of priests whose commitment to the idea of a Catholic outreach to American society overshadowed their concern for the maintenance of the Catholic community within the parish and the diocese. They viewed the laity both as a constituency whose needs they must meet and as a segment of the church whose contributions were necessary to meet the needs of those still outside the fold. And finally, they viewed the laity as a constituency with a vast untapped potential for service *and leadership*.

Judge and Dietz sought out lay leaders and innovators and recognized their efforts. In the early twentieth century lay activists were not hard to find. For example, by 1915 there were 14,215 active members of the St. Vincent de Paul Society in the United States, united under one superior council and engaged in the same kind of home visitations as the Cenacle members.[21] Nevertheless, this figure is misleading as an indication of lay people's willingness to serve in the arena of social reform, because it fails to acknowledge the many women who wished to join the society on an equal basis with men.

At the national conference of the St. Vincent de Paul Society held in Boston in 1911, Father William Kerby argued strenuously that women's auxiliaries should be established wherever a men's chapter existed. He insisted that women could contribute a great deal, especially in the area of "preventive charity," because of their expertise in domestic chores, nursing, and child care, as well as women's natural tenacity, good humor, tact, and patience. Kerby's argument failed to persuade, however, and opposition to women's full membership persisted until the general council held in 1968.[22] This policy of excluding women or denying them full membership helps to explain why Judge and Dietz, who did not originally intend to foster single-sex movements, attracted such a large proportion of women.

By the early twentieth century, a growing number of Catholic women were joining their Protestant sisters in the temperance crusade and other social reform movements, and seeking a greater role in the governance of women's service organizations within the church. Some pioneers, like the members of the alumnae sodality of the Chicago Academy of the Sacred Heart, had followed the example of Protestant women and established settlement houses.[23] Nonetheless, many women remained frustrated with the limits placed upon their participation in Catholic organizations. Outspoken women, such as the temperance and labor activist Leonora Barry Lake and the Boston antisocialist lecturer Martha Moore Avery, registered protests. "Who have built the churches?," Lake asked the male delegates at the Catholic Total Abstinence Union convention in Hartford in 1901. "If you answer truly, you must say 'the woman.' Who makes a man go to Mass of a Sunday morning? Who sends the children to Sunday school? The woman." And on these grounds she urged equal treatment for women in the CTAU.[24] Even in a diocese headed by a booster of lay activism, a lay woman could feel her efforts sharply curtailed. In 1918 Martha Moore Avery, active in a plethora of Catholic women's organizations in O'Connell's Boston, told a friend in exasperation, "The Cardinal laid down the *law* under which a Catholic club must operate. If . . . there are women who mean to work on their *own will, they are not wanted*. It was said as bluntly as that."[25]

Lake and Avery struggled with clerical boosters of lay organizations who sought to keep a tight rein on the activities of the people in the pews. Women on the fringes of the parish system necessarily played a more active role in the charitable, catechetical, and pastoral outreach of the church. In 1915 Thomas Augustine Judge found Mrs. John O'Brien serving as the pastor to the twenty-five Catholics in the tiny milltown of Tallassee, Alabama. When the itinerant pastor came to town each month, he said Mass in O'Brien's home. On other Sundays Mrs. O'Brien led her flock in hymns, the rosary, and recitations from the catechism. During Lent she led them in the stations of the cross. "She is a living St. Vincent de Paul Society," Judge affirmed. "When Mrs. O'Brien is seen on the street, the people say: Somebody is sick or dying, there goes Mrs. O'Brien." Women like Mrs. O'Brien, working on their own initiative on the frontiers, prior to the establishment of parish and diocesan programs, were, quite literally, the pillars and cornerstones of the expanding parish system. An example from turn-of-the-century Syracuse illustrates this point. Out of a catechism class for poor children of the Grove's Tract section of town, established by Lillie Burns in her home in 1889, grew a Sunday school sponsored by the cathedral chapter of the St. Vincent de Paul Society. This program evolved into a mission and in 1894 it became a parish.[26]

In a sense, the Cenacle and the White Cross Nurses were also able to point to new and expanding models of lay commitment because they, too, existed on the frontier, whether they were in the urban frontier doing work with immigrants or in "no-priest-land" in the Protestant south. In the movements nurtured by Judge and Dietz, lay people not only served in a variety of functions that would be classified as lay ministries in the 1970s, but they did so with a self-conscious sense of vocation and a spiritual foundation absent in the organizational approach to lay activism. Clerical midwives like Judge and Dietz encouraged lay people to expand their concept of their own vocation in the church and society. In order to do so, they had to expand their own understanding of their priestly vocation so that it could be coterminous with that of the laity. "I want the Church to get all it can out of my Priesthood, and let the Church get all it can out of yours," Judge told Cenacle members in 1913. "My Priesthood is yours and yours is mine."[27] This statement, incomprehensible to most of Judge's clerical contemporaries, still sounds visionary in the 1980s. Judge, Dietz, and subsequent generations of clerical midwives opened up a whole range of new questions about the status and vocation of the laity, questions that today's Catholics are still in the process of answering.

12

THE HEYDAY OF CATHOLIC ACTION AND THE LAY APOSTOLATE, 1929–1959

During the middle decades of the twentieth century there continued to be two competing visions of the role of the laity held by American Catholic bishops and clergy. Clerical boosters of lay activities continued to marshal the energies of their constituencies into massive diocesan displays of faith and charity, and the bishops found new ways to incorporate lay organizations into the proliferating agencies of the NCWC. Another generation of clerical midwives, the successors to Judge and Dietz, assisted at the birth of new movements in which small groups of lay pioneers expanded the boundaries of their leadership potential and vocational self-consciousness. Despite this element of continuity, it is, nevertheless, accurate to say that the American Catholic laity entered a new era in the late 1920s, an age in which the responsibilities of the people in the pews were taken increasingly seriously, or at least discussed with growing frequency under the rubric of the lay apostolate and Catholic Action.

Although it is premature for historians to presuppose any sense of consensus concerning what constitute the major milestones in the history of the American laity, it is clear that sometime in the late 1920s, the laity turned a corner and saw its own situation, both within American society and within the church, from a new perspective. During the first half of the decade, legislation restricting immigration brought an end to the immigrant church. The strides made toward Catholic assimilation into the American mainstream during the First World War continued apace, and middle-class Catholic families became increasingly visible in the suburbs of cities like Chicago.[1] When Al Smith, the Catholic "wet" candidate, ran for president in 1928, upwardly mobile Catholics in an age of expanding expectations felt the sting of unaccustomed prejudice. Karl Rogers, a retired advertising executive from the Philadelphia suburb of Narberth, described the reaction of many Catholic businessmen and professionals. He was shocked and disappointed to watch "non-Catholic fellow-townsmen with whom we had often played golf and bridge, folks who seemed like us, [go] to the poles [sic] with fire in their eyes to vote against the Pope."[2] Precisely because they found themselves in a new situation within American society, Rogers and his friends did not react by retreating into the ghetto, or by hurling bricks and bottles at their hostile neighbors, as earlier generations of Catholic Philadelphians had been forced to do. Instead, they experimented with new ways to explain their Catholic faith to their neighbors, and hoped to convert a few of them in the process.

The depression was another important catalyst in the changing self-perceptions of the Catholic community. It reawakened the social consciences of the laity, prompting what Donald Thorman described as the rebirth of the lay apostolate,[3] virtually dormant (as a mass movement) since the demise of the lay congresses in the 1890s. Members of parish St. Vincent de Paul societies and lay people active in the National Conference of Catholic Charities (1910) accelerated their efforts to provide for the hungry and homeless. Others, like Dorothy Day and the Baroness Catherine de Hueck, sought new alternatives, smaller movements that required a full-time commitment to the poor, and the spiritual discipline of voluntary poverty. This new impulse toward a more strenuous effort to promote social justice among the urban poor was reinforced by the appearance of the social encyclical *Quadragesimo Anno* in 1931, but it arose primarily from the needs of lay people seeking a more satisfactory way to serve God and humanity in the midst of a crisis.

Alongside these domestic factors that contributed to the changing situation of the American laity, three "new" themes imported from European Catholicism during the late 1920s and early 30s became prominent within the American Catholic community and helped to transform the laity's perceptions of the church and their role within it. These included the statements of the "Catholic Action pope," Pius XI, on the lay apostolate, a renewed emphasis upon the communal, participatory nature of the eucharist fostered by the liturgical revival begun at the European abbeys of Mont César and Solesmes, and the rediscovery of the Pauline concept of the church as the mystical body of Christ. Although it took decades for these three "imports" to become familiar to the American Catholic community at large, their impact upon selected lay pioneers and clerical midwives was already being felt by the end of the 1920s.

From the 30s through the 50s, the terms "Catholic Action" and "lay apostolate" were extensively used by Catholic bishops, priests, and lay people to refer to the laity's recently rediscovered responsibility to take action on the church's behalf. Pius XI (1922–39) made the lay apostolate and Catholic Action papal priorities, and thereby ensured that these ideas penetrated beyond a select cadre of laity and clergy to the priests and people of the parishes, but his dedication to the lay apostolate had clear precedents, especially in the statements of Leo XIII and Pius X. As early as 1917, the lay evangelists David Goldstein and Martha Moore Avery launched their Catholic Truth Guild, confident that they were acting upon Leo XIII's statement in 1890 that "private individuals" and "especially those on whom God has bestowed gifts of mind with the strong wish of rendering themselves useful" may assist in the pastor's office of teaching the truths of the faith. Leo XIII made a clear distinction between the office of pastor, which was restricted to ordained clergy, and "the [lay apostles'] task of communicating to others what they . . . have received," functioning, in effect, as "living echoes of their masters in the faith."[4] Nevertheless, this distinction did not detract from the specific papal mandate for lay activism that Goldstein and Avery found in the document.

In the encyclical *Il fermo proposito* (1905), Leo XIII's successor, Pius X (1903–14), addressed the goal of Catholic Action: "the restoration of all things in Christ." Pius X declared that he needed "the cooperation" of both the clergy and the faithful in fulfilling his pastoral office. He added that "in truth, we are all called . . . to build up that unique body of which Christ is the Head, a body which is highly organized . . . and well coordinated in all its movements."[5] Pius XI built upon this tradition of papal support for the lay apostolate when he addressed the topic of Catholic Action in his first encyclical, *Ubi arcano* (1922). He applauded the "apostolic spirit" that he perceived to be "far more widespread than before" and maintained that when the faithful "take part" in the work of the bishops and clergy "by carrying abroad the knowledge of Christ and teaching men to love Him, then they are indeed worthy of being hailed as 'a chosen generation, a kingly priesthood, a holy nation, a purchased people.'" Although Pius XI underscored the fact that the laity were *participating* in the apostolate of their bishops and pastors, he also made it clear that in certain cases, the laity, "thanks to their very condition, can sometimes accomplish things which are impossible to the clergy, however willing these might be." In these situations, the pontiff stated, lay people engaged in a "sacerdotal ministry . . . more than ever fitted to the needs of our time."[6]

In these statements and in the countless references to Catholic Action found in the writings of Pius XI, critical questions were raised about the potential priesthood of the laity, its relationship to the sacerdotal ministry of the ordained clergy, and the unique contribution made by the lay apostle. Catholics who read the statements of Pius XI and his predecessors could draw their own conclusions. Beyond the generic definition of Catholic Action as "the participation of the laity in the apostolate of the hierarchy," Pius XI left the specific nature of Catholic Action flexible. He acknowledged that it "must adapt itself to difference [sic] of age, sex, and circumstances of time and place."[7] Clergymen and lay people in the field could focus upon the process of commissioning apostles, or upon the specific mission entrusted to the lay apostle, depending upon their own experience and perspective.

Because Pius XI self-consciously promoted the terms "lay apostolate" and "Catholic Action," they became the accepted way for bishops to describe whatever the laity were doing under their jurisdiction, whether or not it had been informed by the statements of Pius XI. In Syracuse in 1934 Bishop Duffy responded to the papal call for Catholic Action by adopting the same policy that O'Connell and Mundelein had embraced decades before: the organization of parish Holy Name Societies into a diocesan federation, which could then be incorporated into the NCWC. Father Daniel A. Lord, S. J., who had to confront many a bishop in his effort to rebuild the moribund Sodality of Our Lady starting in the late 1920s, asserted that he was "convinced that [Catholic Action was] merely anything the local bishop happens to want."[8] For the growing circle of priests and lay people who were familiar with the liturgical renewal and the theology of the mystical body, however, Catholic Action had a very different meaning.

This brings us to the second theme from within European Catholicism that was imported into the American Catholic community during the late 1920s: liturgical renewal. In a sense, the laity's desire for more participation in the liturgy had its roots in the policies of Pope Pius X, who encouraged frequent communion and maintained, in his 1903 motu proprio on church music, that "active participation in the sacred mysteries and in the solemn and public prayer of the Church is the primary and indispensable source of the true Christian spirit."[9] Mrs. Justine Ward and Mother Georgia Stephens, who established the Pius X School of Liturgical Music in 1916, responded to the papal mandate and planted the seeds for the liturgical renewal that would begin in the American Catholic Church a decade later. The chief catalysts for the American liturgical renewal movement were Father William Busch, who opened up the topic for public debate in a letter to the editors of *America* in 1924, and the Benedictine priest Virgil Michel of St. John's Abbey in Collegeville, Minnesota. Michel launched the journal *Orate Fratres* in 1926 to popularize the liturgical renewal that he had encountered on a trip to Europe the year before, and it soon became a primary catalyst in the American Catholic liturgical movement.[10]

According to Paul Marx, a historian of the American liturgical renewal, "a surprising number of the original subscribers" to *Orate Fratres* were lay people.[11] Another example of lay support for liturgical reform was the establishment of the Liturgical Arts Society in New York in 1928 by a group of Catholics in the arts. This enthusiasm displayed by a select but expanding group of the laity for better liturgies and more lay participation in them is important. It indicates that even as early as the 1920s and 30s, at least a small minority of those in the pews felt responsible for the quality of their parish liturgy. Lay people acted upon this sense of responsibility not only by subscribing to *Orate Fratres* or *Liturgical Arts* but also by writing to *Commonweal*, a lay-edited journal that provided a forum where the voices of dissenting Catholics might be heard.

In the late 1930s *Commonweal* received a flurry of letters to the editor demanding vernacular liturgies. In 1939 Hazen Ordway recommended a *Missa Recitata* "every Sunday in every parish," as part of "a movement aimed at full liturgical life for all." Some who were actively engaged in other apostolates disagreed. Two years before, in a letter to the editors of *Commonweal*, Anthony Traboulsee had insisted that the laity should avoid the "exotic" liturgical movement and turn to more pressing, practical concerns such as a "crusade" to help the starving. John Cort's letter written to *Commonweal* in 1939 suggests the wider implications of the liturgical movement for Catholics who were trying to understand how they should serve both the church and society. Cort asserted that it was "hard to see how the Church [could] hold the working class in America or realize that revival of faith necessary for a Christian reconstruction of the social order without somehow breaking down the terrible wall of incomprehension that now stands between the altar at Sunday Mass and so many of our Catholic congregations."[12]

The third new theme from European Catholicism, the theology of the mystical body of Christ, was intimately related to the liturgical reforms. Virgil Michel had come into contact with both developments on his trip to Europe in 1925 and from the start he made the mystical body a central focus in the new vision of the liturgy that he sought to promote. When, in 1929, *Commonweal* editor George Shuster lamented the loss of the "communal aspects" of the liturgy, Michel publicly concurred. He suggested that "the sacred ministrant" was in danger of becoming a "functionary" rather than the "mediator" that he was intended to be. Michel added: "some day an 'official teacher' will have to reutter the age-old Catholic doctrine that the layfolk are not merely trained dogs but true living members of the Church."[13] For those who took seriously the doctrine of the mystical body, the meaning of church *membership* assumed a whole new dimension not necessarily appreciated by everyone who spoke of church (or parish) membership.

One important way in which the theology of the mystical body was disseminated among a select but growing minority of American Catholics from the 1930s through the 50s was through the publications of Sheed and Ward. When the New York branch of Sheed and Ward opened in 1933, it made available to American Catholics the classics of the European Catholic intellectual revival, which was well underway by the late 1920s. The revival was not a unified movement, but rather a cluster of movements, including the Thomistic revival of Etienne Gilson and Jacques Maritain, the historical revival associated with Christopher Dawson, and the literary revival, connected with G. K. Chesterton, Hilaire Belloc, Sigrid Undset, François Mauriac, and others too numerous to mention.[14] Ann Harrigan, a Brooklyn teacher and an avid reader of Sheed and Ward authors in the 1930s, attested to the "electric" effect that the writers of the Catholic intellectual revival had upon her "generally obedient, subservient" middle-class Catholic circle of friends.

Harrigan maintained that among the most important ideas propagated by Sheed and Ward was the doctrine of the mystical body of Christ, which Maisie Ward and Frank Sheed had originally encountered in Robert Hugh Benson's *Christ in the Church*, first published in 1911. In her memoirs, Harrigan quoted a passage from Benson's book that had had a profound impact upon her vision of the church:

> In not one of the great world religions, in not one of the smallest and most arrogant sects, has the proclamation ever been made that the Founder lives a mystical but absolutely real life in a Body composed of his followers . . . that the great bulk of the faithful compose a living organism whose head is Divine.[15]

In this passage, one is struck by the certainty and confidence with which Benson affirms the uniqueness of the Catholic Church. This certainty and confidence was especially appealing to the self-conscious Catholics like Harrigan who frequented the Sheed and Ward bookstore in New York. In other writings by Sheed and Ward authors, one finds variations on the same message—for example, Belloc's insistence that the Catholic Church was the only ideology or institution capable of imposing order upon modern civilization. "Outside it," Belloc maintained, "is the night."[16]

Harrigan and other lay persons who envisioned the church as a living organism, the liturgy as a celebration of human solidarity in

Christ, and Catholic faith as the only means of restructuring modern society, had to look beyond the parish for ways to live out their commitment to the church and humanity. Although the parish was proclaimed to be a fundamental unit of the mystical body, the parish system was not ready to accommodate lay people eager to respond to the mandate for Catholic Action. Led with a tight rein by a generation of "ombudsman" priests,[17] most American parishes resisted lay initiative until the demands of the 1950s rendered the beginnings of parish reform unavoidable. This helps to explain why there were a variety of attempts by lay apostles to form small alternative communities on the fringe of the parish. Even as late as the 1950s, there were only a few self-conscious efforts (e.g., Joseph Gremillion's parish in Shreveport, Louisiana) to restructure the parish in the image of the mystical body.

An exception was *The Lay Apostolate* (1929) by Father John Harbrecht, who was professor of social ethics at Mount St. Mary Seminary in Cincinnati. Harbrecht's book is a rare, ambitious, and unheeded early proposal for a parish-based form of lay ministry that "[realized] the mystical body of Christ." Drawing upon the ideas of his teacher, Professor Franz Keller of the University of Freiburg, Harbrecht asserted that the laity's primary responsibility within the parish should be the organization of charity. He proceeded to define charity in the broadest possible terms as:

> Free and spontaneous service rendered to our neighbor in need, under the influence of divine grace as an expression of our supernatural understanding of how Christ loved us and of our consequent social ethical relations as His disciples in the Christian Community.

Harbrecht maintained that lay apostles should not engage in the "standard and permanent" lay activities pursued by parish societies, but instead should seek to stimulate and coordinate new ways for individuals and Catholic societies to meet the growing needs of the community. Lay apostles should be the leaders of the laity, the nurturers of lay vocations. They should evaluate their own work according to the single criterion of whether it enhances the "spiritual welfare" of the individuals they serve.

Harbrecht's most important models for his vision of the laity were the Salvation Army and a German lay apostolate called the Free Union for Helping the Cure of Souls through Charity, established in 1911. Harbrecht insisted that none of the American Catholic lay apostolates that he had examined even approached his vision. The St. Vincent de Paul Societies and the National Conference of Catholic Charities placed inadequate stress upon the "cure of souls." The NCWC had yet to "accept its responsibilities in the parish." The Holy Name Society, Harbrecht asserted, "[was] unadaptable for the parish Lay Apostolate since it [consisted] only of men." Sodalities had real possibilities, but their potential was untapped in most parts of the country. Harbrecht affirmed that what was missing in the parishes of the United States was a well-trained force of lay workers, consisting of both paid professionals and volunteers. After examining the programs currently open to lay people—schools for social workers at Fordham and St. Xavier College in Cincinnati, the Bureau of Social Service in Hartford, and the National Catholic Social Service School for women established by the NCWC—he dismissed all of them as inadequate for the training of parish workers.

Harbrecht's skeletal outline of a curriculum geared to the needs of parish lay apostles, which included courses in scripture, doctrine, social ethics, social pathology, community organizations, the principles and methods of charity, civil and canon law, sociology, psychiatry, and industrial relations, attests to his conviction that properly educated lay people should play a far more active role in the pastoral care of the local parish than American Catholic bishops and pastors could envision in 1929, or even decades later. From personal experience, Harbrecht knew that it was difficult to attract men to professional charity work, but he insisted: "there are many young women in our parishes who do not feel called to the religious state, yet are willing to dedicate their whole life, or a span of years, to the service of the Lord in aiding the pastor in the cure of souls. . . . They need but be marshalled for professional service in the Lay Apostolate."[18]

There is no evidence to suggest that Harbrecht's proposals were known or respected by the vast majority of parish priests, or even bishops, of his time. Harbrecht's views on the training and mobilization of the laity sound modern even to Catholics of the 1980s. They must have appeared highly unrealistic to his clerical contemporaries. American Catholic bishops and pastors of the 1930s believed that the way to marshal the forces of the laity—aside from soliciting their financial support—was to involve them in the two major priorities of the hierarchy: works of charity and the religious education of the Catholic population. During the period between the 1930s and the 50s, there were successful efforts to expand and centralize existing programs in these two areas on the national and diocesan level within the National Conference of Catholic Charities (NCCC) and the Confraternity of Christian Doctrine (CCD). Two other prominent examples of lay societies engaged in educational and charitable activities were the sodality movement solidified by Daniel Lord, S. J., during the late 1920s, and the elaborate network of lay organizations that had evolved in the archdiocese of Chicago by the early 1930s.

The NCCC, established in 1910, arose, in part, out of frustration that Thomas Mulry and Edmond J. Butler, regional leaders within the St. Vincent de Paul Society, felt with the parochial orientation of the movement. Mulry and Butler were not alone in their concern that the lay leadership in their movement might be attracted to more organized and autonomous non-Catholic movements for social reform. They rightly suspected that the St. Vincent de Paul Society's skepticism concerning the professionalism of social services would alienate potential volunteers. By 1930, two decades after the establishment of the NCCC, the centralization of Catholic charities along diocesan lines had progressed to the point that there were sixty-eight diocesan bureaus in thirty-five states. This made it possible for dioceses to eliminate overlapping agencies, do more "preventive" charity, and seek to promote social legislation in line with Catholic social teachings.[19]

The centralization of Catholic charities presented some problems on the local level, however. Some St. Vincent de Paul Societies continued to support and expand model programs such as the St. Vincent de Paul Workingman's Club in Denver, for men who found themselves hungry and homeless during the depression. In other places where funding was scarce, local pastors and parish St. Vincent de Paul Societies cut back on their programs, secure in the knowledge that there was now a diocesan agency that could fill the gap.[20] At the executive committee meeting of the NCCC in 1943, Miss Marguerite Boylan called attention to still another problem. Priests and sisters had emerged as the visible leaders of the conference, while lay people remained concentrated within the lower echelons of the volunteer work force. On the national level, the conference had failed to nurture "a devoted, intelligent, strong lay group."[21]

A second example of the bishops' efforts to organize the laity during the era of Catholic Action was the establishment of the central bureau of the CCD within the NCWC in 1935, chaired by Bishop Edwin V. O'Hara. O'Hara's vision of the laity's potential as religious educators, derived from his observation of Lutheran summer schools during his boyhood in Minnesota, had been confirmed by his experience with the National Catholic Rural Life Conference (NCRLC) rural vacation schools. With the help of volunteers from the NCCW, which was an affiliate of the NCRLC, the vacation schools for rural Catholic youth grew from three schools containing 47 students in 1921 to 6,112 schools serving 547,000 students in 1938. As Bishop of Great Falls, Montana, O'Hara had likewise nurtured lay leadership in a CCD adult education program organized on the parish level. In 1935, there were seven hundred adult discussion clubs in parishes of the Great Falls diocese meeting regularly to examine the portrayal of early church history in their text, the Acts of the Apostles.[22] The CCD flourished, in part, because it promoted collaboration between lay organizations. By 1938, the CCD had a college section coordinated with the Newman movement. A parent-educator committee focused upon the role of parents in the religious education of their children, which had formed in 1930 within the NCRLC, took root in the CCD movement. It paved the way for the programs and publications[23] later sponsored by Cana conferences.

The CCD made a major contribution to the development of lay leadership on both the parish and the national level in the age of Catholic Action. Starting in 1947, the national center of the CCD, in conjunction with the Catholic University of America, sponsored summer leadership courses (for college credit) to educate the lay people who trained CCD teachers for work in the parishes. During the late 1940s and the 1950s some Catholic colleges were offering free tuition, room, and board to participants in these intensive summer courses lasting for several days. By the 1950s, the CCD on the parish level had evolved into a broad-based program divided into six specialized sections, each with a different function. *Fishers* conducted the parish census. *Helpers* distributed the census information to other groups. *Parent-Educators* distributed literature on their program, served as P-Es in their own homes, and sponsored family oriented events (e.g., Babies' Days) in the parish. *Teachers* trained others to teach religion in parochial schools, rural vacation schools, programs for Catholics in public schools, and through correspondence courses. A *discussion clubs group* sponsored discussions for adults. Finally, the *Apostles of Good Will* planned and publicized programs on Catholic beliefs for interested non-Catholics.[24] The case of the CCD illustrates how a traditional Catholic organization with roots stretching back to the sixteenth century could be remodeled to meet the needs of the twentieth-century American Catholic community and become a training ground for lay leaders.

The Jesuit Sodality of Our Lady, which also had sixteenth-century origins, illustrates the same point. When Father Daniel Lord was placed at the head of the national office of the Sodality of Our Lady in St. Louis in 1925, he investigated the condition of the sodalities in parishes and schools across the country. He was disillusioned to find the sodality movement almost dead in the schools and parishes, with neither priests nor members mourning the impending loss. Lord was convinced that the sodality was misunderstood; according to its original manual, it was not supposed to be "a cluster of the devoutly pious but a regiment of the apostolic alert." Lord had a vision of the sodality as a "spiritual council" at the center of Catholic schools and parishes, a core group of competent lay leaders anxious to act upon their faith.

The centerpiece of the national sodality movement was the Summer School of Catholic Action held annually from 1931 until 1968, and attended by over two hundred thousand priests, sisters, and lay people. Each of the summer schools had the same goal: the spiritual and practical training of a new cadre of Catholic leaders. The sodality, which promoted lay autonomy in a free-standing movement separate from the NCWC, provoked jealousies within the episcopal leadership of the lay apostolate. Archbishop John T. McNicholas of Cincinnati, head of the Catholic Student Mission Crusade, banished Lord's sodality from his jurisdiction in order to eliminate potential competition for his pet organization. By 1932 the sodality was banned by seven bishops. According to Lord, this kind of reaction only confirmed his worst fears, that through the NCWC and the Catholic University of America, the bishops were "determined to control all activities and discountenance all activities they cannot control." In 1950, after a quarter century of promoting lay leadership within the sodality movement, Lord was asking "if our inevitable division into ordained and unordained . . . into the clerical class and the lay class . . . may not make us priests forget that we are One Body in Christ . . . and that the laity are really members of the priesthood of Christ."[25]

On the diocesan level, the organization of the laity during the age of Catholic Action varied greatly from place to place, depending upon the priorities of the ordinary. In the archdiocese of Chicago, where the seeds were planted by Mundelein's policies as a booster of lay activism, lay organizations were especially well developed from the 1930s through the 1950s. On June 11, 1930, one of Mundelein's auxiliaries, Bishop Bernard J. Sheil, formally established the Catholic Youth Organization (CYO), a vast network of smaller youth organizations. Although the CYO began as an assortment of athletic activities designed to woo young Catholic men away from the temptations of the streets (and the equally pernicious influence of the YMCA), its focus became increasingly social in the late 1930s. By the middle of the next decade, the CYO was sponsoring Rita Clubs (residences for working women), halfway houses for ex-convicts, the Nisei Center for Japanese-Americans recently released from internment camps, and an adult education center that specialized in Catholic social teachings and labor issues.

In the early 1930s, Sheil also became the sponsor of another important network, the Chicago Inter-Student Catholic Action (CISCA). An archdiocesan outgrowth of a student organization (Chicago Catholic Student Conference on Religious Activities, or CISCORA) formed at Loyola University in 1927, CISCA became the training ground for a whole generation of lay activists in the Chicago area. The wide range of activities sponsored by CISCA, from collecting used foil for salvage and selling the *Catholic Worker* to holding a mock court dealing with racism, testifies to the sense of lay initiative and social responsibility fostered by this student organization.

Another network of lay movements that took root in the archdiocese of Chicago was the Jocist movement, founded just before the First World War in the working-class parish of a Belgian priest, Joseph Cardijn. The term Jocist, an abbreviated form of *Jeunesse Ouvrière Chrétien*, or Young Christian Workers, became synonymous with Cardijn's "inquiry method" in which small cells of parishioners met regularly to discuss how the gospel might be applied to the particular problems they faced at work. The Jocist movement, never a dominant force in the American lay apostolate, became an important priority of Reynold Hillenbrand, rector of Chicago's St. Mary of the Lake Seminary from 1936 to 1944.[26] As a result, one generation of Chicago priests was exposed to an alternative model of the lay apostolate, which emphasized small groups, the development of lay leadership and initiative, and the laity's duty to transform the world in the image of God. This new model was also propagated by Louis Putz at the University of Notre Dame, Donald Kanaly of Oklahoma, and a handful of other priests across the nation. It resurfaced in the Christian Family Movement (CFM), an indigenous adaptation of the Jocist movement for married couples, which became a catalyst in the changing role and consciousness of the laity in the pivotal decade of the 1960s.

While some of the laity responded to the call for Catholic Action by joining the sodality movement, the parish CCD, or local affiliates of the NCCC, other Catholics preferred another approach: the formation of small, grass-roots lay movements that reflected the style and talents of their leaders and clerical midwives. These movements grew up on the fringes of the parish system and attracted lay apostles who did not fit neatly into the larger diocesan and national movements. Some of them also provided a niche for the growing lay minority, especially women, targeted by Harbrecht in 1929, those who wanted to commit themselves full-time as *lay people* to the apostolate.

One area in which smaller, lay-led movements developed alongside larger hierarchically controlled organizations was in the field of evangelization. During the 1930s as the CCD expanded and consolidated, there were also several grass-roots lay efforts to propagate the faith underway within the American Catholic community. A brief look at David Goldstein's Catholic Campaigners for Christ, Rosalie Marie Levy's Catholic Lay Apostle Guild, Karl Rogers's Catholic Information Society of Narberth, and the Catholic Evidence Guild, imported to the United States by Sheed and Ward, should indicate both the variety within the field of lay evangelism during this period and the growing sense of initiative and responsibility that all lay evangelists shared.

Goldstein launched his street preaching career in 1917 on Boston Common, among the socialist soapboxers and Salvationists. His trademark, a yellow and white Model T lecture car, self-consciously painted the colors of the papal flag, and festooned with the Stars and Stripes and quotations from George Washington and Cardinal O'Connell, aptly symbolized the aggressive, confident, posture that he believed the Catholic Church should assume in the propagation of the faith. From 1931 until 1942, Goldstein crisscrossed the nation in a series of yellow-and-white lecture cars, delivering "Catholic Outdoor Lay Missions." At his missions, which met on several consecutive evenings, Goldstein taught basic Catholic doctrine and even plunged into the controversial issues of communism and contraception. Although he was known for his provocative presentations and the freewheeling "quiz period" that always followed, Goldstein also met privately with individuals who had specific questions or were considering converting to Catholicism. On rare occasions he would replace his prepared lecture with a spontaneous public recitation of the rosary.[27]

Rosalie Marie Levy, a convert and a single woman who had supported herself as a stenographer and a chiropractor, worked full-time as a free-lance lay apostle from 1929 to 1941, propagating the faith and fighting the communists. At great personal sacrifice she gave hundreds of lectures, wrote books, and acted as a heckler at ex-nun lectures delivered by women with names like "Miss Good News" in New York City in the 1930s. Levy organized a group of outdoor speakers who, carrying the American flag and wearing the blue sashes of the Catholic Lay Apostle Guild, answered questions about the church and provided a distinctly Catholic presence in Union Square starting in 1936.[28]

Like Levy, Karl Rogers of Narberth, Pennsylvania, sought to dispel false stereotypes of the church during the period of resurgent anti-Catholicism that followed the Al Smith campaign. Rogers and fellow parishioners from St. Margaret's in Narberth launched a "Catholic advertising" campaign in pamphlets and the secular press. Non-Catholics in Narberth received discreetly hand-addressed envelopes containing pocket-sized tracts "so brief that they may be read between the orange juice and the oatmeal," with snappy titles—for example, "Do Catholic Medals Keep Off Lightning?" and "Dickie, a Buick, and the Pope." Rogers and the members of the Catholic Information Society of Narberth (nicknamed the Narberthians) asked other Catholics to help support their efforts by donating the cost of a soda or a pack of cigarettes each month. By 1935 there were thirty-nine such societies modeled on the Narberthians sponsored by Catholic high schools, Holy Name Societies, sodalities, and at least one Council of Catholic Women. By 1942, the year Rogers died, advertisements based upon the Narberthian pamphlets appeared in 383 newspapers across the United States, and reached a readership of 2,793,059.[29]

The fourth lay evangelistic movement, the Catholic Evidence Guild, was actually a whole network of local, grass-roots movements modeled upon the original guild that had been sponsoring Catholic lectures at Speakers' Corner in London's Hyde Park since 1918. The guild was imported to the United States in the late 1920s due to the combined efforts of Frank Sheed, the Paulist Elliot Ross, and Father (later Bishop) Francis Clement Kelley of the Catholic Extension Society. Guilds established in Baltimore (1931), Washington, D. C. (1931), Oklahoma City (1932), Detroit (1934), Philadelphia (1935), and Buffalo (1935),[30] used *Catholic Evidence Training Outlines*, written by Frank Sheed and Maisie Ward as a training manual for the Hyde Park speakers. The movement received the strong support of a handful of priests, including Stephen Leven in Oklahoma, Charles H. Hart of the Catholic University of America, and the Jesuit Francis Le Buffe in New York City, and attracted Catholic college students at Catholic University, Fordham University, Trinity College, Washington, D. C., and Rosary College, River Forest, Illinois.

From 1935 through the late 1940s, members of the Rosary College Catholic Evidence Guild, accompanied by sisters from the faculty, spent summers street preaching in rural outposts in Oklahoma, North Carolina, and Louisiana. With their own renditions of "God Bless America," "You Are My Sunshine," "Beer Barrel Polka," and "The Bells of St. Mary's," they attracted crowds all across the Bible Belt. And after the singing stopped, listeners stayed to hear about Catholic beliefs and practices, and to watch the students demonstrate the sacrament of baptism on a plastic baby doll many times christened Frances Sheila.[31] There is no way to estimate accurately how many people joined the American branches of the Evidence Guild; their numbers were certainly never large. More important than numbers, however, was the impact of the experience upon guild members and their audiences. The Rosary College street preachers were engaged in what might accurately, if anachronistically, be called a team ministry with Father Leven in Oklahoma in 1935. The recollections of one veteran of that summer's work, written in the first person plural, testify both to the achievements of the group, and to one participant's perception of what they were doing:

> In spite of all odds (heat, dust, noise, and tornados) we managed to deliver a talk each night to several hundred. . . . Before we left [Jennings, Oklahoma], many marriages had been blessed, many babies and adults were baptized, and in general there was a much better understanding of Catholic doctrine.[32]

Although, technically speaking, Father Leven had performed the baptisms and blessed the marriages, they appear, in this account, to be the work of the whole group. And, in a larger sense, they were.

The vitality of the Evidence Guild during the 1930s and the early 1940s, before it became primarily an extracurricular activity for seminarians, illustrates the way in which the spirit of a zealous minority within Catholic colleges resonated with that of the Catholic intellectual revival. Sheed and Ward, the popularizers of the revival, were also the chief boosters of the Evidence Guild. Reynold Hillenbrand, who spread the Jocist ideal among Chicago priests, was also the first trainer of the Rosary College Evidence Guild. Each of these four lay evangelistic movements engaged in activities that offended less courageous Catholics, and Goldstein even offended his fellow lay evangelists with his sensationalism, his gimmicks, and his open admiration for the Salvation Army and the Protestant evangelist Aimee Semple MacPherson.[33] The lay evangelists were, nonetheless, the wave of the future. By the 1950s their evangelistic zeal, as well as the innovation and initiative they displayed, were acknowledged in some places to be the desirable traits for the average parishioner, not merely the lay apostle on the frontier.

The lay evangelists themselves were, in some sense, factors in this change, but there were other small grassroots apostolates that were even more important in paving the way for the "emerging" laity of the late 1950s. Two types of apostolates belong in the latter category: those that popularized the new currents of thought associated with the liturgical renewal, the mystical body ecclesiology, and the Catholic intellectual revival among an everwidening circle of the laity, and those (e.g., the Catholic Workers, Friendship House, and the Grail) that inspired a new vision of the role of the laity, an alternative to the one operative in traditional parish and diocesan societies.

The contribution made by the publishing firm of Sheed and Ward in heightening American Catholic awareness of the intellectual revival and the mystical body has already been mentioned. The Catholic bookstores that sold Sheed and Ward publications and sponsored lectures and public discussions played a crucial role in changing the laity's perceptions of the church and their place within it. The 1930s witnessed the appearance of a new breed of Catholic bookstore, run by educated lay people who were familiar with the changing currents in theology and viewed their stores more as apostolates than as businesses. In 1933 Sara Benedicta O'Neill opened the St. Benet's Library and Book Shop in Chicago, which became both a resource center and meeting ground for members of the burgeoning Chicago apostolates. Three years later in Cambridge, Massachusetts, Evangeline Mercier, Mary Stanton, and Martha Doherty launched the St. Thomas Lending Library and Bookstore, which likewise became the hub of the Catholic student community at Harvard and the surrounding colleges. In 1942, in South Bend, Indiana, the Aquinas Library and Book Shop performed the same function in another region especially rich in lay apostolates during the late 1930s and 1940s.[34]

The informal networks of lay people who congregated at these and other Catholic bookstores attest to the popularization of the Catholic intellectual revival by the eve of the Second World War. Catholics influenced by these networks gained a broader vision of the church and the laity's dynamic role within it than could be gleaned from participation in parish societies or diocesan lay organizations. Both from the content of their reading and from their connection with the community that formed around the bookstores and allied apostolates, they became convinced that American Catholicism, like American democracy, was inherently participatory. Especially among the younger Catholics who were reading Sheed and Ward books and discussing the implications of liturgy and the mystical body, there was a hunger for more strenuous, personalized, and concrete ways to act upon their faith outside the parish, in the community at large.

The Catholic Worker movement, established by Dorothy Day and Peter Maurin in 1933, was among the first to call attention to this hunger for alternative apostolates. Dorothy Day was a radical journalist who converted to Catholicism in 1927. Once within the fold, she longed for the intense community and shared commitment to justice that she had left behind in the communist movement. Day was an activist by temperament and past experience, and no amount of "quiet reading and prayer" could make up for the void she felt after she had left the activist life behind. Her frustration with the church reached its climax in 1932 when she covered a communist hunger march in Washington, D. C., for a Catholic journal and was forced to sit on the sidelines and watch the others protest social injustices. She asked herself, "Where was the Catholic leadership in the gathering of bands of men and women together, for the actual works of mercy that the comrades had always made a part of their technique in reaching the workers?" She realized that she had become "puny", "self-centered", and "ingrown" since her conversion; she had lost her "sense of community." Convinced that a life of spiritual reading and writing for Catholic journals was not sufficient for her, she sought a better way to serve.[35]

Day found the way soon after when she met Peter Maurin, a French peasant in his fifties who has been aptly described as "a cross between a bum and a twentieth-century Isaias."[36] The result was a penny paper, *The Catholic Worker*, and a series of Houses of Hospitality in New York City where a kaleidoscopic group of workers and students lived in voluntary poverty feeding the poor and supporting the struggle for social justice. The movement started out as an extended family: Day, her daughter Tamar, her brother John, and Maurin. It grew larger, adding a former policeman, a Lithuanian woman from the Pennsylvania mines and her infant daughter, and finally, generation upon generation of Catholic college students and recent graduates. The movement spread to Chicago, Buffalo, Boston, Seattle, St. Louis, and beyond. Catholic Worker Houses provided food and clothing for the poor, and food for thought for the Catholic activists who participated in the (formal and informal) discussions of liturgy, theology, social reform, and the writers of the Catholic intellectual revival that took place at Catholic Worker Houses across the country.

The Catholic Worker movement became the prototype of the independent lay apostolate. Always more of an organism than an organization, it spawned new movements with their own identities that went their separate ways. The Association of Catholic Trade Unionists (ACTU), established by John Cort and ten fellow union activists in 1937 in the kitchen of the Mott Street House of Hospitality in New York, provided a Catholic presence in the CIO. As Dietz's Militia of Christ had done in an earlier era, the ACTU "helped dispel the image of Catholics as a passive presence in American unionism." Unlike the Militia of Christ, the ACTU affirmed that Catholics had a *duty* to organize and to strike for a just cause. When, in the early 1940s, the ACTU turned its attention to combatting communism in the CIO, resemblance to the Militia became even more striking. The tension between the Catholic Workers' agrarian utopianism and the ACTU's dedication to reforming the existing urban-industrial society increased as the Second World War approached. The ACTU and the Catholic

Worker movement finally parted company over the issues of the ACTU's partisan position in the CIO and its support for weapons production. Dorothy Day's position was inflexible: "we are not interested in increasing armaments jobs, going along with big business, and perpetuating the *status quo*."[37]

Another example of how the Catholic Worker gave birth to lay movements that found their own distinct vision can be seen in the case of the Chicago Catholic Worker House. Started in 1936 by a black Catholic physician, Dr. Arthur Fall, the movement attracted an impressive community of bright, mostly young, working-class Catholics, including Ed Marciniak, Alex Reser, James O'Gara, and John Cogley. Marciniak's recollections of the early period are reminiscent of Ann Harrigan's remarks concerning her experience of the Sheed and Ward bookstore in New York during the same period. Marciniak asserted that through the Chicago Catholic Worker he "discovered . . . a church [he] had never heard about, never knew existed." The movement introduced Marciniak and the others to a "new world . . . of great intellectual vitality." He and the others "read avidly, every learned Catholic magazine [they] could locate . . . raised every question . . . challenged every conceivable position." "We subjected the church to so much scrutiny," Marciniak insisted, "because we loved her so much."[38] The Chicago Catholic Workers disbanded in the early 1940s in the wake of a serious disagreement with Dorothy Day on the question of pacifism. Veterans of the movement took with them the sense of solidarity in the mystical body that they had affirmed as Catholic Workers. Marciniak himself went on to establish *Work* (1943–60), a Catholic labor journal that promoted the solidarity and dignity of workers and later moved into the area of interracial solidarity.

On the masthead of the *Catholic Worker*, Christ stands arm in arm with two laborers: a black man and a white woman. From the beginning, the rejection of racial distinctions within the mystical body was an important aspect of the Catholic Workers' Christian witness in the inner city and on the picket lines. The 1930s brought other new beginnings in the American Catholic community's awareness of racism within the church and American society. In 1934, the Catholic Laymen's Union, a group of black businessmen and professionals who had been working with the Jesuit John LaFarge on a program of Catholic social action, issued an appeal. Addressing a large Catholic audience assembled in the New York Town Hall, they called for a "thoroughgoing policy of Christian justice and Christian charity toward the Negro race." This was the birth of the New York Catholic Interracial Council, a cooperative effort by black and white Catholics to promote justice in race relations. Under the leadership of LaFarge and George Hunton, and popularized by its journal, the *Interracial Review*, the idea behind the council spread. By 1954 there were twenty-three Catholic Interracial Councils, including four in the south. Hunton also encouraged Catholic colleges and alumni groups to become involved in the fight against racism. As early as 1937, the Catholic Students' Mission Crusade tackled the problem of racial equality in religious education.[39]

Like Dorothy Day and the growing number of Catholics attracted to the Catholic Worker movement, Catherine de Hueck yearned for the opportunity to work for racial equality on a full-time basis in a community of like-minded individuals, rather than as a member of a council or a large Catholic organization. On Valentine's Day 1938 de Hueck established the first Friendship House in the United States on West 138th Street in Harlem, with financial assistance from the Columbia University Newman Club. Like the Catholic Worker movement, this interracial apostolate rooted in a community of dedicated individuals living in solidarity with blacks attracted Catholic college students from across the nation. Students flocked to Friendship House from nearby Columbia, Hunter College, NYU, Manhattanville, and St. John's University (Brooklyn), and from as far away as St. Benedict's College in Minnesota.

At the Friendship House in Harlem, and at others established in Chicago (1942), Washington, D.C. (1948), Portland, Oregon (1951), and Shreveport, Louisiana (1953), lay people lived in voluntary poverty in black neighborhoods, promoting social justice and desegregation. At Friendship Houses, blacks and whites shared meals, studied scripture together, and collaborated in planning religious and cultural programs. The work at the Harlem Friendship House received moral support from LaFarge and a handful of sympathetic priests, but it also met with some resistance. When the pastor of St. Mark's parish, Harlem, who had cooperated with Friendship House, was replaced by a new priest from Arkansas, the relationship between the movement and the parish deteriorated. Reflecting upon the situation in her diary in the early 1940s, Ann Harrigan, who was then a volunteer in the Harlem House, observed that some clergy "dislike [Friendship House] intensely," fearing that it "smacks of Evangelism, Protestantism, Heresy, Unorthodoxy, Radicalism . . . and God knows what else." Nevertheless, Harrigan remained convinced that it was "a far more perfect reproduction of Christ's way than anything else."[40]

When de Hueck married the journalist Eddie Doherty and founded Madonna House (1947), a training center for the lay apostolate in Ontario, the movement lived on without her. Its influence spread beyond the individual houses, in part, through the *Catholic Interracialist*, published by the movement, and in part through the network of Outer Circles for fellow travelers that grew up around the movement. In New York, the Outer Circle met in the apartment of Frank Sheed and Maisie Ward, and allied itself with the local Catholic Evidence Guild. In Chicago, it took the form of a study group that sponsored wide-ranging discussions of liturgy and social justice. In South Bend, black and white couples met in each other's homes for study and collaborated in social service projects.[41] De Hueck's aspiration to achieve in Friendship House the kind of solidarity expressed in the mystical body and the U. S. Constitution was never fully realized in a movement that remained heavily white, female, and middle-class.

Another attempt to extend the boundaries of the lay apostolate and create a movement deeply informed by the mystical body ecclesiology was the Grail, founded in the Netherlands by Jacques van Ginneken in 1921 and transplanted to the United States in 1940. Under the leadership of still another pioneering lay woman, Lydwine van Kersbergen, the Grail set out self-consciously to nurture the liturgical renewal and the concept of the church as the mystical body through collaboration with parishes, dioceses, and other Catholic organizations. At Doddridge Farm, outside Chicago in the early 1940s, and later at its permanent headquarters at Grailville near Loveland, Ohio, the Grail sponsored specialized programs for the spiritual formation of lay women who would later serve as leaders and "leaven" in lay apostolates across the United States and throughout the world.

The Grail's efforts to heighten lay women's consciousness of the intimate connection between the liturgy and their lives were not clearly understood by some of the bishops and clergy. When the Grail offered its first summer program at Doddridge Farm in June 1942, they issued a crisp, upbeat flyer outlining the goals of the program, and received a swift, negative response from the local chancery. It was doctrinally incorrect, Grail leaders were informed, to suggest that their two-week program would aim at "developing a strong, dynamic, living faith" when "faith is an infused supernatural gift which we do not develop." The sentence in the flyer that read "Together we will celebrate the Holy Mysteries," drew especially strong criticism. "The faithful assist at Mass," Archbishop Stritch reminded van Kersbergen, "but they do not celebrate Mass, which essentially consists in acts of exclusively priestly power." In response to the archbishop's suggestion that such a flyer should have an imprimatur, van Kersbergen discreetly apologized, and declared that she had no idea that one needed an imprimatur for a flyer.[42]

Nevertheless, Grailville went on to become a center for the education of lay women in matters of theology and liturgy. The dialogue Mass, offertory processions, and congregational singing were incorporated early into the Grailville liturgies celebrated by visiting priests such as the liturgist Martin Hellriegel. For participants in the Grailville programs, the liturgy assumed a new level of meaning both because of the emphasis upon lay participation and planning of the liturgies and because of the self-conscious way in which the leaders at Grailville discussed the relationship between liturgy and the work the women did everyday in the kitchen and on the farm. One young woman who took part in the Grail's "Forward the Land" program in 1942 and its "Harvest" program the following year, attested to the "vision of the great beauty and splendor of the church in her liturgy," which she had gained from the intense experience of liturgy-centered communal living. She added, "For the first time in my life, I began to understand something of the nature of women."[43]

Some visitors, like Janet Kalven, an alumna of the pioneering Great Books program at the University of Chicago in the middle 1930s, came for a summer and stayed on. Kalven, impressed by the Grail's educational and spiritual ideals, joined the movement permanently in the early 1940s, and often went on the Catholic women's lecture circuit as part of the Grail outreach. Kalven's remarks addressed to a diocesan council of Catholic women in the midwest in the spring of 1942 illustrate how the Grail approached catechetics, women's role, and the family. "The family is a little church," Kalven asserted, "the Mystical Body in miniature. Hence it should act like a cell of the Mystical Body." By incorporating the family into the framework of the mystical body ecclesiology, Kalven and the Grail not only enhanced the spiritual role of women but also helped to form the vanguard of the family-oriented apostolates that would occupy center stage in the American Catholic community after the Second World War.

In the same speech, Kalven also reminded her female audience that "confirmation is a kind of ordination," which represents "a real sharing in the priesthood of Christ." Although she included the proper terminology and referred to "Catholic Action undertaken at the call of the hierarchy," one suspects that there were those who would have quibbled with her descriptions of the laity as "co-offerers of the Holy Sacrifice of the Mass," and as "lay priests [sharing] in Christ's mission as prophet and teacher." Through its programs at Grailville as well as its publications and sponsored lecturers, the Grail helped to expand lay women's consciousness of the role they might play in the church. Grail members like Kalven were acting upon the advice of forward-looking spiritual advisors such as Martin Hellriegel who urged them not to be "pious goody-goodies," but dare to be "women with intelligence and holy impertinence . . . women with vision and radical conviction . . . who are determined to live on principle twenty-four hours a day."[44]

It is not coincidental that the Grail chose to make its permanent headquarters a working farm. The Grail allied itself to the NCRLC and always sent delegates to its meetings. Many of the young women who came into contact with the movement during its early days did so primarily because of its reputation as a training center for rural Catholic women. "There is something almost sacramental about country life," Bishop Wehrle had declared at the first meeting of the NCRLC in 1923, and this agrarian ideal became the unifying theme linking a spectrum of experimental lay apostolates of the 1930s and 40s. Both Eugene McCarthy and Emerson Hynes, self-conscious lay apostles who were inspired by the liturgical renewal at St. John's College in Minnesota in the 1930s, proceeded during the following decade to move "back to the land." In her autobiography, Abigail McCarthy explains that she and her husband were "very serous about building a home life based upon the Benedictine ideal of mixed prayer and work, of lives which combined both intellectual and manual work . . . eager to have the house furnished so we could, as the Rule says, 'pursue hospitality.' "[45] The search for spiritual community at the center of the Catholic Worker movement and Friendship House had likewise assumed the form of farming communes and rural enclaves such as Madonna House.

It was not the agrarian element itself that was the sine qua non of the alternative apostolates built by lay pioneers such as Day, de Hueck, and van Kersbergen. Lay apostles embraced the agrarian ideal because of the three elements that agrarian apostolates brought together so naturally: lay activism, an emphasis upon the sacramental character of everyday life, and the community of the small group. The presence of these three elements, not available in most parish situations, explains the attraction that the Catholic Worker, Friendship House, and the Grail held for so many young Catholics in the age of Catholic Action. Whether they were physically isolated from the mainstream parish subculture, or merely intellectually aloof by virtue of their membership in one of the small-group apostolates, Catholics in the social apostolate developed a critical perspective on the institutional church that would be vocalized with increasing frequency as the twentieth century wore on.

The Second World War represents another milestone in the developing vocational self-consciousness of the laity. The emphasis placed upon the leadership potential of the laity by Sheil, Lord, and the clerical boosters of the Jocist movement combined with the growing involvement of lay people in religious education and evangelization only served to raise the expectations of Catholics for even more opportunity to serve the church on the parish level and beyond. The challenges faced by postwar parishes in an era of suburban growth brought the demise of the self-sufficient ombudsman pastor, and ushered in a new age of lay involvement in parish affairs. Lay people trained in the CYO, CISCA, the Summer Schools of Catholic Action, the Jocist movement (and the armed services) often had more formal training in organizational skills than their pastors. This generation of increasingly suburban Catholics made new demands upon their parishes and made subtle but significant changes in the traditional relationship between pastor and parishioner.

The 1950s placed a severe strain upon the American Catholic parish system, both upon the urban parishes whose constituencies were moving to the suburbs and upon the new suburban parishes that were being built to care for the swelling suburban population during the first wave of the baby boom. Catholics in Skokie, Illinois, watched two new parishes spring up in 1951, only to discover their parish schools overcrowded the following year. In the introduction to *The Living Parish* (1959), Leo Ward enumerated the most serious problems plaguing the parish in the 1950s: decreasing contact between priests and parishioners, the loss of a sense of community both in the rapidly expanding suburban parishes and those with a dwindling urban population, serious and unrelenting financial problems, complaints about the quality of worship services, and the "complacency" that Will Herberg had isolated as the chief danger facing the postwar Catholic community.[46]

Andrew Greeley, who served as assistant pastor in a suburban Chicago parish in the 1950s, elaborated upon some of these problems in *The Church and the Suburbs* (1959). He saw the vast potential for lay initiative and leadership stifled by the lack of channels for meaningful participation in parish governance. He recognized that the needs of the best and brightest among the laity were not met by the kinds of organizations and activities that existed on the parish level. In the age of "disengagement" following the war, a growing number of increasingly educated Catholics were saying that they simply did not want to "get too involved" in parish life. And the parish priest, no longer viewed as the obvious leader or the best educated person in the community, could no longer assume that the old patterns of lay-clergy relations would continue to apply.[47]

These very problems also brought new and creative solutions. One postwar success story was St. Joseph's parish, established by Father

Joseph Gremillion in suburban Shreveport, Louisiana. Gremillion, part of a national network of priests who had worked collaboratively with lay people as midwives to apostolates such as the NCRLC, the Grail, the Catholic Workers, and Friendship House, made a self-conscious effort to organize his new parish in a manner compatible with the mystical body ecclesiology. Gremillion referred to his parish as a "family of families, the basic organ and working unit of the Mystical Body." And he worked to increase his parishioners' awareness of their family ties far beyond the parish.

Working within existing organizations, as he had learned to do in his student days in the Future Farmers of America, Gremillion set out to find the existing leaders in his local community and aggressively sought to involve them in activities rooted in the parish. He organized a "think group" of ten men between twenty-five and forty years of age, bright, educated men who were already in positions of responsibility. This group met for several hours every other week to discuss social problems from vote-buying and family income to racial prejudice and each time they decided upon a specific course of action. In collaboration with the Louisiana Knights of Columbus, Gremillion launched a leadership workshop for Catholic men held at his parish in 1953. He established an evening lecture series called the Collegium, which stimulated the cooperation of Catholics and non-Catholics in social outreach in the surrounding community.

In an effort to promote lay activism in the pivotal area of race relations, Gremillion helped to bring Friendship House to Shreveport for a brief period in the mid-1950s until it was forced out of town by threatened violence in the local press. He insisted that Friendship House did the sort of work that "the lay leader can do over and above the work of the Priest and Sister through the parish alone." Informed by his extensive experience with nonparochial apostolates like Friendship House, Gremillion was prompted to ask whether the traditional view of the parish as the "fundamental unit" of the church was adequate in the complex world of postwar America.[48] Like Abbé Michonneau, who had posed the same question in France in the mid-1940s, Gremillion could answer in the affirmative only if he presupposed a restructuring of the relationship between priest and parishioner.

During the decade following the Second World War, a change in the relationship between clergy and laity became apparent in some parishes, and especially within the family apostolates that grew up on the fringes of the parish system. This change was, in part, a reaction to the new challenges faced by the postwar Catholic community in the midst of suburbanization and the baby boom, but it was also an outgrowth of developments underway within the lay apostolate at least since the early 1930s. Both the pioneering small group apostolates and the large centralized lay organizations had encouraged lay initiative and leadership in the so-called secular arena beyond the boundaries of the local church. Archbishop Ireland, Pope Pius XI, and other kindred spirits within the hierarchy had long urged the laity to consider the world outside the church their special responsibility. This message, combined with the mandate to restore all things in Christ, the solidarity of all members of the mystical body, and the growing emphasis upon the connection between everyday work and the liturgy, became the fundamental components of a new vision of the lay vocation, and a nascent theology of the laity that began to emerge in the 1950s.

Not all parishes responded to the changes of the postwar era in the same way or at the same time. As late as 1955, in the lay-edited journal *Integrity*, John W. Nevin could air his complaints about parish clergymen who were far more concerned about finances than about lay participation. According to Nevin, "too often the spark of Catholic Action [was] gotten outside the parish and then smothered by parish inactivity."[49] In many overburdened parishes, however, pastors gratefully accepted the help of the laity. Parishioners of Detroit's Holy Trinity Parish, a formerly Irish parish in a declining neighborhood, launched a whole array of projects to care for the poor in their midst, including a food cooperative, a chapter of Alcoholics Anonymous, a clinic, a maternity guild, an employment agency, a legal aid society, a credit union, a "gospel inquiry group," and a Puerto Rican cell of CFM. In the late 1950s, lay leaders of St. Richard's, a new expanding "semisuburban" parish on the growing edge of Jackson, Mississippi, began to assume several of the functions formerly performed by priests. In collaboration with their pastor, they consolidated the parish organizations into three main branches: the men's council, the women's auxiliary, and CCD. Within these three groups, and their many subdivisions, the complex needs of the parish were met. CCD took charge of the weekly inquiry class and the parish census. The men's council included a people's eucharistic league, and also supervised ushers, accounting, scouting, and publicity. The women's auxiliary cared for the altar, as usual, but was also responsible for the nursery, school activities, and the PTA. Moreover, through the CCD the parish was divided into several zones that were, in effect, miniparishes each with its own separate discussion groups, parent-educators, and so on.[50]

During the postwar era, the increasingly autonomous and active laity of changing parishes like St. Richard's also made great strides in the field of evangelization. In the mid-1950s members of St. Richard's CCD launched a systematic home visitation program encompassing all six thousand families (of all denominations) within the parish boundaries, and they repeated the whole procedure in the early 1960s. Parishes across the nation were sponsoring similar convert crusades and holding inquiry classes for non-Catholics under the auspices of the CCD and the Legion of Mary. Encouraged by priests such as John A. O'Brien of Notre Dame and John E. Odou and Erwin Juraschek, founders of the Convert Makers of America (1944), these parish-based efforts evolved into an evangelization movement of national proportions, a network of lay evangelists working in close collaboration with priests for the conversion of America.[51]

Some of the overextended postwar parishes came close to realizing Canon Cardijn's ideal of "the parish community . . . [as] a great team, based on a number of small specialized teams . . . complementing and supporting each other, all reaching out to the same goal, the establishment of God's kingdom among all men."[52] Sometimes "free-standing" lay apostolates worked in collaboration with parishes: the Grail's city center movement, active in Detroit, Cincinnati, Philadelphia, Lafayette (Louisiana), and New York City, was established to promote this sort of teamwork. As a result, Grail volunteers found themselves on the cutting edge of the Catholic social apostolate in the 1950s, working in urban renewal, the civil rights movement, and lay campus chaplaincies at non-Catholic colleges. In Detroit, a single Grail member became the nucleus of Gateway House, which, by 1954, had a staff of fourteen running an ambitious program that included a cooperative, family services, a home visitation program, a "Christian culture" program, and a liturgical renewal program. The Cincinnati Center, Gabriel House, gave birth to a grass-roots movement for liturgical reform in a local parish, which was considered "meddlesome" by other parishioners.[53]

The Grail's attempts to promote liturgical change within their own home parish, St. Columba's in Loveland, Ohio, also caused resentment. Other parishioners complained that Grail members sought to take over their church. The report on the dispute sent by the pastor, Joseph Urbain, to Archbishop Karl Alter of Cincinnati, hints at the uphill battle Grail members were fighting as a women's apostolate seeking liturgical and spiritual renewal. Urbain recommended that the Grail should "not [be] so intimately connected with the parish." He also suggested that such a "group of women being led by women" really needed to have their "capacities, ambitions, talents, and love for the liturgy . . . channeled by judicious priestly direction."[54]

The Catholic Church in America had long considered itself the defender of the family against the threats of free love, divorce, contraception, and mixed marriages, and its concern for the family intensified noticeably in the postwar era. In 1956 John Cogley, a former Chicago

Catholic Worker on the staff of *Commonweal*, noted a basic shift in the lay apostolate "from social movements to family movements, from the house of hospitality in the slums to the ranch-style house in the suburbs," and he appeared less than sanguine about the change.[55] Father Andrew Greeley intimated that his parishioners were beginning to think of the parish as a "glorified day nursery and the priests and nuns as highly trained baby sitters." He also made an important distinction when he noted that there were couples clamoring for cub scout troops "who wouldn't touch CFM with a ten-foot pole."[56] There were two kinds of demands placed upon the parishes by the parents of the baby boom era: demands for services (e.g., cub scouts, parochial schools, athletic programs) and demands for family-oriented apostolates, such as the Cana movement and CFM. While both provided the opportunity for lay people to serve as leaders and help fill the gaps in services provided by the parish, it was the new family apostolates on the fringes of the parish that served as major catalysts in restructuring the relationship between the priests and the parishioners.

The Cana movement had its origins in a series of retreats called "Family Renewal Days" for married couples given in New York by Father John Delaney, S. J., in 1943. Soon both the format and the leadership changed. Cana became a lay-led movement in which small groups of couples met regularly to discuss family-related issues. Out of the meetings came the idea for pre-Cana, a program of premarital instruction for Catholic couples planned and run by married Catholic couples. Although Cana had a nominal link to the parish in the priest-moderators, the movement took place on the fringe of the parish system and its agenda extended beyond parish boundaries. Cana couples sought primarily to "become better husbands and wives, better parishioners with full and active participation in parish life, and better citizens." They sought to provide each other with the spiritual formation necessary for responsible action.[57]

The same year that Delaney launched his Family Renewal Days also marked the birth of CFM in Chicago out of an all-male Jocist cell composed of two lawyers, a former seminarian, a statistician, a journalist, and an investment counselor. Following the Jocist pattern, they tried to decide upon an experience that they had in common and chose to focus upon family life. The group was reconstituted as a couples cell, a revolutionary departure from the single-sex orientation of the Jocist cells (and most traditional Catholic organizations for the laity). At roughly the same time, another all-male Jocist cell in South Bend formed a couples movement. The idea spread, and by the time CFM held its first convention at Childerly Farm near Chicago in 1949, thirty-seven couples representing cells from eleven cities elected the first executive couple, Pat and Patty Crowley from Chicago. The same year, the first published edition of the CFM handbook, *For Happier Families* sold twenty-five hundred copies. CFM continued to expand in the 1950s. By 1952 it included five thousand couples in the United States and seven foreign countries. Nine years later it reached its peak with forty thousand couples.[58]

The CFM idea appealed to many young Catholic couples who found themselves uprooted after the war, far from their roots and their families, and anxious to get involved in their new communities. Each cell was composed of several couples and had a chaplain, and usually a nominal affiliation to a parish. Sometimes the cells crossed parish boundaries. The chaplain's input at the meetings was welcomed during the brief "gospel inquiry" at the beginning of a meeting, but the bulk of the session was left in the hands of the leader couple for that week. Leader couples shifted continuously and cell membership was intentionally reshuffled from time to time to help the movement to expand and maintain its grass-roots character.

The "inquiry method" led cells to launch a variety of projects. Initially CFMers focused upon local concerns. South Bend cells addressed the need for a school for retarded children, a swimming pool in a neighborhood without recreational facilities, baby-sitting services for couples who needed a night out together.[59] The emergence of annual program books for CFM couples throughout the country naturally fostered broader social concerns. In 1956, for example, CFM couples were encouraged to address the problem of racism. Couples in Dubuque prompted a city council investigation of segregation in the area. Clinton, Iowa, couples planned an ecumenical, integrated symposium on religion and race, held in a Catholic parish hall.[60] This kind of activity paved the way for more CFM social activism, increasing ecumenical cooperation and polarization in the movement between those who approved the social orientation of the movement and those who wanted a narrower emphasis upon family issues.

During the 1950s Cana remained closely concerned with family issues, and became increasingly associated, in minds of Catholics outside the movement, with the pre-Cana program. CFM, on the other hand, was always expanding the boundaries of the social apostolate. In a certain sense, however, both groups were catalysts in the changing relationship between clergy and laity, and both were factors in the development of a theology for the laity. These couples movements established to deal with family issues not being adequately addressed by existing parish societies indicate the new level of lay leadership and initiative achieved in the postwar Catholic community. Both groups assigned to the priests an unaccustomed supporting role in their activities. In the arena of family, marriage, and sexuality, the married couples quite naturally assumed an expertise and inherent authority that their pastors could not claim, and this resulted in a subtle, but significant change in the dynamic of clergy-lay relationships. It was the lay people in the Cana Conference who worked out the theology of marriage taught in the pre-Cana program.[61] And it was the lay people in CFM and the Jocist movement who reflected upon the theological significance of the changes they were promoting in the social arena.

In a sense, Cana and CFM represented a new phenomenon, an apostolate based in the homes of married Catholic couples. In another sense, it was simply the next stage in the development of the apostolates of lay people who had, in their high school and college days, been involved in CICSA, CYO, the Jocist movement, or who had had a brief exposure to the Grail, Friendship House, and the Catholic Worker. The family apostolates of the postwar era represented another set of options for an increasingly self-conscious and pluralistic lay population. By the early 1950s, Americans in the lay apostolate were becoming aware that they were part of an international movement. American delegates attended the first and second world congresses of the lay apostolate held in Rome in 1951 and 1957. Americans discovered new patterns of Catholic Action at these international meetings. The Brazilian Catholic Action movement was organized into a "national team" that combined activism rooted in the gospel with social criticism. The Belgian and German Jocists had served in the resistance, smuggling Jews out of Nazi Germany.[62]

By the end of the 1950s, exposure to international Catholic Action and the contacts fostered by CFM and the Jocist movement had given a whole new meaning to the lay apostolate that far outstripped the familiar formula: "the participation of the laity in the apostolate of the hierarchy." This new meaning was expressed both in the actions of lay apostles who continued to seek new ways to serve at home and abroad, and in the emergence of the beginnings of a theology for the laity. Inspired, in part, by the example of the medical missionary Dr. Tom Dooley, young Catholics joined a variety of missionary training and placement programs during the 1950s. The Grail had sent one of its members to Hong Kong as early as 1946, and in 1950 it opened a school of missiology at Grailville. The same year, at Regis College in Weston, Massachusetts, a mission unit established eight years before blossomed into a placement program for Catholic college graduates from across the nation who wished to serve as volunteers overseas or in underdeveloped parts of the United States and Canada.

Between 1950 and 1975, the Regis Lay Apostolate alone placed two hundred lay missionaries in the field.[63] In 1955 one observer of lay missions estimated that there were at least twenty lay missionary societies, including eight that specialized in medical missions. Countless other small groups of lay people were working with individual missions—for example, with the Jesuits in Jamaica and the Caroline Islands, Maryknollers in Mexico and Latin America, and Marists in the Solomon Islands. Andrew Greeley held out hopes that when these missionaries returned home, they could be the leaven that would renew the spirituality of the suburban parishes that Herberg had found so complacent.[64] The Papal Volunteers for Latin America, established in 1960, placed the papal seal of approval upon the lay missionary efforts already underway, but it was by no means the initial impulse for lay involvement with Third World peoples.

And out of this flurry of lay activism came the beginnings of a theology of the laity. By 1950 sociologist Dorothy Dohen, who had considerable knowledge of the international dimension of Catholic Action, was articulating a vision of lay responsibility that sounds very close to the concept of praxis at the heart of the liberation theologies of the 1970s and 1980s. In her book *Vocation to Love* (1950) Dohen urged that "our action be a preparation for contemplation." She insisted that the active apostolate "will bear more fruit if it is the overflow of our contemplation." Vincent Giese, writing in *Worship* in 1953, underscored the liturgical dimension of this kind of theology. He spoke of the continuity between inwardly and outwardly oriented movements within the church, between the spiritual renewal of the laity and the social apostolates. Giese affirmed: "The actions of one day become the offertory gift of the next day's Mass."[65] The actions that Giese had in mind were not individual actions, but the actions of social groups and movements, taken in a spirit of solidarity rooted in the mystical body.

Although it would be anachronistic to suggest that a full-blown theology of the laity had emerged by the late 1950s, it is accurate to suggest that the raw materials for that theology began to be apparent during this period. While small-group apostolates began to reflect upon the theological significance of their work and their state in life, others, like Dohen, made pioneering attempts to write about the special vocation of the laity. The journal *Integrity* (1946–56), edited by Dohen in its later years, made an especially self-conscious effort to discuss the lay vocation and the theology implicit in it. *Integrity* was read by those who wished to understand how "holiness" comes from "wholeness,"[66] how Catholics must integrate the various components of their lives (e.g., work, family, and spiritual life) into a unity. This message reinforced the theme of the sacredness of everyday work affirmed by lay apostles in a whole spectrum of small group movements from CFM and Cana to the Grail and the Jocists. At times, *Integrity* appeared to espouse an insular, excessively narrow vision of Catholic life and culture, but it influenced a much broader spectrum of social activist Catholics than the small minority that identified wholeheartedly with its entire platform.

A turning point in the evolution of the American theology of the laity came in 1956 with the English translation of Yves Congar's *Lay People in the Church*, whose subtitle, *A Study for the Theology of the Laity*, conveyed its transitional, experimental nature. Congar's willingness to write on the topic gave the nascent theology of the laity a new respectability. Congar reminded Catholics that the Greek word *laos* signified "the people of God," and carried with it serious responsibilities. Regarding the lay apostle's specific obligations in the church, Congar maintained that the realm of "Society, the World, Mankind [and] History" represented "so many faces of God." He asserted that those who were not "withdrawn" from the temporal realm "by a higher order" have a divine mandate to see that God's will is done in the secular arena.[67]

The theology of the laity that began to emerge in the late 1950s indicates a new awareness of the lay vocation on the part of both the clergy and the laity. In one sense, Congar, Giese, and Dohen were no further advanced in their understanding of the laity's potential and proper status within the Catholic community than Thomas Augustine Judge had been in 1913 when he reminded Cenacle volunteers of their common priesthood. In another sense, however, the proliferation of small-group autonomous lay apostolates from the 1930s through the 50s had changed the whole context in which one discussed the role and status of the laity. Members of the small-group social apostolates, along with their clerical midwives, gained a sense of critical distance from mainstream "parish Catholicism" that empowered them to dream new dreams and glean a new vision of the responsibilities of the laity. A substantial segment of the American Catholic laity entered the 1960s with the soaring confidence that they would be called upon to serve their church in countless unforeseen capacities in the years to come.

13

THE LAITY IN THE AGE
OF AGGIORNAMENTO, 1960–1969

The decade of the 1960s represents a watershed in the history of the American Catholic laity. This fact was as apparent to Catholics living in that pivotal era as it is to historians in retrospect. The consensus ends there, however. What is much less clear is precisely what happened to the laity in the 1960s. On the one hand, it was a time of expanding options and optimism. Mary Daly, whose subsequent writings hardly waxed enthusiastic about the future of the Catholic Church, ended her first book, *The Church and the Second Sex* (1968), with the hope that Catholic men and women will work together to reach "a higher order of consciousness," in which "alienating projections" are overcome and "wholeness, psychic integrity achieved." Others, including the historian Philip Gleason, look back upon the 1960s as a period of "demoralization and collapse," a "devastating" era in which Catholics faced the "utter decomposition . . . [of] faith itself."[1]

Although it is premature, and in a sense perilous, for historians to risk generalizations about such a controversial decade, this task is nonetheless incumbent upon those who wish to understand how the lay apostolate, which was flourishing in the 1950s, gave way to a whole new vision referred to under the rubric of lay ministry by the early 1970s. It would be too simplistic to suggest that those who had been active in pioneering apostolates greeted the changes of the 1960s far more enthusiastically than those who had been inactive or involved in traditional lay organizations. It would be too neat an explanation to maintain that the optimism of the first half of the decade gave way to pessimism and disillusionment during the second half, that the enthusiasm generated by the Second Vatican Council could not be sustained during the ensuing disputes about the implementation of the conciliar statements. In the last analysis, none of these half-truths begin to penetrate into the profound transformation experienced by the Catholic community during the pivotal 1960s.

A sizeable segment of the American Catholic laity entered the 1960s with a new sense of confidence in their own potential as leaders within the Catholic community, agents of the church's mission in American society and throughout the world. They had had the experience of collaborating with priests in small group apostolates such as Cana and CFM. They had begun to speculate about a possible theology and spirituality of the laity. During the 1960s, however, they faced new challenges and unanticipated roadblocks, and began to pose new questions, (or, perhaps, make explicit, questions that lay pioneers and clerical midwives had been confronting implicitly for some time). Among the most important questions, three stand out. What is the proper arena for the activism of the lay apostle: the church or the world? Is there an inherent difference between the vocation of the priest and the vocation of the lay person? And finally, can the structures of the institutional church, including the parish and the diocese, be adapted to accommodate the "emerging" laity, or should alternatives be explored?

It would be inaccurate to portray these kinds of questions as merely the fallout of the Second Vatican Council; articulate lay people and theologians interested in the theology of the laity were raising these questions in the early 1960s, before the conciliar documents were published. The conciliar debates covered in the Catholic and secular press only served to extend the ongoing discussions of these issues. Two books published early in the decade popularized the intramural debate about the laity: Donald Thorman's *The Emerging Layman* (1962) and Daniel Callahan's *The Mind of the Catholic Layman* (1963).

Thorman's book emphasized a theme that might almost be considered the slogan of the Second Vatican Council. Reechoing the words of Pope Pius XII, Thorman declared, "We no longer *belong* to the Church. We *are* the Church." Invoking the doctrine of the mystical body, he reminded the laity that they were "literally Christ-bearers" who "cannot remain aloof from the world, uninterested and not caring, any more than Christ could." Thorman affirmed that there was a vital link between the passivity of the laity in the liturgy and the general lack of enthusiasm for the social apostolates. Quoting Virgil Michel, he insisted that "the entire life of the true Christian . . . must be a reflection and a further expression of his life at the altar of God." Already, in 1962, Thorman spoke of educated and experienced lay apostles whose efforts to form family apostolates or participate more fully in the Mass were being rebuffed by their pastors. There was a "cultural lag," Thorman maintained, between "the directives and desires of the church on the highest levels" and their "actual implementation . . . on the local, parochial scene." He further lamented that "a generation of spiritually starved lay people [were] asking for divine bread" and receiving "watered-down" clerical spirituality from their pastors.[2]

Daniel Callahan likewise complained about the limitations of the parish in nurturing lay apostolates. Acknowledging the alienation of a growing number of the laity from the local parish, he offered a partial explanation: "For anyone who is well-versed in the liturgical movement, the Church's social teaching, and the recent ecumenical theology, the realities of the parish can only come as a profound shock."

Callahan outlined four goals for the American Catholic Church: the creation of a "genuine spiritual community" in the place of an "artificial sense of group identity," the development of a "healthy independence" with respect to both the nation and the papacy, the reinterpretation of ecclesiastical authority in order to promote authentic cooperation between the clergy and the laity, and finally, the nurturing of "a mature, faithful and responsible laity." In an effort to explain why the laity had embraced change in the church before most of their bishops and clergy, Callahan blamed the structures and mores of the institutional church. "The clergy inhabit a different institutional world than the laity," he asserted. "It is a world slow to change, resistant to innovation, and settled in its traditions." Because of this discrepancy, Callahan was uneasy about the fate of the "lay renaissance" he saw on the horizon. He warned that if the lay renaissance could not "come into full bloom, then it is difficult to see how anything else in the Church can either."[3]

In an article published in *The Thomist*, theologian Edward Schillebeeckx characterized the pregnant and potentially confrontational atmosphere within the lay apostolate on the eve of the council. He maintained that neither the laity nor the theologians knew precisely "where the limits of the [laity's] active function in the Church lie." He urged that the laity be given "time and room so that they may feel their way . . . towards their own function" with the help of theologians ("not necessarily priests"), and under the guidance of the Holy Spirit. Reminding his fellow priests that the priesthood had had to go through the same historical process, he counseled them not to "be waiting to pounce" if the laity inadvertently " 'clericalize' [themselves] and act as if [they] were parish [priests]."[4]

One apostolate that raised unforeseen questions about the vocation of the laity, the relationship between the church and the world, and the adequacy of existing structures within the institutional church, was the field of catechetics. By the early 1960s, a catechetical revolution was underway. Forward-looking catechists like Mary Perkins Ryan had abandoned the question-and-answer method in favor of an approach that focused attention upon the centrality of scripture and liturgy to the total life experience of the Christian. The goal was not intellectual assent to the doctrines of the church but "arousing persons to intelligent and whole-hearted cooperation with the work of Christ and His Spirit."

The priests, religious, and lay people who embraced this new approach ultimately found themselves questioning structures and practices that had long been considered fundamental components of the church, including the CCD and the parish school system. Catechists challenged the competence of their bishops to pass judgment on new methods and texts. They rejected the notion that religious education was essentially the function of CCD and the parochial school, and preferred to think of it as an essential and ongoing process of spiritual formation for all adult Catholics. In 1963 the pioneer catechist Gerard Sloyan affirmed that "there is no effective catechesis . . . that does not speak God's Word to every age group, every kind of learner, every human condition." Catechesis represented the "human response to God's Word which is a call." This radical expansion of the concept of catechetics, and of the vocational self-consciousness of the lay catechist, would have important implications for the evolution of lay ministries by the early 1970s.[5]

The fundamental questions being raised by Americans active in the lay apostolate were rendered all the more urgent and difficult to resolve by the context in which they were raised. Both within American society and within the universal Catholic Church, the 1960s witnessed accelerating and unabated turbulence and change. Motivated by their training in small group apostolates such as CFM and the Catholic Workers, Catholics joined the struggles for peace and social justice underway in the United States during the 1960s. The CFM inquiry book, *Politics and Race*, issued for the year 1964, stated that "every member . . . must take an active part in the organized movement for civil rights." CFMers marched in Selma and Montgomery, worked to register black voters in Mississippi, and supported the nationwide home visitation program between black and white families that had been launched by Friendship House. Pat Crowley represented CFM at the pioneering ecumenical Conference on Race and Religion held in Chicago in 1963 to commemorate the centennial of the Emancipation Proclamation. He also joined the board of the National Conference on Religion and Race that was formed as an outgrowth of that meeting.[6]

The enthusiastic participation of CFMers, Friendship House volunteers, and the tiny minority of Catholics who belonged to the network of Interracial Councils affiliated with the National Catholic Conference for Interracial Justice during the 1960s was hardly typical of the average Catholic in the parish. Although the American bishops had issued a public statement in 1958 stating that "enforced segregation" was incompatible with Christianity, Catholic parishes and schools across the south remained segregated. As late as 1967, historian William Osbourne affirmed that there was "more *de facto* segregation" in the parishes than ever. Even in the north, members of a recently formed parish CFM cell on Long Island in 1962 opted to join a non-denominational civil rights effort rather than risk the interference of their pastor or the life of their new —and vulnerable—parish couples group. After examining the history of Catholic involvement in race relations through 1967, Osbourne concluded that the vast majority of parishes had remained completely aloof from the struggle for justice for blacks. He insisted that "given the state of mind of Catholics and the bureaucratic structure of diocese and parish," it was "simply incongruous to expect the members of the typical parish Rosary or Holy Name Society even to discuss nonviolent resistance, much less join a picket line."[7]

The same pattern, minus the episcopal support for activism, applies in the case of Catholic involvement in the peace movement. The tiny Catholic Association for International Peace (1928) and the Catholic Workers were the two most visible components of the American Catholic peace apostolate until the 1960s, when the movement suddenly took off. In 1960 the number of participants at the annual protest sponsored by the Catholic Workers, the Fellowship of Reconciliation, and the War Resisters' League in New York City during the civil defense drill skyrocketed from fourteen to five hundred. The following year the figure quadrupled.[8] The self-immolation of Catholic Worker Roger Laporte in front of the United Nations Building on November 9, 1965, and the actions of the Catonsville Nine on May 17, 1968, transformed the peace movement even as they dramatized the escalation of the extraparochial social apostolates during the turbulent 1960s.

The most important catalyst for change within the American Catholic community during the 1960s was the Second Vatican Council. The council addressed itself to the social, theological, and ecclesiological questions on the minds of the most active and articulate members of the laity, and shocked some Catholics with the idea that even fundamental aspects of Catholic belief and practice were subject to reinterpretation and change. Two groundbreaking documents, *Gaudium et Spes*, on the church in the modern world, and *Apostolicam Actuositatem*, on the apostolate of the laity, focused an unprecedented amount of attention upon the unique responsibilities of the lay apostle in the secular arena. The former document emphasized the dignity and solidarity of all of humanity, and the vital link between spiritual responsibilities and public life in the social, political, and professional spheres. Article 43 underscored the obligation of the laity "to be witnesses to Christ in all things in the midst of society." The latter document stated explicitly that "the renewal of the temporal order" was the laity's "own special responsibility," and emphasized the duty of "every prosperous person and nation" to provide food, clothing, education, housing, medicine, and employment to all who were in need.[9]

Lumen Gentium, the Dogmatic Constitution on the Church, likewise called attention to the unique responsibility of the laity to see that God's will is done in the secular arena. Chapter 2 outlined an inclusive, scripture-based, communal model of the church as "the people of God," while chapter 3 rehearsed the traditional exclusive, hierarchical model, which sharply distinguished the status of the laity from that of the ordained priesthood. Even in the earlier chapter that contained the more inclusive ecclesiology, there was an attempt to clarify the distinctions within the priesthood of the "people of God"; the "common priesthood of the faithful," rooted in baptism, and the "ministerial or hierarchical priesthood," with its foundation in holy orders, "[differed] from one another in essence and not only in degree." Chapter 4 contained admonitions to members of the laity to express their needs and desires to the clergy and the suggestion that some of the laity were qualified to "express [an] opinion on things which concern the good of the church."[10] Nonetheless, the latter statements can only be understood in the light of the distinctions previously discussed.

Theologian Joseph Komonchak has called attention to the fact that the conciliar documents are far from univocal in their treatment of the relationships between the church and the world and between the clergy and the laity. Moreover, he maintains that the council fathers did not throughly escape from a dualistic perspective that polarizes church and world, emphasizing the respective responsibilities of the clergy in the former and the laity in the latter. According to Komonchak, the hierarchy's difficulties in understanding the church as a worldly, historical, political entity are directly related to its inability to transcend a dualistic perspective on the respective roles and status of the clergy and the laity.[11]

Although the conciliar documents do not unequivocally affirm the shared political stance of all Christians within the secular sphere, they do call attention to the laity's special role as agents of the church in the secular realm. They also touch upon the variety of ways in which the laity may act out their Christian commitment within the institutional church. The decree on the lay apostolate mentions that the hierarchy "entrusts to the laity some functions which are more closely associated with pastoral duties, such as the teaching of Christian doctrine, certain liturgical actions, and the care of souls." In *Lumen Gentium* the laity is explicitly included in "the saving mission of the Church." The document also mentions the possibility of "a more direct form of cooperation in the apostolate of the hierarchy" over and above the responsibility of all of the laity to be a Christian presence in the world. In *Ad Gentes*, the decree on missions, the work of lay catechists and missionaries is explicitly acknowledged. Finally, *Sacrosanctum Concilium*, on the liturgy, goes beyond urging the full participation of the laity to a recognition of the "genuine liturgical ministry" of servers, lectors, commentators, and members of the choir.[12]

The self-conscious laity of the 1960s was enthusiastic about the process of aggiornamento underway at the Second Vatican Council, and generally grateful for the attention paid to the role and status of the laity by the council fathers. From the start, however, certain tensions and polarizations became apparent. As early as August 1962, Daniel Callahan expressed concern about the laity's escalating hopes. He insisted that "the layman has been incited by the Church to ask for, and anticipate, a freedom and responsibility which, in the end, the contemporary Church is hardly prone to give him." On the eve of the council, Donald Thorman maintained that even those who were active in the lay apostolate did not feel that they had the right or the opportunity to make their feelings known to the council fathers.[13]

The number of the laity present at the council increased from the delegation of twenty who attended the first session to a total of forty-two auditors and nine guests at the final session. Although commentators in the press called attention to the innocuous character of the hand-picked lay delegation, the mere presence of that delegation at the council was a visible reminder of the changing relationship between the clergy and the laity. One of the American auditors, Martin Work, recounted for readers of the Kansas City *Catholic Reporter* a widely circulated joke about a bishop who went to confession at St. Peter's to repent of having twice contradicted a lay man, only to be told that that sin was now reserved for the Holy Office. Work added that the joke's popularity with the council fathers could be an indication that the "ice [was] getting a bit thin."[14]

Efforts to implement the conciliar decrees on the home front took a variety of forms. It soon became apparent that the existing structures of the parish, the diocese, and affiliated lay organizations needed to be changed and supplemented in the interests of aggiornamento. Some, which had long been fixtures in the Catholic community, were tried and found wanting in the wake of the council by lay critics and priests sympathetic to their cause. Even within the most progressive of the preconciliar lay apostolates, the council ushered in a process of structural reform and self-examination.

The decree on the lay apostolate had urged the laity "to collaborate energetically in every apostolic and missionary undertaking sponsored by their local parish." It called for the establishment of diocesan and parish councils to promote and coordinate collaboration between the laity, priests, and religious.[15] By 1966 ten dioceses already had pastoral councils, and their numbers increased in the years that followed. Many of these pastoral councils assisted in the formation of parish councils that were intended to provide opportunities for lay involvement in the pastoral care and decision-making of the parish. As the example of parish response to the bishops' 1958 statement on segregation makes clear, however, parish reform is totally contingent upon the inclinations of the parish priest. Evidence that lay expectations for more opportunities to serve in the parish setting were not being met can even be found in less than liberal Catholic newpapers such as the Brooklyn *Tablet*. In June 1965 the *Tablet* printed a modest proposal that the laity be given "responsibilities . . . more agonizing than the annual bazaar and something a little more profound than handling the roll call at the Holy Name meeting." The article suggested that at the very least the laity should have some influence in planning the time of Masses and confessions and in proposing topics for Sunday sermons.[16]

Within individual dioceses there were grass-roots transparochial efforts to hold "little councils," groups of interested priests, religious, and lay people who met to discuss the implementation of the council on the local level. The case of the St. Louis "little council" illustrates the maxim that both diocesan and parochial reform depended ultimately upon the good will of the man who was in charge. In January 1965 an ad hoc group of thirty members of the St. Louis clergy and laity, who had been meeting during the third session of the council, submitted a plan for reform to their ordinary, Cardinal Ritter. The cardinal rejected the proposal, insisting that it be simplified and place more emphasis upon parishes and official lay organizations. Members of the original "little council" felt betrayed that the cardinal, when it came to implementation on the diocesan level, appeared to be turning his back on the progressive positions he was supporting in Rome. The following September the cardinal wrote a letter announcing *his* idea for a "little council" to be read by all pastors at Sunday Mass. The resulting program, which included orientation programs for pastors in theology, catechetics, liturgy, and scripture, was lauded by the Catholic press as an "ambitious attempt . . . to extend the concept of archdiocesan colle- giality into the grass roots." It might have been more efficient for the cardinal to propagate the new ideas of the council through diocesan and parochial structures. Nonetheless, Ritter's actions made a strong implicit statement on the limits of lay leadership even within the rela- tively progressive Catholic community in postconciliar St. Louis.[17]

Another effort to supplement the existing church structures and provide a national forum for lay leaders was the National Association of Laymen (NAL), which convened its inaugural meeting on June 23, 1967, in St. Paul, Minnesota. The 225 members of the laity who launched the NAL openly acknowledged the need for "an authentic, free, and responsible lay voice," and a means of facilitating dialogue "on every level within [the Christian community] and without." It is significant that the new organization did not seek to be incorporated within the National Conference of Catholic Bishops, or any other na- tional Catholic organization, but instead hoped for a liaison with the hierarchy and other appropriate Catholic societies. The workshops at the conference—focused upon women in the church, racism, student power, experimental communities, war and peace, the Hispanic com- munity, and the urban crisis—provide some indication of the breadth of the NAL vision. Some, like the Catholic journalist Dale Francis, ob- jected to the fact that delegates to the NAL were not chosen on a dem- ocratic basis on the parish level. Francis accurately predicted that without the official support of the bishops, the NAL could not succeed.[18] Nevertheless, the stories of the St. Louis "little council" and the NAL both attest to the perceived need for new structures in the latter half of the 1960s, structures that might respond to the needs of those who found the old parish and diocesan organizations obsolete.

During the conciliar era, Martin Work suggested that any lay orga- nization without "a spiritual and apostolic formation program"—that is, without "biblical, liturgical, catechetical, ecumenical, and social" components—should "consider dissolving itself." He added that any organization that "thinks only of its internal role in the Church's life" was already half dead.[19] The Holy Name Society, which had been a source of Catholic visibility and pride since the days of O'Connell and Mundelein, waned in the 1960s, as did the Knights of Columbus, the St. Vincent de Paul Society, and the Rosary and Altar Society. In 1964 William J. Whalen, former Knight of Columbus, published an article in the *U.S. Catholic* that straightforwardly posed the question: "The Knights of Columbus: Are They Obsolete?" He recommended that the knights dispense with all vestigial ceremonies and focus their attention upon ecumenical cooperation. In 1969 the knights, who, in the past, had rallied the laity in the fight against socialism and secularism, and sponsored extensive Catholic advertising campaigns, declared themselves enemies of "lawlessness . . . injustice, poverty, discrimination . . . neglect, lack of concern, and lack of dialogue."[20]

At the 1963 convention of the NCCM, John Egan, a priest who had been involved in the Cana Conference and a number of other Chicago social apostolates, challenged the relevance of all Catholic organizations originally intended "to insulate men . . . against unnecessary social contacts with non-Catholics." In so doing, he was calling into question a whole range of traditional lay organizations. Catholics who agreed that the older lay societies organized to meet the needs of the insular immigrant church were inappropriate—and even an embarrassment—in the church of the 1960s, had three choices. They could join with their non-Catholic neighbors in movements for peace, civil rights, and other social justice and civic issues. Or they could confine themselves to the newer apostolates like CFM, which were already increasingly flexible and ecumenical. The only other option was to remain aloof from Catholic groups and organizations and become "deinstitutionalized Catholics" whose religious commitment ended with Mass and the sacraments.[21]

Even the small group apostolates, which were much more attuned to the spirit of aggiornamento than their older counterparts, made structural and policy changes in response to what they perceived to be the mandate of the council. In 1951 the Grail in the United States had followed the lead of the international movement and established a core group of full-time members ("the nucleus") who expressed their total dedication by living lives of chastity. By the 1960s, however, they were submitting this hierarchical structure to serious scrutiny. In October 1962, on the eve of the Second Vatican Council, a meeting of over two hundred members convened in Grailville to discuss the future. Out of their own internal process of aggiornamento emerged a new vision of the Grail, organized increasingly by region rather than around city centers so that married women could participate more fully in the life of the movement.

The Grail replaced the city centers with "community based social programs" across the nation. In Louisiana, they worked with the Southern Consumers Cooperative; in Clermont County, Ohio, with health clinics; in Cincinnati, with Seven Hills Neighborhood House; in Brooklyn and East Harlem, with inner city schools; and in San Jose, with the Hispanic community. They studied group process and the principles of community development. They read the works of the pedagogical pioneer Paulo Freire, and began "to see [themselves] less as teachers and more as evokers of knowledge from experience already present in the other." In 1967 they launched at Grailville a program in which college students earned credit for a combination of academic study of contemporary issues and related work experience in the local community. During this period, the Grail became increasingly self-conscious about its special obligations as a movement for lay women in a time of intense social change. In 1969, after a near unanimous vote of the general assembly, the Grail began to admit Protestant women. Grail members look back upon the 1960s as "a time of disruption and loss, but also a time of openness, discovering each other's religious journey and search for authentic faith."[22] The story of Grail's renewal in the 1960s provides an example of the kind of thoroughgoing restructuring and reform that could occur in an autonomous and self-conscious lay movement during the age of aggiornamento.

Like the Grail, CFM reexamined its former identity and witnessed the exodus of some of its most dedicated members in the 1960s. As the movement devoted increasing attention to social activism, some members resigned in protest. Some insisted that CFM should return to its original narrower focus upon family issues. These disagreements took their toll, and membership figures began to decline after the peak year in 1963. Nevertheless, the movement had a profound impact upon tens of thousands of middle-class Catholic couples. The annual conferences, featuring speakers like Senator Eugene MacCarthy, Senator Mark Hatfield, Representative John Brademas, and Sargent Shriver, exposed CFMers to a vision of lay activism and service that was far broader than the one they encountered in the Sunday sermons in their home parishes. For many couples, CFM became the starting point for even broader commitments, rather than an end in itself.[23]

In the mid-1960s CFM played a central role in the controversy over birth control, which has been viewed by some as the real turning point in the American Catholic laity's struggle for autonomy. Because of their experience as CFM executives, Pat and Patty Crowley were named to the Birth Control Commission established in 1963 by Pope John XXIII. So that they might represent the opinions of their constituency, they published a questionnaire in the CFM journal *Act* to solicit the views of American Catholic married people concerning the rhythm method. On the basis of the responses they had received, they recommended that the church change its prohibition of artificial birth control.

When Pope Paul VI issued *Humanae Vitae* in 1968, reiterating the Catholic prohibition of artificial birth control, the Crowleys joined a prominent minority of two hundred American Catholics who publically took exception to the document. In an interview in *The National Register*, Patty Crowley affirmed that the encyclical was a departure from the spirit of aggiornamento. She noted "a negative element in the encyclical which reflects a negative approach to the concept of marriage itself—and this in spite of the positive approach taken in the Vatican II documents." Crowley predicted, quite accurately, that "trained and educated younger couples will not forget that sense of responsibility given them by the Council Fathers and will maintain that the problem is one for solution by their own consciences."[24]

Perhaps even more demoralizing than the pope's unexpected dismissal of the commission's recommendations was the response of Monsignor Hillenbrand to the Crowley's dissent from *Humanae Vitae*. Hillenbrand, one of the midwives of CFM and its staunch supporter for decades, first reprimanded and then ignored the Crowleys. Their years of training in the "observe-judge-act" approach to moral and social problems had finally led the Crowleys to a protest against an injustice within the church itself. Like many couples in CFM, the Crowleys moved on. They contributed to other causes and entertained countless dinner parties for Cesar Chavez, Bernadette Devlin, the early ecumenical dialogues between Rabbi Robert Marx and Father John Pawlikowski, the Catholic Interracial Council, and the Illinois Human Rights Commission. Like many of their counterparts in CFM, the Crowleys took the conciliar mandate for lay activism in the secular arena so seriously that they soon found themselves working within an expanding ecumenical network for social change.[25]

The incident over *Humanae Vitae* illuminates the growing polarization within the American Catholic community during the latter half of the 1960s. Those who left CFM in protest against the movement's increasing social activism and pioneering stand on the race question were, in some sense, more in tune with the currents of change in the church and the nation than the Crowleys themselves. By the late 1960s the pendulum was already beginning to swing away from activism and back toward introspection. This period witnessed the emergence of three new movements, Marriage Encounter, Cursillo, and the Catholic charismatic renewal, whose swelling popularity attested to the fact that they were meeting pressing needs not recognized by the local parish or existing alternative movements.

Marriage Encounter, a spin-off of the Spanish CFM, was transplanted to the United States with the help of the Crowleys in 1968. In a very real sense, it represented the sequel to the story of CFM, for those who flocked to the Marriage Encounter Weekends did so to experience a kind of renewal not available either in their parishes or in CFM or Cana. The appearance, and almost immediate popularity of Marriage Encounter, heralds a profound change of direction within the American Catholic community in the 1960s. In sharp contrast to the social activism and self-conscious egalitarianism of CFM, the lay people who ran the Marriage Encounter weekends functioned as a tiny cadre of paraprofessionals ministering to the large groups of couples in their care. By the late 1960s the activist model of CFM was on its way out and the introspective, therapeutic model of Marriage Encounter was just beginning to ride the crest.

The roots of the Cursillo movement in the United States date back to 1957 when the first Cursillo ("little course in Christianity") was held in Waco, Texas, among Spanish-speaking Catholics. The first English Cursillo took place in San Angelo four years later. Like some other contemporaneous Catholic movements, Cursillo was essentially a supplement to the parish and diocesan lay activities for those who wanted something more. An individual's involvement in Cursillo begins with an intense, single-sex, weekend experience structured around lectures (called *rollos*) and intermittent opportunities for individual and group response. Cursillo leaders are carefully trained in the techniques to be used in the lectures and discussions. Out of Cursillo weekends emerge small groups that share common interests, groups intended to reinforce the community-building and spiritual formation begun on the weekend. Through Cursillo, many Catholic lay people of the 1960s began to discover the ongoing spiritual renewal available in small, autonomous, Bible-based, intentional communities. Although the literature on Cursillo published by its national secretariat directly addresses the relationship between Cursillo and renewal in the church and society,[26] the popularity of the movement appears to be rooted in the fact that Cursillo fosters a level of community and spiritual intensity unavailable in most parishes. Cursillo's scripture-based lay spirituality also represented a viable alternative to the clerical vision of Catholic spirituality traditionally nurtured within the parish system.

Cursillo is related to another movement whose emergence in the late 1960s signals a new emphasis upon introspection within the church: the Catholic charismatic movement. An important catalyst in the growth of the charismatic movement within the American Catholic community was the national Cursillo convention held in the summer of 1966. Lay faculty members from Duquesne University left the Cursillo convention with a new interest in seeking the gifts of the Holy Spirit, which finally came to fruition during the famous "Duquesne weekend" in February 1967.[27] The weekend led to others at Notre

Dame, Michigan State, and beyond. The movement soon expanded beyond the selective constituency of students and faculty members to transform the spiritual lives of a broad spectrum of middle-class Catholics.

It is not surprising that Ann Swidler, one of the authors of *Habits of the Heart* (1985), chose to examine Marriage Encounter as part of her effort to understand individualism in contemporary America.[28] Marriage Encounter, Cursillo, and the Catholic charismatic movement were all signals of a turning away from the broad agendas of movements like CFM and the Catholic Workers, and from the institutional atmosphere of the large parish or lay organization. All three movements became popular because they responded to the hunger for community and sanctity that was not being satisfied elsewhere in the American Catholic community. This heightened awareness of individual and family concerns, which was by no means unique to the Catholic community, had important implications for the parish and other established Catholic institutional structures. In an age of the "voluntary parish," the increasingly educated, assimilated American Catholic population went shopping for parishes—or surrogates—that suited their needs and even their personal styles.[29]

In 1969 in *Commonweal*, theologian Gregory Baum asserted that "when we ask the question, where in fact the Catholic people are being inspired, instructed, nourished, and built up in Christ, we no longer point to the parish." Instead Catholics sought help in "a wide network of centers, chapels, discussion groups, lecture series, press columns, radio and television programs, worship centers in different places, private conversations and ... books."[30] The end of the 1960s was characterized by an unprecedented restlessness, a search for alternatives, for genuine community. As Baum's statement indicates, pluralistic American Catholics were increasingly divided on the question of where to find the meaning and belonging that eluded them. And this same sense of fragmentation and polarization gripped the lay apostolate itself. Although it was not clear to all interested observers in the late 1960s, the illness afflicting the lay apostolate was terminal. It was the dawn of the new age of lay ministries.

14

THE LAY MINISTRY
EXPLOSION, 1970–

By 1970 the American Catholic Church had taken the shape that we now associate with postconciliar Catholicism:

> A weakening . . . authority structure, a decline in traditional devotional practices . . . instability in marriage . . . theological dissent and catechetical uncertainty . . . a decrease in attendance at weekly Mass and an even sharper decline in the reception of the sacrament of Reconciliation, and especially a dropoff in vocations to the ordained priesthood and the religious life.[1]

Catholics of the early 1970s were no closer to finding answers to the three questions that had occupied center stage during the age of aggiornamento than they had been a decade before. They were still debating whether the only proper arena for lay activism and leadership was the secular realm. They were still struggling with the relationship between the vocation of the priest and that of the dedicated lay person. And they had only begun to explore potential avenues of structural change within the church.

One change became increasingly apparent in the Catholic Church of the 1970s, however, and that was the frequent use of the term "ministry" to describe the work of the laity. Just as Catholic Action and the lay apostolate had been the accepted terminology for the discussion of the role of the laity from the 1920s through the 50s, lay ministry became the new catchword, to be used and abused by the increasingly polarized American Catholic community in its various efforts to define, expand, and contain the laity's participation in the church and the world. Only gradually did it dawn upon Catholics that the new terminology had come to signify a new set of aspirations embraced by lay ministers and their fellow travelers.[2] When this awareness became widespread in the latter part of the decade, it merely underscored the extent to which the unanswered questions of the 1960s had festered.

By the early 1980s the term "lay ministry" had become, for some, the watchword of a movement to explode the false polarization between church and world, to clarify the relationship between lay and priestly vocations, and to reshape the ecclesiology of the church.

The documents of the Second Vatican Council had delineated two paths for the laity who wished to serve the church: the familiar model of "christianizing the social order," implicit in the mandate for the lay apostolate since the era of Leo XIII, and the less familiar model of working within the ecclesiastical sphere. In the immediate aftermath of the council, a tiny minority chose the second option and became the pioneer full-time lay ministers of the American Catholic Church. Lay people were employed as director of finances for the archdiocese of Chicago, supervisor of real estate in the diocese of Seattle, and director of public relations in the diocese of Fort Wayne, Indiana.[3] Starting in 1960, married Catholic men were attending the Institute for Catholic Laymen at the University of San Francisco in preparation for careers as full-time "pastor's lay assistants." Graduates of the institute worked primarily in evangelization efforts within parishes and dioceses—conducting and organizing home visitations, running inquiry forums, assisting the pastor in "demonstration Masses" for non-Catholics, planning days of recollection for lay people, and generally serving as "[mediators] between the Church and the world."[4]

During the 1970s a growing number of schools of theology, even some diocesan seminaries, opened their doors to lay people. One such institution, Immaculate Conception Seminary in New Jersey, which first admitted lay people in 1975, thoroughly rewrote the statement of purpose in their catalogue in order to remove exclusivistic language equating ministry with ordained priesthood. By the following September, the seminary was describing its task as the development of "a life-giving environment: spiritually vigorous, theologically sound and creative, pastorally sensitive, responding to the need of priests, religious and laity who, in the spirit of faith, vision, and love are desirous of solid preparation for Christian ministry."[5] This revision speaks eloquently about the profound transformation underway within some forward-looking graduate theological programs of the 1970s where lay people and seminarians took common courses and began to share common concerns.

Prominent among those who were seeking advanced training in theology were the progressive catechists who were beginning to occupy new positions as parish directors of religious education or religious education coordinators. In *Emerging Lay Ministries* (1979) Dennis Geaney calls the parish religious education coordinator "the most revolutionary breakthrough in the emerging concept of nonordained ministry."[6]

By the early 1970s leaders in the field of religious education, such as Gabriel Moran, were engaged in a wide-ranging critique of the whole system of Catholic education, from the parochial school and CCD all the way to the newly established parish coordinator positions. Moran, who had shocked many in the field of Catholic education in 1968 by proclaiming that "the problem of catechetics is that it exists," reiterated that point in *Design for Religion* (1970), and proceeded to make the same basic statement about the parish system. Moran insisted that the church should stop to restructure the parish before hiring parish religious education coordinators whose work was otherwise doomed from the start. The first step, Moran maintained, was a major reallocation of funds to make them available for the "extensive and expensive" education of religious educators. The second step was a fundamental change in the balance of power within the parish. Moran asserted that a parish director of religious education "must share the directing job of the community or parish" in order to be effective. "Instead of a pastor and his flock," Moran suggested, "we shall have a community with a small team of leaders (men and women) to direct liturgy, education, social action, etc."

Moran's skepticism about the system extended to the whole mentality of the average parochial school and CCD religion teacher. By way of illustration, he recounted the following conversation that he had engaged in several times:

> Question: How do you teach the sacrament of penance to a third grader? Answer: You don't. It is impossible. Stop teaching it. Question: I agree with you in theory, but what do you teach in practice? Answer: Nothing. Question: I understand all that theory, but my problem is *how* do you teach it? Answer: There's no answer to that question. Question: That's the trouble with you theorizers. You don't know the practical difficulties of teaching the third grade. When is someone going to do something practical and come out with good lesson plans for teaching penance to third graders?

For Moran, the real challenge was the formation of adult Catholics and the prospects for this task were improved by the fact that "competing structures" such as CCD were not already in place. The problem was that the parish clergy would never allocate enough money for the task, preferring the thriftier route of hiring a single parish coordinator who then became either a token or a scapegoat.[7] The catechists who represented the foundation for lay ministry in many a parish soon found themselves at odds with pastors and existing parish personnel on issues far more essential than the content of lesson plans.

The early 1970s, then, witnessed two parallel developments. On the one hand, lay people were gradually, but steadily, acquiring the training necessary for service in new, professional capacities within the parish and the diocese. On the other hand, the experiences of lay ecclesial ministers within the institutional church raised fundamental questions concerning the adequacy and flexibility of the parish and diocesan systems.

An analogous pattern can be seen in the hierarchy's treatment of the role of the laity during the early 1970s, which combined some fundamental questioning with gradual concessions to lay ministry. The 1971 Synod of Bishops in Rome took a close look at the "crisis in the priesthood," and at the related question of the difference between clergy and laity. Edward Schillebeeckx maintains that although most of the assembled bishops were "open to new practices in the ministry," the "official organs of the church [were] a serious hindrance to these desires and new visions." According to Schillebeeckx, the bishops' fear of encouraging the involvement of priests in grass-roots Christian communities displayed itself in a reluctance to "[connect] Christian identity with human integrity and liberation."[8] The end result was the further reinforcement of the polarization between the church and the world and between the clergy and the laity.

This debate among the bishops in 1971 illuminates the two documents expanding the role of the laity issued by Pope Paul VI in the following year: *Ministeria Quaedam* and *Ad Pascendum*. The former document stated that the offices of lector and acolyte no longer needed to be reserved for seminarians in training for the priesthood; henceforth, lay people could be installed in these offices without changing their lay status. The latter document, in conjunction with *Sacrum Diaconatus Ordinem*, issued in 1967, made the permanent diaconate accessible to lay men. With the publication of *Immensae Caritatis* on extraordinary eucharistic ministers in 1973, the machinery was in place for ecclesial lay ministers to take a few short steps into the sanctuary. These were important steps, but when viewed against the backdrop of the 1971 synod, Moran's critique of the parish system, and growing speculation about the *ordination* of lay ministers,[9] the documents issued in 1972 and 1973 appear to be a new way of limiting as well as expanding the role of ecclesial lay ministers.

Nevertheless, the 1970s and the 80s saw the rapid proliferation of a wide spectrum of lay ministries. Many who had been involved in a variety of activities within the parish from organizing recreation and administering the finances to teaching CCD came to see their tasks as ministries rather than committee work. Between the mid-1970s and the mid-1980s, the number of lay ministers and the varieties of lay ministry burgeoned. The Notre Dame study of Catholic Parish Life states that by the 1980s lay ministers were responsible for 83 percent of the leadership within the parishes.[10] Youth ministry, family ministry, liturgy and music planning, religious education, spiritual direction, hospital and campus ministries: all of these opened up to the laity, both to the volunteer and to the full-time professional. It is difficult to generalize about lay ministry because it varies with the context, and ranges from positions within the diocesan bureaucracy to free-standing individualized ministries without either a diocesan or a parish base. *Why We Serve* (1984), a collection of the personal stories of full-time lay ministers, edited by Douglas Fisher, suggests certain patterns in the evolution of lay ministry within the lives of individuals, and some of the common problems and concerns of lay ministers.

One pattern apparent within Fisher's book is that a multiplicity of ministries issued forth from the common font of religious education. The position of parish director or coordinator of religious education was a first step for several of the lay ministers whose careers are covered by Fisher. It was also a transitional stage for the former seminarians and women religious who enriched the pool of pioneer lay ministers in the early 1970s. Both those who stayed in these positions and those who moved beyond to other ministries—within dioceses or religious conference centers—had some common complaints about the state of lay ministry during the 1970s and 80s. Salaries were too low for those who wished to raise a family. There were unrealistic expectations placed upon the overburdened parish personnel by pastors who were not used to the collaborative style of leadership. On the diocesan level, lay ministers noticed a double standard, which meant that lay people were the last to be promoted, regardless of their education and experience.[11]

The laity made important strides in family ministries for many of the same reasons that Catholics of the postwar era flocked to the family apostolates. Advocates of family ministries, such as Delores Curran, emphasize the breadth and integration of the ideal family ministry program, which should include:

> parenting education . . . sexuality education for children or parents; ministry to the separated and divorced; family faith enrichment ministry; youth ministry; young adult ministry; ministry to the interfaith married; family communication classes; marriage and family counseling; supportive ministry for the single parent; marriage enrichments; aid for parents in dealing with pressures against family life like drugs, cults, television, overscheduling, teen alienation,

changing attitudes toward women and mobility, and programs for the committed single.

In a vein similar to that of the catechetical innovators who lamented that pastors and CCD directors reduced religious education to lesson plans for grade school children, Curran, and others in the field, complain of the inability of most pastors and parish personnel to "disassociate family ministry from the religious education of children." In 1980 Curran could only find about fifty parishes in the whole United States whose programs reflected an understanding of "total family ministry."

Like the new vision of catechetics, the new model of family ministries was (and is) more than a demand for an increase in specialized parish services catering to the beleagured family. Family ministries point to needs both within the parish and within the family that simply cannot be met by the traditional parish. Among these are the need for families to minister to the parish, and vice versa, in a mutual pastoral relationship.[12] Family ministry by its very nature tends to be team ministry taking place in a small arena. One pilot program launched in the early 1970s in Good Shepherd parish in Mount Vernon, Virginia, illustrates the alternative ecclesiology implicit in the emerging family ministries. The parish was subdivided into "family learning teams" composed of about fifteen family units (with family defined broadly as "any household of faith"). One family within each subdivision would act as "steward" to the other fourteen, not just in the area of religious instruction but in a much broader process of promoting a living, active faith. In some sense, family learning teams are reminiscent of the pioneering CCD programs that emerged after the Second World War, which likewise attempted to break down bloated parishes into smaller units in order to promote efficiency in evangelization and intensify the sense of community within the parish. Nevertheless, the way in which the family learning teams at Good Shepherd envisioned the parish staff as resources, assistants, and facilitators to the family learning teams signals a significant shift in the laity's perceptions of what it was doing in parish subgroups, a shift that crosses the threshold between the lay apostolate and lay ministry.[13]

An important family ministry that grew up on the fringes of the parish system is the ministry to divorced and separated Catholics. One of the changes that had accompanied Catholic assimilation into the American mainstream by the 1960s was the dramatic increase in the number of divorced Catholics. Although there were earlier groups such as the Judeans and the Fabiolas, intended to meet the spiritual needs of divorced women, it was only in the 1970s, and not within the parish and diocesan structures, that the first lay ministry to divorced

Catholics surfaced. In 1971 the Paulist Center in Boston sponsored a support group composed of divorced Catholics who sought to help others in the midst of divorce proceedings. From this pioneering group evolved a full-fledged program intended to address the needs of divorced Catholics. Other groups sprang up across the country, and conferences were organized featuring clergy, divorced persons, and professionals in marriage and family life. By 1975 a coalition of local ministries, the North American Conference of Divorced and Separated Catholics, was established. Among the outgrowths of this movement were *Divorce*, a newsletter intended to facilitate the education and training of lay ministers to divorced Catholics, and a weekend retreat program, the "Beginning Experience," derived in part from the Marriage Encounter model.[14] Faced with the indifference of their pastors and bishops to their special needs, divorced Catholics of the 1970s trained themselves to minister to other divorced Catholics.

The proliferation of lay ministries in the 1970s and 80s represented still one more instance of the search for new church structures that had also preoccupied a prophetic minority of the clergy and laity during the 1890s, the 1930s, and the 1960s. As in the past, the search for structures took place simultaneously on two planes. Large coalitions of lay people formed—usually in combination with priests and sisters—to speak out on issues of common concern within the church and society. Meanwhile, small groups of Catholics joined together to create new opportunities for a high level of spiritual formation and service in a communal context. Self-conscious groups of lay ministers were prominent in both kinds of movements.

One effort to promote lay organizations on the international level was the Council of Laity set up in Rome in 1971 to coordinate the activities of officially recognized international lay organizations. In 1977 this body was incorporated into the Vatican administrative structure and renamed the Pontifical Council of the Laity. Ironically, church law precluded lay members in a council of this magnitude and so the lay people on the council had to be replaced with clergy.[15] Parallel efforts to provide an institutional link between the laity and the American hierarchy resulted in the establishment of the Secretariat of the Bishops' Committee on the Laity within the National Conference of Catholic Bishops. Delores Leckey, a lay woman with a wide range of experience in social apostolates, pastoral ministries, and the mass media, was chosen to be the first director.

The secretariat sponsored five major conferences in its first decade. The first, held in Annapolis in April 1978, brought together leaders of forty national Catholic organizations to promote dialogue and collaboration among them, and between them and the hierarchy. The second, a consultation of diocesan councils of laity, met in Washington in September 1978 to continue the discussion between selected lay leaders and bishops. A third consultation convened in February 1980 in Washington to focus upon the problems posed for the laity, clergy, and religious when they experimented with shared ministries. A fourth consultation focused upon spirituality took place in Adrian, Michigan, in June 1981. Finally, a fifth conference organized around the theme of work and faith met at the University of Notre Dame in October 1983. Through these meetings and the publications issued by the secretariat, the Bishops' Committee on the Laity sought new ways to promote dialogue between the laity and the hierarchy, and to provide a platform for lay leaders within the institutional church.

The National Office for Black Catholics (1970) and the three National Encuentros comprised of Hispanic Catholics, which met between 1972 and 1985, represent two more national structures established in the 1970s through which the views of important segments of the lay population could reach the hierarchy. In response to the Third National Encuentro (1985), the American hierarchy formulated a pastoral plan for Hispanic ministry that took into account the opinions expressed by the twenty-five thousand Hispanic Catholics who had met in consultations across the country. Two salient features of the pastoral plan approved by the bishops were a strong emphasis upon collaboration in ministries extending from the local to the national level, and a recognition of the essential role played by smaller communities within the parish in meeting the pastoral needs of the Hispanic community.[16]

Implicit in the pastoral plan for Hispanic ministry is an appreciation of the fact that for the Hispanic community the small "intentional community" is, in a very real sense, *even more fundamental* than the parish itself. This theme surfaces again and again in the literature on lay ministry published in the 1970s and 80s. One estimate placed the number of intentional communities in the American Catholic Church as high as fifteen thousand in 1979, and the number continued to rise steadily during the next decade. Some of these communities had their roots in movements like Cursillo, on the fringe of the parish system, while others were outgrowths of movements within the parish, such as Renew. Still others were generated by special concerns that the members shared for women's issues, the peace movement, or the economy. Bernard J. Lee and Michael A. Cowan, authors of *Dangerous Memories*, a study of intentional communities, maintain that many of the small "regathering groups" of the 1970s were created by educated, middle-class Catholics who "[were] accustomed to stating and resolving the issues of their lives on their own terms," people who "[were] anxious to preserve their autonomy in the face of larger religious and social units." For these people, intentional communities provided opportunities for relationships of collaboration, mutuality, and service not available within the parish system.

In their discussion of intentional communities, Lee and Cowan resurrect the organic imagery of the church, or community, as a body in which all are members, language that had been especially significant to the Catholic Workers, Friendship House, and the other small communal apostolates that had emphasized the mystical body.[17] James and Evelyn Whitehead likewise underscore the appropriateness of body imagery to today's community-centered lay ministries. In the process, they call attention to the critique of the traditional hierarchical model of the church that is implicit in the renewed emphasis upon the church as the body of Christ. In *The Emerging Laity*, the Whiteheads affirm that "if *all* the authority resides in the administrative arm of the body Christian (we do not say 'head,' since Christ is the head), the authoritative contributions of the other members of the body are depreciated."[18]

Women were especially attracted to the communal, nonhierarchical models of the church gaining prominence in the 1970s and 80s. Although the Notre Dame study of Catholic Parish Life estimated that women constituted 58 percent of all parish leaders (aside from the pastor),[19] for increasing numbers of women, ministry within the parish became increasingly problematic. As Mary Jo Weaver put it in her book *New Catholic Women* (1985).

> Women in the parish are in a tragic double bind; whatever choice they make forces them to deny some part of their identity. If they stay within the institution they have to repress any consciousness of women's questions . . . and embrace a tradition that defines them without consulting them. If they leave it, it appears that they have given up on their heritage and denied their Catholicity.

Weaver noted that many Catholic women dealt with the problem by joining the Womanchurch movement.[20]

The Womanchurch movement has its roots in the general ferment of the mid-1970s, as well as in one particular discussion of the issue of Catholic women's ordination convened by Mary Lynch in Chicago 1974, which led to a conference of twelve hundred women in Detroit the following year. In Detroit, Rosemary Ruether asserted that the drive for Catholic women's ordination was premature: women needed first to scrutinize the prevailing ethos of clericalism within the structures of the church, and its deep roots "in sexist symbols of domination and passivity." The heated discussion in Detroit produced important results. It planted the seeds for the Women's Ordination Conference and Womanchurch Speaks, a mass meeting held in Chicago in November 1983. Participants at the conference did not focus upon how women might join the clergy or hierarchy, but how the Catholic women's community assembled as Womanchurch could take the initiative in liberating the church and its most fundamental institutions from the bondage of patriarchy.[21]

The emergence of the Womanchurch movement signaled one critical source of polarization within the American Catholic community in the 1970s, but Catholic feminism and the drive for women's ordination were by no means the only divisive issues. The latter part of the decade also witnessed the emergence of other coalitions that sought to arrive at a new structural framework for Catholic leadership in the church and society. Three significant efforts were the "Call to Action" Conference held in Detroit 1976, the Chicago Declaration of Christian Concern issued in 1977, and National Association for Lay Ministry Coordinators, with its roots in a meeting in Philadelphia 1977.

The Call to Action was preceded by three years of wide-ranging consultation, including three national conferences designed to provide a forum for the input of all sectors of the church, including the laity. In this discussion, and the climactic meeting in Detroit 1976, movements aimed at the full participation of American Catholics in social reform and those focused upon the need for more opportunities for lay ministry intersected. At the mass meeting in Detroit's Cobo Hall, the delegates passed a spectrum of resolutions too numerous to be mentioned here. Some of these were intended to remove basic inequities rooted in the hierarchical, celibate, white, male leadership of the church. There was a call for economic justice for church employees, affirmative action for racial and ethnic equality in all ecclesial ministries, "pastoral understanding" for divorced and remarried Catholics, a reexamination of *Humanae Vitae*, pastoral sensitivity to the needs of "sexual minorities," and ratification of the ERA. Other resolutions condemned nuclear weapons and asked for a national commission on economic justice.

According to David O'Brien, who attended the Call to Action, the meeting represented a "revelation of new possibilities" for cooperation and compassion within the Catholic Church. Delores Curran, another participant, was a bit less sanguine, and expressed concern that the high percentage of church employees made the Call to Action Conference appear more revolutionary than it really was. Reflecting back upon the proceedings, Curran insisted that "until we can come up with resources to allow laity not employed by the church to attend such gatherings, issues will continue to be judged primarily from an insider's perspective."[22] The Call to Action set important precedents, however, and focused public attention upon the need to examine the relationship between social witness and ecclesial ministries. It also reechoed the three unsolved questions left over from the 1960s concerning the appropriate arena for lay activism, the distinction between lay and clerical vocations, and the need for alternative structures to supplement the parishes.

The year after the Call to Action the publication of the Chicago Declaration of Christian Concern called attention to another abiding polarization, that between the church and the world. The declaration, signed by forty-seven prominent Chicago Catholics—clerical, religious, and lay—underscored the unique responsibility of the laity to act as agents of peace and social justice in the world. It celebrated Chicago's tradition of "dynamic lay leadership" and "priests who saw their ministry as arousing the laity to the pursuit of justice and freedom, who served the laity without manipulating them." It lamented the dissipation of the energies of the laity in internal church issues, including women's ordination, and cautioned against the "devaluation of the unique ministry of lay men and women" that had accompanied the rise of lay ecclesial ministries. At the heart of the current identity crisis of the church, the declaration's signers maintained, was a retreat from lay leadership in the secular realm, a problem exacerbated by the new opportunities for the laity to serve as paraprofessionals in the ecclesial realm.[23]

Lay ecclesial ministries continued to expand and flourish, however. Late in 1977, the same year that the Chicago declaration was published, a group of priests and religious who were engaged in setting up training programs for lay ministry held an informal meeting in Philadelphia. Out of this meeting grew the National Association for Lay Ministry Coordinators, established in 1981. This movement, which changed its name three years later to the National Association for Lay Ministry (NALM), grew into an inclusive coalition of lay ministers, lay ministry coordinators, and supporters of lay ministries within the Catholic Church. It has promoted dialogue on lay ministry, enhanced the visibility of issues pertaining to lay ministry, and nurtured discussions concerning the structural changes that are necessary within the church if the potential within lay ministries is to be realized.

NALM provided a platform for ecclesial lay ministers within a church that had yet to provide channels for the airing of their grievances. In 1980, for example, *Origins*, an organ of the National Catholic Documentary Service, published the full text of an address that Suzanne Elsesser had delivered at the Fourth Annual Conference of Lay Ministry Coordinators in Washington, D.C., in June 1980. Elsesser discussed the problems that lay ministers were having gaining acceptance in the church they sought to serve. Other lay people treated them as impersonators, or minions, of the clergy and religious, or accused them of promoting a dangerous "new clericalism," which would only further polarize the laity. Elsesser maintained that all lay ministers could tell "horror stories" about collisions between colleagues in lay ministry and pastors who were not ready for their services. Elsesser explained:

> If a priest is not as certain as he once was about who he is as a priest and what he is supposed to be doing, it can be very threatening to have ecclesial ministers, or any lay person, express clear ideas about who they are and what they should be doing.

Elsesser maintained that new ways of formalizing the commitment of lay ministers were needed, along with clearer policies regarding the education, recruitment, placement, and accreditation of lay ministers.[24]

The same year that Elsesser made these recommendations the American Catholic bishops took an important step to enhance the recognition of ecclesial lay ministries with the publication of a pastoral on the laity entitled *Called and Gifted*. Published to coincide with the fifteenth anniversary of the conciliar decree on the lay apostolate, *Apostolicam Actuositatem*, the bishops' pastoral focused upon four aspects of the lay vocation: the call to adulthood, to holiness, to ministry, and to community. Like the Chicago declaration three years before, *Called and Gifted* acknowledged the laity's "privileged position" in the secular arena and its responsibility to transform the world in the image of the kingdom of God. Unlike the declaration, however, the pastoral treated ecclesial lay ministries as an equally legitimate way for the laity to fulfill their Christian mission.

In the pastoral, the bishops admitted that the role of lay ecclesial ministers still needed to be clarified, and that policies related to the employment and benefits of lay ministers still had to be worked out. They acknowledged the "tensions and misunderstandings" that continued to impede women's full participation in ministry. Finally, they officially recognized the ongoing efforts of lay people to seek a level of community unavailable within the parish in intentional communities, maintaining that these efforts represented a mandate for an "ongoing review of parish size, organization, priorities, and identity."[25] Although its implementation remains problematic, *Called and Gifted* represents a high water mark in the institutional response to the laity's struggle to serve the church in postconciliar America.

EPILOGUE

During the seven years between the pastoral *Called and Gifted* and the Synod on the Laity held in Rome in 1987, the fragmentation within the Catholic community that had emerged in the 1960s and escalated in the 1970s did not disappear. The increased degree of episcopal leadership in the socio-economic arena evidenced by the pastorals on peace and economic justice might have added a new dimension to the polarization of the laity. The unanswered questions posed in the 1960s appeared all the more urgent. Where might the laity best serve: in the secular arena or the sanctuary? Is there an abiding and inherent difference between the vocation of the ordained clergyman and that of the lay minister? Can the institutional structures of the church accommodate an expanding vision of the laity's vocation? In 1987 references to "the clericalization of the laity," "professional Catholics," and "grown-up altar [boys]," could be found in such middle-of-the-road Catholic publications as *Maryknoll* and *Our Sunday Visitor*.[26] A vocal segment of the church remains comfortable assigning complementary roles and separate realms to the clergy and the laity, to men and women.

Meanwhile, the search for new structures that provide a sense of community and mutuality absent in the parish and the diocese is still underway. The elaborate regional and national consultations sponsored by the National Conference of Catholic Bishops in anticipation of the Synod on the Laity and the even more protracted process of listening to Catholic women that preceded the publication of the bishops' pastoral on women only called attention to the fact that *normal* channels of dialogue within the American Catholic community were sorely inadequate. For a growing number of Catholic feminists in the 1980s, consultations initiated by the hierarchy are not the solution; they merely point to the problem inherent in the fundamental structure of the church from the parish through the papacy. As Mary Hunt of the Women's Alliance for Theology, Ethics and Ritual (WATER) has affirmed, feminists are not leaving the church; rather, "the church has left [them]." According to Hunt, the exodus of Catholic women to the womanchurch movement underscores the fact that "women as women cannot be full religious agents in the patriarchal church and therefore, the only way we can be church is to be Womenchurch [sic]."[27]

The Synod on the Laity held in Rome in October 1987 in the wake of carefully planned consultations with the American laity was, by almost all accounts, a failure. In the words of Peter Hebblethwaite, it "expired quietly... unloved, unmourned, largely unreported." Lay leaders, such as Edward Sellner of NALM, who had participated in pre-Synod consultations in Belleville, Illinois, and South Bend, could not help but express profound disappointment. After the synod Sellner speculated that "unless something does change, it seems educated and committed Roman Catholics, especially women and young people, may increasingly become indifferent to an apparently uncaring institutional church."[28]

One can only speculate about the sentiments of the anonymous laity engaged in localized ministries, the constituency whose concerns were so eloquently expressed by Rosemarie Brickley in a letter to *Commonweal* in 1985. Brickley spoke on behalf of the "Rodney Dangerfields" of the American Catholic community, "yanked around, patronized, disdained, demeaned," who somehow still had the faith and the stamina "to keep showing up to pray, to iron the altar linens, to clean up the used tissues, to visit the sick, give food to the hungry, and to do anything else that needs doing."[29] But as Brickley's article suggests, and the 1987 study of Catholic beliefs, practices, and values published by Gallup and Castelli reiterates, Catholic dissent and discontent do not mean an impending exodus from the church. Gallup and Castelli acknowledged that there is strong evidence of important areas of disagreement within the Catholic community. Nonetheless, they insist that their research shows that "neither criticisms nor disagreements have changed [American Catholics'] sense of belonging to the Church, indeed their sense of ownership of the Church." In fact, Gallup and Castelli maintain that "because they have institutionalized a sense of change" in the church, most Catholics of the late 1980s believe "that their criticisms will eventually be heard."[30] Somewhere in the midst of the fragmented American laity, among the professional ecclesial ministers represented by Sellner, the alienated women of the Womanchurch movement, and the Rodney Dangerfields of the local parish, lurks invincible the spirit of the American laity. The "sleeping giant" that captured the attention of Thomas Augustine Judge three-quarters of a century ago is wide awake and trying to rouse the institutional church.

· PART IV ·

American Catholics in a Changing Society: Parish and Ministry, 1930 to the Present

This essay is divided into three sections. The first section will focus on the 1940s and seek to recapture the spirit and nature of American Catholicism at that time. In doing so it will provide some context for other chapters in this book, as well as examine more specifically the relationship between the parish and ministry at that time. The second section will turn to the 1980s and present a "state of the church" analysis, emphasizing the changes that have occurred since the 1940s, especially in the area of parish and ministry. The final section will explain why these changes took place.

15

THE 1940s

The Boston Brahmins had never seen anything like it. One hundred thirty thousand Catholics parading through the streets of the old Puritan citadel. It was a sight to behold. Priests decked out in frock coats and top hats marched along the streets of Boston; numerous politicians worked the crowds lining the streets. The Boston Irish loved it. Yankee Protestants tried to ignore it. But it was hard to ignore the biggest parade in Boston's history, a parade that featured 106 bands, 75 floats, and lasted for eight hours. It was the final spectacle of the national convention of the Holy Name Society, the major religious society for Catholic men. Over a hundred thousand men from all across the country had gathered in Boston for the convention. For four days in October 1947 they attended meetings, held a huge outdoor rally and holy hour in Fenway Park, and listened to bishops extol the greatness of Catholicism and Americanism.

The theme of the convention was "For Faith and Freedom" and the new archbishop of Boston, Richard Cushing, gave a rousing talk on Thursday evening, underscoring the loyalty of Catholics to the nation and the church. For Cushing and many others the memories of the 1928 Al Smith campaign and its bitter anti-Catholic tone were still alive and in 1947 many Protestants continued to question the national loyalty of Catholics. Cushing resented this, and so did most Catholics. As far as he was concerned no one could be more American than him. "My religious faith, Catholicism; my civil and political faith, Americanism," was the way he put it. The outdoor rally at Fenway Park on Friday evening emphasized the same theme; over five hundred papal and American flags decorated the stadium. The theme of Sunday's grand parade was "Walk with Christ for Faith and Freedom." The floats depicted religious themes but red, white, and blue buntings and flags celebrated national pride and loyalty.[1]

These were heady times for Catholics. They felt very much at home in the United States and when their loyalty was questioned, they did not hesitate to defend their record as Americans. The Holy Name Society symbolized the militant confidence of Catholicism in the 1930s and 40s. Its members, respectable lower- and middle-class men, pledged to honor both God and country. They could do this in the privacy of the home or the church, but most often they honored God and country in large public gatherings such as the parade and rally in Boston. These demonstrations of faith by hundreds and even thousands of men gave Catholicism a muscular quality, a respectable but confident dignity that would not back down when challenged by charges of un-Americanism.

Catholic intellectuals showed a similar confidence. They believed Western civilization was crumbling and the key to its survival was Roman Catholicism. Joseph Fichter, a young Catholic sociologist, stated that he was convinced that "Roman Catholicism is the institution with the best possible prospect of reintegrating Western culture."[2] Few Catholics would disagree. World War I and more recently World War II had demonstrated how fragile the future of Western civilization was and the urgent need for order and stability. Some individuals turned to Marxism and the communist system as the answer to the world's problems. Many Catholics believed that religion, in particular Roman Catholicism, was the solution. Fortified with a philosophical system of thought known as neo-scholasticism, Catholics believed that they could reintegrate Western culture, a culture that seemed to be coming apart in the mid-twentieth century. The Jesuit scholar, John Courtney Murray, was attempting to do this in the area of church-state relations; the French philosopher, Jacques Maritain, wrote about the Catholic view of art and poetry; Etienne Gilson celebrated the cultural and intellectual unity of the medieval period in his writings and offered to his readers a model for the reintegration of Western culture. Numerous people read these authors, Gilson in particular, and began to see "the world in a new way, saw explanations where there had been frustrating mysteries and alluring mysteries where there had been unsatisfying explanations." "For the first time," wrote one convert after he had read Gilson's book, *The Spirit of Medieval Philosophy*, "I saw the supernatural as real, not a myth . . . and this was the source of both my excitement and 'initial belief.' "[3]

In the political arena Catholic confidence took flesh in an aggressive campaign to gain public funds for parochial schools. This "cultural offensive," as one critic described it, scared a lot of people.[4] In fact, shortly after the Holy Name convention in Boston a group of sixty Protestant leaders met in Washington, D.C., and made plans to establish Protestants and Other Americans United for the Separation of Church and State (POAU), the twentieth-century version of the militantly anti-Catholic American Protective Association. The confidence and smugness of Catholics had clearly frightened some important Protestant leaders and they were convinced that something had to be done about it.

Helping to guide the Catholic "cultural offensive" was a new breed of bishops. Richard Cushing in Boston, Francis Spellman in New York, Edward Mooney in Detroit, Samuel Stritch in Chicago, and Joseph Ritter in St. Louis were the most prominent of this group. Educated and articulate, these men became spokesmen for the new Catholic offensive and defenders of the national loyalty of Catholics. Born and raised in the United States, they were well assimilated into the American mainstream. They were not leaders of an immigrant church; they were leaders of an American church. Wrapping themselves in the flag, they preached a gospel of American patriotism, praising the separation of church and state. Their strong stance against communism enhanced their reputation for loyalty to the nation. But they could be equally adamant in their desire for public funds for Catholic schools, and political and diplomatic recognition of the Vatican. This was the bone that stuck in the throat of many Protestants.

Bishops like Mooney and Spellman were also gifted administrators and they guided the church through a period of incredible growth. The postwar baby boom had a substantial impact on the church, and the Catholic population rocketed to over forty million people by 1960, a 100 percent increase in twenty years. New parishes were organized at the rate of three or four a week in the 1940s and 50s. In addition, ground was broken for two or three new parochial schools each week. New high schools and colleges opened their doors in the postwar period, and seminaries and convents expanded their facilities to make room for the numerous men and women who wanted to enter religious life.

In the 1930s and 40s Catholics were still very much tied to their immigrant roots. This was especially true of the more recent arrivals, the Italians and the East Europeans. Polish parishes still had sermons and hymns in Polish; so did the Hungarians and Italians. The majority of immigrants continued to marry within their own ethnic group, and city neighborhoods featured the sights and sounds of Old World villages. The vast majority of Catholics worked with their hands, with two-thirds of them in the ranks of the lower class at this time. In addition, only 7 percent of the Catholic population in 1940 had graduated from college; the corresponding figure for Protestants was 15 percent.[5]

In the 1930s and 40s the parish continued to be the focal point of Catholic life. One contemporary sociologist described the importance of the parish in the following manner:

It is the place where the great majority of people, both Catholic and non-Catholic, have their only contact with the Church. It is the locus of life and work and play for pious Catholics and renegades, for prospective converts and hardened sinners. The beliefs, the behavior, and the worship of the Catholic faith are exhibited here in the parish, or they simply are not exhibited at all.[6]

The parish church was where people came to pray and worship; this was where babies were baptized, lovers were married, and the dead were buried. But the parish was more than just a religious institution; it was a key social institution that brought people together through a network of societies and clubs; it was also a major educational institution that instructed generations of Catholics in the truths about God and country.

Sunday was the big day in the parish. Crowds attended one of several morning Masses. Though the church always seemed to be full, never more than half the parishioners regularly went to Sunday Mass. Often another type of service would take place on Sunday afternoon; this might be a holy hour or benediction of the blessed sacrament. But these afternoon services attracted small numbers of worshipers. Next to Sunday the next busiest day in the parish was Saturday—the time for marriages and confessions. Marriages took place in the morning and large parishes could have as many as three on one day. Confessions were heard in the afternoon and evening, and crowds could be significant especially before the holidays of Christmas and Easter.

During the week religious services were generally limited to early morning Mass and one or two evening devotional services. Mostly women attended these weekday Masses and devotions. In large parishes priests were busy many weekday mornings burying the dead. Though men were much more involved in parish life in the 1930s and 40s than previously, their sphere of activity centered around the Holy Name Society, weekend spiritual retreats, and nocturnal adoration societies. These adoration societies were thought to be especially appropriate for men, for they needed volunteers to come to church for prayer and adoration of the eucharist throughout the night. Devotion to Christ in the eucharist was central to Catholic spirituality in these days and it was mainly associated with the ritual of benediction of the blessed sacrament. This ritual was second only to the Mass in frequency of celebration and just about every public ceremony in church concluded with benediction. Devotion to Mary was also very popular. Every Catholic owned rosary beads and many recited the rosary in honor of Mary. Each church had a shrine to Mary and parishioners could be found praying there at any time of day. Evening novena devotions were very popular in the 1930s and early 40s and most often they centered on a devotion honoring some aspect of Mary's life. The parish mission or revival was another feature of parish life at this time; this was when visiting preachers came to the parish to preach a revival of religion. The goal was the spiritual renewal of the parish and it was achieved primarily through instruction in the spiritual life and a confession of one's sins.

In those days the parish school was as important as the church and almost half the parish budget went to support the school. In fact, the parish was a child-centered institution at that time, with the parochial school being the centerpiece of this culture. Despite the emphasis on Catholic schools, however, only about half the parishes in the country had a school and never much more than half the eligible number of children attended a Catholic school. To reach the children who attended public schools, parishes organized religious education programs and these could be very extensive. Known as the Confraternity of Christian Doctrine (CCD), it was generally the one area in parish life where lay people could become involved in some type of apostolic activity, in this case teaching religion to children. The CCD enjoyed its brightest moments in the 1940s and 50s.

As a social institution the parish provided an array of activities for both young and old. Religious societies had their communion breakfasts on Sunday morning after Mass and these were always special occasions. Holy Name societies often used such occasions to march through neighborhood streets, proud as peacocks to be Catholic and well dressed. Dances, card parties, bingo, and fashion shows always attracted a crowd. The young had the Catholic Youth Organization (CYO), which sponsored all types of athletic activities, from boxing to camping. Bowling leagues were also popular as were men's smokers.

From one perspective the parish of the 1930s and 40s was not very different from its late nineteenth-century predecessor. Its religious, educational, and social calendar had not changed much from the turn of the century and priests were giving the same advice that their predecessors had given fifty years earlier; in fact, some parish bulletins reprinted verbatim pastoral advice that was sixty years old.[7] Given the Catholic commitment to tradition, such continuity with the past was not surprising. As far as religion was concerned change was not part of the Catholic vocabulary in the 1930s and 40s. Yet the parish had changed in some very subtle ways.

In the nineteenth century most parishes were organized according to nationality because of the strong desire of the people to maintain their particular ethnic culture. For this reason immigrant Catholics emphasized the need to preserve the language of the old country; as so many of them put it, "language saves faith" and without the language and the cultural network that sustained it religion would surely be lost. As time passed, however, Old World loyalties weakened and the importance of ethnic identity diminished. Catholics were becoming more American and began to identify themselves as Catholic and American. Though there might be a twinge of ethnic loyalty among the third and fourth generations, most Irish and Germans identified themselves as American Catholics, not Irish or German Catholics. The same was becoming true for Italians, Poles, and other East European groups. The last to arrive in the New World, they would be the last to lose that powerful link with the culture of the old country. But by the 1940s these bonds were growing weaker for them as well. As Catholics became more American and less ethnic, the parish changed. Its role as the ethnic fortress diminished and it became a religious fortress. It was no less insular than its immigrant predecessor, but now its insularity was defined religiously more so than ethnically.

This shift helps to explain the strong Catholic sense of confidence and even militance in the 1920s, 30s, and 40s. Catholic loyalty or religious loyalty had replaced ethnic loyalty; pride in religion had surpassed pride in ethnic identity. As this developed, people transferred their loyalty from a particular ethnic group to their church and their nation. St. Patrick's Day parades and Italians festas still took place, but they now had to compete with Holy Name parades and stadium rallies where Catholics honored God and the American flag.

This shift from ethnic loyalty to denominational loyalty meant that the parish had fewer claims on the people. As an immigrant institution the parish was as much a cultural institution as it was a religious institution; it could appeal to people's ethnicity or nationality as well as their religion. In fact, it was very difficult to separate the two. As ethnicity weakened in the middle decades of the twentieth century the parish increasingly became centered on its religious function and this limited its appeal with the people.

Another development was taking place that was not so subtle. Like many Americans, Catholics were moving to the suburbs. Life in suburbia was quite different from the old city neighborhoods. The single family dwelling emphasized the private side of life and potentially the insularity of the family from the larger society. The pervasiveness of the automobile and the car-pool culture of suburbia diminished the importance of neighborhood as it enabled residents to travel far from home for work and play. The absence of sidewalks and boulevards weakened the public dimension of surburban living. Who had ever heard of a parade in a cul-de-sac! In the suburbs everything—houses and people especially—looked alike. Homogeneity and middle-class domesticity had replaced the diversity of city life. Yet, when it came time to begin a parish in the suburb, very few people thought about the need for change in this new social environment. The parish was the same everywhere and at all times, regardless of the environment. At least that was the way it seemed as church after church sprouted up in the suburbs and no one seemed to notice that maybe something different was needed in these bedroom communities. City parish and suburban parish were all the same in the 1940s, or so it appeared. As suburbs grew and parish populations increased, people began to acquire a "filling station mentality." They came to church to be refueled spiritually, but they remained on the periphery of parish life. The sense of community, evident in the immigrant parish, was not very visible in the suburban parish. The privatism and individualism nurtured in the suburbs certainly were responsible for this, partially if not totally.

Another important change was the continuing emergence of a church beyond the parish. For most of the nineteenth century the parish was the church; that was all there was to the church. In the twentieth century the church bureaucracy expanded with each passing decade and by the middle of the century there was much more to church than just the parish. One of the fastest growing areas was Catholic charities. When the archbishop of New York, Patrick Hayes, established the Catholic Charities of the archdiocese of New York in 1920, he was setting up a separate empire that would administer the operations of as many as eighty-one institutions and ninety-three agencies that cared for the sick, aged, orphans, and delinquents; its annual budget was in the millions of dollars and hundreds of people, both volunteers and employees, were involved in this enterprise. Another area of growth was education. High schools and colleges increased in the twentieth century and the parochial school had ballooned into a full-fledged school system; in some cities it was larger than the public school system. Foreign missions was another growth industry and it too had its own bureaucratic network. Social action had acquired more importance with Catholics and a large network of voluntary societies and movements developed around such issues as race relations and the rights of labor. What this all meant was that some of the most dynamic features of Catholic life in the 1930s and 40s were totally separate from what was going on in the parish. The church had become larger than the parish and many Catholics could find an outlet for their apostolic energies in arenas beyond the parish.

In some ways the parish of the 1930s and 40s was a carbon copy of the parish of the 1880s and 90s. Sunday Masses still attracted large crowds, Saturday confessions kept priests busy, and people still came to church to be baptized, married, and buried. But significant changes had taken place. Denominational loyalty was replacing ethnic allegiance; suburban parishes were growing more rapidly than city parishes; and beyond the parish Catholic life and activity was booming. Clearly the influence of the parish was decreasing and its role in Catholic life was shrinking. Some Catholics recognized what was going on. A handful of "pioneer priests," as Scott Appleby called them, promoted a new vision of Catholicism that was energized by the concept of the church as the mystical body of Christ. Equipped with this vision they wanted the parish to break out of its increasingly insular posture and be a launching pad for service to the world. Debra Campbell's lay activists, engaged in apostolates beyond the parish, also tried to move the people in the parish to new horizons and new levels of apostolic activity. Indeed, noises of reform were in the air and rumors of renewal were going about, but not until the middle and late 1950s would more than a small number of pioneer priests and lay activists think seriously about the future of the church in the United States. That was not surprising. It was hard to think about change in October 1947 right after thousands of Catholic men had publicly demonstrated their faith in the streets of Boston. The sounds of triumphal Catholicism drowned out any noises of reform.

In the 1940s the vast majority of priests were engaged in parish work. They defined themselves as "parish priests" and this was where they lived and worked, day and night. The people had put them on a pedestal and they enjoyed widespread respect and popularity. Hollywood sensed this and began to celebrate the work of the Catholic priest on the screen. In 1944 Bing Crosby won an Oscar for best actor when he charmed the hearts of millions as Father O'Malley in the award-winning movie *Going My Way*. A year later Crosby and Father O'Malley returned to the screen and starred with Ingrid Bergman in *The Bells of St. Mary's*. Crosby's portrayal of Father O'Malley "became an important icon in American culture. His bold optimism and unflagging faith in the powers of good kindled a real popular affection for this archetypal man of the cloth."[8] The Catholic priest could do no wrong in the sugarcoated universe that Hollywood had created for him. He was worldly, but not too worldly. The seminary had instructed him to be in the world, but not of it. His model of priesthood dated from the seventeenth century when the modern seminary was formed. It was a monastic model that stressed piety over learning and separation from the world rather than involvement. O'Malley personified these virtues and Catholics applauded. Virtue had triumphed over vice. Take away some of the schmaltz and Hollywood's priest bore a resemblance to the model promoted by the seminary.

Hollywood's glorification of the priest confirmed the grandiose view that most Catholics had. In a statement symptomatic of the age, Bishop Walter Foery of Syracuse proclaimed that the "history of the Catholic Church is essentially the history of the priesthood." The reasons for this were clear according to Foery. "Priests are the living instruments through whose ministry Christ's mystical presence abides in the church until the end of time. The priest is the accredited teacher of the word of God. He is the dispenser of the mysteries of God. He is the witness of Christ. Where the spirit of priestly life flourishes, there the church flourishes. Where it grows cold, lifeless, and indifferent, there the church suffers tremendous loss. Destroy the priesthood and the bond between heaven and earth is broken."[9]

Such a close identification between priest and church, an identification that gave him alone the power to activate the "divine economy of religion and salvation," also meant that he alone could exercise ministry in the parish. Since he alone was regarded as the "other Christ," only he could represent Christ and his priestly ministry. Thus, he gobbled up all ministries and left little for anyone else. He was the sacramental minister who celebrated Mass and provided the sacraments for the people; he was the one who preached the word; he was the spiritual counselor and comforter of the sick; and he was the primary teacher, though here he had a lot of help, given the large numbers who needed to be taught. But his ministry did not stop there. He had to preside at monthly communion breakfasts; he was chaplain to all the parish societies and had to show up at their meetings; he supervised the youth athletic programs and often ended up bowling in the parish bowling league; and of course he trained the altar boys. In addition to all this, the priest had to administer the affairs of the parish, seeing that building repairs were done and bills were paid. The priest was all things to all people and as a result there was little left for anyone else to do. Moreover, many parishes had a staff of priests that included a pastor and two, four, or even more assistant pastors. Such an abundance of priests persuaded people who wanted to become apostolically involved to look beyond the parish.

One further point is worth noting as regards the relationship between the parish and the priest in the 1930s and 40s. The parish was his personal benefice, awarded to him in return for his services. This meant that all income of the parish derived from the offerings of the people belonged to him and after expenses were met, he could pocket the surplus if he so chose. This was a practice left over from medieval times. In Boston, church law endorsed this tradition until the 1950s, but in other places where the law was not so generous the custom still prevailed. In other words, the priest not only controlled the parish, he effectively owned it. Though his name might not appear on the title to the land, no one doubted who the landlord was.

Such total control of the parish by the priest was the norm in the 1930s and 40s and very few people complained. But it did make the lives of one group very difficult. These were the women religious or the sisters as they were then called. In a book that I wrote a few years ago I called the sisters "the Catholic serfs." I have found no reason to change that opinion. They had fewer rights than priests, brothers, or lay people. One reason for such subordinate status was their relationship to the pastor of the parish. In the 1930s and 40s most sisters taught in parish schools. The school was their life, the center of their universe. But for all practical purposes the pastor was the headmaster of the school, the local superintendent of education. He paid the bills and was responsible for the maintenance of the building and the playground. He hired the sisters and no one doubted that he could fire them if he so desired. Because of their economic dependence on the pastor, he held great power over them. He was the boss and they were his employees. This could be a benign relationship, a father-daughter type of relationship as Patricia Byrne suggests, or it could be a cold, distant relationship that resembled that between the lord of the plantation and his serfs. Both types existed and in each situation the sisters were in a position of dependence and subordination. Such a state of dependence gave the pastor a great amount of control over the lives of the sisters in the parish.

Another major formative influence on the lives of sisters at this time was the concept of the cloister. Like the priests the role model for sisters was a monastic one and the convent was for all practical purposes a monastery. Except for the chapel and a parlor or two, it was off limits to lay people and priests. Sisters lived in a closed society, cut off from the world. Unlike the priest they could not travel about in their own automobiles, listen to the radio, enjoy the theater and movies, the horse races or sporting events. When they left the convent, they had to go in pairs lest the sight of a solitary sister walking the streets give scandal to the faithful. Even in the parish their activity was limited; they were "in the parish but not of it." Their domain was the school; the parish—the church and its ministries—was the priest's domain.

As Patricia Byrne noted, it was this conflict between the cloister and the competitive marketplace that increasingly made religious life more and more of a struggle for sisters. They were like Martians on earth, struggling to survive in an alien world. Because of their commitment to education, sisters had to keep up with their profession and with each passing decade of the twentieth century they did become more engaged in the world of education and learning, and with each passing decade more and more cracks appeared in the walls of the cloister. In the 1960s the walls finally collapsed and the world rushed in to change the lives of sisters.

The persistent strength and totality of this cloister culture had protected the sisters from the modernizing trends in both church and society. When the walls did collapse, the sisters had much more catching up to do than the priests. Since the cloister culture had stunted their growth intellectually and culturally, they needed to be reeducated and retooled as sisters of the twentieth century and they set about doing this with the same intensity and commitment that they exhibited in the convent and the school. As a group they soon passed the priests in terms of modernization and commitment to church renewal. In fact, they became the vanguard of the new Catholicism that surfaced in the United States in the late 1960s and 70s.

The changes in the life and work of sisters provided the most striking contrast of changes in the church after the Second Vatican Council and the reason for this is apparent. They had moved from a medieval cloister to the modern marketplace in a very brief period of time. The most dramatic symbol of this shift took place in a matter of moments when sisters took off their medieval habits and put on modern clothes. A simple everyday act, but it was invested with momentous symbolism and meaning. All of a sudden the church of the 1930s and 40s had become history.

While the sisters were struggling with the pastor and the cloister, lay people were busy trying to decide which parish organization they would join. They certainly had many from which to choose. But the parish organizations for the laity were mostly devotional types of societies such as the ladies' sodality or the Holy Name or St. Vincent de Paul organizations for men. Teaching catechism was popular with the women while men did other types of work such as visiting homes in search of lapsed Catholics. Since the parish was the domain of the priest, lay people were looked upon as his helpers. They took their mandate from him much like the sheep followed the voice of the shepherd. That was how Pope Pius X described the position of the laity in the early twentieth century. Their one duty was, in the pope's words, "to allow themselves to be led, and, like a docile flock, to follow the Pastors."[10] But they wanted more and they found it in movements and organizations that were sprouting up beyond the parish.

Catholic Action was a movement that attracted many young people in the 1940s. Promoted by the papacy and many American bishops, it sought to engage lay people in a more active role in the mission of the church. It was one other aspect of the Catholic "cultural offensive" in the 1930s and 40s, and it reflected the confidence and enthusiasm of Catholics who sought to save Western civilization from destruction. Their goal was "to restore all things in Christ"; this phrase, popularized by Pope Pius X, became the motto of the Catholic Action movement.

In becoming more apostolic lay people worked under the direction of the priest and shared in his apostolate. As one favorite saying put it, "Everything by themselves. Nothing without the priest." Nonetheless, it was clear, as Debra Campbell noted, that a new understanding of the laity and the church was emerging. Lay people were being told that in some mysterious way, they were the church. Pope Pius XII said as much in 1946 when he wrote, "The laity must above all have a conviction . . . not only of belonging to the Church, but of being the Church, that is to say, the community of faithful on earth under the leadership of the common head, the Pope, and the bishops in communion with him. They are the Church."[11] It appeared that the laity were more than just sheep, as far as Pius XII was concerned. Indeed, they remained subordinate to the hierarchy, but they received much more encouragement to become active apostles in the world in order "to restore all things in Christ."

This atmosphere of increased concern for the mission of the church in the world encouraged the emergence of new movements and organizations. The Catholic Worker movement, Friendship House, and labor schools were founded in the 1930s and 40s as the issues of poverty, race, and work captured the attention of Catholics. As Debra Campbell and Scott Appleby indicated, priests were very important in promoting these causes. The liturgical movement also had a substantial influence. By promoting a richer understanding of the Mass and the sacraments, it gave to these Catholic activists a stronger grounding in the spiritual life and helped to inspire them in their work as lay apostles.

As Debra Campbell noted, the increased activity in the lay apostolate in the 1930s and 40s had very little to do with the parish. For the most part it took place beyond the parish. The reason for this is not hard to discover. The parish was the domain of the priest and lay leadership was not to be found in an institution controlled by priests. In the parish the old adage of "pay, pray, and obey" still prevailed as far as the laity was concerned.

Rumors of reform were beginning to circulate throughout Catholic convents and rectories in the 1940s. Lay people began to talk a new language; Catholic action, the lay apostolate, and how to restore all things in Christ became topics of conversation around some kitchen tables. As old city neighborhoods changed and new suburban developments appeared, the parish acquired new functions. The more people reflected upon the church and society, the more they realized that the depression of the 1930s and the changes ushered in by World War II had radically altered the American landscape. What this would mean for the Catholic Church was not yet clear. What was becoming increasingly clear, however, was that religion in the United States was moving into a new age.

16

THE 1980s

In September 1987, almost forty years to the day after the Holy Name convention in Boston, Pope John Paul II visited the United States. On Sunday, September 13, the fourth day of his nine-city tour the pope stopped in San Antonio, Texas. Thousands of people lined the streets to get a glimpse of the pope as he rode through San Antonio in his specially constructed popemobile. After a six-mile tour through the city John Paul II celebrated Mass in a large field where an estimated three hundred thousand people had gathered in ninety-five degree heat. Newspapers claimed that this was the largest religious event in Texas history. What was particularly noteworthy about the pope's visit to San Antonio was his desire to recognize the vitality and strength of the Hispanic Catholic community. San Antonio was the showcase of Hispanic Catholicism in the United States. Spanish-speaking Catholics had lived in San Antonio for over two hundred years. In the 1980s 75 percent of the city's population was Hispanic and most of them were Catholic. The church in San Antonio, led by its archbishop, Patricio Flores, was very active in the life of the community. A major reason for such activity was the community organization known as COPS, Communities Organized for Public Service. Based in thirty parish communities and supported by Archbishop Flores, it was a grass-roots political organization that had substantial influence on the public life of the city.

In recognizing the vitality of the Hispanic Catholic community Pope John Paul was acknowledging the importance of their presence in the cultural mosaic of American Catholicism. When he arrived in Los Angeles a few days later, he underscored this point very emphatically. "Today in the church in Los Angeles," he said, "Christ is Anglo and Hispanic, Christ is Chinese and black, Christ is Vietnamese and Irish, Christ is Korean and Italian, Christ is Japanese and Filipino, Christ is Native American, Croatian, Samoan, and many other ethnic groups." In acknowledging the ethnic universality of the church, the pope urged the people to have a "keen sensitivity to authentic cultures"; he urged them to proclaim the gospel in the language of the people and in a manner that incorporates the distinctive symbols and traditions of various ethnic groups.[1]

The contrasts between San Antonio 1987 and Boston 1947 are striking. In 1947 the pope was still a prisoner in the Vatican and only rarely did he leave his palace. But Pope John Paul's trip to the United States was the 36th major journey that he had taken in his nine years as pope. In the course of these trips he had visited Catholics in just about every major country in the world. This was his second trip to the United States and in traveling to such cities as Miami, New Orleans, San Antonio, Phoenix, Los Angeles, and San Francisco the pope was recognizing the growing importance of the church in the southern and western parts of the nation. Most especially he was recognizing the importance of the rapidly expanding Hispanic Catholic community. The dominance of the Irish-American style of Catholicism, personified by Archbishop Cushing and the Boston Irish, was history, silently put to rest along with Father O'Malley and *Going My Way*. In 1947 Archbishop Cushing had proclaimed his Americanism; forty years later the pope was celebrating the ethnic pluralism of Catholicism in the United States and warning about the dangers of American capitalism. In 1987 few Americans questioned the loyalty of Catholics. In fact, when people brought up the topic of Catholic loyalty, what they usually meant was the loyalty of Catholics to the church; in 1987 the one who raised this question most often was the pope and his aides in the Vatican. They did so with good reason for as one survey revealed "an overwhelming 93% of those who say they consider themselves Catholic believe 'it is possible to disagree with the Pope and still be a good Catholic.' "[2]

The militant and triumphal style of Catholicism, so evident in the 1940s, was gone by the 1980s. In its place was a widespread recognition of the value of religious freedom and religious pluralism. Gone too was the confidence and smugness of the Catholics of the 1940s who believed that Roman Catholicism was the single best hope of Western civilization. Replacing it was a belief in toleration, the toleration of other religious traditions as well as other cultural traditions. One sure indicator of this was the increase in the number of religiously mixed marriages. In the 1940s a mixed marriage for most Catholics meant that an Irish boy was marrying an Italian girl. Marrying someone who was not Catholic was so frowned upon that those who did had to get married in the parish rectory or some secondary location in the church, but never at the altar during mass. By the 1980s a sizable number of Catholics were marrying individuals from another religious tradition; one study estimated that "the present rate for Catholic inter-marriage is about 40%." Moreover, an overwhelming number of Catholics (89 percent) approved of religiously mixed marriages.[3]

In the 1940s the POAU feared a Catholic "cultural offensive." In the 1980s such a cultural offensive was noticeable to be sure, but it was not focused on public aid for parochial schools or the official appointment of an American representative to the Vatican. The public policy concern of Catholics in the 1980s centered on such issues as abortion, war, and the economy. In the 1980s Catholics were especially concerned about issues of social justice. One of the most dramatic turnarounds had taken place in their attitude toward war. In the 1940s and 50s Catholics were super hawks, but by the 1980s most had become doves. This dramatic shift prompted one commentator to conclude that "the sea change in attitudes toward war and peace among Catholics . . . is one of the most significant public-opinion shifts in recent decades."[4]

In the 1940s and 50s the Catholic population was increasing at a rate of 5 percent per year; in the 1960s, 70s, and 80s the increase had slowed to 1 percent per year. Reflecting this slow growth rate new parishes were established at the rate of one or two a week in the 1960s, 70s, and 80s, or about half the rate of the 1940s and 50s. In 1987 just forty-one new parishes were established. The statistics for parochial schools for the 1960s and 70s were much more startling. In the 1970s schools closed at the rate of three a week; twenty years earlier schools had opened at the rate of three a week. As the Catholic population moved to the suburbs in the post–World War II era, the presence of the church in the city became problematic. This became especially dramatized in 1988 when the archbishop of Detroit announced the closing of forty-six parishes in the inner city of Detroit. Such a massive closing of churches was unprecedented. Furthermore, it underscored the challenges that church leaders faced as they sought to shape the church for a new generation of Catholics. American Catholicism was clearly moving into a new age. The pattern of extraordinary growth in population and institutions was over as an era of consolidation replaced an age of expansion.

In looking at the Catholic people in the 1980s it is obvious that as a group they were much better educated than the previous generation. In fact, more than one-third of the nation's college students in 1988 were Catholic.[5] As Catholics became more educated, they moved up the social and economic ladder. Surveys done in the 1980s found that 30 percent of the Catholic working population was employed in business and the professions, a percentage slightly higher than the figure for all Protestants. Reflecting the large presence of recent immigrants, principally of Hispanic background, 39 percent of the Catholic population comprised manual workers, a percentage slightly lower than the figure for all Protestants. What these data suggest is that a large segment of the Catholic community has made it into the middle class; another sizable segment has not. In other words, in terms of income and class, the Catholic Church is divided into two churches. One is white, middle-class, and suburban; the other is brown or black, lower-class, and urban. More importantly the danger of a "severe cleavage into two churches radically disjointed in terms of class differences, attitudes, desires, hopes, and aspirations" is a strong possibility.[6]

With all the changes taking place in the Catholic community, it was not surprising that priests began to reexamine their own position in the church. As Scott Appleby has shown, this evaluation process persuaded many priests to leave the priesthood and pursue other careers. This exodus was most pronounced in the late 1960s and early 1970s, but it has continued throughout the 1980s. Coupled with this was a decline in the number of vocations to the priesthood. The combination of these two forces has led to a serious shortage of clergy in the American Catholic community. In addition, the median age of the clergy has increased significantly during the past quarter-century and this has compounded the problem of clerical leadership.

At the very moment when priests began to reevaluate their ministry, the laity discovered a new church, a church that claimed to be the people of God and a church in which lay people were suddenly thrust upon center stage. As the laity acquired a new self-understanding they began to seek new roles in the church. When this happened the understanding of ministry in the Catholic church underwent substantial change. Suddenly the priest was no longer alone in the parish or in the sanctuary; numbers of lay people appeared on the scene and were eager to take over his work. This new understanding of church and ministry posed serious challenges to the priest who in the not so distant past was accustomed to being the one and only person identified with parish ministry. As the people's understanding of priesthood changed, priests began to reexamine their own understanding of priesthood and many found this especially difficult. In addition to a more comprehensive understanding of church and ministry, Catholics have continued to debate the issues of a married clergy and the ordination of women. The raising of these issues has also challenged the traditional understanding of an ordained priesthood that is both celibate and male.

In the past quarter-century the traditional understanding of priesthood has been reshaped in a very substantial manner. Nevertheless, a satisfactory definition of ordained priesthood still remains as elusive as a fistfull of water. The very fluidity of the discussion and the elusiveness of a satisfactory definition or consensus has contributed to an identity crisis, or at least identity dilemma, among American Catholic priests.

One trend Scott Appleby pointed out was that by the 1980s priests had begun to reemphasize the importance of the parish. With the move toward professionalization in the 1960s and 70s and the popularity of various apostolates or ministries not associated with the parish, parish ministry had become unpopular. This changed in the 1980s as priests increasingly began to define their work in terms of the sacraments. No longer the ombudsman who was all things to all people, the priest concentrated on his role as sacramental minister and the center for this ministry has traditionally been the parish.

One other notable development in the past decade or so has been the strong desire of priests to revitalize and renew themselves both spiritually and professionally. The more the priesthood came under scrutiny and criticism, the more priests and bishops began to call for renewal. This call for renewal has resulted in the establishment of a variety of continuing education programs for priests. Such programs have had a decidedly positive effect on the morale of the clergy and the effectiveness of clerical ministry.

As significant as change has been with priests, it has been even more radical for sisters, or women religious as they are commonly known in the post–Vatican II era. The most obvious change, besides the abandonment of the traditional habit, has been the decline in the number of sisters; in 1987 there were 74,509 fewer women religious than in 1966. Obviously fewer women were entering religious life, with the result that the median age of women religious has increased with each passing year. In addition, convent life has changed so dramatically that the convent itself, as it was known in the 1940s, has virtually disappeared. As Patricia Byrne suggests, the main reason for this was the abandonment of the culture of the cloister. Though not as visible and publicized as the abandonment of the habit, the dissappearance of the cloister culture has had very profound effects on the lives of women religious. Coupled with this has been the self-awakening that has taken place as a result of the women's movement. Then add to this the de-emphasis on teaching in the parochial school and what resulted was a way of life for women religious that was radically different from that of the 1930s and 40s.

One obvious difference was the type of work in which sisters became involved. No longer confined to teaching in the parochial school, by the 1980s sisters could be found working in a wide variety of ministries, from caring for the aged to working with convicts. Parish ministry continued to attract sisters and because of the shortage of ordained priests a number of sisters have even been appointed as pastors of parishes. As their work has changed, so too has their style of living. In the 1940s a life beyond the convent was unknown. By the 1980s many sisters were living alone in rented apartments; this has forced them to reevaluate the need for community and the sense of identity gained from belonging to a religious order. In many respects the difference between sisters and apostolic lay women has vanished; the dress and style of life of most sisters was no longer that distinctive. In the case of many sisters all that separated them from their lay counterpart, who in many instances may have been a colleague in ministry, was their vow of celibacy and a vaguely defined relationship with a specific religious order. For many women that was not a strong enough incentive to remain in religious life. For others it was not distinctive enough to persuade them to enter religious life.

It is clear that Catholic sisters and priests have undergone major changes in the last fifty years or so. Continuities remain to be sure. The priest still celebrates the eucharist, or says Mass as they used to put it; he hears confessions, and marries and buries the faithful. He is celibate and is still a he and not a she. But the Catholic priest no longer sits perched on his pedestal, the idol of the people; he has come down from this lofty perch and is searching for his niche in the new church. With the sisters change has certainly overshadowed the sense of continuity. In fact, the changes have been so profound that the very future of religious life for women is even questioned. Whatever the long term resolution of this may be, women religious in the year 2010 will bear little resemblance to their predecessors of the 1930s and 40s.

As far as the laity of the 1980s is concerned, the changes in the past quarter-century were not so dramatic. Changes there were to be sure—Mass in English, altars turned around to face the people, hawks becoming doves, and numerous others. But as regards apostolic involvement in the mission of the church, or what can be called in the language of the 1970s and 80s involvement in ministry, continuity with the past rather than a decisive break with the past has been the pattern. In fact, as Debra Campbell has shown, the heyday of the lay apostolate was in the 1929–1959 era and this era paved the way for subsequent developments in the self-understanding of the American Catholic laity.

As lay people began to appropriate a more comprehensive understanding of ministry, they became much more involved in the life of the parish. One study done in the mid-1980s found that 83 percent of those people named as the "most influential leaders" in the parish were lay persons. Some of these parish leaders were on the payroll and others were volunteers. Those on the payroll were most often individuals educated and trained in such areas as liturgy, religious education, and counseling. The professional full-time lay minister was a new phenomenon in the 1970s and 80s. They supplemented the work of the parish priest and soon became a permanent fixture in the Catholic parish. Women were especially active in this area with three out of five recognized parish leaders being female.[7]

As Debra Campbell has argued, many Catholics still look beyond the parish for their area of ministry. This was certainly true in the 1929–1959 era of the lay apostolate and has remained so throughout the 1980s. Heirs of the 1940s lay apostolate, many Catholics in the 1980s still look to the family, neighborhood, and workplace as the areas of primary responsibility for the laity. These people have become involved in such issues as shelters and housing for the homeless; they belong to political action groups concerned with issues like civil rights, abortion, the environment, and jobs. The women's movement and its concern for equal rights has also attracted the attention of many Catholics in recent decades. These people are carrying on a venerable tradition in American religious history—involvement in the voluntary society.

In the early nineteenth century many Americans joined voluntary societies in order to promote the values of the Protestant Christian religion. They banded together to promote the Sunday School; they organized to abolish slavery and to evangelize China. In the late nineteenth and early twentieth century the trend continued as the idea of a more public, social Christianity took hold. Women became especially involved in the settlement house movement and the temperance crusade. Such involvement did not suggest a rise in religious indifference. On the contrary, it suggested a religious awakening and a new understanding of the public dimension of religion. But as the voluntary society or the organized movement took on the role of promoting the public or social dimension of religion, the congregation increasingly became "an enclave of inwardness." With Catholics a similar awakening took place in the twentieth century as more and more of them looked beyond the parish to the voluntary society or organization as the catalyst for their involvement in the public arena. The Catholic Action movement that Debra Campbell discussed was part of this awakening and it has continued to the present day as many Catholics search for involvement in some type of social gospel. As was true in the 1940s many parishes in the 1980s were "enclaves of inwardness"; their main concerns focused on the religious needs of the individual. For this reason people seeking a more public expression of their faith continued to join the voluntary society. This was a major shift in the way Catholics organized themselves in order to promote a more public, social gospel. The decisive moment of this shift would be in the 1930s and 40s and, as was true with Protestants, it was not a sign of religious indifference, but an indication of a religious awakening.[8]

The development of the lay apostolate was part of the religious awakening that took place among Catholics in the post–World War I era. It was most pronounced in France and Germany, and reached the United States in the 1930s. As this awakening developed the parish began to come under scrutiny. The book, *Revolution in a City Parish*, written by a French parish priest, Abbé Michonneau in 1946 and published in English translation in 1949, was the key book that persuaded a number of Catholic priests to rethink the role of the parish in the modern world. Joseph Fichter, S.J., was the first American scholar to give serious attention to the study of the parish. His first work, *Southern Parish: Dynamics of a City Church*, appeared in 1951. Since then many studies of the parish have taken place. Protestants have also directed a great deal of attention to the study of the local congregation. This began with the work of Paul Douglass in the 1930s and has also continued to the present day. The most recent major study of the Catholic parish was the Notre Dame Study of Catholic Parish Life. Initiated in 1981 by Philip Murnion, a priest-sociologist from New York, the study underwent considerable expansion in 1983 when the Lilly Endowment provided funding for a long-term and large-scale project. David Leege, a political scientist at the University of Notre Dame, became the senior research director for the project and guided it through to its completion. This study has produced a remarkably rich profile of the American Catholic parish in the 1980s.

Certain features of the parish of the 1980s stand out when compared to the parish of the 1930s and 40s. First of all, the 1980s parish is a remarkably diverse institution. Various types of parishes have existed throughout history; even in the United States where Catholicism has a relatively brief past, different types of parishes have existed. In the immigrant era the ethnic and cultural heritage of the people was the major distinguishing feature of the parish. Moreover, parishes always reflected regional and geographical diversity; a southern parish differed from a northeastern one just because of its geographical location. An urban parish was very different from a rural parish, and the same was true of the suburban congregation. But by the 1980s parishes within the same region, be it urban or suburban, southeast or northeast, were very diverse from each other. As one study put it, there were varieties of religious presence. The same city, Hartford, Connecticut, for example, could have one parish that was an enclave of inwardness and another that was active in the world beyond the parish. Some parishes have enthusiastically embraced the liturgical and theological changes initiated by the Second Vatican Council and others, except for a few cosmetic changes, act as if the council never happened. Such diversity becomes even clearer when parish programs are examined. About 18 percent of the parishes studied offered "little more than Mass and religious education for the young." But 37 percent of the parishes were incredibly busy and offered a wide range of programs, including a parish school. The remaining parishes had a moderately complex range of programs. Such diversity was not present in the 1930s and 40s. The personality of the pastor did give a certain tone to parish life, but beyond this measure of difference parishes were strikingly similar in those years and the sameness of the Latin Mass underscored this quality of parish life.[9]

Moreover, in the 1980s diversity was even present within the same parish. Most often this showed up in the different types of liturgies celebrated in the parish. Thus, people began to speak of a 9:30 congregation or a Saturday evening congregation and what they were referring to was the presence of different congregations or communities within the same parish and each of these congregations had its own style of liturgy. In the 1930s and 40s parishes did serve different constituencies, but most often the measure of difference was age. In the 1980s more than age was involved. Most often it was a point of view and an understanding of the role of religion in modern life. One pundit, using the soda industry as his inspiration, described such diversity among Roman Catholics as R. C. Classic, R. C. Light, and R. C. Free.

Sunday is still the most important day in the parish. But what happens on Sunday in a 1980s parish was quite different from the 1940s. The main difference was not just the celebration of the liturgy in English, but an entirely new form of the Mass. The devotional life of the parish has also changed; gone are the popular Marian devotions of the 1930s and 40s and the ever present benediction of the eucharist. In their place are prayer services in which the Bible has a central place; seasonal pentitential services, in Lent and Advent most generally, followed by confession have replaced the popularity of the weekly Saturday confession. Mary still occupies a central place in the personal prayer life of Catholics, second only to Jesus, but parish-sponsored

Marian devotions were not common in the 1980s. When 1940 devotions take place in the 1980s, older women make up the majority of the congregation. "Well over half," noted David Leege, "and sometimes as high as 85% of young Catholics rarely or never participate in stations, public rosary, novenas, or benediction."[10] Part of growing up Catholic in the 1940s was participation in such classic Catholic rituals; that was no longer true in the 1980s. The contemporary Catholic was more interested in spiritual renewal programs or Bible study groups.

Two very important changes in the parish centered on new types of involvement of the laity. The most celebrated change was that noted by Debra Campbell, the explosion of lay ministry. As the Notre Dame study observed, the most noteworthy feature of the 1980s parish was that "unpaid lay persons conduct many of the important ministries of the parish." This could range from visiting the sick to acting as a eucharistic minister at Mass. In addition, many parishes, an estimated three out of ten, have a salaried lay person on the pastoral staff.[11] The other area of unprecedented involvement was the parish council. Three out of four parishes have a parish council in which lay people, together with the pastor, make decisions affecting the life of the parish. Such involvement of lay people in the planning and decision-making of parish life was unknown in the 1940s, though there were precedents for this in the early nineteenth century when lay trustees were very much a part of parish life. The increasing involvement of the laity in the parish has meant that much of the leadership in the parish has passed to lay people. This was quite different from the days when the pastor ruled the parish much like the master lorded it over his plantation.

As was true in the past, women were very active in the parish in the 1980s. They outnumber men at Mass and at such devotions as stations of the cross, the public rosary, and novenas. They were also recognized leaders with three out of five leaders in the parish being women. Nonetheless, when it came to power and authority, men controlled the parish. This situation has produced noticeable dissatisfaction among women parish workers.[12]

A major area of lay involvement in the parish was education. The parish has always been an important center for formal education. The parochial school developed in the nineteenth century and became the great achievement of American Catholicism. In the twentieth century the Confraternity of Christian Doctrine took hold in the United States and lay people, women especially, became most involved in this work of religious instruction. As more and more schools closed in the 1970s and 80s, parishes turned to comprehensive religious education programs that were directed to adults as well as children. Studies indicated that all parishes, be they simple or complex in their range of activities, traditional or progressive in their understanding of religion, have religious education programs. Most often a professionally trained lay woman or sister will be in charge of this work.

The increased involvement of women in the parish points to one of the major changes in American Catholicism in the period from the 1930s to the 1980s. Women no longer sit in the back of the church piously and quietly watching the world go by; they have become very active in a variety of parish ministries and are now recognized leaders in many parish communities. Such an awakening among lay women has had its counterpart among women religious and this has resulted in the most momentous changes in religious life since the days of the sixteenth-century Catholic reform movement. Priests have also undergone their own transformation during this era. While a new understanding of ministry was reshaping the Catholic community, economic and educational forces were also at work. Since the 1930s Catholics have climbed up the educational and economic ladder and now rank alongside or ahead of most Protestants. Such change has produced a large dose of individualism among priests, sisters, and lay people. It has also created a great deal of diversity among Catholics; the homogeneity of the past has vanished, swept aside by a rage for pluralism.

Whether such change has been good or bad for Catholicism in the United States is a question that will be debated well into the twenty-first century, but no one can doubt the fact that change has transformed American Catholicism in the past fifty years. A key question that remains is: Why did such substantive and dramatic changes take place at this particular moment in time? That is a question that deserves an answer.

17

A QUESTION IN
SEARCH OF AN ANSWER

Any fifty-year period in history is going to have significant change. But some eras are clearly more significant than others, because the changes that took place were so dramatic and revolutionary. The 1770 to 1820 era immediately comes to mind as a key epoch in history. An age of democratic revolution, it transformed the history of both Europe and America. Much the same can be said of the period 1930 to 1980. As was true in the eighteenth century the major catalyst for change in this era was war. World War II redrew the map of Europe and transformed international politics. It was a turning point in U.S. history and initiated changes that, as historian William Chafe put it, "helped to create the structural preconditions for long-range developments that would, potentially at least, change America more than almost any event since the Industrial Revolution."[1] Such changes have permeated the whole of American society. They have transformed life in the kitchen and the bedroom, the schoolhouse and the workplace. Change has also reshaped religion in America. The annihilation of the Jews in Europe during the war transformed Judaism like no other previous event. Protestants have also experienced many changes since the war, though none so decisive as the Jewish holocaust. A major realignment of denominations has taken place as evangelicalism has pushed some churches to the forefront and relocated others to the sidelines. The women's movement has altered the understanding of ministry and opened the door to the ordination of women; by the late 1980s more than twelve hundred women labored as ordained priests in the American Episcopal Church; a similar pattern has developed in other Protestant denominations.

The recent history of American Catholicism must be understood against this backdrop of epochal change. The Catholic Church was not the only institution that underwent substantial change in the past fifty years nor was Catholicism the only belief system that experienced transformation. A whole host of forces has reshaped and refashioned American Catholicism. Some of these forces were present in other nations as well, and led to similar transformations of church and religion. But in the United States the nature of the changes had their own history and the consequences were particularly distinctive for the simple reason that they were linked to the social and cultural forces that were reshaping American society in these decades.

In trying to put the past fifty years of American Catholic history in context, it is important to realize that the Second Vatican Council was only one of several major influences on the transformation of American Catholicism. In fact, it is fair to say that World War II had as much influence on the reshaping of contemporary American Catholicism as did the Second Vatican Council. Another way of putting this is to state that social and cultural forces were as important as theological developments in transforming American Catholicism. Thus, in seeking to understand why such decisive changes took place in the course of the past forty to fifty years, it will be helpful to focus on these three categories—social, cultural, and theological. They can serve as generic categories in which are included several specific forces, each of which had a major influence on the transformation of contemporary American Catholicism and in particular the parish and the understanding of ministry.

Upon examining the *social* forces that have helped to change American society since World War II, three stand out above the rest—class, race, and gender. By class I simply mean the economic factors that result in distinctions of wealth, occupation, and status. When I speak of race I am referring to what has happened among blacks and Hispanics in particular; as for gender I mean women and their changing role in American society since the 1940s.[2]

In the late 1930s the nation was in the midst of a severe economic depression and the New Deal of President Roosevelt was going sour. World War II changed everything. The massive mobilization for war gave the economy the boost it needed and before long factories were working double shifts and paychecks got fatter and fatter. A new prosperity took hold across the land, and wages and salaries more than doubled by the end of the war. Americans had more money to spend and for the first time in many years the purchase of a new home or a new car became a possibility for many families. With only a few interruptions the age of new prosperity continued through the decade of the 1950s. William Chafe described this economic bonanza in the following manner:

> The astonishing growth of the American economy represented the single most impressive development of the postwar years. The gross national product soared 250 percent between 1945 and 1960. Ex-

penditures on new construction multiplied nine times, while consumption of personal services increased three times. By 1960 per capita income was 35 percent higher than even the boom year of 1945. . . . As a result of the postwar boom, nearly 60 percent of the American people had achieved a "middle-class standard" of living by the mid-1950s . . . in contrast to only 31 percent in the last year of prosperity before the Great Depression. By the end of the decade 75 percent of American families owned their own car, 87 percent their own TV set, and 75 percent their own washing machine.[3]

With the new prosperity came a new middle class. They settled in the suburbs that were sprouting up across the country. They owned their own home, had a two-car garage, a backyard patio, and bedrooms filled with children and decorated with college pennants.

In the 1970s economic progress slowed considerably, beginning with the Arab oil embargo in 1973. Inflation rose to double digit figures and the number of the unemployed increased. In the 1980s balance of trade figures worsened and the national debt reached unparalleled levels. Americans then began to talk about the distribution of wealth in the United States and how the rich were getting richer and the poor were becoming more numerous. A congressional study done in 1986 finally confirmed what many had suspected. Between 1963 and 1983 the wealthiest 10 percent of the nation had increased its share of wealth by 7 percent while the remaining 90 percent of the population lost 7 percent of its share of wealth. Another way of putting this is to say that in 1963 the wealthiest 10 percent of the nation owned 65 percent of the wealth and in 1983 they had increased that to 72 percent; the other 90 percent owned 35 percent of the wealth in 1963 and twenty years later their share had declined to 28 percent.[4] Indeed, the rich were getting richer and everyone else was getting poorer. To combat this economic reversal many mothers went to work to supplement the family income.

There is a congruence between class and race. Even though many white Americans lived in poverty, the overwhelmingly majority of the poor were black or Hispanic and the vast majority of them, about 70 percent, lived in the city, and half of them lived in female-headed households. Poorly housed, poorly educated, and struggling to survive they made up the underclass of American society. It was obvious that as the economic reversal of the 1970s took hold, American society became more and more segmented by race and class. This was not something new; it had begun in the late nineteenth century but the prosperity of the post–World War II era reversed the trend. But another reversal took place in the 1970s and Americans then began to speak about the United States as a two-tiered society. For those on top who had an education, skills, and a good family background to give them a head start, the chances of success and prosperity were decent. For those on the bottom, alienation and hopelessness were much more likely than economic prosperity.

As bleak as this picture appears, there was another side to the story. Since the 1960s many black Americans have experienced success and prosperity. The civil rights movement of the 1950s and 60s helped to launch this success story with the result that "35 to 45 percent of black families succeeded in achieving a middle-class lifestyle during the seventies."[5] Like their white counterparts they settled in the suburbs and distanced themselves from the poor blacks in the inner cities. In doing so they helped to widen the chasm separating the urban poor from the rest of society. Another chapter in this success story was the involvement of scores of blacks and Hispanics in the civil rights movement. They experienced a new self-consciousness in the 1960s and translated it into an aggressive campaign for equal rights and recognition of their cultural values. This campaign transformed the workplace, the schoolhouse, and even reached into the corporate boardroom and the church sanctuary.

These changes in the areas of economics and race touched every phase of American life. As for the Catholic Church the impact was substantial. Catholics shared in the economic boom as much as anyone, with the result that the church had become a very middle-class institution by the 1980s. Catholics had more money and were better educated than ever before. As this new middle class settled in the suburbs, the church's center of gravity shifted from the old inner city to the new suburban rings that were growing up around the nation's cities. This economic and geographic development produced a new type of parish, the suburban parish, and like the people it served it became a captive of the suburb.

The growth of the suburbs has encouraged a polarization of the metropolis as income, race, and lifestyle defined the distance between city and suburb. The suburbs were white, middle-class, and nurtured a more private lifestyle. The bond between neighborhood and parish, so visible in the immigrant neighborhood, did not exist in the suburb and the way that people lived changed dramatically. As the historian of the suburbs, Kenneth Jackson, put it:

> Our lives are now centered inside the house, rather than on the neighborhood or the community. With increased use of automobiles, the life of the sidewalk and the front yard has largely disappeared, and the social intercourse that used to be the main characteristic of

urban life has vanished. Residential neighborhoods have become a mass of small, private islands; with the back yard functioning as a wholesome, family-oriented, and reclusive place. There are few places as desolate and lonely as a suburban street on a hot afternoon.[6]

The privatization of life showed up in the suburban parish as a noticeable lack of concern for issues of social justice. Concern for the common good did not go much beyond the parish and seldom did it bridge the chasm separating the urban church from the church in the suburbs. The liturgy celebrated in the churches reinforced this privatization of religion with the result that "the intrinsic link between liturgy and social action, so characteristic of the American liturgical movement, was largely lost in the postconciliar period."[7]

Those who wanted to break free from the captivity of the suburbs and its privatized culture joined the voluntary society and became involved with groups that were concerned with social justice issues. Such an organization was tailor-made for the middle-class activist and it enabled many people to get involved in issues that transcended the parochial concerns of the suburban church.

As society became divided along racial and economic lines, a two-tiered church emerged. One level is white, middle-class, and suburban; the other is brown and black, lower-class, and urban. Neither one talks very much to the other and the lower class church feels especially alienated from the rest of the American Catholic Church. Bridging this gap and effectively responding to the needs of lower-class, black and brown Catholics is perhaps the greatest challenge church leaders face as American Catholicism enters the closing years of the twentieth century.

As racial and economic forces changed the city in the 1950s and 60s, a new type of ministry developed, urban ministry. This attracted both priests and nuns as well as lay people. These Catholic activists helped to redefine the nature of ministry in the church and they pushed church leaders to attempt to meet the challenges that the city presented. Some urban parishes became centers of neighborhood renewal and even took on the task of building new housing. The federal government's war against poverty encouraged this trend, but as the money ran out and the problems became more overwhelming, urban ministry lost its appeal except among the old guard and the occasional new activist.

The racial and ethnic awakening of the 1960s had a profound effect on black and Hispanic communities in the Catholic Church. This was especially evident among Hispanics. Since the early 1970s three national Hispanic pastoral meetings have taken place and a national pastoral plan has emerged from these gatherings. Hispanic priests have been promoted to the hierarchy and a new sense of pride in being Hispanic and Catholic has surfaced. Hispanics have emphasized the importance of their cultural and religious traditions, and with this has come renewed support for the concept of the parish as a national and cultural center as well as a religious congregation. The link between these developments and the ethnic awakening that swept the country in the 1960s and early 70s is clear. Within the black community a similar awakening has taken place, but it gathered momentum more slowly, though no less dramatically. The high point of this was the National Black Catholic Congress of 1987, the first such congress since the late nineteenth century. As was true with Hispanics, power and authority in the church has been an important issue in the black Catholic awakening and this has resulted in the appointment of black bishops and the establishment of a national office for black Catholics. Like Hispanics, blacks have emphasized the importance of their own religious and cultural traditions, most especially in the liturgy, and this has turned attention to the need for parishes in the black community that are organized not by territory but by culture and race. The small number of black priests has made the issue of lay leadership an important priority; the same is true among Hispanics.

Another major social change since the Second World War has been the emancipation of women. Once they left the home to work in the factory during the war, women began to think differently about their place in society. In the 1960s an organized women's movement took hold and eventually propelled women into leadership positions in government, education, business, and religion. Though the advance in the Catholic Church has not been as great as in other churches, women have assumed leadership roles in the parish to the extent that they now have a dominant role in the varieties of parish ministry. The women's movement has also helped to transform the world of women religious. As they abandoned the cloister women religious took on the independent spirit of their sisters in the women's movement and sought a more just and equitable place in the church. The sense of solidarity that has emerged within the women's movement has given women religious a great deal of support in their efforts to make the church more responsive to the needs of women. Women have pushed for a reevaluation of the sacrament of ordination and an exclusively male priesthood. This debate has advanced the frontiers of theological thought and challenged the bishops of the church to consider an issue that was unimaginable in the 1940s.

As the social forces of economics, race, and gender transformed American society in the post–World War II period, another major development was also taking place and this too was tied to the war and its aftermath. This was the educational revolution. As a social force education not only helped to improve the national I. Q., but it also brought about important *cultural* changes.

The major catalyst for the educational revolution was the G.I. Bill. After the war the federal government provided a bushel basket of benefits for returning veterans; chief among them was government-supported education. The influx of so many new students into the nation's colleges gave higher education an enormous boost and this marked the beginning of a major educational awakening. By the 1950s 2.6 million people were enrolled in higher education; after modest growth in the 1950s a massive expansion took place in the 1960s and by the end of the decade 8.6 million people were enrolled in the nation's colleges and universities; that was an increase of 139 percent in one decade. Though the expansion slowed in the 1970s, the number of college students reached the 12.4 million level by 1982.[8]

The sociologist Robert Wuthnow argues that this enormous expansion of education has produced a "new class," people with a college education, and as this new class developed "a new basis of cultural cleavage" took place, "a cleavage that fell largely along educational lines and that cut through most of the established religious organizations."[9] Education now became an important "mode of religious differentiation" within denominations and its impact has been substantial.

Wade Clark Roof and William McKinney, authors of an important study of American religion, summarized the impact of the educational revolution and the cultural cleavage it produced:

> For organized religion the consequences have been important. It has had to try to accommodate a more informed and less parochial constituency; adjust to new cultural orientations and values brought on by expanding scientific and technological constituencies; bridge growing gaps between the better educated and the lesser educated on a wide range of social, political, and moral issues; and confront continuing, and at times tense, divisions between those arguing for symbolic interpretation of the Scriptures and those insisting upon a more literal approach.[10]

Within the Catholic Church the changes brought about by this educational transformation have been particularly significant. With the emergence of the new class local congregations began to evidence more and more cleavage as subcommunities developed along educational lines. In some parishes these subcommunities even became identified with specific Sunday liturgies and as Roof and McKinney suggest, such cleavage could be a divisive force in the parish.

A major conclusion of both Scott Appleby and Patricia Byrne is that the educational awakening of the post–World War II era had an enormous influence on the understanding of ministry among priests and women religious. In fact, I would argue that education was the single most important catalyst for change among sisters and priests for the simple reason that it opened new horizons for them. For sisters education was the highway to the modern world and with it came a major reevaluation of the work and culture of religious life. The code word was "professionalization," but the reality was educational advancement and as this took place religious life for women changed slowly but decisively. This transformation among sisters took place much earlier than it did among priests. With the sisters it began as early as the 1940s and gained considerable momentum in the 1950s and 60s. As for priests, they caught the education bug much later, in the mid to late 1960s. A remark by Joseph Fichter captured this new mentality very neatly. He said that in the modern world of the post–Vatican II church, "no longer can the priest be just a priest." It is hard to imagine Father O'Malley or any priest in the 1940s making such a statement. But the times had changed and the priest now had to be someone "who does something," as Fichter put it, and in order to do something he needed further education so that he could gain some expertise beyond what he got in the seminary. In this way he became the true professional and as this took place the understanding of priesthood changed.[11]

Lay ministers also caught the education bug and were busy taking courses to become certified as directors of religious education, of liturgy, of youth ministry, and the like. The need for professionalization, encouraged by the culture of the new class, had obviously transformed parish ministry and it created an entirely new phenomenon, the institute for education and training in parish ministry.

As education changed the nation it produced certain alterations in the cultural psyche of the people. One major change was an increase in individualism. Americans have always been known for their spirit of individualism. Alexis de Tocqueville and numerous other European visitors noticed this trait and never ceased to comment on it. But in the 1960s and afterwards individualism intensified. There was talk of the "me generation," "doing your own thing," and the "liberated person." Twenty years of survey data substantiated this development and it has obviously permeated the nation's churches. Robert Wuthnow described this as "a mode of cultural adaptation" on the part of the churches, one that would "greatly influence the character of American religion." Robert Bellah and his colleagues studied such highly individualized faith and the dangers it presented to the common good of society. The principal focus of the study by Roof and McKinney was this "new individualistic ethos" or what they labeled as "the new voluntarism in American religious life."[12]

Particular studies of the Catholic population have come up with similar conclusions and the implications are enormous.[13] The more that religion became privatized and self-centered, the more people challenged the authority of the institution. Among Catholics this was especially poignant because it meant that they could, and indeed did, disagree with such an authority figure as the pope on a variety of issues, and still consider themselves to be loyal Catholics. As for disagreeing with the pastor, the authority figure in the local parish, this became even less of a problem. The individualistic ethos also meant that believing became more important than belonging. In fact, belonging to a congregation "was no longer viewed as a presumed outgrowth of belief; it has become a matter of taste."[14] All of this encouraged the development of a new type of Catholic, one whom Andrew Greeley labeled "the communal Catholic," a person who is culturally and religiously Catholic but lives on the fringe of the institutional church. This trend is especially noticeable among younger Catholics who are not married and traditionally have had a very distant relationship with a parish. The rise in individualism also accounts for the religious diversity that is evident among regular church-goers.

For Catholics there is a paradox in all this. The Catholic tradition has a strong social and communitarian quality, and this has grown stronger in the past half-century as the liturgical movement has taken hold along with an increased concern for social justice. Yet this tradition exists in the midst of the individualistic environment of the United States. As a result of this, Catholics have learned to speak two languages, that of the self-centered person and that of the more socially oriented individual. The Notre Dame Study of Catholic Parish Life put it this way:

> On the one hand, the symbols of the Church are communitarian. On the other hand, the values of the culture, the economy, and the polity are very self-centered and individualistic. Catholics use the symbols of the former to set expectations of the local church. Catholics use the values of the latter to describe their deepest religious concerns.[15]

The rising tide of individualism has also reshaped ministry in the church. As one priest put it to me "every priest is defining his own priesthood." Though this may be an exaggeration, it hits the nail on the head. Given the lack of consensus on the meaning of ordained priesthood in the 1970s and 80s, such individualism is not surprising. Among women religious a similar individualism exists reminiscent of the rugged solitary individual who blazed new trails along the American frontier. Living apart from her religious community and engaging in new forms of ministry, the American sister was bound to get caught up in an individualistic ethos. As for the laity individualism necessarily weakened the hold of the parish; as parish loyalty diminished, lay people developed a greater sense of freedom to join organizations beyond the parish where they could become involved in causes of their own choosing.

Another major cultural development since World War II was the decline of denominationalism. In the 1950s denominationalism was quite strong and people readily identified themselves as Protestants, Catholics, or Jews. As Will Herberg suggested, religion had replaced ethnicity as a person's badge of identity. By the 1970s such intense identification with a particular denomination was on the wane. In the 1980s "a greater degree of social and cultural homogeneity now seems to characterize the various denominations and faiths."[16] People switched denominations more readily and marriages between Catholics and Protestants had become very common. Coupled with this was the rise of what Robert Wuthnow called "the special purpose group."

The special purpose group resembles the voluntary society in many ways and it has a long history in this country and elsewhere. Speaking about the contemporary situation Wuthnow goes so far as to say that "as a style of organization, the growth of special purpose groups constitutes a significant form of social restructuring in American religion." He notes that "their causes range from nuclear arms control to liturgical renewal, from gender equality to cult surveillance, from healing ministries to evangelism."[17] These groups can have a very positive influence on the church at both the local and national level. By supporting such special purpose groups and providing a forum for their cause, the local congregation can offer to its constituents a new way to intensify their religious commitment. Many parishes have done this by supporting a variety of such groups, ranging from Marriage Encounter to Bread for the World. This too contributes to the diversity of parish life and the encouragement of different communities or constituencies within the same parish.

The presence of special purpose groups can also reinforce the cultural and educational cleavage that is already present in parishes throughout the country. According to Wuthnow the distinguishing mark that put people on either side of this divide was their orientation to either liberalism or conservatism. This polarization between liberals and conservatives represents the major realignment that religion in America has undergone since World War II. It is clearly expressed in the often repeated dictum that "conservative Catholics have more in common with conservative Protestants than they do with liberal Catholics." Of course the same can be said about liberal Catholics and their relationship with conservative Catholics.

What this all means is that denominationalism is a less important badge of religion than it was fifty years ago and special purpose groups can often serve as a surrogate denomination or parish. This obviously undermines the central position of the parish in the lives of the people and forces it to compete with these groups for religious loyalties. As the special purpose groups grow in popularity, the parish will cease to be the vital center of religion for many people. Priests and sisters also join special purpose groups and the more intense their involvement is, the less their involvement in the parish. Moreover, by their very involvement in these groups they are reshaping their ministry. They too become less concerned about denominational boundaries and frequently discover that their closest colleagues in these groups are people from other religious traditions.

In emphasizing the influence of social and cultural forces on the development of American Catholicism since the 1930s, I do not want to ignore the dynamic forces within the church itself. Social and cultural forces did influence both the institution and people in the manner of a stimulus on the part of society and culture that evoked a response or reaction on the part of the church and its members. But during this period of history Catholicism was doing more than just responding to the challenge of these external forces. It had its own inner dynamic or spirit of renewal that also led to change and adaptation. The principal catalyst for this was the Second Vatican Council that took place from 1962 to 1965. This brings us to the third major reason for change in American Catholicism: *theology.*

Theological reform was in the air long before Pope John XXIII opened Vatican Council II in October 1962. What the council did was to channel these currents of reform into the mainstream of Catholic thought and give them the church's seal of approval. Nor did theological renewal end with the council. Theologians have continued to explore the mystery of the church and the meaning of Christian faith in the modern world and this continuing quest of "faith seeking understanding" has influenced the meaning of ministry and parish.

The major theological development that has transformed American Catholicism since the 1940s was the new understanding of church or what theologians like to call a new ecclesiology. This new description of the church took a more biblical approach, describing the church as "the people of God." It also stressed the idea of collegiality in the church, or the spirit of cooperation between clergy and laity as well as bishops and priests. Since the parish is the embodiment of the church at the local level, this new ecclesiology had enormous influence on the parish. In many ways the parish became a much more open institution; it became the people's church and ceased to be the private preserve of the priest. Lay people became more involved in the parish and a new spirit of cooperation between priest and people developed.

Parish councils represented the institutional response to this new understanding of church, but it really meant so much more than just shared decision-making or consultation with the laity on the part of the clergy. Where this was most evident was in the celebration of the liturgy. The Vatican Council was very important in this regard. It set the agenda for liturgical reform and in doing so revolutionized the public worship of Catholics. As a result of this the laity became much more involved in the celebration of the liturgy and before long lay people were taking active roles in the celebration as readers of the scriptures and ministers of the eucharist; they also planned parish liturgies and promoted congregational singing. Added to this was a renewed emphasis on the importance of baptism and the charism of the priesthood of all believers that comes from this sacrament. In elevating the importance of baptism as the rite of initiation into the church, theologians were deemphasizing the centrality of the sacrament of orders and placing it in a larger context within the church. This encouraged the idea of lay ministry and gave theological endorsement to the ministry explosion of the 1970s and 80s.

These changes in ecclesiology, liturgy, and sacramental theology, especially the importance of baptism, have transformed the self-understanding not only of lay Catholics, but also of priests and sisters. The essays of Appleby and Byrne clearly suggest this.

Another important development of Vatican Council II was the church's desire to be a servant church, an institution involved in and concerned about the world and its problems. This self-understanding of the church established new horizons for all Catholics—priests and sisters as well as lay people—and it encouraged them to move beyond the cultural confines of the institutional church and become involved in the redemption of the world through a variety of ways. This new social vision blended in with the increase in special purpose groups and together these two developments inspired Catholic activists to become involved in issues and causes that pushed them beyond the parish.

The increase in individualism within American society coincided with the Catholic Church's endorsement of religious freedom at the Second Vatican Council. The council emphasized the rights of the individual in the area of religion and spoke out against forcing people to believe one way or another. Though such a declaration balanced the excesses of authoritarianism, it also posed a challenge to bishops and priests, not to mention the pope, who for so long had presumed that Catholics would accept what they said simply because they were bishop, priest, or pope. Religious freedom was something new for Catholics and it was going to take some getting used to for everyone. More than any other theological development, this endorsement of religious freedom has altered forever the traditional understanding of authority in the church.

The document on religious freedom also changed the way Catholics viewed Protestants and people of other religious traditions. The church's endorsement of the ecumenical movement reinforced this and Catholics learned that Protestants were not that bad after all. They began to pray together and eventually they began to marry one another.

There were many other theological changes that reshaped Roman Catholicism. For example, people thought differently about the Bible, sin, confession, the eucharist, and popular devotions. Taken together, all these developments suggest that the spirit of renewal was working overtime in the church in the past half-century. When these developments are joined with the social and cultural changes of the past fifty years, then the extent of the transformation of American Catholicism becomes even greater.

Though this study has examined the forces of change separately, in a logical and discrete manner, they did not function that way in reality. Most often they intersected and acted in concert to influence human lives. Theological change took place in the context of social and cultural change, sometimes challenging these changes and at other times reinforcing them. The same was true of social and cultural changes in relation to developments in theology. A clear example of this interaction of theological, social, and cultural forces is the women's movement in the Catholic Church.

The Second Vatican Council said nothing about the role of women in the church. Nonetheless, the new theology of church and ministry that came from the council influenced the role that women would have in the church by giving them a new self-understanding as Catholics. Add to this the change in the status of women initiated by the Second World War and the subsequent awakening that women first experienced in the 1960s, and the result was a feminist movement within American Catholicism. This movement has transformed the role of lay women in the church, and in doing so has reshaped the parish and forced the leaders of the church to examine the issue of women in ministry. It has also had an enormous influence on the life and culture of women religious. Thus, the interaction of social and theological forces came together to produce a truly revolutionary moment for Catholic women.

The close relationship between religion and society explains why the changes in religion that have taken place in the recent past are often described as "revolutionary." The United States has experienced a major turning point in its history in the post–World War II era, a turning point that some suggest ranks with the Industrial Revolution in terms of influence. For Roman Catholics an era of their church's history was also coming to an end in these years; the Tridentine church, the church born in the Reformation of the sixteenth century, was being transformed into a new church. This was a special moment for both Americans and Catholics, a time when a new age was coming to life. This was particularly challenging for Catholics, and indeed "revolutionary," because change in the church took place at the precise moment that society was being transformed from top to bottom. This combination of changes turned American Catholicism inside out and radically transformed the church and the people. As this was taking place the parish and the understanding of ministry began to change.

This process of change, begun in the 1930s and 40s, gained momentum in the 1950s as the post–World War II era took shape and Catholic reformers began to raise their voices; Vatican Council II accelerated the changes for Catholics and the social reform of the nation in the 1960s served to reinforce many of these changes. Since then the spirit of social reform and religious renewal have lessened somewhat, but social and religious transformation still continue. Continuity with the past rather than radical change is the catchword of the 1980s, but it is the new past of the Vatican II church rather than the Tridentine church that now provides the benchmark for continuity and tradition. That is the Catholic revolution of the twentieth century.

NOTES

Part I / Present to the People of God:
The Transformation of the Roman Catholic Parish Priesthood

Introduction

1. Rev. Arthur J. Serratelli, personal interview, Orange, New Jersey, March 26, 1987.
2. Rev. Bruce A. Dreier, personal interview, San Francisco, May 18, 1987.
3. Jay P. Dolan, "A Catholic Romance with Modernity," *Wilson Quarterly*, Autumn 1981, pp. 120–33. On the three-tiered church, see Karl Adam, *The Spirit of Catholicism* (Garden City, N.Y.: Image reprint, 1954), pp. 114–58.
4. The classic exposition of the "paradigm shift" is found in Thomas Kuhn, *The Structure of Scientific Revolutions* (Chicago: University of Chicago Press, 1962). This interpretation has been applied frequently to twentieth-century Roman Catholicism, most recently in Lester R. Kurtz, *The Politics of Heresy: The Modernist Crisis in Roman Catholicism* (Berkeley: University of California Press, 1986), pp. 167–89. Jay Dolan describes the "New Catholicism" of "The Catholic Reformation, 1960–84" in *The American Catholic Experience* (Garden City, N.Y.: Doubleday, 1985), pp. 421–54.

Chapter 1. The Era of the Ombudsman, 1930–1954

1. Msgr. John Mattie, personal interview, Seattle, May 11, 1987.
2. Rev. Michael Pflieger, *Priestly Existence* (Westminster, Md.: Newman Press, 1957), pp. 12–13.
3. Rev. John A. O'Brien, *The Priesthood in a Changing World* (Paterson, N.J.: St. Anthony Guild Press, 1943), p. 3.
4. On the ideal of priestly sanctity, see "The Holiness of the Priest," in Fulton J. Sheen, *The Priest Is Not His Own* (New York: McGraw-Hill, 1963), pp. 67–85. Rev. M. D. Forrest, M.S.C., provides the standard theological description of priest-as-sacrificial-victim in *The Clean Oblation* (St. Paul, Minn.: Radio Replies Press, 1945), pp. 119–30. The survival of the "priest-as-Christian gentleman" approach is apparent in the pages of the *Homiletic and Pastoral Review*. For a recent presentation, see Robert J. Fuhrman, "The Priest, a Call to Perfection," *Homiletic and Pastoral Review* 85 (October 1984), pp. 28–32.
5. Joseph White, "The Diocesan Seminary in the United States: A Historical Introduction" (an unpublished paper); chapters 11 and 12 discuss, respectively, "Model Priest and Seminary" and "Clerical Learning."
6. Quoted in Philip Murnion, *The Catholic Priest and the Changing Structure of Pastoral Ministry, New York, 1920–1970* (New York: Arno Press, 1978), p. 127.
7. Quoted in *Sermons and Addresses of His Eminence William Cardinal O'Connell, Archbishop of Boston*, 11 volumes (Boston: Pilot Publishing Co., 1911–38), vol. 10, p. 102.
8. Robert E. Sullivan, "Beneficial Relations: Toward a Social History of the Diocesan Priests of Boston, 1875–1944," in Robert E. Sullivan and James O'Toole, eds., *Catholic Boston: Studies in Religion and Community, 1870–1970* (Boston: Archdiocese of Boston), p. 219.

9. See Gabriel Daly, *Transcendence and Immanence: A Study in Catholic Modernism and Integralism* (Oxford: Clarendon Press, 1980), pp. 7–25, for a discussion of neo-scholasticism and extrinsicism.

10. See John M. Huels, O.S.M., *The Popular Appeal of the Sorrowful Mother Novena* (Rome: Edizioni Marianium, 1976), p. 191, and Adam, *Spirit of Catholicism*, pp. 114–18.

11. Rev. John Tackney, personal interview, Brookline, Massachusetts, March 17, 1987. On the St. Vincent de Paul Society, see Most Rev. Amleto Giovanni Cicognani, D.D., "Parish Charity," in *A Call to Catholic Action: A Series of Conferences on the Principles Which Should Guide Catholics in the Social-Economic Crisis of Today*, 2 volumes (New York: Joseph F. Wagner, 1935), vol. 2, pp. 205–12. Cicognani, at that time apostolate delegate to the United States, discussed, in these pages, the proper role of the St. Vincent de Paul Society exclusively in terms of charity.

12. Jerome D. Hannan, "Anticlericalism in the United States," *America* 62 (April 8, 1930), p. 8.

13. On the homogeneity of the rural Catholic parish, see Douglas Ensmiger, "The Rural Church and Religion," in Carl C. Taylor et al., *Rural Life in the United States* (New York: Alfred A. Knopf, 1949), pp. 122–23. The "ecclesial presence" provided by women religious was stressed by Rev. Joseph Keenan, personal interview, Camden, Mississippi, April 29, 1987.

14. Jeffrey M. Burns, "Building the Best: A History of Catholic Parish Life in the Pacific States," in Jay P. Dolan, ed., *The American Catholic Parish: A History from 1850 to the Present* (New York: Paulist, 1987), vol. 2, pp. 22–23.

15. Stephen J. Shaw, "The Cities and the Plains, A Home for God's People: A History of the Catholic Parish in the Midwest," in Jay P. Dolan, ed., *The American Catholic Parish*, vol. 2, pp. 338–39.

16. Quoted in Edward R. Kantowicz, *Corporation Sole: Cardinal Mundelein and Chicago Catholicism* (Notre Dame: University of Notre Dame Press, 1983), p. 150.

17. See Joseph H. Fichter, *Religion as a Social Occupation: A Study in the Sociology of Professions* (Notre Dame: University of Notre Dame Press, 1961), pp. 213–54. James Hennesey, S.J., *American Catholics: A History of the Roman Catholic Community in the United States* (New York: Oxford University Press, 1981), pp. 236–37, 243, 287, captures a sense of the institutional expansion coincident with general lack of regional or national planning.

18. Sullivan, "Beneficial Relations," pp. 210–16; personal interview, Boston, March 19, 1987.

19. Murnion, *Catholic Priest*, p. 151.

20. Rev. Howard Bleichner, S.S., personal interview, Menlo Park, California, May 19, 1987.

21. Personal interview, New Orleans, Louisiana, April 21, 1987.

22. Rev. Bruce Dreier, personal interview, May 18, 1987.

23. Max Kassieppe, O.M.I., *Priestly Beatitudes* (New York: Herder, 1953), pp. 249–55.

24. Rawley Myers, ed., *The Greatest Calling* (New York: McMullen Books, 1951).

Chapter 2. Pioneers of Renewal, 1930–1954

1. Msgr. John J. Egan, personal interview, Notre Dame, Indiana, April 9, 1987.

2. William Halsey, *The Survival of American Innocence: Catholicism in an Era of Disillusionment, 1920–1940* (Notre Dame: University of Notre Dame Press, 1980), pp. 67, 119–20, 126–52.

3. David O'Brien, *American Catholics and Social Reform: The New Deal Years* (New York: Oxford University Press, 1968), pp. 44, 47–69. Also see Joseph M. McShane, S.J., *"Sufficiently Radical": Catholicism, Progressivism, and the Bishop's Program of 1919* (Washington, D.C.: Catholic University Press, 1986), pp. 239–82. McShane, pp. 7–56, explicates the convergence of American natural law traditions, Catholic natural law traditions, and progressive reform thought in the programs of the NCWC Social Action department during the interwar years.

4. Thomas E. Blantz, C.S.C., *A Priest in Public Service: Francis J. Haas and the New Deal* (Notre Dame: University of Notre Dame Press, 1982), pp. 22–46, discusses Ryan's influence on Haas; Dolan summarizes O'Grady's career in *The American Catholic Experience*, p. 403. On Ligutti, see Vincent A. Yzermans, *The People I Love: A Biography of Luigi G. Ligutti* (Collegeville, Minn.: Liturgical Press, 1976).

5. Gerald M. Costello, *Without Fear or Favor: George Higgins on the Record* (Mystic, Conn.: Twenty-Third Publications, 1984), pp. 14–28.

6. William H. Chafe, *The Unfinished Journey: America Since World War II* (New York: Oxford University Press, 1986), pp. 111–45, provides a rich description of the impact of technological advances upon American culture.

7. David J. O'Brien summarizes this development succinctly in "The American Priest in Social Action," in John Tracy Ellis, ed., *The Catholic Priest in the United States: Historical Investigations* (Collegeville, Minn.: Saint John's University Press, 1971), pp. 444–48.

8. Recounted in Leo Klein, "Gerald Ellard, Pioneer of Renewal," *America* 127 (May 26, 1973).

9. Aaron I. Abell, *American Catholicism and Social Action* (Notre Dame: University of Notre Dame Press, 1960), pp. 200ff.

10. Virgil Michel, "The Liturgical Movement," in Benjamin L. Masse, S.J., ed., *The Catholic Mind Through Fifty Years, 1903–1953* (New York: The America Press), pp. 173–88.

11. Kantowicz, *Corporation Sole*, pp. 173–88.

12. Steven M. Avella, S.D.S., " 'I've Brought You a Man with Imagination': The Life and Career of Reynold Hillenbrand Until 1944," unpublished paper, 1982.

13. Ibid., pp. 22–25.

14. On Hillenbrand's influence, see Pam Bauer, "Hillenbrand 'Anticipated Vatican II,' " *National Catholic Reporter*, June 1, 1979; Robert McClory, "Hillenbrand: U.S. Moses," *National Catholic Reporter*, September 7, 1979; and Reynold Hillenbrand, "Meaning of the Liturgy," National Liturgical Conference: *Proceedings of the Liturgical Week of 1941* (Benedictine Liturgical Conference, Newark), pp. 20–26. On labor schools, see Neil Betten, *Catholic Activism and the Industrial Worker* (Gainsville, 1976), pp. 108–23. On Carrabine and Dowling, see Andrew M. Greeley, *The Catholic Experience: An Interpretation of the History of American Catholicism* (Garden City, N.Y.: Doubleday, 1967), pp. 248–49.

15. Greeley, *Catholic Experience*, pp. 252–53. Possible reasons for the surprise dismissal include: Hillenbrand alienated the Jesuits on the faculty by emphasizing Benedictine liturgical reform, downplaying traditional Ignatian spirituality, and attracting diocesan priests in his mold to the faculty; his increasing national responsibilities kept him away from the day-to-day operations of the seminary too frequently; his protégés were "troublemakers" in Chicago parishes and their pastors complained incessantly to Stritch; and finally Hillenbrand's personal style of leadership tended to be inflexible and autocratic.

16. For a treatment of this process whereby "plausibility structures" are built up and reinforced in inchoate groups, see Peter L. Berger and Thomas Luckmann, *The Social Construction of Reality: A Treatise on the Sociology of Knowledge* (Garden City, N.Y.: Doubleday, 1966).

17. William I. Lonergan, S.J., "Catholic Action in the United States," *America* 44 (January 3, 1931), pp. 308–9.

18. Doran Hurley, "Mr. Patrick Donahoe Lived Catholic Action," *America* 61 (January 14, 1939), p. 346.

19. John LaFarge, S.J., "How Catholic Action Triumphs Through Conquest," *America* 61 (February 4, 1939), pp. 412–13.

20. Abbe G. Michonneau, *Revolution in a City Parish* (Westminster, Md.: Newman, 1956), pp. 47ff.; John LaFarge, "Let's Build the Spiritual Front," *America* 85 (August 19, 1950), p. 500.

21. Reynold Hillenbrand, "The Priesthood and the World," *Worship* 26, no. 2 (January 1952), p. 52.

22. Ibid., p. 53.

23. See Joseph White, "The Diocesan Seminary in the United States: An Historical Introduction," ch. 12.; Joseph H. Fichter, *America's Forgotten Priests: What Are They Saying?* (New York: Harper and Row, 1968), pp. 80–87.

24. Emerson Hynes, "The Parish in the Rural Community," in C. J. Neusse and Thomas J. Harte, C.Ss.R., *The Sociology of the Parish* (Milwaukee: Bruce, 1951), pp. 101–21.

25. Father Thomas A. Judge, C.M., *Father Judge Teaches Ministry* (Holy Trinity, Alabama: Missionary Cenacle Press, 1983), pp. 13–15; Mother Boniface Keasey, *Led By the Spirit* (New York: Gardner Press, 1984), pp. 357ff. Also Rev. Joseph Keenan, personal interview, Camden, Mississippi, April 29, 1987.

26. Joseph J. Casino, "From Sanctuary to Involvement: A History of the Catholic Parish in the Northeast," in Dolan, ed., *The American Catholic Parish*, vol. 1, pp. 73–74. See also Charles Kraut, *Depression-Era Boston* (New York, 1980); Robert E. Sullivan, "Beneficial Relations," in *Catholic Boston*, p. 227.

27. Jeffrey M. Burns, "Building" (chap. 1, n. 14, above), pp. 25–32, 49–75. Richard Parle, personal interview, Seattle, Washington.

28. For an example of the perdurance of the church-world and clergy-laity dualism in the preconciliar church, see Msgr. Pierre Veullot, ed., *The Catholic Priesthood According to the Teachings of the Church: Papal Documents of Pius XII* (Westminster, Md.: Newman Press, 1964). Also see Joseph Komonchak, "Clergy, Laity, and the Church's Mission to the World," *The Jurist* 41 (Fall 1981), pp. 422–47, for a comparison before and after the council.

29. William H. Russell, *Christ the Leader* (Milwaukee: Bruce, 1937), p. vi.

30. Ibid., p. 94.

Chapter 3. Priesthood Reconsidered:
Presence Beyond the Parish, 1954–1962

1. J. B. Gremillion, *Journal of a Southern Pastor* (Chicago: Fides, 1957), pp. 71–72.

2. Dolan, "A Catholic Romance with Modernity," pp. 122–33.

3. On the changes in Catholicism in the conciliar era, see Peter Hebblethwaite, *The Runaway Church* (New York: Seabury, 1975); Langdon Gilkey, *Catholicism Confronts Modernity* (New York: Seabury, 1985); Peter Chirico, "Dynamics of Change in the Church's Self-Understanding," *Theological Studies* 39 (1978), pp. 55ff.; Karl Rahner, S.J., "Toward a Fundamental Theological Understanding of Vatican II," *Theological Studies* 40 (1979), pp. 721–32.

4. John Tracy Ellis, "American Catholics and the Intellectual Life," *Thought* 30 (1955), pp. 351–88.

5. These developments are summarized in T. M. Schoof, *A Survey of Catholic Theology, 1800–1970* (Glen Rock, N.J.: Paulist Newman Press, 1970), pp. 102–45; and in Roger Aubert, *The Church in a Secularized Society* (New York: Paulist, 1978), p. 614.

6. Gremillion, *Journal of a Southern Pastor*, p. 94.

7. Ibid., pp. 9–10.

8. Ibid., pp. 19–20.

9. Ibid., pp. 69–70.

10. On the role of CCD in shaping lay apostles, see Marian Frances Margo, C.D.P., "Religious Education Outside the Parochial School," in Marvin Bordelon, ed., *The Parish in a Time of Change* (Notre Dame: Fides, 1967), pp. 68–86.

11. Gremillion, *Journal of a Southern Pastor*, p. 71.

12. J. B. Gremillion, "The Parish Is Christ," *Our Sunday Visitor* (diocese of Alexandria, Louisiana), January 6, 1957, pp. 6–7; Joseph H. Fichter, S.J., *Dynamics of a City Church* (New York: Arno Press, 1978), Preface to Arno Press reprint.

13. Gremillion, *Journal of a Southern Pastor*, p. 71.

14. J. B. Gremillion papers, University of Notre Dame Archives (UNDA).

15. Msgr. George A. Kelly, *The Battle for the American Church* (Garden City, N.Y.: Image, 1981), pp. 213–14.

16. Charles W. Dahm, *Power and Authority in the Catholic Church: Cardinal Cody in Chicago* (Notre Dame: University of Notre Dame Press, 1981), pp. 3–4, 28–29, situates Egan's achievement in the context of Chicago's ecclesiastical and city politics.

17. Form letter, Rev. John J. Egan, June 27, 1955; Rev. J. B. Gremillion to Most Rev. John J. Wright, February 28, 1955; "Priests Attending Worcester Meeting" (J. B. Gremillion, private circulation, 1955); Louis Putz, C.S.C., to Rev. Joseph Gremillion, March 27, 1955; Godfrey Diekmann, O.S.B., to Rev. John J. Egan, January 26, 1959. These personal correspondences were made available to me through the generosity of Msgr. J. B. Gremillion from his personal files. More information on the participants and agendas of these meetings is available in the Joseph Gremillion files, UNDA.

18. "Mayslake Retreat House–Hinsdale, Illinois," circular, July 16–17–18, 1957 (J. B. Gremillion personal files).

19. Msgr. John J. Egan to Rev. John C. Murray, S.J., February 2, 1959 (J. B. Gremillion personal files).

20. Msgr. John J. Egan, personal interview, Notre Dame, Indiana, April 9, 1987.

21. John D. Donovan, "The Social Structure of the Parish," in Nuesse and Harte, *Sociology of the Parish*, pp. 88–93, passim.

22. Quoted in David J. O'Brien, *Faith and Friendship: Catholicism in the Diocese of Syracuse, 1886–1986* (Catholic Diocese of Syracuse, 1987), p. 241.

23. David H. Fosselman, C.S.C., "The Parish in Urban Communities," in Nuesse and Harte, *Sociology of the Parish*, pp. 133–52.

24. David J. O'Brien, "The Future of Ministry: Historical Context," in *The Future of Ministry* (New York: Sadlier, 1985), p. 37.

25. Records of the National Catholic Education Association, 1955–1965, Catholic University of America Archives (CUA).

26. On the impact of Catholicism as a "mainline" American religion, see Martin Marty, "Protestant and Jewish Relations," in Edward C. Herr, *Tomorrow's Church: What's Ahead for American Catholics?* (Chicago: Thomas More Press, 1982), pp. 223–26.

27. Daniel Callahan first articulated the dissatisfaction of "the new laity" with traditional parish roles and the clergy in *The Mind of the Catholic Layman* (New York: Scribner's Son's, 1963), pp. 103–47.

Chapter 4. Priesthood Reformed:
Experiments in Parochial Presence, 1962–1972

1. Msgr. Russell B. Collins, personal interview, Reading, Massachusetts, March 14, 1987.

2. Peter Berger, *The Heretical Imperative: Contemporary Possibilities of Religious Affirmation* (Garden City, N.Y.: Doubleday, 1979), pp. 1–31.

3. *Lumen Gentum: The Dogmatic Constitution on the Church in the Modern World*, in Austin P. Flannery, ed., *Documents of Vatican II* (Grand Rapids, Mich.: Wm. B. Eerdman's, 1975), p. 364.

4. John A. Coleman, S.J., *An American Strategic Theology* (N.Y.: Paulist, 1982), p. 131.

5. See "Man's Needs and Aspirations," in Joseph Gremillion, ed., *The Gospel of Peace and Justice* (Maryknoll, N.Y.: Orbis, 1976), pp. 10–13, for an exposition of this conciliar theme.

6. On Rahner, see "Introduction: Rahner's Philosophical Theology," in Gerald A. McCool, ed., *A Rahner Reader* (New York: Seabury, 1975), pp. xiii–xvii.

7. Gregory Baum, *Man Becoming: God in Secular Experience* (New York: Herder and Herder, 1970), p. ix.

8. Garry Wills, *Bare Ruined Choirs: Doubt, Prophecy, and Radical Religion* (New York: Dell, 1971), p. l.

9. Quoted in Wills, *Bare Ruined Choirs*, pp. 4–5.

10. Joseph Cunnane, "The Theology of the Priesthood," in Denis E. Hurley, O.M.I., and Joseph Cunnane, *Vatican II on Priests and Seminaries* (Dublin: Scepter Books, 1967), p. 23.

11. There was also talk of a "vocation crisis" in the early 1950s. Pope Pius XII and Cardinal Stritch both spoke of the crisis in 1954. See Rev. George L. Kane, ed., *Meeting the Vocation Crisis* (Westminster, Md.: Newman Press, 1956).

12. David J. O'Brien, "The Future of Ministry: Historical Context," in *The Future of Ministry*, p. 38.

13. Rev. Gary Morelli, personal interview, Tacoma, Washington, May 1987.

14. See Philip Slater, *The Pursuit of Loneliness: American Culture at the Breaking Point* (Boston: Beacon Press, 1970); Theodore Roszak, *The Making of a Counterculture* (Garden City, N.Y.: Doubleday, 1969); and Charles Reich, *The Greening of America* (New York: Random House, 1970) on the motivations behind the counterculture of the 1960s.

15. Andrew M. Greeley, *Confessions of a Parish Priest: An Autobiography* (New York: Simon and Schuster, 1986).

16. On these developments as perceived at the time, see Joseph J. Blomjous, *Priesthood in Crisis* (Milwaukee: Bruce, 1969). For a contemporary retrospective on these developments, see Archbishop Daniel Pilarczyk, "The Changing Image of the Priest," *Origins* 16, no. 7 (July 3, 1986), pp. 137–40.

17. John J. Egan, Peggy Roach, and Philip J. Murnion, "Catholic Committee on Urban Ministry: Ministry to the Ministers," *Review of Religious Research* 20, no. 3 (Summer 1979), p. 279.

18. Ibid., pp. 280–81.

19. Ibid., pp. 282–83.

20. Blomjous, *Priesthood in Crisis*, pp. 63–104, 128–34, 201–13.

21. Russell Collins, personal interview, March 15, 1987.

22. Ibid.

23. On the impact of Catholic priests and nuns joining the peace movement, see Howard Zinn, *A People's History of the United States* (New York: Harper and Row, 1980), p. 479; on the Berrigans, see Francine du Plessix Gray, *Divine Disobedience* (New York: Random House, 1969); also see John Tracy Ellis, "The Church in Revolt," *Critic* 28 (January 1970), p. 21.

24. For an informed treatment of the contribution to urban renewal possible given denominational cooperation, see George D. Younger, *The Church and Urban Renewal* (New York: J. B. Lippincott, 1965), pp. 122–96.

25. For a nuanced description of ministerial "types" in the priesthood and the questions about their continued efficacy, see John A. Coleman, S.J., "The Future of Ministry," *America* 134 (March 28, 1981), 243–49.

26. Quoted in William H. Cleary, ed., *Hyphenated Priests: The Ministry of the Future* (Washington, D.C.: Corpus Books, 1969), p. xi.

27. Joseph H. Fichter, *Organization Man in the Church* (Cambridge, Mass.: Schenkman, 1974), p. 4.

28. Quoted in C. J. McNaspy, "Hyphenated Priests: Past, Present, and Future," in Cleary, *Hyphenated Priests*, p. 2.

29. Geno Baroni, "Catholic Initiatives," in Louis J. Luzbetak, S.V.D., ed., *The Church in the Changing City* (Techny, Ill.: Divine Word Publications, 1966), p. 117–21.

30. Sister Marie Augusta Neal, S.N.D., "Parish Structures," in Luzbetak, *Church in the Changing City*, pp. 66–67, passim.

31. "Decree on the Ministry and Life of Priests," in Hurley and Cunnane, *Vatican II on Priests and Seminaries*, p. 93.

32. Charles A. Gallagher and Thomas L. Vandenberg, *The Celibacy Myth: Loving for Life* (New York: Crossroad, 1987), pp. 12–14, summarize this reaction to imposed celibacy.

33. Andrew M. Greeley, *New Horizons for the Priesthood* (New York: Sheed and Ward, 1970), p. 22.

34. Philip Rieff, *The Triumph of the Therapeutic: Uses of Faith After Freud* (New York: Harper and Row), p. 12.

35. John L'Heureux, "The Reality of the Myth: Person as Hyphen," in Cleary, *Hyphenated Priest*, pp. 44–46, passim.

36. Cited in Fichter, *Organization Man*, p. 21.

37. Andrew Greeley, *The Catholic Priest in the United States: Sociological Investigations* (Washington, D.C.: U.S. Catholic Conference Publications, 1972), pp. 53–70. See also Eugene C. Kennedy and Victor J. Heckler, *The Catholic Priest in the United States: Psychological Investigations* (Washington, D.C.: United States Catholic Conference Publications, 1972), pp. 3–16.

38. Greeley, *Catholic Priest in the United States*, pp. 56, 71–79.

39. Ibid., p. 113.

40. Personal interview, New Orleans, Louisiana, April 22, 1987.

41. A historical precedent for clerical representation in American Catholicism is presented in Nelson J. Callahan, *A Case for Due Process in the Church: Father Eugene O'Callaghan, American Pioneer of Dissent* (New York: Society of St. Paul, 1970).

42. "Position Paper on the Priesthood," in "Report of Committee for Age Group II," Priest's Senate File Box, Archives of the Archdiocese of San Francisco (AASF).

43. "Diocese of Providence: Job Specifications for Parish Priests," June 1969, Priest's Senate File Box, AASF.

44. "Proposed Guidelines for Parish Ministry," Priest's Senate File Box, AASF.

45. Michael J. McNally, "A Peculiar Institution: A History of Catholic Parish Life in the Southeast (1850–1980)," in Dolan, ed., *The American Catholic Parish*, vol. 1, p. 201. Also see Dahm, *Power and Authority in the Catholic Church*, for a detailed picture of the same process in Chicago in the formation of the Association of Chicago Priests (ACP).

46. Rev. Howard Calkins, "Jesus Caritas, Fraternity of Priests," *Clergy Report* (Archdiocese of New York) 12, no. 6 (June 1982), p. 2.

**Chapter 5. The Absent Priest and the Floating Parish:
The Possibilities and Predicaments of Crisis, 1962–1972**

1. Andrew M. Greeley, "The Parish Assistant," in Gerald Sloyan, ed., *Secular Priest in the New Church* (New York: Herder and Herder, 1967), pp. 160–61.

2. H. Richard Niebuhr, "The Protestant Movement and Democracy in the United States," in James Ward Smith and A. Leland Jamison, eds., *The Shaping of American Religion* (Princeton: Princeton University Press, 1961), pp. 38–39.

3. Quoted in John C. Haughey, "The Underground Church," *America* 118 (May 18, 1968), p. 664.

4. Encyclical Letter of Pope Paul VI, *Humanae Vitae* (Of Human Life) (pamphlet, NC News Service translation, printed by Daughters of St. Paul, 1968), p. 6.

5. Quoted in Paul Wilkes, "Profiles: Parish Priest," *The New Yorker* (June 13, 1988), p. 70.

6. "Letter of Pope Paul VI on Priestly Celibacy," in *The Teachings of Pope Paul VI* (Vatican City: Libreria Editrice Vaticana, 1970) pp. 456–59, passim.

7. "1971 Synod of Bishops: The Ministerial Priesthood," in Odile M. Liebard, *Official Catholic Teachings: Clergy and Laity* (Wilmington, N.C.: McGrath Publ. Co., 1978), pp. 329, 340.

8. Charles E. Curran, *The Crisis in Priestly Ministry* (Notre Dame, Ind.: Fides, 1972), p. 31. Also see Karl Rahner, S.J., "What Is the Theological Starting Point for a Definition of Priestly Ministry?" *Concilium* 153 (1969), pp. 86ff.

9. Joseph H. Fichter, S.J., *Priest and People* (New York: Sheed and Ward, 1965), pp. 185–92.

10. Eugene Schallert, S.J., "A Study of the Diocesan Priesthood, Archdiocese of San Francisco," AASF.

11. J. F. Powers, "One of Them," in *Look How the Fish Live* (New York: Alfred A. Knopf, 1975), p. 87.

Chapter 6. The Emergence of the Orchestra Leader, 1973–
1. Paul Wilkes, "Profiles," p. 40.
2. Joseph Byrne, "How Far Is Up?" *America* 116 (January 6, 1988), p. 8.
3. Richard Schoenherr and Annemette Sorenson, "Social Change in Religious Organizations: Consequence of Clergy Decline in the U.S. Catholic Church," *Sociological Analysis* 43 (Spring 1982), pp. 23–52.
4. Eugene F. Hemrick and Dean R. Hoge, *Seminarians in Theology: A National Profile* (Washington, D.C.: United States Catholic Conference, 1985).
5. Dean R. Hoge, *The Future of Catholic Leadership: Responses to the Priest Shortage* (Kansas City: Sheed and Ward, 1987), p. 10.
6. Ibid.
7. On this last point, see Robert G. Howes, "The Parish Priest: Endangered Species?" *Homiletic and Pastoral Review* 133 (November 1982), pp. 20–26.
8. Jeffrey M. Burns, "Building the Best: A History of Catholic Parish Life in the Pacific States," in Jay P. Dolan, ed., *The American Catholic Parish*, vol. 2, p. 68.
9. Hoge, *The Future of Catholic Leadership*, p. 40; Joseph J. Casino, "From Sanctuary to Involvement: A History of the Catholic Parish in the Northeast," in Jay P. Dolan, ed., *The American Catholic Parish*, vol. l, p. 85.
10. Rev. Floro Arcamo, personal interview, Seattle, Washington, May 11, 1987.
11. Burns, "Building the Best," pp. 69–70.
12. Casino, "From Sanctuary to Involvement," p. 86.
13. Thomas P. Leonard, "Parish and Housing: Community Involvement," *Clergy Report* (Archdiocese of New York) 11, no. 1 (January 1981), p. 1.
14. Roberto Gonzalez, O.F.M., "Parish and Housing: Work and Ownership," *Clergy Report* (Archdiocese of New York) 11, no. 1 (January 1981), p. 8.
15. Rev. Thomas Farrelly, personal interview, New York City, March 11, 1987.
16. Sister Dorothy Trosclair, personal interview, Sligo, Louisiana, April 21, 1987.
17. The question as to whether or not these should be included under the rubric "lay ministries" is a terminological can of worms opened of necessity by Debra Campbell in chap. 13 of this volume.
18. For an example of the papal rhetoric on this point, see "Address of Pope Paul VI to a General Audience on the Layman's Task, April 23, 1969," in Liebard, "1971 Synod," pp. 296–99.
19. Dennis Geaney, *Emerging Lay Ministries* (Kansas City: Andrews and McMeel, 1979), p. 51.
20. "Decree on the Apostolate of the Laity," in Austin P. Flannery, ed., *Documents of Vatican II* (Grand Rapids, Michigan: William B. Eerdmans, 1975), p. 791.
21. Bernard Lyons, *Parish Councils: Renewing the Christian Community* (Techny, Illinois: Divine Word Publications, 1967), pp. 32ff.
22. Maria Harris, *The DRE Book: Questions and Strategies for Parish Personnel* (New York: Paulist Press, 1976), p. 185.
23. Personal interview, Reading, Massachusetts, March 16, 1987.
24. Richard J. Pettey, *In His Footsteps: The Priest and the Catholic Charismatic Renewal* (New York: Paulist Press, 1977), p. 69.
25. Personal interview, Seattle, Washington, March 23, 1987.
26. "Bulletin: Vatican II Institute" (private circulation, 1977); personal interview, Rev. Howard Bleichner, S.S., Menlo Park, California, May 18, 1987.
27. Archbishop Raymond Hunthausen, personal interview, Seattle, Washington, May 12, 1987.
28. Rev. Gary Morelli, personal interview, Seattle, Washington, May 11, 1987.
29. Archbishop Daniel Pilarczyk, "The Changing Image of the Priest," *Origins* 16, no. 7 (July 3, 1986), p. 139.
30. Quoted in Rodger Van Allen, "The Chicago Declaration and the Call to World

Holiness," in Robert J. Daly, ed., *Rising From History: U.S. Catholic Theology Looks to the Future* (Lanham, Md.: University Press of America, 1987), p. 159.

31. "Darlington School of Theology Bulletin, 1975–1976" (private circulation); "Immaculate Conception Seminary Graduate School of Theology: Bulletin, 1976–1977" (private circulation).

32. Letter, Msgr. Ray P. Hebert to the author, April 22, 1989.

33. David J. O'Brien, *Faith and Friendship: Catholicism in the Diocese of Syracuse, 1886– 1986* (Catholic Diocese of Syracuse, 1987), pp. 324–25.

34. On expectations of parish leadership, see David C. Leege, "Parish Life Among the Leaders," in David C. Leege and Joseph Gremillion, eds., *Notre Dame Study of Catholic Parish Life*, report no. 9 (University of Notre Dame, December 1986).

Part II / In the Parish but Not of It: Sisters

Introduction

1. James Hennesey, S.J., "A Look at the Institution Itself," *New Catholic World* 231 (January/February 1988), p. 9.

2. Helen Rose Fuchs Ebaugh, *Out of the Cloister* (Austin: University of Texas Press, 1977), pp. 13–18, 51; Mary Aloysius Schaldenbrand, S.S.J., "Asylums: Total Societies and Religious Life," in *The New Nuns*, ed. M. Charles Borromeo Muckenhirn, C.S.C. (New York: New American Library, 1967), pp. 115–27.

3. Sister Ursula Grimes, C.S.J., interview with the author, Baden, Pennsylvania, April 20, 1977 (emphasis in original).

4. Marie Augusta Neal, S.N.D. de N., *Catholic Sisters in Transition: From the 1960s to the 1980s* (Wilmington, Del.: Michael Glazier, 1984), pp. 24–25; and *Official Catholic Directory* (New York: P. J. Kenedy & Sons, 1966, 1981).

Chapter 7. Saving Souls and Educating Americans, 1930–1945

1. Francine Cardman et al., "In Solidarity and Service: Reflections on the Problem of Clericalism in the Church," in *Religious Life at the Crossroads*, ed. David A. Fleming, S.M. (New York/Mahwah: Paulist Press, 1985), p. 81.

2. Neil G. McCluskey, S.J., *Catholic Education Faces Its Future* (Garden City, N.Y.: Doubleday, 1969), p. 99.

3. *Official Catholic Directory* (New York: P. J. Kenedy & Sons, 1940).

4. Instructions Preparatory to Perpetual Vows by Sister Superior Rosalia, Waltham, July 1930, Provincial Superiors File, Archives of the Sisters of Notre Dame de Namur, Ipswich Province (hereafter cited as ASND, Ipswich).

5. Mother Ann Sebastian to Dear Sisters, Nazareth, Kentucky, Spring 1939, Circular Letters 1931–1940, Archives of the Sisters of Charity, Nazareth, Kentucky (hereafter cited as ASCN).

6. Mary J. Oates, " 'The Good Sister': The Work and Position of Catholic Church Women in Boston, 1870–1940," in *Catholic Boston: Studies in Religion and Community, 1870–1970*, ed. Robert E. Sullivan and James M. O'Toole (Boston: by the Roman Catholic Archbishop of Boston, 1985), p. 178.

7. Ibid., p. 175.

8. Patricia Byrne, C.S.J., "French Roots of a Women's Movement: The Sisters of St. Joseph, 1650–1836," Ph.D. Dissertation, Boston College, 1986, pp. 203–13; and Ann Curry, P.B.V.M., *Mother Teresa Comerford: Foundress of the Sisters of the Presentation, San Francisco, California* (San Francisco: Sisters of the Presentation, 1980).

9. *Constitutions of the Sisters of Charity Established in the State of Kentucky* (Cincinnati: Benziger Brothers, 1878), pp. 4–5; *Constitutions of the Sisters of Charity of Nazareth (Kentucky)* (Rome: Vatican Polyglot Typography, 1922), p. 17.

10. Sister Thaddea Kelly, P.B.V.M., interview with the author, San Francisco, March 11, 1987.

11. Sermon preached by Monsignor J. M. Byrne on the Occasion of the Formal Distribution of Our Revised Constitution, April 10, 1937, Mother House Annals, vol. 3,

1936–1942, Archives of the Sisters of the Presentation of the Blessed Virgin Mary, San Francisco (hereafter cited as APBVM).

12. James W. Sanders, *The Education of an Urban Minority: Catholics in Chicago, 1833–1965* (New York: Oxford University Press, 1977), pp. 101–8.

13. Cited by Mother Eucharista Galvin, "Problems and Answers," in *The Education of Sister Lucy: A Symposium on Teacher Education and Teacher Training*, National Catholic Educational Association, Philadelphia, April 21, 1949 (Notre Dame, Ind.: Saint Mary's College, 1949), p. 11.

14. Bertande Meyers, D.C., *The Education of Sisters: A Plan for Integrating the Religious, Cultural, Social, and Professional Training of Sisters* (New York: Sheed and Ward, 1941), pp. 29–30.

15. Harold A. Buetow, *Of Singular Benefit: The Story of Catholic Education in the United States* (New York: Macmillan, 1970), pp. 221, 246, citing Irwin Shephard, "Continuous Sessions in Normal Schools," *Journal of the Proceedings and Addresses of the Thirty-Eighth Annual Meeting of the National Education Association*, Los Angeles, July 11–14, 1899 (Chicago: University of Chicago Press, 1899), p. 893; Meyers, *Education of Sisters*, pp. 17–19, citing W. W. Parsons, "The Normal School Curriculum," *N.E.A. Proceedings for 1890* (Topeka, Ks.: Kansas Publishing House, 1890), pp. 718–24; and E. S. Evender, G. C. Gamble, and H. G. Blue, *National Survey of the Education of Teachers: II, Teacher Personnel in the United States*, Bulletin, 1933, no. 10 (Washington, D.C.: Government Printing Offices, 1935), p. 40.

16. A Report of the Experiences of the Sisters Attending the Early Summer School Sessions, collected by Sister Genevieve Tebedo, 1961, Vacation School File, Archives of the Sisters of Charity of Leavenworth, Leavenworth, Kansas (hereafter cited as ASCL).

17. Mother [Mary Berchmans Cannan] to Dear Sisters, Leavenworth, Kansas, May 23, 1924, Circular Letters 1907–1934, ASCL.

18. Buetow, *Of Singular Benefit*, p. 248.

19. Vital Personal Statistics, File on Deceased Sisters, APBVM; and Deceased Sisters File, Archives of the Sisters of St. Joseph, Baden, Pennsylvania (hereafter cited as ACSJ).

20. Myers, *Education of Sisters*, pp. 42–43.

21. Sister Mary Berchmans to Rt. Reverend Msgr. Patrick McInerny, LL.D., Leavenworth, Kansas, May 16, 1932, Circular Letters, 1907–1934, ASCL.

22. Buetow, *Of Singular Benefit*, p. 226, who lists 14,121 religious to 2,663 lay teachers in 1,945 secondary schools.

23. Meyers, *Education of Sisters*, p. 44.

24. Rose Dominic Gabish, S.C.L., "The Story of Sister Rose Dominic Gabish, SCL as of February 1982," p. 33, typed, spiral-bound MS, 215 pp., ASCL.

25. *Notable American Women: The Modern Period*, s.v. "Wolff, Sister Madeleva (Mary Evaline)," by Karen Kennelly; and [Wolff], M. Madeleva, C.S.C., *My First Seventy Years* (New York: Macmillan, 1959).

26. Philip Gleason, *Keeping the Faith: American Catholic Past and Present* (Notre Dame: University of Notre Dame Press, 1987), p. 146.

27. In 1938 Rev. Merlin J. Guilfoyle was appointed to teach senior religion at Presentation Academy, San Francisco, "at the repeated request of the principal, Sister Mary Regina, that a member of the Clergy be appointed in that capacity" (Mother House Annals, Feb. 23, 1938, vol. 3, 1936–1942, APBVM).

28. Joseph H. Fichter, *Parochial School, A Sociological Study* (Notre Dame: University of Notre Dame Press, 1958), pp. 428–29.

29. Oates, "Good Sister," p. 184, and Appendix C-1, "Corporate Receipts, Sisters of St. Joseph, Archdiocese of Boston, 1938–39," p. 199.

30. Mary Jo Weaver, *New Catholic Women: A Contemporary Challenge to Traditional Religious Authority* (San Francisco: Harper and Row, 1985), pp. 20, 25.

31. The material on Sister Mary Isabel Concannon, C.S.J., is from an interview with the author, Pittsburgh, April 28, 1987. Sister Mary Isabel died July 19, 1988.

32. Cardman, "In Solidarity," pp. 66–67, 83–84.

33. Sister M. Paulinus to Dear Sisters, Baden, Pennsylvania, June 6, 1939, Letters of the Superior General to the Community, 1934–1961, 01.01, ACSJ.

34. Jay P. Dolan, *The American Catholic Experience: A History from Colonial Times to the Present* (Garden City, N.Y.: Doubleday, 1985), p. 289.

35. Financial Report, July 1, 1934, to June 28, 1937, Financial Reports, ACSJ.

36. Sister James Maria Spillane, S.C.N., interview with the author, Nazareth, Kentucky, April 7, 1987.

37. Mother House Annals, Oct. 29, 1938, vol. 3, 1934–1942, APBVM, and interviews of the author with Sisters Kathleen Healy and Margaret Cafferty, P.B.V.M., San Francisco, March 11 and 13, 1987. Both sisters are graduates of Presentation high schools and spoke of their experience as teenagers.

38. M. M. Carthagh to Dear Sister Superior [San Francisco], January 20, 1943 (copy), Mother House Annals, vol. 4, 1943–1945, APBVM.

39. Sister Mary Bernadette Giles, P.B.V.M., interview with the author, San Francisco, March 9, 1987.

40. Fichter, *Parochial School*, p. 370, and David J. O'Brien to the author, July 1988.

41. History of the Religious Instruction Vacation Schools in the Diocese of Leavenworth, compiled by Sister Leo Gonzaga, SCL, 1945, Vacation Schools—History, Vacation School File, ASCL.

42. *Manual of Religious Vacation Schools* (Washington, D.C.: Rural Life Bureau, NCWC), pp. 3–6.

43. Excerpts from letters, n.d., Vacation Schools—History, Vacation School File, ASCL.

44. Questionnaire for Religious Vacation Schools, Baldwin, Kansas, Annunciation Parish, 1931, Vacation Schools File, 1929–1937, ASCL (emphasis in the original).

45. Regulations Adopted in Conference, Nazareth, Easter Sunday, 1914, [signed] Mother Rose, Circular Letters 1911–1923, Archives of the Sisters of Charity of Nazareth, Nazareth, Kentucky (hereafter cited as ASCN).

46. Sandra M. Schneiders, I.H.M., *New Wineskins: Re-Imagining Religious Life Today* (New York: Paulist Press, 1986), p. 25.

47. Ebaugh, *Out of the Cloister*, pp. 13–18, 40.

48. Directions and Resolutions—Mother House, n.d., [signed] Sr. M. Reginald [Superior General 1928–1934], APBVM.

49. A Missionary, "Failures of Religious Vocations," *Sponsa Regis*, June 1931, reprinted in *Blow the Trumpet at the New Moon: A "Sisters Today" Jubilee*, ed. Daniel Durken, O.S.B. (Collegeville, Minn.: Liturgical Press, 1979), p. 55.

50. Sister Mary Ambrose, P.B.V.M., directed the children's choir of St. Patrick's School, San Jose, in a Solemn Mass in honor of St. Patrick, broadcast on March 17, 1938, while sisters at the motherhouse listened; also entry for March 2, 1939, Mother House Annals, vol. 3, 1936–1942, APBVM.

51. Mother Ann Sebastian to Dear Sisters, Nazareth, Kentucky, January 1938, Circular Letters 1931–1940, ASCN.

52. Conversations of the author with Sister James Maria Spillane, S.C.N., Nazareth, Kentucky, April 7, 1987, and Sister Consuelo Heaps, C.S.J., Baden, Pennsylvania, April 24, 1987.

53. Sister M. Adrian to Dear Sisters, Baden, Pennsylvania, November 21, 1936; and Sister M. Adrian to Dear Sisters, Baden, Pennsylvania, December 15, 1936, Letters of the Superior General to the Community 1934–1961, 01.01, ACSJ.

54. V. Rev. J. P. Cronin to Dear Mother, Louisville, Kentucky, June 19, 1922 (copy), Circular Letters 1911–1923, ASCN.

55. Mother M. Josepha to Dear Sisters, Leavenworth, Kansas, September 4, 1935; repeated in Mother M. Francesca to Dear Sisters, Leavenworth, Kansas, December 1, 1938, Circular Letters 1935–1950, ASCL.

56. "It will be a surprise to you to learn that next week our dear Sisters are to leave West Lynn, the scene of their many years of self-sacrifice and devotedness. The new

convent is almost ready for occupying and the Sisters of St. Joseph who are to teach in the Boys' High School at Lynn will reside there" (Sister Rosalia of the B[lessed]. S[acrament]. to My dear Sister Superior, Waltham [Massachusetts], July 8, 1930, Provincial Superiors File, Archives of the Sisters of Notre Dame de Namur, Ipswich, Massachusetts) (hereafter cited as ASND, Ipswich).

57. [Sister Rosalia of the Blessed Sacrament], Instructions Preparatory to Perpetual Vows by Sister Superior Rosalia, Waltham, July 1930, Provincial Superiors File, ASND, Ipswich.

58. Mary McGill to Wilfrid Parsons, S.J., October 1929, cited in James Hennesey, *American Catholics: A History of the Roman Catholic Community in the United States* (New York: Oxford University Press, 1981), p. 221; see Hennesey, "A Look," pp. 254–57.

Chapter 8. Success and the Seeds of Change, 1945–1960

1. James Hennesey, *American Catholics* (New York: Oxford University Press, 1981), p. 283.

2. Philip Gleason, *Keeping the Faith: American Catholicism Past and Present* (Notre Dame: University of Notre Dame Press, 1987), p. 65.

3. Mother House Annals, 1941, vol. 3, 1936–1942, APBVM.

4. Mother House Annals, August 14, 1945, vol. 4, 1943–1945, APBVM.

5. Sister Augusta of the S[acred]. H[eart]. to Dear Sister Superior and Sisters, Waltham, Massachusetts, Ash Wednesday, 1942, Provincial Superiors File, ASND, Ipswich.

6. Mother M. Francesca to Dear Sisters, Leavenworth, Kansas, October 7, 1944, Circular Letters 1935–1950, ASCL.

7. Sister Mary Kevin Hollow, S.C.L., interview with the author, Leavenworth, Kansas, March 27, 1987.

8. The Historical Lines of Presentation Foundations and Schools, APBVM.

9. *Official Catholic Directory* (New York: P. J. Kenedy & Sons, 1945, 1950, 1960).

10. Community Statistics, 1945–46; and Mother M. Francesca to Dear Sisters, Leavenworth, Kansas, January 9, 1946, Circular Letters 1935–1950, ASCL.

11. Neil G. McCluskey, *Catholic Education Faces Its Future* (Garden City, N.Y.: Doubleday, 1969), p. 140.

12. Mother Ann Sebastian to Dear Sisters, Nazareth, Kentucky, March 15, 1947, Circular Letters, 1947–1953, ASCN.

13. Sister M. Emerentia to Dear Sisters, Baden, Pennsylvania, May 18, 1946; November 4, 1946; November 30, 1946; January 14, 1947; January 28, 1947; March 3, 1947; March 30, 1947; May 25, 1947; June 5, 1949, Letters of the Superior General to the Community 1934–1961, 01.01, ACSJ.

14. To Dear Sisters, Nazareth, Kentucky, March 15, 1947, Circular Letters 1947–1953, ASCN; and Sister Emerentia to Dear Sisters, Baden, Pennsylvania, July 12, 1947, Letters of the Superior General to the Community 1934–1961, 01.01, ACSJ.

15. "Problems and Answers," in *The Education of Sister Lucy: A Symposium on Teacher Education and Teacher Training*, National Catholic Educational Association, Philadelphia, April 21, 1949 (Notre Dame, Ind.: Saint Mary's College, 1949), p. 11.

16. Harold A. Buetow, *Of Singular Benefit: The Story of Catholic Education in the United States* (New York: Macmillan, 1970), p. 251; Bertrande Meyers, D.C., *The Education of Sisters: A Plan for Integrating the Religious, Cultural, Social, and Professional Training of Sisters* (New York: Sheed and Ward, 1941), pp. 116–18; and Sister Patricia Ann Cloherty, P.B.V.M., interview with the author, San Francisco, March 9, 1987.

17. Hennesey, *American Catholics*, p. 283.

18. M. Madeleva [Wolff], C.S.C., *My First Seventy Years* (New York: Macmillan, 1959), p. 110.

19. M. Madeleva [Wolff], C.S.C., "The Education of Our Young Religious Teachers," in *The Education of Sister Lucy*, p. 9.

20. Ibid., p. 10.

21. Summary of the Proceedings of the General Chapter, July 1942, Nazareth, Kentucky, Circular Letters 1941–1943; G.E.D. Tests, undated letter, filed under 1949; and Mother Bertrand to Dear Sisters, Nazareth, Kentucky, April 1949, Circular Letters 1947–1953, ASCN.

22 "The Preparation of Teachers of Religion in College," in *The Education of Sister Lucy,* p. 35.

23. Helen Rose Fuchs Ebaugh, *Out of the Cloister* (Austin: University of Texas Press, 1977), p. 80.

24. Sister Emerentia to Dear Sisters, Baden, Pennsylvania, June 4, 1948, Letters of the Superior General to the Community 1934–1961, 01.01, ASCJ.

25. Sisters Mary Daniel Turner, S.N.D. de N., and Lora Ann Quinonez, C.D.P., former executive directors of LCWR, conversation with the author, Silver Spring, Maryland, February 27–28, 1988.

26. Mother M. Francesca to Dear Sisters, Leavenworth, Kansas, October 7, 1944. In her letter of August 20, 1946, she quoted a retreat master: "Your spiritual life is *first* and your work *second*" (Circular Letters 1935–1950, ASCL).

27. Mary Schneider, O.S.F., "The Transformation of American Women Religious: The Sister Formation Conference as a Catalyst for Change," Working Paper Series, series 17, no. 1, Cushwa Center for the Study of American Catholicism, University of Notre Dame, Spring 1986, p.7.

28. Mother Olivia to Sister Superiors, San Francisco, September 12, 1949, and March 10, 1950, Circular Letters 1949–1955, APBVM; and Sister Patricia Ann Cloherty, P.B.V.M., interview with the author, San Francisco, March 9, 1987.

29. A. Plé, "Spiritual Responsibilities," *Sponsa Regis* 20 (May 1949), p. 203.

30. J. Creusen, S.J., "Adaptation," *Review for Religious* 8 (1949), pp. 86–96.

31. *Laetanti admodum animo,* in *The States of Perfection: Papal Teachings,* ed. Benedictine Monks of Solesmnes (Boston: St. Paul Editions, 1967), p. 381; hereafter cited as *States of Perfection.*

32. Allocution to members of the General Congress of Religious Orders, Congregations, Societies, and Secular Institutes, December 8, 1950, in *States of Perfection,* p. 407.

33. September 13, 1951, in *States of Perfection,* p. 413.

34. Arcadio Larraona, C.M.F., "Opening Discourse of the Most Reverend Secretary of the Sacred Congregation of Religious" (August 10, 1952), in *Religious Community Life in the United States: Proceedings of the Sisters' Section of the First National Congress of Religious in the United States* (New York: Paulist Press, 1952), p. 21.

35. Sister Mary Patrick, I.H.M., "Share the Sisters," in *Religious Community Life in the United States,* p. 135; and Mother Bertrand to Dear Sisters, Nazareth, Kentucky, October 23, 1959, citing Sister Mary Emil Penet in *Proceedings III* of the Sister Formation Conference (Washington, D.C.: NCWC, 1959).

36. Sister Loretto Julia to Dear Sister Superior, Waltham, Massachusetts, January 21, 1959, Provincial Superiors File, ASND, Ipswich.

37. Edwin A. Quain, S.J., "The Selection of Religious for Graduate Study," in *The Mind of the Church in the Formation of Sisters,* selections from addresses given during the six regional conferences and the first national meeting of the Sister Formation Conference, 1954–1955, edited by Sister Ritamary, C.H.M. (New York: Fordham University Press, 1956), pp. 267–68.

38. The history of the Sister Formation Conference is from Mary Schneider's essay, "The Transformation of American Women Religious," which provides a well-documented account of the years 1954–64.

39. Sister Mary Kevin Hollow, S.C.L., interview with the author, Leavenworth, Kansas, March 27, 1984; see Schneider, "Transformation," pp. 6ff.

40. Cited in Sister Mary Emil, "The Sister Formation Conference of the National Catholic Educational Association," Introduction, *The Mind of the Church in the Formation Sisters,* ed. Sister Ritamary, C.H.M. (New York: Fordham University Press, 1956), p. xv.

41. Wolff, *My First Seventy Years*, p. 113.

42. "Share the Sisters," in *Religious Community Life in the United States*, p. 134.

43. Wolff, *My First Seventy Years*, p. 113.

44. Surveys conducted in May and October 1952 by a six-member volunteer committee of sisters authorized by the NCEA, *The Mind of the Church in the Formation of Sisters*, pp. xvii–xviii.

45. Sister M. Adrian to Dear Sister [Baden, Pennsylvania], November 1935; Rules and Regulations Which Are to Be Observed [Baden, 1953]; Sister M. Benigna to Dear Sisters, Baden, Pennsylvania, August 8, 1956, Letters of the Superior General to the Community, 1934–1961, 01.01, ASCJ; Mother Mary Ancilla to Dear Sisters, Xavier, Kansas, August 15, 1954, Circular letters 1935–1959, ASCL; Sister Loretto Julia to Dear Sister Superiors and Sisters, Waltham, Massachusetts, February 11, 1959, Provincial Superiors File, ASND, Ipswich.

46. *Review for Religious* 17 (1958), pp. 317–18, reprinted in *Questions on Religious Life, Compiled from 'Review for Religious' 1942–1961* (St. Mary's, Ks.: *Review for Religious*, 1964), pp. 125–26.

47. John Tracy Ellis, "American Catholics and the Intellectual Life," *Thought* 30 (1955), pp. 351–88; see Hennesey, *American Catholics*, pp. 300–301; and Gleason, *Keeping the Faith*, pp. 72–78.

48. Formation Program of the Sisters of Charity of Nazareth, n.d. [evidently 1953 or 1954], ASCN; Mother M. Benigna to the Most Reverend Coleman F. Carroll, D.D., Baden, Pennsylvania, January 11, 1957 (copy), Correspondence of the Major Superiors, ACSJ; Mother Bertrand to Dear Sisters, Nazareth, Kentucky, September 1959, Circular Letters, 1959–1960, ASCN: and Mother Mary Ancilla to Dear Sisters [Leavenworth, Kansas], February 2, 1959, Circular Letters, 1959, ASCL.

49. Sister Loretto Julia to Dear Sister Superior, Waltham, Massachusetts, August 4, 1959, ASND, Ipswich.

50. Sister Ursula Grimes, C.S.J., interview with the author, Baden, Pennsylvania, April 20, 1987.

51. Sister Clare Reese, C.S.J., interview with the author, Baden, Pennsylvania, April 26, 1987.

52. Sister Mary Grace to My dear Sisters, Baden, Pennsylvania, May 21, 1951, Letters of the Superior General to the Community, 1934–1961, 01.01, ACSJ; and Sister Ursula Grimes, C.S.J., interview with the author.

53. Ebaugh, *Out of the Cloister*, pp. 94–98.

54. Schneider, "Transformation," p. 20; and Sister Mary Kevin Hollow, S.C.L, interview with the author, Leavenworth, Kansas, March 28, 1987.

55. Sister Marie Joseph to Dear Sister Superior, Waltham, Massachusetts, February 9, 1952, Provincial Superiors File, ASND, Ipswich; Sister Mary Annetta to Dear Sister Superior, San Francisco, April 16, 1957, Local Superiors (Form Letters Sent), July 1955–December 1959, and Mother House Annals, 1955–1961, APBVM; and Good Spiritual Books, February 2, 1959, Circular Letters 1959, ASCL.

56. Elizabeth Carroll [R.S.M.], "Reaping the Fruits of Redemption" in *Midwives of the Future: American Sisters Tell Their Story*, ed. Ann Patrick Ware (Kansas City, Mo.: Lerner Press, 1985), p. 59.

57. Sister M. Benigna to Dear Sisters, Baden, Pennsylvania, September 8, 1955; August 14, 1957, Letters of the Superior General to the Community 1934–1961, 01.01, ACSJ.

58. Hugh Nolan, "Native Son," in *History of the Archdiocese of Philadelphia*, p. 411, cited in Hennesey, *American Catholics*, p. 287.

59. Jay P. Dolan, *The American Catholic Experience: A History from Colonial Times to the Present* (Garden City, N.Y.: Doubleday, 1985), pp. 381ff.

60. McCluskey, *Catholic Education*, p. 108.

61. See Joseph H. Fichter, *Parochial School: A Sociological Study* (Notre Dame: Univer-

sity of Notre Dame Press, 1958), pp. 429–37; and David J. O'Brien, "The Future of Ministry: Historical Context," in *The Future of Ministry: The New England Symposium Papers*, ed. Joseph P. Sinwell and Billie Poon (New York: Sadlier, 1985), p. 37.

62. Fichter, *Parochial School*, p. 433.

63. See Fichter, ibid., p. 345, and McCluskey, *Catholic Education*, pp. 114–15.

64. Gleason, *Keeping the Faith*, p. 170.

65. Sister Rose Matthew, I.H.M., "Sister Teachers in the United States: A Study of their Status and Projected Role," in *Planning for the Formation of Sisters: Studies on the Teaching Apostolate and Selections from Addresses of the Sister Formation Conferences 1956–1957*, ed. Sister Ritamary, C.H.M. (New York: Fordham University Press, 1958), pp. 97–99, 106, 116.

66. Sister Clare Reese, C.S.J., interview with the author, Baden, Pennsylvania, April 26, 1987.

67. Sister Loretto Julia to Dear Sister Superior and Sisters, Waltham, Massachusetts, June 7, 1958, Provincial Superiors File, ASND, Ipswich.

68. Sister Michelle Prah, C.S.J., interview with the author, Notre Dame, Indiana, April 12, 1987.

69. David J. O'Brien, "Choosing Our Future: American Catholicism's Precarious Prospects," in *Rising from History: U.S. Catholic Theology Looks to the Future*, ed. Robert J. Daly, Annual Publication of the College Theology Society, vol. 30 (Lanham, Md.: University Press of America, 1987), pp. 20–23.

70. James W. Sanders, *The Education of an Urban Minority: Catholics in Chicago, 1833–1965* (New York: Oxford University Press, 1977), pp. 202–4.

71. The Historical Lines of Presentation Foundations and Schools, APBVM; and John F. Dearden to Mother M. Benigna, Pittsburgh, October 26, 1956; December 27, 1956, Correspondence of the Major Superiors, ACSJ.

72. Mother Mary Ursula to Rev. Marcel J. Fourcade, San Francisco, September 2, 1959 (copy), Letters from Pastors 1958–1964, APBVM.

73. Mother M. Olivia to Rev. Thomas A. Murphy, San Francisco, July 22, 1954 (copy), Letters from Pastors to 1958, APBVM.

74. School Year 1955–56, Statistics File, ASCL; and Ordinances—Chapter 1960 and Report of Growth 1954–60, ASCN.

75. Sister Mary Grace to My dear Sisters, Baden, Pennsylvania, July 25, 1950; Rules and Regulations Which Are to Be Observed, n.d. [1953]; and A Financial Memoranda [signed] Sister M. Benigna, n.d. [June 2, 1956]. Letters of the Superior General to the Community 1934–1961, 01.01, ACSJ.

76. Sister Mary Emil, I.H.M., Introduction, *The Mind of the Church in the Formation of Sisters*, p. xviii.

77. Sister Mary Emil Penet, "Progress Report on Sister Formation," *Sister Formation Bulletin*, Supplement (Summer 1956), p. 1, cited in Schneider, "Transformation," p. 8, and idem, Introduction, *The Mind of the Church in the Formation of Sisters*, p. xxxi.

78. Ebaugh, *Out of the Cloister*, p. 50.

79. Emily George, R.S.M., "Canonical Status," in *Turning Points in Religious Life*, ed. Carol Quigley, I.H.M. (Wilmington, Del.: Michael Glazier, 1987), p. 176.

80. Sister Mary Isabel Concannon, C.S.J., interview with the author, Pittsburgh, April 28, 1987.

81. Sacred Congregation of Religious to Superiors of Institutes of Perfection, August 6, 1957, in *The States of Perfection*, pp. 636–69. Auxiliary Bishop of Pittsburgh, Coleman F. Carroll, reminded the sisters that this obliged them under pain of mortal sin, quoted by Sister M. Benigna to Dear Sisters, Baden, Pennsylvania, March 6, 1968, Letters of the Superior General to the community 1934–1961, 01.01, ACSJ.

82. Sister Loretto Julia to Dear Sister Superior and Sisters, Waltham, Massachusetts, Advent 1958, Provincial Superiors file, ASND, Ipswich.

83. O'Brien, "Choosing our Future," in *Rising from History*, p. 22.

Chapter 9. A Tumultuous Decade, 1960–1970

1. Letters of the Superior General to the Community 1934–1961, 01.01, ACSJ.

2. Address of Pope Paul VI to Religious Women (as archbishop of Milan, Paul VI gave this address in 1961 and repeated it in Rome in 1965), typescript, kindly provided by Sister Ann Grady, S.N.D. de N., Ipswich.

3. Here and throughout this chapter, I am greatly indebted to the helpful critique of David J. O'Brien.

4. Philip Gleason, *Keeping the Faith: American Catholicism Past and Present* (Notre Dame: University of Notre Dame Press, 1987), p. 84.

5. David J. O'Brien, "Choosing Our Future: American Catholicism's Precarious Prospects," in *Rising from History: U.S. Catholic Theology Looks to the Future*, ed. Robert J. Daly, Annual Publication of the College Theology Society, 1984, no. 30 (Lanham, Md.: University Press of America, 1987), p. 18.

6. Mother Leo Frances to Dear Sisters, Xavier, Kansas, August 7, 1962, Circular Letters 1962, ASCL; and Decrees of the General Chapter, 1961, ASCJ.

7. Interview of the author with Sisters Katharine Hanrahan, S.C.N., Nazareth, Kentucky, April 6, 1987; Bette Moslander, C.S.J., Concordia, Kansas, March 23–24, 1987; Kathleen Healy, P.B.V.M., San Francisco, March 11, 1987; Clare Reese, C.S.J., Baden, Pennsylvania, April 26, 1987; and Teresa Bernard Daly, S.N.D., Ipswich, Massachusetts, May 4, 1987.

8. Marcelle Bernstein, *The Nuns* (Philadelphia and New York: J. B. Lippincott, 1976), p. 236.

9. Joan A. Chittester [O.S.B.], "No Time for Tying Cats," in *Midwives of the Future: American Sisters Tell Their Story*, ed. Ann Patrick Ware (Kansas City, Mo.: Leaven Press, 1985), p. 7.

10. Announcements, December 15, 1965, Baden, Pennsylvania, Letters of the Superior General to the Community 1961–1967, ACSJ.

11. Mother Lucille to My dear Sisters, Nazareth, Kentucky, April 2, 1962, and idem, April 4, 1962, Circular Letters 1960–1965, ASCN; and interview of the author with Sister Katharine Hanrahan, S.C.N., Nazareth, Kentucky, April 6, 1987.

12. Chapter Statement, 1968, ASCL.

13. Entries for August 18–19, 1962, January 10, 1963, and February, 1963, Mother House Annals 1962–1964, APBVM; and Reading List for Sisters under Temporary Vows, 1965, Circular Letters 1960–1966, ASCL.

14. Sister Virginia Mulhern, S.N.D. de N., interview with the author, April 30, 1987.

15. To Dear Sister Superior and Sisters, Ipswich, Massachusetts, Visitation 1964, Provincial Superiors File, ASND, Ipswich.

16. John W. O'Malley, S.J., "Reform, Historical Consciousness and Vatican II's Aggiornamento," *Theological Studies* 32(1971), p. 574.

17. Cardinal Leon Joseph Suenens, *The Nun in the World: New Dimensions of the Modern Apostolate* (Westminster, Md.: Newman Press, 1963; London: Burns & Oates, 1962), pp. 4, 5, 123.

18. In Sister Gertrude Joseph Donnelly, C.S.J.O., *The Sister Apostle* (Notre Dame, Ind.: Fides, 1964), p. 9.

19. Sandra Schneiders, I.H.M., *New Wineskins: Re-Imagining Religious Life Today* (New York: Paulist Press, 1986), pp. 23–25; see Doris Gottemoeller, R.S.M., "The Changing Missions of Religious Life," in *Starting Points: Six Essays Based on the Experience of U.S. Women Religious*, ed. Lora Ann Quinonez, C.D.P. (Washington, D.C.: LCWR, 1980), pp. 21, 25ff.

20. Dogmatic Constitution on the Church, no. 40, in *The Documents of Vatican II*, ed. Walter M. Abbott, S.J. (New York: America Press; An Angelus Book, 1966), p. 67.

21. [Sister Eleanor Joseph] to My dear Sister Superior and Sisters, Ipswich, September 7, 1963, Provincial Superiors File, ASND, Ipswich; see James Hennesey, *American Catholics* (New York: Oxford University Press, 1981), p. 309.

22. In Abbott, *Documents*, pp. 199–200.

23. [Sister Eleanor Joseph] to My dear Sister Superior and Sisters, Ipswich, September 7, 1963, Provincial Superiors File, ASND, Ipswich.

24. Mother Mary Ursula to My dear Sisters, San Francisco, September 20, 1962, Local Superiors (Form Letters Sent) 1960–62, APBVM; [Sister Eleanor Joseph] to Dear Sister Superior and Sisters, Ipswich, Massachusetts, September 12, 1964, Provincial Superiors File, ASND, Ipswich; Mother Leo Frances to Dear Sisters, Xavier, Kansas, January 28, 1966, Circular Letters 1966, ASCL; Guidelines for a Self-Study, p. 1, and Eleventh General Chapter, July 1966, p. 12, ASCN; and Program for Renewal 1968–1969, Sisters of the Presentation, San Francisco, August 15, 1968, "Other Apostolates," p. 47, APBVM.

25. *Ecclesiae Sanctae: Motu Proprio for Implementing Four Council Decrees,* August 6, 1966, no. 3, in *Vatican Council II: the Conciliar and Post-Conciliar Documents,* ed. Austin P. Flannery, O.P., rev. ed. (Grand Rapids, Michigan: William B. Eerdmans, 1984), pp. 625–27.

26. Conversations of the author with Sister Margaret Cafferty, P.B.V.M., San Francisco, March 12, 1987; and Sisters Mary Daniel Turner, S.N.D. de N., and Lora Ann Quinonez, C.D.P., Silver Spring, Maryland, February 17–28, 1988.

27. Sister Marie Augusta Neal, S.N.D. de N., interview with the author, Boston, February 4, 1987; Neal, *Catholic Sisters in Transition from the 1960s to the 1980s* (Wilmington, Del.: Michael Glazier, 1984), pp. 9–10; idem, "The Relation Between Religious Belief and Structural Change in Religious Orders: Developing an Effective Measuring Instrument," *Review for Religious Research* 2 (1970), pp. 2–16; 12 (1971), pp. 153–64; the insight about the effect of the "survey" on sisters is from Sister Bette Moslander, C.S.J., interview with the author, Concordia, Kansas, March 23–24, 1987.

28. Ed. Sister M. Charles Borromeo Muckenhirn, C.S.C. (Notre Dame, Ind.: Fides, 1965).

29. See *The New Nuns* (Intro., Part II, n.1, above), p. iv.

30. Chapter Statement, 1968, Report of Commission Three: How Do We Form and Develop Ourselves as Sisters of Charity in the Church and in the World?, p. 5, ASCL; and Sister Mary Cele Breen, S.C.L., interview with the author, Leavenworth, Kansas, March 31, 1987.

31. Elizabeth Carroll [R.S.M.], "Reaping the Fruits of Redemption," in Ware, *Midwives of the Future,* pp. 58–59; and Sister Ursula Grimes, C.S.J., interview with the author, Baden, Pennsylvania, April 20, 1987.

32. Suzanne Campbell-Jones, *In Habit: A Study of Working Nuns* (New York: Pantheon Books, 1978), p. 203.

33. Talara Log [Fall 1963], Circular Letters 1963, ASCL.

34. Las cinco peruanas gringas [written by Sister Marie Colombiere] to Mother Leo Frances, Sisters, Juniors, and Novices, Talara, Peru, April 11, 1964, Circular Letters 1964, ASCL.

35. "Conclusions and Recommendations," in *Priests and Religious for Latin America,* Proceedings and Conclusions of the First Inter-American Conference of Religious, Mexico City, February 8–12, 1971 (Washington, D.C.: U.S. Catholic Conference, Division for Latin America [1971]), p. 72.

36. Mother Patricia Barrett, R.S.C.J., "Nuns in the Inner City," in *The New Nuns,* pp. 99–102.

37. Margaret Ellen Traxler [S.S.N.D.], "Great Tide of Returning," in Ware, *Midwives of the Future,* p. 132.

38. Sister Margaret Cafferty, P.B.V.M., interview with the author, San Francisco, March 13, 1987.

39. Barrett, in Muckenhirn, *The New Nuns,* p. 105; see Sister Matthias Rinderer, O.S.F., "One Sister's Chicago Education," ibid., pp. 112–13.

40. Correspondence of David J. O'Brien with the author, October 1987.

41. Sister Mary Bernadette Giles, P.B.V.M., interview with the author, San Francisco, March 9, 1987; "New Member of City's Rights Group," *San Francisco Chronicle,* January 20, 1966; Photo Essay, *The Monitor,* June 29, 1967, pp. 9–10; "The Kid's Cool Summer," *The Monitor,* August 1, 1968, pp. 6–7; "Right to Read," *The Monitor,* July 9, 1970, pp.

6–7; "Women Here Unite for Soviet Jewry," *San Francisco Jewish Bulletin*, December 3, 1971; "'Summer of Love' Means Chance to Learn for 3,000 S.F. Children," *The Monitor*, June 20, 1974, p. 8.

42. Sister Judy Raley, S.C.N., interview with the author, Nazareth, Kentucky, April 7, 1987.

43. Sister Betty Blanford, S.C.N., interview with the author, Nazareth, Kentucky, April 9, 1987.

44. The Long Beach, California, *Independent* carried a photograph and article on the change of habit by the Presentation Sisters the day preceding the actual event, slated for July 31, 1965.

45. John M. Lozano, C.M.F., "Trends in Religious Life Today," in *Religious Life at the Crossroads*, ed. David A. Fleming, S.M. (New York/Mahwah: Paulist Press, 1985), pp. 149–57; reprinted from *Review for Religious* 42 (July/August 1983), pp. 481–505; see Schneiders, *New Wineskins*, pp. 26–27, and Mary Jo Weaver, *New Catholic Women: A Contemporary Challenge to Traditional Religious Authority* (San Francisco: Harper and Row, 1985), pp. 78–79.

46. See Ebaugh, *Out of the Cloister*, p. 48; and Campbell-Jones, *In Habit*, pp. 134, 144, 155–56.

47. M. Peter Traxler, S.S.N.D., ed., *New Works of New Nuns* (St. Louis/London: B. Herder Book Co., 1968).

48. Mary Luke Tobin, S.L., "The Mission of the Religious in the Twentieth Century," in *Vows but No Walls: An Analysis of Religious Life*, ed. Eugene E. Grollmes, S.J. (St. Louis/London: B. Herder Book Co., 1967), pp. 203, 206, 207–9.

49. Novak, reprinted in *The New Nuns*, p. 30.

50. Mother Mary Isabel to Dear Sisters, Baden, Pennsylvania, December 8, 1965, Letters of the Superior General to the Community 1961–1967, ASCJ.

51. Ebaugh, *Out of the Cloister*, pp. 33, 38.

52. Sister Alice Adams, S.C.N., interview with the author, Nazareth, Kentucky, April 8, 1987.

53. Mother Leo Frances to Dear Sisters, Xavier, Kansas, October 23, 1965.

54. Buetow, *Of Singular Benefit*, p. 304, citing Mark J. Hurley, ed., *The Declaration on Christian Education of Vatican Council II* (Glen Rock, N.J.: Paulist Press, 1966), pp. 157 and 305.

55. Sister Michelle Prah, C.S.J., interview with the author, Notre Dame, Indiana, April 12, 1987.

56. Mother M. William to Dear Sisters, San Francisco, July 23, 1964, Local Superiors (Form Letters Sent) 1963–64, APBVM.

57. Mother Mary William to Dear Sisters, San Francisco, December 17, 1965, Local Superiors (Form Letters Sent), APBVM. Sister Nancy McLaughlin, P.B.V.M., interview with the author, San Francisco, March 10, 1987; Guidelines for a Self-Study, August 1967, ASCN; and Mother Leo Frances to Dear Sisters, Xavier, Kansas, May 12, 1965, Circular Letters 1960–66, ASCL.

58. Apostolic Exhortation on the Renewal of Religious Life, *Evangelica Testificatio*, June 29, 1961, no. 18, in Flannery, p. 688.

59. Sister Mary Linscott to My dear Sisters, Rome, July 6, 1969, General Officers File; and Sister Marie Julienne to Dear Sisters, Ipswich, Massachusetts, July 19, 1969, Provincial Superiors File, ASND, Ipswich.

60. Jack Starr, "Trouble Ahead for the Catholic Schools," *Look*, October 22, 1963, pp. 37–45.

61. *Official Catholic Directory*, 1964.

62. From the Desk of the Provincial, February 21, 1961, citing the January 1961 issue of the *Sister Formation Newsletter*, Provincial Superiors File, ASND, Ipswich; and *Official Catholic Directory*, 1969.

63. Mother Mary Isabel to Dear Sisters, Baden, Pennsylvania, July 31, 1961, Letters of the Superior General to the Community, 1961–1967, ACSJ.

64. "Our school has been completed for about nine months and is not yet occupied," John J. Boland to Mother Ursula, St. Patrick's parish, Cote Madera, California, October 3, 1961, Letters from Pastors 1958 to 3/19/64, APBVM.

65. Mother Lucille to My dear Sisters, Nazareth, Kentucky, April 9, 1962, Circular Letters 1960–1965, and General Chapter, July 1966, ASCN.

66. Buetow, *Of Singular Benefit*, pp. 284, 288, 295.

67. Report to Mr. Edgar J. Roy, Jr., NCEA Study of Catholic Higher Education, St. Louis University, April 16, 1966 (copy), Statistics, ASCL.

68. Active Sisters in Community Apostolates [1968–1974], Statistics, ASCL.

69. *Official Catholic Directory*, 1960, 1965, 1969, 1970.

70. Neal, *Catholic Sisters in Transition*, pp. 20–21.

71. Joseph H. Fichter, *Religion as an Occupation* (Notre Dame: University of Notre Dame Press, 1961), p. 133.

72. Ebaugh, *Out of the Cloister*, pp. 5–6, 30, 46–47, 53–54, 89–94.

73. Sanders, *Education*, p. 230; see pp. 255ff.

74. Quoted from *The Catholic Mind*, January 1968, p. 3, in McClusky, *Catholic Education*, p. 105.

75. *Official Catholic Directory*, 1966, 1971; and Neal, *Catholic Sisters in Transition*, pp. 20–21.

76. Report of the General Government 1983–88, Sisters of St. Joseph, Baden, Pennsylvania, ACSJ.

77. Guidelines for a Self-Study, 1965–66, Committee IV: The Apostolate of the Congregation, pp. 20–21, ASCN.

78. Sister Joan Murphy to Cardinal James Francis McIntyre, San Francisco, January 16, 1970 (copy), Local Superiors (Form Letters Sent) 1969–1970, APBVM; Mother Leo Frances to Very Reverend Msgr. Henry Gardner, Archdiocesan Superintendent of Schools, Kansas City, Kansas (Leavenworth, Kansas), January 5, 1970 (copy), Correspondence File #30, 1970, ASCL; Sister Mary Kevin Hollow to The Most Reverend Raymond Hunthausen (Leavenworth, Kansas), May 6, 1969, Files of the Secretary General, Sisters of Charity of Leavenworth, Leavenworth, Kansas; and "Bishops, Educators Issue Statement on Future of Catholic Schools in Butte," *Montana Catholic Register, Western Edition*, Friday, February 28, 1969; and "2 Catholic Schools to Close," ibid., Friday, March 14, 1969.

79. Sister Kathleen Healy, P.B.V.M., interview with the author, San Francisco, March 11, 1987.

80. Examples are *Second Look*, by the Sisters of Charity of Leavenworth, 1971; *Present Perspectives*, Sisters of Notre Dame, Massachusetts Province, 1972; the two-year self-study done by the Sisters of St. Joseph of Baden in conjunction with Mr. Richard Cassidy's New York firm, Decision Research, Inc., ASCL, ASND, Boston; and Sister Michelle Prah, C.S.J., interview with the author, Notre Dame, Indiana, April 12, 1987.

81. Research and Development, ACSJ.

82. Campbell-Jones, *In Habit*, pp. 146, 155–56, 167; Ebaugh, *Out of the Cloister*, pp. 38, 48, 134, 144; Juliana Casy, I.H.M., "Emmanuel: A Reflection," in *Starting Points*, pp. 1–14; and Sister Margaret Ann Leonard, L.S.A., interview with the author, Roxbury, Massachusetts, February 6, 1984.

83. Comments of Philip Gleason, advisory meeting, Notre Dame, Indiana, October 16, 1984.

84. Sister Margaret Cafferty, P.B.V.M., interview with the author, San Francisco, March 13, 1987.

Chapter 10. Diminishment, Disillusion, Discovery, 1970–

1. David J. O'Brien, "Choosing our Future: American Catholicism's Precarious Prospects," in *Rising from History*, p. 28; Jay P. Dolan, *The American Catholic Experience*, p. 428, and Thomas F. O'Meara, O.P., comments to the author, July 31, 1988.

2. Dolan, *American Catholic Experience*, p. 423; see p. 453.

3. Neal, *Catholic Sisters in Transition*, pp. 20–21.

4. Sister Rosalie Curtin, S.C.L., interview with the author, Leavenworth, Kansas, March 31, 1987.

5. Chapter Report, 1986: Presented to the Eleventh General Chapter of the Sisters of the Presentation, p. 38, APBVM (hereafter cited as Chapter Report 1986).

6. Statistics, 1967–1986, Office of the Provincial Secretary, Sisters of Notre Dame de Namur, Ipswich.

7. Chapter Report 1986, APBVM.

8. Ibid., p. 2.

9. Sister Mary Kevin Hollow, S.C.L, interview with the author, Leavenworth, Kansas, March 27, 1987.

10. Neal, *Catholic Sisters in Transition*, p. 43.

11. Interviews of the author with Sisters Judy Raley, S.C.N., Nazareth, Kentucky, April 7, 1987, and Alice Adams, S.C.N., Nazareth, Kentucky, April 8, 1987.

12. Ebaugh, *Out of the Cloister*, p. 83.

13. *Followers of Christ: Perspectives on the Religious Life* (New York: Paulist Press, 1978), p. 13.

14. David Fleming, S.M., "Community, Corporateness, and Communion," in *Starting Points: Six Essays Based on the Experience of U.S. Women Religious*, p. 37.

15. Sister Patricia Halliday, S.N.D. de N., interview with the author, Boston, May 6, 1987.

16. Campbell-Jones, *In Habit*, pp. 155–56, citing Mary Douglas, Emile Durkheim, Michael Hill, and Peter Berger; see the excellent treatment of medieval women religious in a changing ecclesiastical and social milieu by Caroline Walker Bynum, "Women Mystics in the Thirteenth Century: The Case of the Nuns of Helfta," in her *Jesus as Mother: Studies in the Spirituality of the High Middle Ages* (Berkeley: University of California Press, 1982), pp. 170–262.

17. Sister Michelle Prah, C.S.J., interview with the author, Notre Dame, Indiana, April 12, 1987.

18. Sister James Maria Spillane, S.C.N., interview with the author, Nazareth, Kentucky, April 7, 1987.

19. Sister Mary Kevin Hollow, "Note: this letter was sent to bishops, pastors, principals, school boards and school superintendents," Leavenworth, Kansas, December 16, 1975 (copy), Circular Letters, 1975–1977, ASCL.

20. *Monitor*, April 2, 1981, p. 6.

21. Bernstein, *The Nuns*, p. 236.

22. James L. Connor, S.J., "Response to Ministry and Change in the Future," in *Facets of the Future: Religious Life U.S.A.*, Ruth McGoldrick, S.P., and Cassian Yuhaus, C.P., eds. (Huntington, Ind.: Our Sunday Visitor, 1976), p. 51.

23. Guidelines for Summer Apostolic Service Programs, January 1978, Circular Letters 1978–1981, ASCL.

24. *Constitutions of the Sisters of Charity of Nazareth* (Notre Dame, Indiana: Ave Maria Press, 1966), p. 1; and *Constitutions: Sisters of Charity of Nazareth* (Nazareth, Kentucky: by the author, June 1980), Core Document, p. 1.

25. Divestiture of Hospitals: Why We Do It, Adapted from Statement by Executive Council to Executive Board, February 9, 1985, p. 1, Personal File, Sister Bette Moslander, Concordia, Kansas.

26. *Constitutions*, "Chapter XII. The Apostolate," no. 154, p. 42.

27. Mother Leo Frances to Dear Sisters, Leavenworth, Kansas, July 19, 1973.

28. Chapter Statement, 1968, Report of Commission I: Who Are We as Sisters of Charity of Leavenworth in the Church and in the World?, p. 1, ASCL.

29. Report of Sister Barbara Thomas, Superior General, to the General Assembly of the Sisters of Charity of Nazareth, June 15, 1974, p. 22, ASCN.

30. Ibid.

31. *The Conference Report 1975–76* (Washington, D.C.: Leadership Conference of Women Religious), pp. 6–7.

32. Towards an Understanding of Mission, 1975, Chapter Acts of the Sisters of Notre Dame 1975, p. 14, ASND, Ipswich.

33. *Constitution of the Sisters of Charity of Leavenworth,* "Mission" (Leavenworth, Ks.: by the author, March 25, 1981), p. 5.

34. Form Letter, Washington, D.C., January 11, 1977; and One Response to "The Call to Action," Mission USA, 1977; Province Files, and *Boston Province Newsletter* 4, no. 7 (April 19, 1977), p. 8. Publications, Archives of the Sisters of Notre Dame de Namur, Boston (hereafter cited as ASND, Boston).

35. Sister Ann Victoria Cruz, S.C.N., interview with the author, Nazareth, Kentucky, April 8, 1987.

36. Sister Clare Reese, C.S.J., interview with the author, Baden, Pennsylvania, April 26, 1987.

37. John Deedy, *The New Nuns: Serving Where the Spirit Leads* (Chicago: Fides/Claretian, 1982), pp. 2, 81.

38. Hennesey, *American Catholics,* p. 313.

39. Kathleen Coman, S.C.L., Trends in Church/Congregational Ministries: A Summary, April 1986, Personnel Office Files, Sisters of Charity of Leavenworth.

40. Sister Margaret Eletta Guider, O.S.F., conversation with the author, June 1988.

41. Mary Jo Weaver, "Inside Outsiders: Sisters and the Women's Movement," chapter 3 of her *New Catholic Women,* pp. 71–108; see also Kaye Ashe, *Today's Woman, Tomorrow's Church* (Chicago: Thomas More Press, 1983).

42. Weaver, *New Catholic Women,* p. 76.

43. Sisters Mary Daniel Turner, S.N.D. de N., and Lora Ann Quinonez, C.D.P., conversation with the author, Silver Spring, Maryland, February 27–28, 1988.

44. Cardinal Leon Joseph Suenens, *The Nun in the World: New Dimensions in the Modern Apostolate* (Westminster, Md.: Newman, 1963), pp. 10–16.

45. Teresa Mary Defarrari, C.S.C., "Women Theologians in the Church," *Sisters Today* (July 1966), reprinted in Daniel Durken, O.S.B., ed., *Blow the Trumpet at the New Moon,* pp. 361–66.

46. Mary Aloysius Schaldenbrand, S.S.J., "Freud and Sisters," in *The New Nuns,* pp. 71–82.

47. Esther MacCarthy, S.N.D. de N., "Literature on Ecclesial Role of Women Provides Rich Source for Study," *Boston Province Newsletter* 6, no. 4 (December 16, 1978), p. 8. Publications, ASND, Boston; LCWR, *New Visions, New Roles: Women in the Church* (Washington, D.C.: Leadership Conference of Women Religious, 1975); idem, *Status and Roles of Women: Another Perspective* (Washington, D.C.: Leadership Conference of Women Religious, 1976); Doris Gottemoeller and Rita Hoffbauer, eds., *Women and Ministry: Present Experience and Future Hopes,* Proceedings of the Symposium based on Women and Ministry: A Survey of the Experience of Roman Catholic Women in the United States (Washington, D.C.: Leadership Conference of Women Religious, 1981).

48. Ashe, *Today's Woman,* pp. 161–64; and Weaver, *New Catholic Women,* p. 44.

49. Washington, D.C., October 7, 1979, cited from the Southern Province Bulletin, November 1979, ASCN.

50. Quoted in Council Communications, September 12, 1984, Province Files, ASND, Ipswich.

51. Sister Virginia Scally, S.N.D. de N., interview with the author, Boston, May 6, 1987.

52. Chapter Report 1985, p. 18, APBVM.

53. David C. Legee, "Parish Life Among the Leaders," in David C. Legee and Joseph Gremillion, eds., *Notre Dame Study of Catholic Parish Life,* report no. 9 (University of Notre Dame, December 1986), p. 12; and David C. Legee and Thomas A. Trozzolo, "Participation in Catholic Parish Life: Religious Rites and Parish Activities in the 1980s," *Notre Dame Study of Catholic Parish Life,* report no. 3 (April 1985), p. 7.

54. Dolan, *American Catholic Experience*, p. 442.

55. Chapter Report 1986, pp. 11–12, APBVM.

56. Sister Mary Kevin Hollow, S.C.L., interview with the author, Leavenworth, Kansas, March 27, 1987.

57. Sister Marie Francette Holes, C.S.J., conversation with the author, Ambridge, Pennsylvania, June 1988.

58. Sister Kathleen Healy, P.B.V.M., interview with the author, San Francisco, March 11, 1987.

59. Sister Michelle Prah, C.S.J., to the author, Notre Dame, Indiana, April 13, 1987.

60. Sister Katharine Hanrahan, S.C.N., personal files shared with the author.

61. Sister Judy Raley, S.C.N., interview with the author, Nazareth, Kentucky, April 7, 1987.

62. Sister Ursula Grimes, C.S.J., interview with the author, Baden, Pennsylvania, April 7, 1987.

63. Interviews with the author, Sisters Cleta Herold, P.B.V.M., San Francisco, March 9, 1987; Edna Malloy, S.N.D.de N., Boston, May 5, 1987; and Herman Joseph Koch, S.C.L., Leavenworth, Kansas, March 30, 1987.

64. Sister Patricia Johnson, S.N.D.de N., interview with the author, Boston, April 30, 1987.

65. Sister Ann Victoria Cruz, S.C.N., interview with the author, Nazareth, Kentucky, April 8, 1987.

66. Coman, Trends in Church/Congregational Ministries: A Summary, April 1986; *Wall Street Journal*, May 19, 1986; *New Catholic Reporter*, March 20, 1987, pp. 1, 26, 28; March 27, 1987, p. 8; April 3, 1987, p. 6.

67. Sister Ursula Grimes, C.S.J., interview with the author, Baden, Pennsylvania, April 20, 1987.

68. Chapter Report 1986, p. 10, APBVM.

69. Donna Markham, O.P., "The Decline of Vocations in the United States: Reflections from a Psychological Perspective," *New Catholic World*, January/February 1988, pp. 13–19.

70. Weaver, *New Catholic Women*, p. 86.

71. Coman report.

72. James Hitchcock, *Catholicism and Modernity: Confrontation or Capitulation?* (New York: Seabury Press, 1979), p. 1.

73. Brigid Keough, R.S.C.J., conversation with the author, Tokyo, Japan, August 22, 1986.

**Part III / The Struggle to Serve:
From the Lay Apostolate to the Ministry Explosion**

Introduction

1. Thomas Franklin O'Meara, O.P., *Theology of Ministry* (New York: Paulist Press, 1983), pp. 142, 140.

2. Florence R. Rosenberg, Edward M. Sullivan, and Paul H. Besanceney, S.J., *Women and Ministry: A Survey of the Experience of Roman Catholic Women in the United States* (Washington, D.C.: Center for Applied Research in the Apostolate, 1980), pp. 55–56.

3. Dennis Geaney, *Emerging Lay Ministries* (Kansas City: Andrews and McMeel, 1979), pp. 8–9.

4. National Catholic News Service press release dated July 17, 1981, obtained through the Committee on Doctrine of the National Conference of Catholic Bishops (NCCB). This definition, adopted for in-house use by the NCCB and the United States Catholic Conference (USCC), has been superseded by the American bishops' pastoral, *Called and Gifted*, issued in 1980.

5. See the "Chicago Declaration of Social Concern," reprinted in *Challenge to the Laity,* ed. Russell Barta (Huntington, Indiana: Our Sunday Visitor, 1980), pp. 19–27.

Chapter 11. Lay Organization and Activism, 1889–1928

1. Quoted by David Goldstein in "A Layman's Apostolate," *America* 20 (January 11, 1919), pp. 335–36.

2. Lelia Hardin Bugg, *The People of Our Parish* (Boston: Marlier, Callanan and Co., 1900; reprint ed., New York: Arno Press, 1978), p. 228. Bugg devotes all of chapter 5 to "Our Catholic Societies."

3. Philip Gleason, *The Conservative Reformers: German Catholics and the Social Order* (Notre Dame: University of Notre Dame Press, 1968), p. 119; Christopher J. Kauffman, *Faith and Fraternalism: The History of the Knights of Columbus, 1882–1982* (New York: Harper and Row, 1982), pp. 178–80.

4. Jay P. Dolan and Jeffrey Burns, "Parish History Study" (unpublished, 1982), cited in Jay P. Dolan, *The American Catholic Experience: A History from Colonial Times to the Present* (Garden City, N.Y.: Doubleday, 1985), pp. 120–21.

5. Leslie W. Tentler, "Catholic Women and Their Church: A View from Detroit," Working Paper Series 16, no. 2, Fall 1985, Charles and Margaret Hall Cushwa Center for the Study of American Catholicism, University of Notre Dame, pp. 8–15, 35–36.

6. William Stang, *Pastoral Theology* (New York: Benziger Brothers, 1897), p. 153.

7. Sister Joseph Miriam Blackwell, M.S.B.T., *Ecclesial People: A Study in the Life and Times of Thomas Augustine Judge, C.M.,* 2nd ed. (Holy Trinity, Alabama: 1984), pp. 89–90.

8. *Souvenir Volume: Three Great Events in the History of the Catholic Church in the United States,* 2nd ed. (Detroit: William H. Hughes, 1890), p. 18.

9. Edward Kantowicz, *Corporation Sole: Cardinal Mundelein and Chicago Catholicism* (Notre Dame: University of Notre Dame Press, 1983), p. 5.

10. Ibid., pp. 14, 20, 132–38. See chapter 1 regarding Mundelein's first year as archbishop.

11. Quoted in Robert J. Lord, John E. Sexton, and Edward T. Harrington, *History of the Archdiocese of Boston,* 3 vols. (New York: Sheed and Ward, 1944), vol. 3, p. 514.

12. Susan S. Walton, "To Preserve the Faith: Catholic Charities in Boston, 1870–1930," in *Catholic Boston: Studies in Religion and Community, 1870–1970,* ed. Robert E. Sullivan and James M. O'Toole (Boston: Archdiocese of Boston, 1985), pp. 67–119.

13. Donna Merwick, *Boston's Priests, 1848–1910: A Study of Social and Intellectual Change* (Cambridge: Harvard University Press, 1983), p. 161.

14. Transcript of the Founding Meeting of the National Council of Catholic Women, March 4–6, 1920, located at the NCCW Offices, Washington, D.C., p. 112.

15. Cited by Blackwell, *Ecclesial People,* p. 81.

16. James P. O'Bryan, S.T., *Awake the Giant: A History of the Missionary Cenacle Apostolate* (Holy Trinity, Alabama: Missionary Cenacle Press, 1986), pp. 32–33.

17. Ibid., pp. 31, 24.

18. Blackwell, *Ecclesial People,* pp. 124, 147, 180, 169; O'Bryan, *Awake,* pp. 34, 72, 141.

19. Aaron I. Abell, *American Catholicism and Social Action: A Search for Social Justice, 1865–1950* (Notre Dame: University of Notre Dame Press, 1963), p. 173.

20. Mary Harrita Fox, *Peter Dietz, Labor Priest* (Notre Dame: University of Notre Dame Press, 1953), pp. 10, 154, 156, 159, 161.

21. Daniel T. McColgan, *A Century of Charity: The First One Hundred Years of the St. Vincent de Paul Society in the United States,* 2 vols. (Milwaukee: Bruce, 1951), vol. 2, pp. 291–92.

22. Ibid., pp. 392–93; *Rules and Commentaries: Society of St. Vincent de Paul* (St. Louis: Council of the United States, Society of St. Vincent de Paul, 1980), p. 1.

23. Mary Agnes Amberg, *Madonna Center: Pioneer Catholic Social Settlement* (Chicago: Loyola University Press, 1976).

24. Quoted in Joseph C. Gibbs, *The History of the Catholic Total Abstinence Union of America* (Philadelphia: n.p., 1907), pp. 152–53.

25. Martha Moore Avery to David Goldstein, June 16, 1918, David Goldstein Papers, Boston College Special Collections, Chestnut Hill, Massachusetts (hereafter cited as GP).

26. O'Bryan, *Awake*, pp. 149–50; David O'Brien, *Faith and Friendship: Catholicism in the Diocese of Syracuse 1886–1986* (Syracuse: Catholic Diocese of Syracuse, 1987), p. 165.

27. Quoted in O'Bryan, *Awake*, p. 37.

Chapter 12. The Heyday of Catholic Action and the Lay Apostolate, 1929–1959

1. James W. Sanders, *The Education of an Urban Minority: Catholics in Chicago, 1833–1965* (New York: Oxford University Press, 1977), p. 91.

2. Karl Rogers, "Tom, Dick, and Harry Spread the Word," *Homiletic and Pastoral Review* 36 (October 1935), p. 87.

3. Donald J. Thorman, *The Emerging Layman: The Role of the Catholic Layman in America* (Garden City, N.Y.: Doubleday, 1962), p. 30.

4. Leo XIII's encyclical *Sapientiae Christianae* quoted in David Goldstein, *Autobiography of a Campaigner for Christ* (Boston: Catholic Campaigners for Christ, 1936), p. 264.

5. Pope Pius X, *II fermo proposito*, in *The Lay Apostolate* (Boston: St. Paul Editions, 1961), p. 212.

6. Pope Pius XI, *Ubi arcano* and "Letter to the Piedmontese Bishops" (1926), in *The Lay Apostolate*, pp. 273–75, 279.

7. Pope Pius XI, "Letter to Cardinal Bertram" (1928), in *The Lay Apostolate*, pp. 289, 292.

8. O'Brien, *Faith*, p. 205; Thomas F. Gavin, S.J., *Champion of Youth: A Dynamic Story of a Dynamic Man* (Boston: Daughters of St. Paul, 1977), p. 161.

9. Quoted by William O'Shea, S.S., "Liturgy in the United States, 1889–1964," *American Ecclesiastical Review* 150 (March 1964), p. 184.

10. Ibid., p. 185.

11. Paul Marx, O.S.B., *Virgil Michel and the Liturgical Movement* (St. Paul: Liturgical Press, 1957), p. 126.

12. Hazen L. Ordway to the Editors, *Commonweal* 30 (June 23, 1939), p. 238; Anthony Traboulsee, "A Layman's Lament," *Commonweal* 27 (November 19, 1937), p. 100; John Cort to the Editors, *Commonweal* 30 (June 9, 1939), p. 183. Cort noted that in some churches, both in the east and the midwest, a priest standing at the altar rail was providing simultaneous translation of the Latin Mass, and lay people in the congregation were reciting parts of the Mass in English.

13. Quoted in Rodger Van Allen, *The Commonweal and American Catholicism: The Magazine, the Movement, the Meaning* (Philadelphia: Fortress, 1974), p. 81.

14. See, e.g., F. J. Sheed, *Sidelights on the Catholic Revival* (London: Catholic Book Club, n.d.).

15. Ann Harrigan Makletzoff, "Friendship House: The Harlem Years" (unpublished manuscript), pp. 18, 24–25.

16. Hilaire Belloc, *Essays of a Catholic*, quoted in William M. Halsey, *The Survival of American Innocence: Catholicism in an Age of Disillusionment, 1920–40* (Notre Dame: University of Notre Dame Press, 1980), p. 14.

17. See R. Scott Appleby, "Present to the People of God," Part I of this volume.

18. John J. Harbrecht, *The Lay Apostolate: A Social Ethical Study of Parish Charity Organization for Large City Parishes* (St. Louis: B. Herder, 1929), pp. 452, 140–42, 158, 119, 242–44, 359–60, 374, 432–40, 413–14.

19. Donald P. Gavin, *The National Conference of Catholic Charities, 1910–1960* (Milwaukee: Bruce, 1962), pp. 6–7, 22, 92.

20. Willard Motley, "Religion and the Handout," *Commonweal* 29 (March 10, 1939), pp. 542–43; McColgan, *Century of Charity*, vol. 2, p. 363.

21. Gavin, *National Conference of Catholic Charities*, pp. 97, 182–83.

22. *The Confraternity Comes of Age: A Historical Symposium* (Paterson, N.J.: Confraternity Publications, 1956), pp. 34, 16.

23. Mary Tinley Daly, "Parent-Educator Program of the C.C.D.," in *Confraternity Comes of Age*, pp. 57–70.

24. Ellamay Horan, "Developing Lay Catechists," in *Confraternity Comes of Age*, pp. 41–56; Leo R. Ward, *Catholic Life, U.S.A.: Contemporary Lay Movements* (St. Louis: B. Herder, 1959), chap. 9.

25. Gavin, *Champion of Youth*, pp. 73, 100–102, 106–9, 170.

26. Kantowicz, *Corporation Sole*, chaps. 12–13; on CISCA, see pp. 280–81, n. 28.

27. On Goldstein's career, see his *Autobiography of a Campaigner for Christ*.

28. Rosalie Marie Levy, *Thirty Years with Christ* (New York: by the author, 1943), pp. 87–88. Among Levy's popular devotional works were *The Heavenly Road* (1919), a series of *Heart Talks with Jesus* and *Heart Talks with Mary* published in the 1920s, and *Stepping Stones to Sanctity* (1940).

29. Rogers, "Tom, Dick and Harry Spread the Word," p. 89; "Epistle to the Narberthians" (Washington, D.C.: National Council of Catholic Men, n.d.).

30. W. H. Russell, "The Catholic Evidence Guild in the United States," *Lumen Vitae* 3 (1948), pp. 301–17.

31. See Debra Campbell, "Part-Time Female Evangelists of the Thirties and Forties: The Rosary College Catholic Evidence Guild," *U.S. Catholic Historian* 5 (Summer/Fall 1986), pp. 371–84.

32. Sister Lucille Coulihan, I.H.M., to the author, March 25, 1985.

33. Debra Campbell, "A Catholic Salvation Army: David Goldstein, Pioneer Lay Evangelist," *Church History* 52 (September 1983), pp. 322–32.

34. Nina Polcyn Moore to the author, August 12, 1987; Louise Des Marais, "The Early Years: St. Benedict Center, 1941–46," Archives of the Archdiocese of Boston, Chestnut Hill, Massachusetts; Interview with Lucile Weber, Terry Carrico, and Lucile McCullough, South Bend, May 20, 1987.

35. Dorothy Day, *The Long Loneliness* (New York: Harper and Row, 1952), pp. 165–66.

36. Ward, *Catholic Life, U.S.A.*, p. 189.

37. Mel Piehl, *Breaking Bread: The Catholic Worker and the Origin of Catholic Radicalism in America* (Philadelphia: Temple University Press, 1982), pp. 160–63.

38. Quoted in Piehl, ibid., p. 150.

39. John LaFarge, S.J., *The Manner Is Ordinary* (New York: Harcourt, Brace and Co., 1954), pp. 346–47; *Commonweal* 26 (August 20, 1937), pp. 393–94.

40. Diary entry written August 23, 1941, quoted in Makletzoff, "Friendship House," p. 66.

41. Leo R. Ward, C.S.C., *The American Apostolate* (Westminster, Md.: Newman Press, 1952), pp. 99–100.

42. See "The Vineyard," U.S. Grail Movement Records, Flyers, collection 1, box A3, folder 4; Samuel A. Stritch, Archbishop of Chicago, to Lydwine van Kersbergen, May 29, 1942; van Kersbergen to Stritch, June 3, 1942, U.S. Grail Movement Records, Regional Files, collection 1, box 40, folder 4, Grail Archives, Grailville, Loveland, Ohio (hereafter cited as AAG).

43. Grace Elizabeth Gallagher, "New Horizons for Young Women," *The Wanderer*, November 25, 1943, quoted by Alden V. Brown, "The Grail Movement in the United States, 1940–72: The Evolution of an American Catholic Laywomen's Community" (unpublished Ph.D. dissertation, Union Theological Seminary, 1982), p. 20.

44. Janet Kalven, "Disseminating Catholic Truth to Our Children," U.S. Grail Movement Records, Talks, Lectures, Grail Members, collection 1, box 83, folder 19, AAG; Brown, "Grail Movement in the United States," p. 54.

45. Bishop Wehrle quoted in "The Green Revolution," *Commonweal* 31 (March 1, 1940), pp. 395–96; Abigail McCarthy, *Private Faces/Public Places* (Garden City, N.Y.: Doubleday, 1972), p. 118.

46. Leo Ward, C.S.C., *The Living Parish* (Notre Dame: Fides, 1959), pp. vii–xii.

47. Andrew M. Greeley, *The Church and the Suburbs* (New York: Paulist/Deus, 1959; reprint ed., 1963), pp. 84, 135, 56–57.

48. Gremillion, Sermon Notes, Baccalaureate, Dominican College, New Orleans, May

26, 1958, box 2, Addresses and Lectures; Gremillion's presentation to the Catholic Committee of the South, CCS folder; *Collegium Newsletter,* box 2, Scribblings File; (Carbon) Gremillion to Most Rev. C. P. Greco, box 1, Friendship House File; Gremillion Papers, Archives of the University of Notre Dame (hereafter cited as AUND). J. B. Gremillion, *The Journal of a Southern Pastor* (Chicago: Fides, 1957), pp. 231–32, 7.

49. John W. Nevin, Flushing, New York, to the Editor, *Integrity* 9 (April 1955), pp. 5–6.

50. Ward, *Living Parish,* chap. 1.

51. On the postwar convert crusade, see Josiah G. Chatham, "The Total Parish Apostolate," *Worship* 37 (June-July, 1963); John A. O'Brien, ed., *Winning Converts: A Symposium on Methods of Convert Making for Priests and Lay People,* revised ed. (Notre Dame: Notre Dame Books, 1957; reprint ed., 1959); *Convert Making Our Apostolate* (Rome: n.p., 1967).

52. Joseph Cardijn, *Laymen into Action* (London: Geoffrey Chapman, 1964), pp. 123–24.

53. Brown, "Grail Movement in the United States," pp. 140–52.

54. See (Rev.) Joseph V. Urbain to the Most Rev. Karl J. Alter, D.D., May 22, 1957, and Urbain's attached report, "Concerning the Grail, Grailville, Ohio," Archives of the Archdiocese of Cincinnati.

55. John Cogley to Leo R. Ward, December 14 [1956], Correspondence 1955–59, Leo R. Ward Personal Papers, AUND.

56. Greeley, *Church and Suburbs,* pp. 67–68.

57. *Your Cana Club: A Basic Program* (Washington, D.C.: Archdiocese of Washington, 1959), p. 36, provided by Kathleen Enzler.

58. Jeffrey M. Burns, "The Christian Family Movement," Working Paper Series 11, no. 2, Spring 1982, Charles and Margaret Hall Cushwa Center for the Study of American Catholicism, University of Notre Dame, p. 6.

59. Interview with Ralph and Regina Weissert, May 28, 1987.

60. Rose Marciano Lucey, *Roots and Wings* (San Jose: Resource Publications, 1987), pp. 62–63.

61. Interview with Monsignor John Egan, April 13, 1987.

62. Ana Maria Bidegain, "From Catholic Action to Liberation Theology: The Historical Process of the Laity in Latin America in the Twentieth Century," Working Paper no. 48, November 1985, Helen Kellogg Institute for International Studies, University of Notre Dame, pp. 12–14; John Fitzsimons, "The Workers' Apostolate," *Integrity* 1 (November 1946), pp. 42–46.

63. Extensive collected material on the lay apostolate program is available in the archives at Regis College, Weston, Massachusetts.

64. Violet Nevile, "The Laity in the Missions," *Integrity* 9 (February 1955), pp. 6–7; Greeley, *Church and Suburbs,* p. 134.

65. Dorothy Dohen, *Vocation to Love* (New York: Sheed and Ward, 1950), pp. 35–36; Vincent J. Giese, *The Apostolic Itch* (Chicago: Fides, 1954), pp. 19–20. The latter consists of material reprinted from *Worship,* June 1953.

66. *Integrity* 1 (October 1946), p. 3.

67. Yves M. J. Congar, O.P., *Lay People in the Church: A Study for the Theology of the Laity* (London: Bloomsbury, 1956; reprint ed. 1957), pp. 1, 414–15.

Chapter 13. The Laity in the Age of Aggiornamento, 1960–1969

1. Mary Daly, *The Church and the Second Sex* (New York: Harper and Row, 1968), p. 181; Philip Gleason, "In Search of Unity: American Catholic Thought, 1920–1960," *The Catholic Historical Review* 65 (April 1979), p. 188.

2. Thorman, *Emerging Layman,* pp. 14, 84, 31–37, 57–58.

3. Daniel Callahan, *The Mind of the Catholic Layman* (New York: Charles Scribner's Sons, 1963), pp. 140, 182–83, 130, ix.

4. Edward Schillebeeckx, O.P., "The Layman in the Church," reprinted in *Vatican II:*

The Theological Dimension, ed. Anthony D. Lee (Chicago: The Thomist Press, 1963), pp. 281–82.

5. Mary Perkins Ryan, "The Focus of Catechetics," *Worship* 37 (March 1963), p. 238; Gerard S. Sloyan, "Catechetical Renewal," *Worship* 37 (January 1963), p. 102.

6. Lucey, *Roots and Wings*, pp. 64–69; John Kotre, *Simple Gifts: The Lives of Pat and Patty Crowley* (Kansas City: Andrews and McMeel, 1979), p. 140.

7. William A. Osbourne, *The Segregated Covenant: Race Relations and Catholics* (New York: Herder and Herder, 1967), pp. 39–40, 47, 109, 188–89, 236–37.

8. Jim Forrest, *Love Is the Measure* (Mahwah, N.J.: Paulist Press, 1986), pp. 134–39.

9. Walter M. Abbott, S.J., ed., *The Documents of Vatican II* (Piscataway, N.J.: New Century Publishers, 1966), pp. 243, 498–99.

10. Ibid., pp. 27, 64.

11. Joseph A. Komonchak, "Clergy, Laity, and the Church's Mission in the World," *The Jurist* 41 (1981), pp. 435–39.

12. Abbott, *Documents*, pp. 513, 59, 605–6, 614, 147–48.

13. Daniel Callahan, *The New Church: Essays in Catholic Reform* (New York: Charles Scribner's Sons, 1966), p. 22; Thorman, *Emerging Layman*, pp. 40–41.

14. Jean-Guy Vaillancourt, *Papal Power: A Study of Vatican Control over Lay Elites* (Berkeley: University of California Press, 1980), pp. 80–81; Martin H. Work, "An Understanding of the Nature of the Church, " in *The Layman and the Council*, Michael Greene, ed. (Springfield, Illinois: Templegate, 1964), p. 60.

15. Abbott, *Documents*, pp. 501, 515.

16. Cited by Barrett McGurn, *A Reporter Looks at American Catholicism* (New York: Hawthorn Books, 1967), p. 135.

17. William Barnaby Faherty, S.J., *Dream by the River: Two Centuries of Saint Louis Catholicism 1766–1967* (St. Louis: Pirraeus Publishers, 1973), pp. 208–9.

18. On the NAL, see *Catholic Mind* 65 (September 1967), pp. 10–13; David O'Brien, *The Renewal of American Catholicism* (New York: Oxford University Press, 1972), pp. 10–11.

19. Greene, *Layman and Council*, p. 35.

20. Kauffman, *Faith*, pp. 403–8.

21. McGurn, *Reporter*, chap. 11; William J. Nagle, "Failures—Lay and Clerical," in *The Layman in the Church*, ed. James O'Gara (New York: Herder and Herder, 1962), p. 83.

22. Janet Kalven et al., "The Grail Movement in America, 1940–1982," a brief, unpublished history of the American Grail submitted as a contribution to the International History of the Grail, pp. 5–7.

23. "CFM Survey" (Chicago: Christian Family Movement, 1969), pp. 15, 19–24.

24. *The National Register*, August 11, 1968, p. 1, quoted in Kotre, *Simple Gifts*, p. 102.

25. Kotre, ibid., chap. 10.

26. See, e.g., *Our Fourth Day* (Dallas: National Ultreya Publications, 1985), p. 5.

27. Kevin and Dorothy Ranaghan, *Catholic Pentecostals* (Paramus, N.J.: Paulist Press, 1969), chap. l.

28. Robert N. Bellah et al., *Habits of the Heart: Individualism and Commitment in American Life* (Berkeley: University of California Press, 1985; reprint ed., New York: Harper and Row, 1986), p. x.

29. Jay Dolan and Jeffrey Burns, "The Parish in the American Past," in *The Parish: A Place for Worship*, ed. Mark Searle (Collegeville, Minn.: Liturgical Press, 1981), pp. 60–61.

30. Gregory Baum, "Occasional Papers," *Commonweal* 91 (October 31, 1969), p. 127, quoted in Dolly Sokol and Jack Doherty, "The Alternative Parish Experience," in Searle, *The Parish*, p. 155.

Chapter 14. The Lay Ministry Explosion, 1970–

1. Richard P. McBrien, Preface to Dean R. Hoge, *The Future of Catholic Leadership: Responses to the Priest Shortage* (Kansas City: Sheed and Ward, 1987), p. vi.

2. John A. Coleman, "The Future of Ministry," *America* 144 (March 28, 1981), pp. 243–49.

3. McGurn, *Reporter*, p. 206.

4. Alice Ogle, "New Careers for Laymen," *Marriage* 47 (January 1965), p. 55.

5. Catalogue of Immaculate Conception Seminary Graduate School of Theology 1976–77, p. l.

6. Geaney, *Emerging*, pp. 51–52.

7. Gabriel Moran, *Design for Religion: Toward Ecumenical Education* (New York: Herder and Herder, 1970), pp. 9, 160–63.

8. Edward Schillebeeckx, *Ministry: Leadership in the Community of Jesus Christ* (New York: Crossroad, 1981), pp. 105, 113–14.

9. See, e.g., Jan Van Cauwelaert, "The Ordination of Lay People to Ministries in the Church," *Lumen Vitae* 27 (1971), pp. 585–92.

10. David C. Leege and Joseph Gremillion, "The U.S. Parish Twenty Years after Vatican II: An Introduction to the Study," in *Notre Dame Study of Catholic Parish Life*, report no. 1, (December 1984), p. 5.

11. Douglas Fisher, ed., *Why We Serve: Personal Stories of Catholic Lay Ministers* (New York: Paulist Press, 1984).

12. Delores Curran, "Family Ministry and the Parish: Barriers and Visions," in *Family Ministry*, eds. Gloria Durka and Joanmarie Smith (Minneapolis: Winston Press, 1980), pp. 3–6.

13. Mercedes and Joseph Iannone, "Family Learning Teams and Renewed Understanding of the Parish," in Durka and Smith, ibid., pp. 228–48.

14. R. Kevin Seazoltz, "Contemporary American Lay Movements in Spirituality," *Communio* 6 (1979), pp. 346–48.

15. Leonard Doohan, *The Lay-Centered Church: Theology and Spirituality* (Minneapolis: Winston, 1984), p. 6.

16. "National Pastoral Plan for Hispanic Ministry," *Origins* 17 (December 10, 1987), pp. 449, 451–63.

17. Bernard J. Lee and Michael A. Cowan, *Dangerous Memories: House Churches and Our American Story* (Kansas City: Sheed and Ward, 1986), pp. 53–54, 18, 55, 120–22.

18. James D. Whitehead and Evelyn Eaton Whitehead, *The Emerging Laity: Returning Leadership to the Community of Faith* (Garden City, N.Y.: Doubleday, 1986), p. 53.

19. David C. Leege, "Parish Life among the Leaders," in *Notre Dame Study of Catholic Parish Life*, report no. 9 (December 1986), p. 12.

20. Mary Jo Weaver, *New Catholic Women: A Contemporary Challenge to Traditional Religious Authority* (San Francisco: Harper and Row, 1985), p. 64.

21. Ibid., pp. 113, 133.

22. David O'Brien, "A New Way of Doing the Work of the Church," and Delores L. Curran, "If the Bishops Meant What They Said," *Commonweal* 113 (December 26, 1986), pp. 701–2, 705–6.

23. "Chicago Declaration of Christian Concern," in Barta, *Challenge*, pp. 19–28.

24. Suzanne Elsesser, "Full-Time Lay Ministries in the Church," *Origins* 10 (August 14, 1980), pp. 148–49.

25. The American bishops' pastoral *Called and Gifted* (1980) is reprinted in the Appendix to *The Catholic Laity Today*, ed. Francis F. Butler (Washington, D.C.: FADICA, 1982), pp. 57–61.

26. Penny Lernoux, "Conflicting Models of the Church," *Maryknoll*, September 1987, pp. 38–43; Robert P. Lockwood, "The Synod on the Laity: A Curmudgeon's View," *Our Sunday Visitor*, August 2, 1987, p. 7.

27. Mary Hunt, quoted in Adelle-Marie Stan, "A Decade of Dissent," *Conscience* 8 (September-December 1987), p. 25.

28. Peter Hebblethwaite, " 'Unloved' Synod Dies 'Unmourned' with Few Assets," *National Catholic Reporter*, November 6, 1987, p. 1; Edward C. Sellner, "Letter to the Editor," *National Catholic Reporter*, November 27, 1987, p. 1; see Edward C. Sellner, "A Proposed

Agenda for the Synod on the Laity," *Lay Ministry* 5 (March-April 1987), pp. 1–3.

29. Rosemarie Brickley to the Editors, *Commonweal* 112 (December 20, 1985), pp. 690, 711.

30. George Gallup, Jr., and Jim Castelli, *The American Catholic People: Their Beliefs, Practices, and Values* (Garden City, N.Y.: Doubleday, 1987), p. 43.

Part IV / American Catholics in a Changing Society: Parish and Ministry, 1930 to the Present

Chapter 15. The 1940s

1. *The Pilot,* October 3, 1947 and October 10, 1947.

2. Joseph H. Fichter, S.J., *Dynamics of a City Church*, vol. 1 of *Southern Parish* (Chicago: University of Chicago Press, 1951), p. 4.

3. Richard Gilman, *Faith, Sex, and Mystery* (New York: Simon and Schuster, 1986), p. 57.

4. The phrase is from Methodist Bishop G. Bromley Oxnam; quoted in Robert Moats Miller, "Catholic Protestant Tensions in Post-World War II America: The Experience of Methodist Bishop G. Bromley Oxnam," Working Paper Series, 19, no. 1 (Fall 1987), p. 23, Cushwa Center for the Study of American Catholicism.

5. Theodore Caplow et al., *All Faithful People: Change and Continuity in Middletown's Religion* (Minneapolis: University of Minnesota Press, 1983), p. 172.

6. Fichter, *Dynamics of a City Church*, p. 8.

7. Joseph J. Casino, "From Sanctuary to Involvement: A History of the Catholic Parish in the Northeast," in Jay P. Dolan, ed., *The American Catholic Parish: A History from 1850 to the Present*, vol. 1, p. 73.

8. Les and Barbara Keyser, *Hollywood and the Catholic Church: The Image of Roman Catholicism in American Movies* (Chicago: Loyola University Press, 1984), p. 94.

9. Quoted in David O'Brien, *Faith and Friendship: Catholicism in the Diocese of Syracuse 1886–1986* (Syracuse: Catholic Diocese of Syracuse, 1987), p. 343.

10. Quoted in Jay P. Dolan, *The American Catholic Experience: A History From Colonial Times to the Present* (Garden City, N.Y.: Doubleday, 1985), p. 222.

11. Quoted in James O'Gara, ed., *The Layman in the Church* (New York: Herder and Herder, 1962), p. 13.

Chapter 16. The 1980s

1. *National Catholic Reporter,* September 25, 1987; *New York Times,* September 14, 1987; *Origins* 17, no. 18 (October 15, 1987), pp. 307–8.

2. *Time,* September 7, 1987, p. 48.

3. Dean R. Hoge and Kathleen M. Ferry, *Empirical Research on Interfaith Marriage in America* (Washington, D.C.: United States Catholic Conference, 1981), p 1; George Gallup and Jim Castelli, Jr., *The American Catholic People: Their Beliefs, Practices, and Values* (Garden City, N.Y.: Doubleday, 1987), pp. 59–60.

4. Ibid., p. 89.

5. *National Catholic Reporter,* December 2, 1988.

6. Gallup and Castelli, *The American Catholic People,* pp. 5 and 183; John A. Coleman, "Counting Catholic Noses," *Church,* Spring 1988, p. 5.

7. See David C. Leege and Joseph Gremillion, "The U.S. Parish Twenty Years After Vatican II: An Introduction to the Study," in David C. Leege and Joseph Gremillion, *Notre Dame Study of Catholic Parish Life,* report no. 1 (University of Notre Dame, December 1984), p. 5; and David C. Leege, "Parish Life Among the Leaders," *Notre Dame Study of Catholic Parish Life,* report no. 9 (December 1986), p. 12.

8. David C. Leege and Thomas A. Trozzolo, "Participation in Catholic Parish Life: Religious Rites and Parish Activities in the 1980s," *Notre Dame Study of Catholic Parish Life,*

report no. 3 (April 1985), pp. 6–7; and Mark Searle and David C. Leege, "The Celebration of Liturgy in the Parishes," *Notre Dame Study of Catholic Parish Life*, report no. 5 (August 1985), p. 1. The phrase "enclave of inwardness" comes from E. Brooks Holifield, "The Historian and the Congregation," in *Beyond Clericalism: The Congregation as a Focus for Theological Education*, ed. Joseph C. Hough, Jr., and Barbara G. Wheeler (Atlanta: Scholars Press, 1988), p. 96; this essay also discusses the voluntary society and how it altered the role of the congregation in the nineteenth century.

9. David C. Leege, "Parish Organizations: People's Needs, Parish Services, and Leadership," *Notre Dame Study of Catholic Parish Life*, report no. 8 (July 1986), p. 8; see also David A. Roozen, William McKinney, and Jackson Carroll, *Varieties of Religious Presence* (New York: Pilgrim Press, 1984).

10. Leege and Trozzolo, "Participation in Catholic Parish Life," p. 3.

11. Leege and Gremillion, "The U.S. Parish Twenty Years After Vatican II," p. 5, and Leege, "Parish Life Among the Leaders," p. 6.

12. Leege, "Parish Life Among the Leaders," p. 15.

Chapter 17. A Question in Search of an Answer

1. William H. Chafe, *The Unfinished Journey: America Since World War II* (New York: Oxford University Press, 1986), p. viii.

2. See the works of Chafe, *The Unfinished Journey*, and Richard Polenberg, *One Nation Divisible: Class, Race, and Ethnicity in the United States Since 1938* (New York: Penguin Books, 1980).

3. Chafe, *Unfinished Journey*, p. 112.

4. *Wall Street Journal*, August 15, 1986. Wealth is measured as the value of what could be purchased after all debts were paid off and the remaining assets converted to cash.

5. Chafe, *Unfinished Journey*, p. 442.

6. Kenneth T. Jackson, *Crabgrass Frontier: The Suburbanization of the United States* (New York: Oxford University Press, 1985), pp. 279–80.

7. Mark Searle, "Renewing the Liturgy—Again," *Commonweal* 115, no. 20 (November 18, 1988), p. 619.

8. Robert Wuthnow, *The Restructuring of American Religion: Society and Faith Since World War II* (Princeton: Princeton University Press, 1988), pp. 154–55, and Wade Clark Roof and William McKinney, *American Mainline Religion: Its Changing Shape and Future* (New Brunswick: Rutgers University Press, 1987), p. 65.

9. Wuthnow, *Restructuring*, p. 163.

10. Roof and McKinney, *American Mainline Religion*, pp. 65–66.

11. This was quoted by S. Appleby in his essay on priests and it is originally from William H. Cleary, ed., *Hyphenated Priests: The Ministry of the Future* (Washington, D.C.: Corpus Books, 1969), p. xi.

12. Wuthnow, *Restructuring*, p. 57; Roof and McKinney, *American Mainline Religion*, p. 43; and Robert Bellah et al., *Habits of the Heart* (New York: Harper and Row, 1986).

13. See *National Catholic Reporter*, September 11, 1987.

14. Roof and McKinney, *American Mainline Religion*, p. 52.

15. David C. Leege and Thomas A. Trozzolo, "Religious Values and Parish Participation: The Paradox of Individual Needs in Communitarian Church," *Notre Dame Study of Catholic Parish Life*, report no. 4, p. 8.

16. Wuthnow, *Restructuring*, pp. 96–97.

17. Ibid., p. 101.

Selected Bibliography

Part I / Present to the People of God:
The Transformation of the Roman Catholic Parish Priesthood

D'Arcy, Paul, M.M., and Eugene Kennedy, M.M. *The Genius of the Apostolate.* New York: Sheed and Ward, 1965.

Fichter, Joseph H. *America's Forgotten Priests: What Are They Saying?* New York: Harper and Row, 1968.

————— *Priests and People.* New York: Sheed and Ward, 1965.

————— *Religion as an Occupation: A Study in the Sociology of Professions.* Notre Dame: University of Notre Dame Press, 1961.

Gallagher, Charles A., and Thomas L. Vandenberg. *The Celibacy Myth: Loving for Life.* New York: Crossroad, 1987.

Greeley, Andrew M. *The Catholic Priest in the United States: Sociological Investigations.* Washington, D.C.: United States Catholic Conference, 1972.

————— "The Parish Assistant." In *Secular Priests in the New Church.* Edited by Gerald Sloyan. New York: Herder and Herder, 1967.

————— *Uncertain Trumpet: The Priest in Modern America.* New York: Sheed and Ward, 1968.

Gremillion, J. B. *The Journal of a Southern Pastor.* Chicago: Fides Publishers Association, 1957.

Hurley, Denis E., O.M.I., and Joseph Cunnane. *Vatican II on Priests and Seminaries.* Dublin, Ireland: Scepter Publishers, 1967.

Michouneau, Abbe G. *Revolution in a City Parish.* Westminster, Md.: Newman, 1956.

Murnion, Philip. *The Catholic Priest and the Changing Structure of Pastoral Ministry, New York 1920–1970.* New York: Arno Press, 1978.

O'Brien, Rev. John A. *The Priesthood in a Changing World.* Paterson, New Jersey: St. Anthony Guild Press, 1943.

O'Neil, Arthur Barry, C.S.C. *Priestly Practice.* Notre Dame: University of Notre Dame Press, 1943.

Rahner, Karl, S.J. *The Identity of the Priest.* New York: Paulist Press, 1969.

Sweetser, Thomas. *Successful Parishes: How They Meet the Challenge of Change.* Minneapolis: Winston Press, 1983.

Part II / In the Parish but Not of It: Sisters

Buetow, Harold A. *Of Singular Benefit: The Story of U.S. Catholic Education in the United States.* New York: Macmillan, 1970.

"The Crisis in Religious Vocations: An Inside View." *New Catholic World* (January/February 1988).

Ebaugh, Helen Rose Fuchs. *Out of the Cloister.* Austin: University of Texas Press, 1977.

Fichter, Joseph H. *Parochial School: A Sociological Study.* Notre Dame: University of Notre Dame Press, 1958.

Greeley, Andrew M., and Peter H. Rossi. *The Education of Catholic Americans.* Chicago: Aldine, 1966.

McCluskey, Neil G. *Catholic Education Faces Its Future.* Garden City, N.Y.: Doubleday, 1969.

Meyers, Bertrande, D.C. *The Education of Sisters: A Plan for Integrating the Religious, Cultural, Social, and Professional Training of Sisters.* New York: Sheed and Ward, 1941.

Muckenhirn, M. Charles Borromeo, C.S.C., ed. *The Changing Sister.* Notre Dame, Indiana: Fides Publishers, 1965.

————, ed. *The New Nuns.* New York: New American Library, 1967.

National Congress of Religious in the United States. Proceedings. *Religious Community Life in the United States.* New York: Paulist Press, 1952.

Neal, Marie Augusta, S.N.D.de N. *Catholic Sisters in Transition: From the 1960s to the 1980s.* Consecrated Life Studies no. 2. Wilmington, Delaware: Michael Glazier, 1984.

Sanders, James W. *The Education of an Urban Minority: Catholics in Chicago, 1833–1965.* New York: Oxford University Press, 1977.

Traxler, M. Peter, S.S.N.D., ed., *New Works of New Nuns.* St. Louis and London: B. Herder Book Co., 1968.

Weaver, Mary Jo. *New Catholic Women: A Contemporary Challenge to Traditional Religious Authority.* San Francisco: Harper and Row, 1985.

Part III / The Struggle to Serve:
From the Lay Apostolate to the Ministry Explosion

Barta, Russell, ed. *Challenge to the Laity.* Huntington, Indiana: OSV Press, 1980.

Callahan, Daniel. *The Mind of the Catholic Layman.* New York: Charles Scribner's Sons, 1963.

Fisher, Douglas, ed. *Why We Serve.* New York: Paulist Press, 1984.

Geaney, Dennis. *Emerging Lay Ministries.* Kansas City: Andrews and McMeel, 1979.

Greene, Michael, ed. *The Layman and the Council.* Springfield, Il.: Templegate, 1964.

The Jurist 47 (1987): 1 [A special issue on the laity].

The Lay Apostolate. Boston: St. Paul Editions, 1961.

Thorman, Donald J. *The Emerging Layman.* Garden City, N.Y.: Doubleday, 1962.

Ward, Leo, C.S.C. *Catholic Life, U.S.A.* St. Louis: B. Herder Book Co., 1959.

————.*The Living Parish.* Notre Dame: Fides Publishers, 1959.

————, ed. *The American Apostolate.* Westminster, Md.: Newman Press, 1952.

Two useful bibliographies:

Doohan, Leonard, ed. *The Laity: A Bibliography.* Wilmington, Del.: Michael Glazier, 1987.

Snyderwine, L. Thomas, ed. *Researching the Development of Lay Leadership in the Catholic Church Since Vatican II.* Lewiston, N.Y.: Edwin Mellen Press, 1987.

Part IV / American Catholics in a Changing Society:
Parish and Ministry, 1930 to the Present

Bellah, Robert N., Richard Madsen, William M. Sullivan, Ann Swidler, and Steven M. Tipton. *Habits of the Heart.* New York: Harper and Row, 1986.

Chafe, William H. *The Unfinished Journey: America Since World War II.* New York: Oxford University Press, 1986.

Dolan, Jay P. *The American Catholic Experience: A History from Colonial Times to the Present.* Garden City: Doubleday, 1985.

————, ed. *The American Catholic Parish: A History from 1850 to the Present,* 2 vols. New York: Paulist. 1987.

Gallup, George, Jr., and Jim Castelli. *The American Catholic People: Their Beliefs, Practices, and Values.* Garden City: Doubleday, 1987.

Leege, David C., and Joseph Gremillion, eds. *Notre Dame Study of Catholic Parish Life.* Reports Nos. 1–13, December 1984–October 1988. Institute for Pastoral and Social Ministry, University of Notre Dame.

Wuthnow, Robert. *The Restructuring of American Religion: Society and Faith Since World War II.* Princeton: Princeton University Press, 1988.

INDEX